SAVINGS BANKING
An Industry in Change

SAVINGS BANKING
An Industry in Change

Franklin H. Ornstein

**With Research Assistance By
Hugh A. Harris**

RESTON PUBLISHING COMPANY, INC.
A Prentice-Hall Company
Reston, Virginia

To AIMEE
Who Would Have Been
My Banker

10 9 8 7 6 5 4 3 2 1

© 1985 by Reston Publishing, Inc.
   Reston, Virginia
   A Prentice Hall Company

ISBN 0-8359-6883-9

PRINTED IN THE UNITED STATES OF AMERICA

Designed and typeset by Publications Development Co. of
Crockett, Texas, Developmental Editor: Nancy Marcus Land,
Production Editor: Bessie Graham

Preface

As its name implies, the savings industry was spawned from the basic concept that personal savings was a virtue and essential to the growth of the economy. Later, coupled with a commitment to housing built through private investment, savings banking became the vehicle which within 50 years made this nation's people the best housed in the world.

The story of this specialized financial intermediary, its beginnings, its growth and ultimate metamorphosis is set forth in this book. Perhaps, at this time, when savings and loans, savings banks and other similar savings based institutions are faced with changes of an extraordinary nature, it is important to understand the niche that this industry has occupied in the nation's strength. To know how it has functioned may shed some light on its future prospects.

Those of us who have dedicated our lives to this important segment of our financial community view the new powers being granted to the savings banks and savings and loans and the elimination of regulatory constraints as real improvements. We feel that these innovations will bolster those institutions and strengthen them so that they can continue, albeit somewhat modified, to render the service to the community in the manner that has been their legacy for all the years past. The conviction is shared by most of us that the savings industry will emerge from this period of restructuring a stronger, more vibrant and more relevant entity. This book as a historical reference and a working text of the metier of savings banking is a significant contribution to the study of business. Even though the industry is in a constant state of flux and the rules change on a daily basis, what is written here will continue to be a foundation for the understanding of the operation and management of an institution that has occupied an important place in our society.

Bryce Curry
President,
Federal Home Loan Bank
of New York

Contents

Introduction

It is a constant source of amazement to find that the public makes no distinction among the types of financial institutions servicing their needs. Perhaps the dual banking system, so precious to our law makers, and the multiplicity of regulations and regulators tends to create an atmosphere so complex that only the most astute can make a differentiation. Throughout the years in dealing with legislators, it is surprising that even the most informed have a limited knowledge of the consumer banking system in this country. On occasion, even members of banking committees and members of regulatory agencies are unable to comprehend the differences among financial institutions.

This lack of perception is particularly true when the line is drawn on a functional basis between commercial and savings banking. The difference, which can be traced to the origins of savings institutions, has been institutionalized by a series of legislation and subsequent regulations. The historical background and the governmental actions shaping the development of the savings industry is the subject of this book. Hopefully, this book will provide a better understanding of the segment of the financial industry that has played a major role in providing shelter for the American family and in developing the value of savings. Also hopefuly, it will not be an epitaph of what was once a viable business.

The historical background, traced in the early chapters, reveals that while the types of savings institutions have moved closer together in the kind of service they render to the community, taken together they have changed little over a 200-year span. Although savings banks and savings and loans grew from different roots, they eventually developed to serve the community in much the same way. This service was recognized by elected officials and resulted in protective legislation that not only insulated them from competition but assured the continuation of their existence. Governmental protection created an atmosphere of stability for both the customers of the institutions and for their managing officers, and fostered favorable lending conditions for housing. Consequently, savings flowed into the institutions and remained there. With savings as long-term deposits, savings institutions expanded their traditional role of financing home ownership. Governmental guarantees, tax benefits, and the establishment of an unwritten but clear national priority towards housing accelerated this process.

Through the years as the nation's economy expanded and contracted, there were periods of instability when high interest rates caused disintermediation from the banking system and created pressure upon institutions with long-term portfolios to borrow to cover their lack of liquidity. The result was that the cost of borrowing impacted profits of the institutions since the existing loans and investments made for long periods of time were at fixed rates below the cost of acquiring funds. Those periods were short lived, and savings institutions weathered them by reducing lending activity and using repayments to reduce debt. There was, however, a more permanent result that arose out of these dips in the economy.

During these periods of squeeze on earnings, pressure built for an expansion of their powers to improve profits. As a result, while almost 200 years passed without a significant change in the method of doing business, forces were set in motion for the most extraordinary change in the financial industry since the passage of the National Banking Act of 1864. By legislative fiat, first federally chartered savings and loans followed by state chartered savings banks, savings and loans, cooperative banks, building and loans, and the like received expanded powers to function in areas traditionally reserved for the commercial banking community. These powers were, however, only small inroads into these highly new areas and were limited in scope.

During the periods of high interest rates, it also became apparent that a more flexible deposit structure was necessary to allow institutions to compete for depositor funds. A growing concern for the rights of consumers accelerated the demand for more competitive savings rates and for the relaxation and eventual elimination of regulatory control of interest rates on demand and time deposits. Consequently, as the nation entered into another period of high short-term interest rates in 1978, a new savings certificate was introduced in an attempt to prevent disintermediation and to stabilize deposit flows. This certificate, having a rate tied to current market rates and known as the "Money Market Certificate," drastically increased money costs and accelerated the need to increase yields on investments. In a sweeping move, Congress enacted the Depository Institutions Deregulation Act in 1980. The act gave federally chartered thrifts extensive new powers in exchange for the eventual elimination of all deposit rate controls.

The Garn-St Germain Depository Institutions Act of 1982 further liberalized the asset and liability powers of thrift institutions. Federally chartered savings and loan associations were granted the power to make commercial, corporate, business, or agricultural loans up to 5 percent of assets until January 1, 1984 when the limitation would be 10 percent of assets. In addition, demand accounts were permitted, and existing loan-to-value restrictions and first lien limitations on real property loans were removed. A new money market competitive account was authorized, with no interest rate ceiling and minimum deposit requirement of $2,500. The Depository Institutions Act of 1982 also provided capital assistance for distressed savings institutions in order to bolster the net worth positions of these institutions.

As the flood gates open, and savings institutions find themselves still caught with a high percentage of long-term, low-yielding loans unmatched against the costs of deposits and borrowings, it is questionable whether all the newly granted powers and those that are proposed will be of any immediate benefit. What is certain, however, is that the regulation of banking institutions enters an era in which differences are blurred and the delivery of financial services will no longer follow traditional lines.

Acknowledgments

I would like to acknowledge with appreciation the assistance of Hugh A. Harris. During the preparation of the book, the changing nature of the industry required constant revisions of the material. His diligent efforts kept the book timely.

I would also like to thank several individuals who were especially helpful in this publication—Gerald Seixas of the Savings and Loan League in New York, Angelo Vigna of the Federal Home Loan Bank of New York, the staff of the United States Savings and Loan League, and the National Council of Savings Institutions.

Special thanks to Bill Carey of the Federal Home Loan Bank Board in Washington, D.C., and also to Nancy Marcus Land of Publications Development Company of Texas.

Finally, to Sigrid Sprague, who dutifully and patiently organized, typed, and retyped the various drafts of the manuscript, I am truly grateful.

Franklin H. Ornstein
Long Beach, N.Y.

Foreword

While the contemporary mutual savings bank and savings and loan association exhibit similar operational characteristics, as evidenced by their growing structural and functional convergence, an examination of the original purposes and operation of these two financial institutions reveal striking and fundamental differences. The fostering of thrift and the provision of a secure place where small savers could deposit their money and earn some interest, and thus by self-help improve their welfare, were the basic foundation tenets of the mutual savings bank. Mortgage lending was subsequently undertaken as a lucrative means of investing these funds and was, thus ancillary to the original thrift and security motives. Operationally, the early mutual banks were established with the right to self-perpetuation.

On the other hand, the primary raison d'etre for the establishment of the savings and loan association was the facilitation of home ownership among members of the association through the pooling of savings and the allocation of loans for home financing from a common fund. The early savings and loan associations were not organized with the right to a perpetual existence, but rather terminated operations as soon as each member received a loan.

A historical evaluation of the early development of savings and loan associations and mutual savings banks must of necessity, therefore, be charted along two distinct paths.

PART ONE
EARLY HISTORY

Chapter I

Introduction

EARLY DEVELOPMENT

"Building Societies" as the forerunners of the American Savings and Loan Associations were known, existed in England from as early as 1781. The close relationship between the growth of the building and loan association movement and the "Friendly Societies" in England is well illustrated by the fact that building societies in England were originally certified under the Friendly Societies Act of 1834. Bodfish points out, too, that the Chief Registrar of Friendly Societies in England, up to a century later continued to issue an annual report on building societies.[1]

In essence, the Friendly Societies operated similar in function to that of an insurance pool, where members made weekly subscriptions and in cases where unforeseen contingencies developed, such as sickness, death, travelling expenses for members who were unemployed and desired work in other cities, annuities for widows and orphans, payments of weekly allowances were made.

It was largely through membership in these Friendly Societies that the inculcation of the thrift habit through regular contributions and the notion of the co-operative concept were fostered and nurtured.

With the rapid development of the Industrial Revolution in England

---

[1] Bodfish, H. Morton, *History of Building and Loan in the United States*. Chicago, 1931, p. 8.

throughout the eighteenth century and the pervasive changes in migration patterns, employment, family and social life which accompanied this economic transformation, the rising wage-earning class were unable to procure satisfactory housing through existing government and public facilities. It was, therefore, not surprising that given the spirit of co-operative self-help existing at the time, some mutual solution was developed to overcome the housing problem. Such action by one organization of wage earners culminated in the birth of the first documented Building Society in Birmingham, England, in 1781.

The Birmingham Building Society was a mutual association, and its original organizers were the sole owners and only members. "Proprietors" or overseers were elected from members of the Society and were responsible for the regulation of the Society's activities and received no remuneration for their services. The "friendliness" of the Society was evidenced by the fact that the Society was established in a pub, and all subsequent monthly meetings were held there. Nonmembers could not be granted loans, and loans were only made explicitly for the construction of homes. The articles of association of the Birmingham Building Society stated that each member was to contribute 10½ shillings payable to the treasurer at the pub on the first Monday of every month. Failure to make payments due resulted in a fine, and nonpayment for a prolonged period resulted in forfeiture of previously paid balances held in the Treasury. As soon as an adequate sum had been accumulated in the Treasury, a loan was made by lottery to a member which was worth £70 for each share held. A 5 percent interest rate was charged, and monthly payments on principal and interest were required in addition to regular monthly payments on shares. The loan was used for building a house on land leased by the Society, and the mortgage on the house was usually held as security.

As soon as the Treasury had accumulated adequate funds again, the process was repeated until all members had received and repaid a loan. Surplus funds held by the Treasury were then allocated among the members, and the Society ceased to operate. This in capsulized form was the British prototype of the early Building Society.

By the mid-nineteenth century, the spirit of co-operative enterprise was widespread and the purpose of such an organization was also well known. As the movement spread throughout continental Europe, it was only natural and inevitable that the same spirit of cooperation would in due course prevail throughout the United States.

Moreover, economic conditions in the United States were in many respects similar to those prevailing at the time of the Industrial Revolution in England. These conditions were particularly conducive to the growth of cooperation among the rising wage-earning class. While the wage-earning class in America at this time was largely wealthier than its counterpart in England, they, too, were forced to depend on mutual effort for any significant degree of economic advance.

Prior to 1816 in America, the occupational structure of the population was largely confined to that of farmers, fishermen, traders, merchants who normally ploughed back any small surplus into the business in the form of new equipment, stock or additional land. The new employee class did not have access to these traditional methods of saving. Banks at the time, too, were virtually preoccupied with commercial discount or loan business and did not actively seek to solicit small deposits. There was, thus, a pressing need for types of institutions which had not been in existence before this period.

Up to 1831, the United States was basically an agrarian economy and the agriculturist was to a large degree self-sufficient. Several developments, however,—after 1831—provided the stimulus to the growth of a formidable manufacturing sector in America. Firstly, the growth and development of local industry was fostered by the Napoleonic Wars of 1795-1815, which disrupted trade between America and her European partners, particularly England. Secondly, the imposition of a protective tariff effective in 1816, and increased, reaching a high during 1828-1832, further stimulated local manufacturing. The tariff greatly enhanced the competitiveness of American manufacturers who already had some natural protection due to the costs and transportation problems for goods from Europe to the American mainland. Internally, too, transportation inland from the main American ports was also restricted, hence, small local factories could compete with the larger overseas competition.

This rapid manufacturing development pervasive throughout America at this time generated the growth of a wage-earning class and the concomitant concentration of people in urban centers. Both these developments were crucial to the establishment of the building society movement in America. The new wage earners were generally not property owners but received regular wages, which though small allowed the saving of some portion toward a distant goal.

Together with the mass immigration from Europe, local population growth, transportation improvements and the rapid development of large cities, there was thus an acute demand for housing among the thousands who moved to the cities seeking jobs in factories. The factory system also meant that most of the working class energies were expended working full time in factories, with little or no time or effort remaining for individuals to build their own homes as was previously done. With regular wages, the systematic saving of a small portion through some co-operative effort would greatly enhance the ability of the working class to purchase or construct homes.

It is against this historical perspective and economic background that the first building (savings) and loan association was established in Frankford, Pennsylvania, in 1831. Known as the Oxford-Provident Building Association, it was largely structured along lines similar to that of the British prototype. It is significant to note that three of the original founding members were Englishmen. The Association's records preserved by the Pennsylvania Historical Society, dated January 3, 1831, states that "This association shall be known by the name, style and title of the Oxford-Provident Building Association of Philadelphia County.

The association shall be conducted by 13 trustees. The trustees shall not receive either directly or indirectly any compensation for their services. Each member shall pay the sum of five dollars upon each share of stock held by him and a monthly contribution of three dollars.

The association shall continue until every member shall have an opportunity of building or purchasing a dwelling house for each share of stock he may hold in the same, after which the balance in the Treasury shall be equally divided among the members according to their respective shares.

No loan shall be made to a member for the purpose of building a dwelling house at a greater distance than five miles from the borough of Frankford."[2]

At the start of business, the par value of shares was placed at $500 each, and all members were initially required to make a membership payment of five dollars ($5) and pay three dollars ($3) per month subsequently on each share. The maximum number of shares any one member could acquire was limited to five shares.

As soon as the sum of $500 was available for a loan, members submitted bids for the use of the fund to purchase an existing home, or to finance the building of a new home.

_____

[2] Bodfish, *op. cit.,* pp. 37-42.

In February 1832, the first loan of $375 was made to Comly Rich, a member who paid a "premium" or bid of $10 for the loan. An interest payment of 6 percent was charged on the principal, and as soon as the fund totalled $500, the bidding process was repeated. When each member had been granted and repaid a loan, the association was to be terminated. Ten years after its inception, in January 1841, the first Oxford-Provident Association was dissolved.

In 1836, the Brooklyn Building and Mutual Loan Association was organized after a delegation visited Frankford and obtained the necessary operational and organizational information. The third association was established in South Carolina. The movement naturally spread rapidly throughout the United States; and by 1860 before the Civil War, there were associations in several states. By 1880, it was commonly thought that there was probably one association in every state, and in 1888 it was estimated there were 3000-3500 in the United States. By 1893, according to estimates by the U. S. Bureau of Labor, there were 5,600 associations nationwide with over 1.35 million members and assets totalling approximately $475 million.

Influenced by early state laws and customs, these institutions have mushroomed in number, it should be noted under a variety of names—Building Associations, Building and Loan Associations, Cooperative Savings and Loan Associations, Building Societies, Mutual Savings and Loan Associations, and Cooperative Banks. In the case of the latter variation, Massachussetts law requires that these institutions must use the term "Cooperative Bank" in the general title, which is legal testament to the historical sentiment underlying the development of these financial institutions.

EARLY STRUCTURE AND TYPES

The early building and loan associations were all voluntary and unincorporated, operating largely without public supervision. These institutions operated on what was known as the "Terminating Plan." As soon as the goals of the association had been achieved, the association ceased operation and was terminated. In other words, when the last member repaid his loan and the shares matured, the association would unobtrusively go out of business, in many instances without any trace of its previous existence.

Under the terminating plan, the association was usually chartered with authority to issue a fixed and definite amount of stock and to operate for a designated number of years. All stock was issued as of the same dates. New members could join after the initial organization date, but were required to pay "back dues" up to the beginning of the association, plus a bonus in order to preserve equality with the original subscribers.

Bodfish[3] asserts that such a system was wasteful, as the business accumulated during 12 or 15 years of operation was dissipated at the end of the alloted life of the association. Moreover, the goodwill accrued over the years was likely to be lost even if another association with the same name was created.

As a means of preserving and extending such goodwill and facilitating the admission of new members to the association, the serial plan was devised. During the 1850s, the serial plan became popular as the contemporary mode of organization. This plan allowed a certain "continuity of existence" to the association. It is noteworthy that the third Oxford-Provident Association adopted in January 1854 a resolution for the issuance of a series of stock.

The most important distinction between the serial and terminal plans was that in the case of the former, several series of stocks were issued at stated intervals and not only one series of stock as in the latter. Bodfish notes that "The members of each series constitute practically a terminating association among themselves; hence, the serial association is sometimes described as a collection of terminating units."[4]

Under the serial plan, savers could also join the association by paying back dues, but only to the beginning of the last series. Series were issued quarterly, semi-annually, or annually. Dues were required to be paid on a regular basis and delinquent members were subject to fines. Earnings were prorated by a system based on the number of shares held in the series and the age of the series.

Several disadvantages were, however, inherent in this type of organization. In the first place, with the larger associations now, the serial accounting system became increasingly complex and difficult to manage, as the association grew in size and number of accounts. Secondly, the serial plan required the association to acquire large sums of cash at regular intervals in order to accommodate maturities. Finally, some managers desired to sell shares at any time and not

---

[3] Bodfish, *op. cit.,* p. 86.
[4] Bodfish, *op. cit.,* p. 87.

only at prescribed intervals. The desire to overcome these difficulties led to the introduction of the "Permanent Plan" at a later date.

The serial plan, however, provided the mechanism by which some individuals not desirous of acquiring homes could safely invest their savings. The serial plan thus made feasible the notion that the savings of individuals could be pooled in order to provide the financing of homes for other individuals and not necessarily for themselves. Hence, the savings of some individuals who had no desire to purchase homes could be lent to other individuals who had interests in acquiring homes. Members could, therefore, join the association purely on its investment merits.

With the continuing population shifts westward, the savings and loan movement continued to attract new participants and by 1880, the permanent plan of operation was adopted largely in response to the changing environment.

It should be noted, as a matter of historical interest, that the first association operating under the permanent plan actually dated back to 1846. The Charleston Savings Association of South Carolina organized in the 1840s publicly announced that it was both interested in savers as well as depositors. One founding member of the original Charleston Association referred to the "permanent feature by which an individual is enabled to enter the society at any time without being subject to back payments and precisely on the same footing with the original members."[5]

Such developments in South Carolina were, however, largely localized, and it was not until the introduction of the "Dayton Plan" in 1880 that the idea of permanent charters became popular throughout the savings and loan association movement.

The inspiration for the Permanent Plan was derived from a visit to England where the permanent plan was in use. The permanent plan eliminated the series subscription to stock and instead permitted the issuance of shares at any time. The accounts of individual members were kept separately, each member's account being treated practically as a separate series. Net earnings were distributed in the form of dividends, usually semi-annually, and were paid on the balance of shares, including any previously alloted dividends left in the account.

With the introduction of the Dayton Plan by the Mutual Home and Savings Association of Dayton, Ohio, several innovations to the original permanent plan were effected. These included the introduction of optional paid-up stock or "full-paid shares" and the removal

---

[5] Bodfish, *op. cit.,* p. 234.

of restrictive penalties applied to withdrawals. Members were permitted to subscribe for shares, the payment dues on which may be made in any amount and at any time. The paid-up stock issue allowed payment in full at one time and facilitated the investment of lump sums for securing income in the form of dividends and the maintenance of a savings fund. Thus, large and small funds could be invested at the members' convenience. The premium charge on loans was also eliminated. Shares that were matured could also remain within the association.

The permanent plan also introduced the establishment of a contingent reserve fund for losses. Losses were accommodated by establishing a loss reserve fund which was credited with a portion of net income as a safeguard against future potential losses. The balance of earnings was then credited to each individual account at a predetermined rate. By the end of the second World War, virtually all savings and loan associations were operating under permanent charters.

During the 1890s, in some regions of the United States, notably California, Kansas, Ohio, and Oregon, the permanent capital or guarantee capital stock plan was developed. Under this plan, the association issued a non-withdrawable class of stock subscribed and paid for by the founders of the association. Permanent capital associations were useful in areas which were growing rapidly and were subject to continual changes in population.

By 1893 of the 5,598 associations operating as local institutions, 3,600 had been founded between the period 1880-1890.

The history of the savings and loan association movement would be incomplete without some mention of two ancillary developments. The first was the rapid growth of "Nationals"—that is, National Building and Loan Associations, appearing in the late 1880s, a period when speculative ventures were rampant. Operating under the savings and loan plan of investment; that is, monthly installments to build up shares at maturity, the organizers solicited funds on a national basis and also made loans after by mail. These associations were logically "get rich quick" promotional ventures for the benefit of the organizers. Virtually all of these associations were liquidated during the depression of 1893-97, victims of a depressed real estate market, as well as of their own questionable operational practices. Such practices included poorly made loans and widely dispersed and inadequately controlled operations. By 1897, the Nationals all disappeared from the financial scene in America, largely through failure and restrictive legislation. The Nationals, as would be expected, naturally adversely affected the growth of local savings and loan associations for some time.

The second noteworthy development was the formation of the United States League of Local Building and Loan Associations, later renamed the United States Saving and Loan League. This organization was formed largely in response to the development of "nationals" and the need for some kind of cooperative action on the part of local associations.

Since 1892, this League has promoted the development of better quality housing and has provided over the years many specialist and professional services to savings and loan associations.

By 1920, there were over 8,600 associations. For the next decade following, there was a substantial growth in assets and number of associations. In 1929, for example, there were 21,343 associations. The depression and crash of 1929 led to important innovations governing the operations of savings and loan associations.

INVESTMENT POWERS

As noted before, the early associations invested the majority of funds collected in the form of mortgage loans to members desiring to acquire homes. Some assets were also held in the form of cash prior to making a loan or when there was a gap between acquiring cash and the allocation of a loan request. In the interim, short-term loans could be profitably made to members with the savings share balances providing the collateral. Share loans accounted for 5 percent of total assets in 1890. Some real estate was also held, largely the result of foreclosures on mortgages.

United States Government Securities were also held prior to World War I, but it was not until the establishment of the Federal Home Loan Bank System that investments in United States Government Securities were of some prominence.

More recently—as will be discussed later—the investment powers of savings and loan associations have been greatly widened to include activities which were not previously considered as suitable investment holdings for savings and loan associations.

Briefly, the Depository Institutions Deregulation and Monetary Control Act of March 1980, authorized Savings and Loan Associations to invest up to 25 percent of assets in consumer loans, corporate bonds, and commercial paper. Savings and loan associations were also allowed to provide trust and fiduciary powers and to issue credit cards and mutual capital certificates. Restrictions also on the the ability to provide other than first lien residential loans were also removed, as were the dollar limits on residential loans. Other geographic limitations on the granting of loans were also relaxed in addition to increasing the various loan to value rations on single family and multi-family loans. These and other measures were designed to enhance the competitiveness and viability of the savings and loan industry vis-a-vis the commercial banking system. Further deregulation of the investment capabilities of the savings and loan industry was also implemented with the passage in September 1982 of the Garn-St Germain Depository Institutions Act. Title three of the Act provides for fundamental restructuring of the modus operandi of thrift institutions and "represent a competitive emancipation from the laws and regulations that have artificially constrained investments and made thrifts vulnerable to volatile economic conditions."[6] Savings and loan associations under the provisions of the 1982 Act, for example, will be able to make commercial loans, accept demand deposits and provide overdraft facilities. A more detailed analysis of these and other extended powers will be presented in later chapters.

SUPERVISION AND REGULATION

For over forty years, the early savings and loan associations were all voluntary and unincorporated with no public supervision of their activities.

New York was the first state to recognize the growing importance of savings and loan associations and to adopt specific legislative and regulatory measures. In 1875, New York required its building and loan associations to provide annual reports of their condition and financial standing to the State Banking Department. By 1892, annual supervision and inspection by the Superintendent of Banks became compulsory.

Prior to 1890, supervision also developed rapidly in other states. Maine and Michigan enacted legislation in 1887, Minnesota, Wisconsin and the Dakotas in 1889. Other states also passed supervisory legislation during the 1890s; and by 1900, more than half of the

---

[6] Federal Home Loan Bank Board "The Garn-St Germain Depository Institutions Act of 1982: Summary, Text and Selected Legislative History," p. 1.

states had introduced some legislation regulating savings and loan associations.

By 1930, 46 out of 48 states had some degree of legislative supervision. By 1933, with the passing of Federal legislation governing savings and loan associations, several weaknesses in the operational structure of these institutions were reduced or remedied.

Trustee or Director Structure

The general direction and operation of a savings and loan association is usually determined by a board of directors or trustees. The Board in toto constitutes the governing body of the association. Savings and loan associations are in great measure mutual organizations. Members or account holders are, strictly speaking, the owners of the association. The responsibility for the running of the business is delegated to a board of directors composed of prominent or professional individuals in the community.

A description of the duties and responsibilities of the first trustees and officers of the Oxford-Provident Association is contained in the Articles of Association (reprinted by Bodfish in *A History of Building and Loans in the United States,* pp. 37-41). Some indication of the trustee structure can be seen in Figure I-1.

The Board of Directors of early savings and loan associations were not self-perpetuating and were often only elected for a specific period of time. It was not until the adoption of permanent charters that the Boards became more or less self-perpetuating. Although in theory most directors continued to be elected, the majority of members never exercised their right to vote, so that in practice there was, in fact, self-perpetuation of the Board of Directors.

The Board of Directors—in addition to publicizing the policies under which the association operates—is responsible for the selection of effective management to guide the association in the achievement of its stated objectives.

The original articles of association for the Oxford-Provident stated that the trustees "shall not receive either directly or indirectly any compensation for their services."[7] With the later internal development and expenses of associations and their increasing complexity, it became quite common for directors to receive remuneration for services as lawyers and officers of their particular associations. Several were also motivated by strong profit incentives and often used their

[7] Bodfish, *op. cit.,* p. 38.

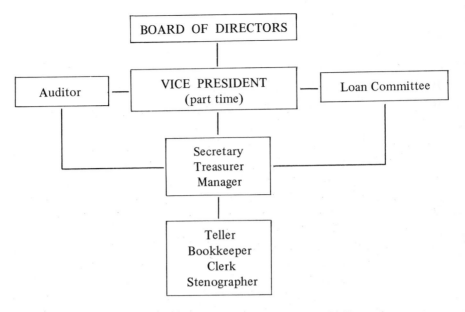

Figure I-1 Illustrative Organizational Chart of a Typical
Savings and Loan Association
(Assets < $1 Million)

position with the association to obtain financial benefits from other businesses which provided services for the association.

Subsequent legislation, in particular the Financial Institutions Regulatory and Interest Rate Control Act of 1978, limited the types of outside business activities bank executive officers could engage in, and also restricted the ability to use their position in the institution for preferential treatment or personal financial gain. Civil penalties incurred for violations were also increased.

Officers of the association were largely responsible for the day-to-day management of the association and usually included a president, departmental vice presidents, a manager, treasurer, and a secretary. A brief description of their respective functions follows.

The president is the chief executive officer and presides at all meetings of the association members as a rule, and also at all meetings of the Board of Directors. He is the titular head of the association and derives his authority from the ratification of his actions and support of his leadership by the board of directors. The powers of a president—although not explicitly nor customarily set out in the charter of by-laws—are far-reaching and very extensive.

The managing officer is the individual responsible for the permanent operations of the association. He represents the institution in its relations with the public. The duties of this officer are similar to those characteristics of what is usually called "top-level management." He is in control of the operational details of the association. With the increasing complexity of operations, such control usually requires assistance by additional administrative personnel, by specialists in lending and savings operations, and by skilled office personnel. In essence, the managing officer may be viewed as the central day-to-day operational supervisor.

A vice president usually has special duties such as responsibility for the mortgage loan department or the savings. He, as the head of the mortgage department, for example, is responsible for checking and verifying records of all payments on loans and to activate corrective measures on delinquent accounts at all times. He is the custodian of loan reports, insurance and tax records. In some smaller associations, the secretary may fulfill these functions.

The treasurer has responsibility for properly supervising and disbursing monies and accounting for the receipts of the association. This is a highly responsible office and presumes a working knowledge of savings and loan accounting. In some associations, the treasurer may supervise teller and window accounting procedures. An assistant may be responsible for recording payments received and withdrawals on accounts and other related matters.

The secretary usually handles the records of the association and the Board, and frequently handles the routine of recording mortgages, deeds, releases of contracts, etc. The secretary may also handle the opening of new accounts and generally supervise other office operations not assigned to other officers. In smaller associations, the secretary may also function as the executive officer.

With larger associations, an auditor may be appointed who assures the managing officer that daily reports are in balance and that financial affairs are properly administered in all departments. He is responsible for instituting internal checks and for general bookkeeping and accounting procedures.

In larger associations, there may be other important officers ranging in functions from principal accountant, personnel officer, chief loan officer, chief investment officer, savings officer, and a principal appraiser. The scope of activities of such officers is usually well defined in the job description.

MUTUAL BANKS

Early History

The early mutual savings banks were largely benevolent institutions, characteristically philanthropic in nature. The savings bank idea first appeared in Continental Europe about 1775, was adopted in England about 1800 and, thence, transmitted to the United States. Historians usually recognize Hugues Delestre as the first proponent of such an organization. In 1610, Delestre proposed the establishment of an institution for the benefit of the "wage worker who might deposit his savings and withdraw them again in part or in whole as he might require, with interest according to the time they had been on deposit; and this institution was designed to take the place of alms giving."[8] Daniel Defoe, Ricardo, and Thomas Malthus also expounded the idea. Malthus, for example, suggested "that of all the plans which have yet been proposed, for the assistance of the laboring class, the savings banks—as far as they go—appear to me much the best and the most likely to effect a permanent improvement in the condition of the lower classes of society."[9]

Historical records indicate that the first basic prototype savings bank was founded in Hamburg, Germany in 1765, though the first institution akin to the modern savings bank was found by the Reverend Henry Duncan in Ruthwell, Scotland in 1810.

The trend towards savings banking spread rapidly throughout Europe, largely nurtured by the philanthropic sense of Christendom and princely patronage. It is widely acclaimed that savings banks received their first literary advocacy in France, their first practical task in Germany and their first statutory regulation in England.

The development of the factory system, expanding industrial production, population growth, and immigration, all contributed to the growth of an ever increasing pool of wage earners who desired some mechanism by which savings could be held safely with some earnings potential. Commercial banks, at the time, were not interested in servicing such small individual accounts, and no governmental agency provided savings deposit facilities. The development of mutual thrift associations thus appeared in response to the need for depository services by a relatively new stratum of society.

---

[8] Hamilton, James H. *Savings and Savings Institutions*, London, 1902, p. 155.
[9] Hamilton, *op. cit.*, p. 150.

Groups of wealthy public-spirited individuals would contribute the necessary capital funds to establish the association, which then accepted deposits of small depositors. Savings banks would encourage thrift, sobriety, virtue, industry, and prosperity.

The first mutual savings bank in the United States was the Philadelphia Saving Fund Society which began business on December 21, 1816. It was organized as a voluntary association and did not receive a charter until 1819. The Provident Institution for Savings in Boston was the first savings bank to be incorporated, having been chartered on December 18, 1816.

The philanthropic nature of the early banks is evident from a publication dated 1816, which stated "It is proposed to form an institution in Boston for the security and improvement of the savings of persons in humble life, until required by their wants and desires . . . . It is not by the alms of the wealthy that the good of the lower class can be generally promoted. By such donations, encouragement is far oftener given to idleness and hypocrisy than aid to suffering worth. He is the most effective benefactor to the poor who encourages them in habits of industry, frugality and sobriety."[10]

The Philadelphia Bank was incorporated by 25 individuals, each contributing $10 toward a fund of $250 to start operations. The State charter limited the number of managers or incorporations to 25, but imposed no restriction on investment powers. Limits were placed on rates of interest, amount of deposits ($300,000 maximum), as well as a ceiling on individual deposits ($500).

In 1818, the Savings Bank of Baltimore was established to be followed by the Bank for Savings in the City of New York, the Society for Savings in Hartford, Connecticut and the Savings Bank of Newport, Rhode Island in 1819. In 1820, the Albany State Bank received its charter.

Parenthetically, it should be noted that most of the early banks experienced difficulty in obtaining charters because of the antipathy with which legislatures regarded all banks at the time; hence, the use of the term "institution or society" in many of the early titles.

Some indication of the rapid growth of mutual banks during the early years is illustrated by the fact that between 1920 to 1930, the number of mutuals increased from 10 in 1820 to over 600 in 1930. The number of depositors grew from 8,600 to over 11,890,000 for the comparable period of time.

---

[10] Sherman, Franklin J. *Modern Story of Mutual Savings Banks*. New York, 1934, Little and Ives Company, p. 71.

The low average deposits indicate that they have largely been held by small savers. Statutory limitations were, however, placed on individual quantity deposits on the notion that large depositors have a wide gamut of financial services available outside of mutual banks. Tax exemption of these deposits have also led to restrictions on their size in order to reduce the incidence of tax avoidance.

Mutual savings banks were firmly established in the northeastern section of the country, in New England and the mid-Atlantic states, by the time of the Civil War. The growth of mutual banks in other areas of the United States had been slow; however, if not non-existent, probably due in part to differing local economic conditions and the organization of stock savings banks in the West.

Contemporarily, the geographic concentration of the mutual savings bank industry is attributable to the influence of economic forces enforced by legislation that allows mutual savings banks to be chartered only in the eighteen states in which they currently operate, in contrast to the wider distribution of savings and loan associations.

CHANGING NATURE

Early Structure and Types

A mutual savings bank's main objective is not that of profit maximization. There are no stockholders and the assets are owned by the depositors and are credited to their accounts after provision for current expenses and additions to surplus. Under state laws, trustees are not permitted to profit from the banks. The funds of a mutual savings bank are, therefore, in effect, trust funds.

In view of the trust nature of the mutual banks, state legislatures have enforced stringent laws regarding their organization and operation. Maryland and Deleware are the only exceptions to the above where the investment of savings banks funds is left entirely to the discretion of the officers of the banks. However, in these states, savings banks are subject to exhaustive examinations by the respective banking departments.

Generally, according to the laws of most states in which mutual savings banks operate, a savings bank may be formed when a designated number of responsible citizens can demonstrate to the state banking commissioner that there exists sufficient need and opportunity for a savings bank in their community. The incorporators must guarantee that all liabilities can be accommodated during the initial starting period and also provide a guarantee (surplus) fund for the protection of the bank until it has built up adequate resources. From the inception of the bank, a part of the earnings must be diverted into a surplus fund until it reaches a stated percentage of total deposits. This percentage differs in various states, some of which stipulate maximum ratios.

In forming a mutual savings bank, a petition is usually made to the Superintendent of Banks with at least thirteen signatures. These thirteen citizens offer their services as trustees, and two-thirds of their number must be residents of the county in which it is proposed to locate the bank. In making a decision on the application, the superintendent considers the desirability of the locality, local economic conditions, denseness of population, the character and social standing of the trustees.

All mutual savings banks established after the Bank for Savings in New York, displayed certain common characteristics which included inter alia, the right to a continued existence, the notion of mutuality, the trustee system, and the method of management.

Up to 1860, commercial banks, as well as the First and Second Banks of the United States, were being granted terminating, serial, or term charters, and most legislators of the time were reluctant to relinquish control over the existing number of banking institutions inherent in the power to deny charter renewal applications. It should be noted parenthetically that Savings and Loan Associations were still operating under serial charters during this period.

The act of incorporation of the Bank for Savings in New York, however, gave to the Board of Trustees the right to perpetual succession which, de facto, gave the bank the right to an infinite existence. The Statute also made the twenty-eight incorporators the first trustees of the bank. Their duties included the overseeing of all the activities of the bank.

The philanthropic nature and disinterested attitude with which the original trustees accepted their responsibilities is clearly revealed by the First President of the Bank who stated "The trustees or directors owe it to both the public and themselves distinctly to declare that they entirely disclaim the idea of receiving any personal emolument or advantage in any shape whatsoever."[11] The Act of Incorporation expressly stipulated that trustees "should not directly or indirectly receive any pay or emolument for their services nor transact any busi-

---

[11] Teck, Allan. *Mutual Savings Banks and Savings and Loan Associations: Aspects of Growth*. New York and London, Columbia University Press, 1968. P. 12.

ness which belongs to or is transacted by the Bank for Savings."[12]

One analyst noted that the "early operation of savings banks, and even the later operations up to 1860, was honest and successful chiefly and predominantly because of the inspired devotion, the integrity and the true beneficience of the men who guided them." He asserts also ". . . . that it must remain a singular chapter in the history of human dealings that notwithstanding ample opportunity for dishonesty and self-aggrandizement, there prevailed a fidelity and uprightness among savings bankers which is almost unbelievable."[13]

As mentioned before, mutual savings banks had no members or stockholders. Depositors provided savings funds and were creditors of the bank. They did not exercise voting rights with regard to the selection of either trustees or management, did not attend meetings and had no authority or obligations for decision-making of any operational significance. Furthermore, depositors had no influence over the way the bank invested money, handled accounts or paid interest. The majority of mutual savings banks established after 1819 were thus based on concepts of perpetual existence, a trustee system and profitsharing among depositors.

Early Structure

The Board of Directors was the governing body of the mutual savings bank as designated in the Act of Incorporation. From the members of the Board, a President, and usually three vice presidents were elected. The By-Laws of the bank also provided for the election of a secretary, a treasurer from the Board, and two permanent committees which were responsible for the operation of the bank. The monthly attending committee composed of three members was responsible for the supervision of the bank during business hours. The three member funding committee attended to the bank's investment portfolio.

The trustees also chose attorneys from among their members who represented the bank in legal matters.

The administrative organization described above which was first adopted by the early savings bank, reflected the charitable interest of their founders; but with expansion and successful operations, such a structure became obsolete and not viable. Rather, professional managements operating these institutions as businesses rather than phil-

---

[12] *Ibid.*
[13] Sherman, *op. cit.*, p. 61.

anthropic enterprises were required, and the present administrative structure of mutual banks gradually evolved in this way. In less than a decade, managerial functions were delegated entirely to trustee appointed salaried officers.

Investment Powers

The investment powers of mutual savings banks were originally stipulated in their respective state charters. However, as was previously noted, some of the early charters left the scope and nature of these powers to the founders themselves, such as in the case of the Philadelphia Saving Fund Society, established in 1819. The Provident in Boston also had no restriction on the society's investment powers, excepting for the proviso that deposits could be accepted and that funds be invested at "best advantage."

Some charters made no provision for holding cash, others required periodic distribution of the surplus, while others did not specifically deal with the use of accumulated surpluses. It should be noted that in the case of the Scottish savings banks, trustees deposited all the funds in joint stock banks and were paid special interest rates. Given the dearth of branches of joint stock banks in America at the time, the Philadelphia Society also first invested in public bonds and made its first mortgage loan in 1818.

As the savings bank grew in number and size, investment problems became more and more acute. In the formative years of their existence, savings banks invested virtually all available funds in government and state bonds in compliance with charter regulation which directed that funds be put into "stocks created or issued under and by virtue of the laws of the United States or of the State and in no other way." In 1820, while there were only nine banks with over a million dollars in deposits, by 1930 deposits had grown to $7 million. With rising expenses and larger funds to allocate, investment decisions by savings banks, thus, became a complex issue.

Mutual savings banks made investment decisions within an expanding framework of legal restrictions imposed by the individual states in order to assure the high quality of savings bank assets. In most states, the statutes specified types of investments savings banks could undertake and ceilings on the proportion of assets or deposits that could be held in each type of investment. Detailed criteria for evaluating eligibility of investments were stipulated, including in the case of mortgages, the type and location of mortgaged property and maximum loan to value ratios. In the case of corporate bonds, the size, earnings and dividend record, and capital structure of issuer were important considerations governing such investments.

All mutual banks are supervised to some degree by their respective State Banking Departments. Management, savings services, and the selection of investment portfolios are all closely regulated by the State Regulatory Authority.

The imposition of strict investment criteria reflects, however, the need of savings banks acting in trust for millions of depositors of modest means to guarantee and secure deposits by maintaining high standards of investment policy. Over the years, savings banks' investment powers have been gradually expanded. Legislation, for example, in the early 1950s allowed mutual savings banks to acquire F.H.A. and V.A. mortgages on out-of-state properties, thus removing the previous restriction to mortgages held on local properties. In certain states—as mentioned previously—savings banks have been granted limited authority to invest a percentage of their funds at their own discretion. In other states, they were permitted to invest in securities not otherwise eligible, by obtaining permission from supervisory agencies.

Some assessment of the changing modes of investment is portrayed by the following chronological survey of the changes in investment capabilities through the years 1819-1864.

1819:   Savings banks were permitted investments only in government bonds and bonds of their particular states. The year was also en passant, the red letter year for legislative approval of savings banks.

1820:   The charter of the Bank for Savings in New York was amended to authorize loaning money to the Corporation of the City of New York.

1827:   Interstate investment is permitted with the Bank for Savings being authorized to invest in the public stocks of the State of Ohio. Albany Savings Bank in New York was also granted the authority to invest in the stocks of banks in Albany and Troy and to loan money to the Corporation of Albany.

1829:   Brooklyn Savings Bank was given the power to invest in "Brooklyn Village Stock," also in the stock of the City of New York. In addition to holding stocks of the State of New York, the Seamen's Bank for Savings was authorized to invest in the stocks of the States of Pennsylvania and Ohio.

1830:   The Bank for Savings in New York is legally permitted to acquire stocks of any State in the Union and to lend to the Public

School Society of New York on satisfactory real security. The above were pioneer legal developments. Statewide investments were approved, and the ability to make mortgage loans was legalized almost ten years after the Bank for Savings had sought legal sanction for such activity.

1831:   Poughkeepsie Savings Bank incorporated this year, allowed to make loans on "bond and mortgage on real estate double the value of the sum loaned." This ratio of the loan to value of the property was stipulated for the first time.

1832:   Brooklyn Savings Bank received legal permission to advance money on bond and mortgage on property double in value the amount loaned. The Seaman's Bank for Savings was also authorized to invest in the stock of any State in the Union.

1833:   Greenwich Savings Bank is given authority to invest in the stocks of the States of Pennsylvania and Ohio and to advance money against the property of the Public School Society of New York.

1834:   Schenectady Savings Banks is granted authority to invest in the stock of any State and to make bond and mortgage loans. The Bowery Savings Bank was also authorized to make bond and mortgage loans on property in New York and Brooklyn valued at twice the amount of the loan.

In addition, the comprehensive Savings Bank Law passed in Massachusetts permitted investments in mortgages on real estate to the total extent of 75 percent of the amount of deposits, and also investments in bank stocks.

1839:   Savings Bank of Utica is given permission to invest in the stock of the City of Utica, and Troy Savings Bank to invest in the stock of the City of Troy in addition to other now familiar provisions.

1857:   Bonds of the county in which the savings bank is located became legal investments.

1863:   Town bonds in which the bank is located are legalized.

1864:   Bonds of counties are a legal investment for savings banks.

The above Survey details the developments, particularly in the State of New York. Comparative changes in investments between 1834 and 1873 for Massachusetts are illustrated in Table I-1.

The rapid increase in the percentage of mortgages to total assets held is clearly discernible rising from 11 percent of total assets in 1834 to over 48 percent in 1873.

Table I-1

Investments ($)	1834	1873
Public funds	2,000	17,500,000
Loans on public funds	–	1,120,000
Bank stock	1,190,000 (34%)	21,700,000 (10%)
Loans on bank stock	560,000	1,570,000
Deposits–bank	520,000	2,370,000
Railroad bonds	–	6,000,000
Loans on railroad stock	–	500,000
Real estate	–	2,275,000
Loans on mortgages	390,000 (11%)	100,000,000 (48%)
Loans to counties, cities, & towns	270,000	14,700,000
Loans on personal security	280,000	35,000,000
Cash on hand	25,000	2,125,000
Surplus	–	3,160,000
Dividends	140,000	11,000,000

Adapted from Sherman, *op. cit.*, p. 75.

Investments permitted by law in the various states up to 1930 is given in Table I-2.

More recently, the Depository Institutions Deregulation and Monetary Control Act also further broadened the investment powers of Mutual Savings Banks and grandfathered many of the existing regulations for federally chartered Mutual Savings Banks. These latter developments will be fully discussed in a later chapter.

Supervision and Regulation

In the early formative years up to the beginning of the Civil War, there was no uniformity and no cohesive organization among the various mutual banks. It was true that most charters were fashioned off the Scottish model, but, nevertheless, there was a bewildering variety of charters.

It should be noted that there was no definitely evolved policy of supervision by the States, nor was there a uniform practice in investment matters. There was so little cogency in the legal operation of a savings bank that often a state law would be passed revoking a right granted by a previously authorized charter, and then the paradox occurred that a savings bank could lawfully indulge in an unlawful practice.

In New York, for example, there were 86 different individual char-

Table I-2

	Cal.*	Conn.	Del.**	Ind.	Maine	Md.***	Mass.	Minn.	N.H.	N.J.	N.Y.	Ohio	Ore.	Pa.***	R.I.	Vt.	Wash.	Wis.
Number of banks	1	75	2	5	32	14	194	1	44	23	144	3	1	7	9	19	3	6
U.S. government bonds	Yes	Yes	Yes	Yes	Yes	Yes	Yes	Yes	Yes	Yes	Yes	Yes	Yes	Yes	Yes	Yes	Yes	Yes
State, county, and municipal bonds	Yes	Yes	Yes	Yes	Yes	Yes	Yes	Yes	Yes	Yes	Yes	Yes	Yes	Yes	Yes	Yes	Yes	Yes
Real estate bonds & mtgs.	Yes	Yes	Yes	Yes	Yes	Yes	Yes	Yes	Yes	Yes	Yes	Yes	Yes	Yes	Yes[1]	Yes	Yes[11]	Yes
Railroad bonds	Yes	Yes	Yes	Yes	Yes	Yes	Yes	Yes	Yes	Yes	Yes	Yes	Yes	Yes	Yes	Yes	Yes	Yes
Equipment obligations	Yes	Yes	Yes		Yes	Yes	Yes	Yes	Yes	Yes	Yes	Yes	Yes	Yes	Yes	Yes	Yes	
Street railway bonds		Yes	Yes		Yes	Yes	Yes		Yes	Yes	Yes	Yes	Yes		Yes	Yes		
Telephone bonds	Yes	Yes	Yes		Yes	Yes	Yes	Yes	Yes	Yes	Yes	Yes	Yes	Yes	Yes	Yes	Yes	
Gas and electric co. bonds	Yes	Yes	Yes		Yes	Yes	Yes	Yes	Yes	Yes	Yes	Yes	Yes	Yes	Yes	Yes	Yes	
Bank and trust co. stocks		Yes	Yes		Yes	Yes	Yes					Yes	Yes		Yes	Yes		
Collateral loans	Yes	Yes	Yes		Yes	Yes	Yes	Yes			Yes	Yes			Yes	Yes	Yes	Yes
Canadian bonds (Dominion & Provincial)	Yes[1]	Yes	Yes		Yes	Yes			Yes			Yes						
Foreign government bonds	Yes[1]	Yes	Yes		Yes	Yes						Yes		Yes	Yes[7]	Yes	Yes[7]	
Acceptances & bills of exchange	Yes	Yes	Yes	Yes	Yes	Yes	Yes	Yes	Yes	Yes	Yes	Yes	Yes	Yes	Yes	Yes	Yes	
Loans on soldier's adjusted service certificates			Yes	Yes	Yes	Yes	Yes		Yes	Yes		Yes	Yes		Yes	Yes	Yes	
Bonds of other corporations		Yes	Yes	Yes	Yes	Yes			Yes	Yes		Yes	Yes		Yes			
Stocks of other corporations		Yes[3]	Yes	Yes	Yes	Yes			Yes	Yes		Yes	Yes			Yes[10]		
Guaranteed mortgage bonds			Yes	Yes	Yes	Yes	Yes[4]		Yes	Yes	Yes	Yes	Yes		Yes[2]	Yes		
Unsecured notes		Yes[3]	Yes	Yes[4]	Yes[4]	Yes	Yes	Yes	Yes	Yes	Yes	Yes			Yes[9]	Yes		
Farm loan bonds		Yes	Yes		Yes	Yes			Yes	Yes	Yes	Yes	Yes	Yes		Yes		
Stock exchange collateral		Yes	Yes		Yes	Yes			Yes	Yes	Yes	Yes	Yes		Yes	Yes		
Participation certificates	Yes		Yes			Yes				Yes		Yes	Yes	Yes		Yes		
Joint stock land bank bonds														Yes				
State land bank bonds		Yes	Yes	Yes	Yes	Yes		Yes	Yes	Yes	Yes	Yes	Yes	Yes				
Judgments against the state		Yes	Yes			Yes					Yes	Yes	Yes					
Federal Land Bank bonds		Yes	Yes	Yes	Yes	Yes							Yes					
Ground rent certification		Yes	Yes			Yes						Yes						

*In addition to the investments listed, the California Savings Bank Law specifies that funds may be invested in any bonds legal in New York and Massachusetts.

**Investment of savings bank funds in Maryland and Deleware left entirely to the discretion of officers and trustees.

***In Pennsylvania several saving fund societies are operating under special charters which permit greater latitude in investments.

[1] If certified by Superintendent of Banks. 2–water companies. 3–joint and several obligations of residents of state. 4–three-name paper. 5–of Federal Land Bank of First Land Bank District. 6–also certain railroad stocks. 7–Dominion only. 8–restricted. 9–six months and under restrictions. 10–included in Real Estate Bonds & Mortgages; certain ones in Vermont and New Hampshire legal. 11–including first mortgage on leaseholds.

Source: The National Association of Mutual Savings Banks.

ters of savings banks in operation. There was, thus, a pressing need for a single Savings Bank Act sufficiently comprehensive and flexible to meet the requirements of every institution in the State of New York, for example. Such an Act would impart uniformity, directness, precision, safety, and efficiency to the management.

A general law was, however, enacted in 1834 in Massachusetts which served as the legal reference for subsequent general state laws.

The main provisos of the 1834 Act were:

- The officers of the bank were to be a president and a treasurer, in addition to others as found necessary, and other trustees or managers as the corporation deemed necessary.
- Officers were selected by the Corporation with the exception of the treasurer who was chosen by the Trustees.
- Individual deposits were limited to $1,000 but not deposits of religious or charitable organizations.
- Officers could not borrow from the bank, but this prohibition did not apply to trustees.
- The income of the bank was to be divided "in just proportion" among depositors, and there was no provision for a surplus fund to be established.
- An annual report was required of all mutual banks.

In 1838, the Massachusetts legislature provided for three bank commissioners who were to examine each savings bank annually. Subsequent charters were simple references to the above Act. Virginia legislators passed a general law in 1838, Connecticut in 1843, Rhode Island in 1858, Maine in 1868, and New York in 1875. With the rapid expansion of the mutual banking industry, ad hoc regulatory extensions and revisions were made in order to ensure the viability and soundness of the banks' operation within a legal framework. Consolidation of chartering regulations and uniformity in supervision was achieved with the granting of Federal charters to mutual savings banks in 1978.

Chapter II

Parallel Development of Banking Systems in the United States

The early commercial banks in the United States such as the Bank of North America founded in 1782, were all state chartered and were authorized by special acts of their respective state legislatures. It was not until 1791 that the first federal commercial bank, the Bank of the United States was established. Chartered for 20 years, the First Bank of the United States, though largely successful, ceased operation at the expiration of its charter in 1811.[1] State banks, though, rapidly increased in number. By 1811, there were 88 such banks in operation. Banks at that time operated under very little regulation, and supervision by the various states—where it existed at all—was inadequate and not well enforced. Notwithstanding several failures, by 1816 there were over 246 banks in existence.

Renewed interest in and support for the creation of another federal commercial bank culminated in the formation of a Second Bank of the United States in 1816. Although 20 percent of the capital stock of the Second Bank was owned by the federal government, the Bank was basically a private institution. Due primarily to improper management, however, the Second Bank was not as successful as its predecessor, and, in 1836, it failed disastrously.

---

[1] For a comprehensive analysis of the operation of the First and Second Banks of the United States, see McConnell, Diane G. "Central Banking in the New Nation," *Banking, Journal of American Banker*, Vol. LXVII, No. 10, October 1975, pp. 34-136.

WILDCAT BANKING

Prior to 1837, a charter to establish a bank could only be granted by a special act of the State Legislature. Such a system engendered corruption and fostered nepotism, bribery, and other abuses. The Michigan Act of 1837 ushered in the era of "free banking" where virtually anyone could obtain a bank charter by satisfying certain requirements.

New York passed a similar law in 1838, and most states followed suit and enacted comparable legislation. By 1840, the number of banks increased from 500 in 1834 to over 900 institutions.

Requirements for the establishment of a bank were not stringent and were often not enforced. Cash holdings were generally very low, and in order to satisfy the bank examiner, funds were usually borrowed prior to his inspection. Free banking opened banking to competition, but the major weaknesses of many of these banks were inadequate capitalization and insufficient provision for the conversion or redemption of notes to specie.

One ingenious method of banking adopted by some promoters was the establishment of banks in isolated locations. This obviously reduced accessibility to the bank and made it virtually impossible for almost all note holders to redeem notes. The term *wildcat banking* was used to describe these operations. The locations in which many of these banks were opened were more accessible by wildcats than by bank customers.

An interesting discourse on the operations of these wildcat banks is contained in the October 1975 issue of the banking magazine published by the *Journal of American Bankers*. As the article states, "There is no standard today against which to measure the impact of wildcat banks. It is hard to say precisely how severe or how deleterious that impact was. . . . Wildcat banking had too much importance but not so much as its appeal to the imagination makes it seem to have had. It belonged to the realm of quackery and its activities had much the same significance in the workings of the economy that noise has in the running of a train."[2]

---

[2] See McShane, Patricia M. "Wild Cat Banks, 1835-1863," *Banking, Journal of American Banker*, Vol. LXVII, No. 10, October 1975, p. 142.

NATIONAL BANKING ACT OF 1864

The necessity for banking reform occasioned by the spurious banking activities of the wildcat banks led to the introduction of the National Banking Act of 1864.

The 1864 Act provided the framework within which the national banking system functioned for half a century until the passage of the Federal Reserve Act of 1913. The Act of 1864 was preceded by a Bill of 1863 which authorized Congress to charter banks that would be required to hold government bonds as security for the issuance of notes. This bill, however, was poorly constructed and was thoroughly revised in 1864. In 1865, as a means of luring banks to convert to a national charter, a 10 percent tax on bank notes issued by state chartered banks was imposed by Congress. State banks, thus, found note issuing unprofitable and converted to national charters. They were, in effect, taxed out of existence.

The National Banking Act was designed to replace the sporadic, haphazard, and largely unsound state banking systems with new banks that would issue safe and uniform currency. Moreover, the issuance of irredeemable notes would also assist in the financing of the war effort.

National banks were to be chartered by the Comptroller as corporate organizations for 20 years. The provisions on management and control in conjunction with other provisions of the Act were intended to provide the community with capable management familiar with local conditions and the protection of the public against mismanagement and fraud.

Minimum requirements on reserves held against liabilities were introduced. Restrictions were also placed on the use of banks' funds, particularly with regard to the type and amount of loans that banks could undertake. All national bank notes, were printed by the Treasury and distributed to national banks in proportion to the value of government bonds purchased by the bank and deposited with the Comptroller of the Currency. The safety and stability of the national banks revealed considerable improvement in comparison to previous state-chartered institutions, due to superior enforcement procedures by the comptroller and its cortege of bank examiners.

The National Banking Act was primarily concerned with note-issue banking. With the rapid development of demand deposits and checking accounts, the extension of credit in the form of demand deposits rather than notes became the major operation of banks. As banks found they did not have to issue notes to make loans, state chartered banks began to reappear since state requirements were less stringent than those governing national banks. By 1870, with the growth of deposit banking, state banks outnumbered national banks. Since 1870, there has, thus, been a dual banking system.

With the money supply tied to government bond issues, seasonal fluctuations in money demand could not be easily accommodated. When the Treasury operated a temporary deficit, banks were flooded with money. Such irregularities often seriously disrupted the money market. A central banking system to manage the over-all operation of the banking system was thus a pressing need. With financial crises arising every decade in 1873, 1884, and 1893, there was widespread recognition of the potential usefulness of some centralized control. In 1907, a severe crisis brought to the foreground the need for a central bank.

FEDERAL RESERVE ACT OF 1913

Legislation was enacted in 1913 creating the Federal Reserve System charged with the responsibility for undertaking central bank functions in implementing national monetary policies. All national banks were required to be members of the Federal Reserve System. State chartered banks were not mandated to join the federal system but could do so on a voluntary basis.

The Federal Reserve Act provided for the strengthening of reserves so that they could be more readily used to facilitate the meeting of obligations by banks instead of suspending cash payments. The Act also sought to develop a flexible currency which could expand and contract according to the needs of the economy.

The Federal Reserve System would also function as a clearinghouse for its member banks in handling checks.

The Board of Governors of the Federal Reserve system is also responsible for general supervision of banking at the federal level, in particular, regulations concerning branching, bank mergers, deposit reserve requirements, international banking activities, and the exercise of broad functions in connection with the money supply. Regulation of maximum limits on the interest paid on savings and time deposits were added to the Federal Reserve's supervisory powers in 1933. A detailed analysis of the Federal Reserve System can be found in *Federal Regulation of Banking* by C. H. Golembe (Federal Reserve Bank Publication). Note that very few state chartered banks have joined the Federal Reserve System. In fact, over the past ten years more than 600 banks have withdrawn from formal membership. This development has severely retarded the ability of the Federal Reserve Board to effectively implement its monetary policies and to regulate the cost, availability, and supply of money within the United States economy. There are approximately 14,600 commercial banking institutions operating in the United States. Of that number, about 4,600 are national banks and ipso facto Federal Reserve members. Of the remaining 10,000 state chartered banks, approximately 100 voluntarily belong to the Federal Reserve system. In 1970, 84 percent of all bank deposits were held by member banks. Currently, the comparable figure is approximately 71 percent. Moreover, in the first months of 1980, there were over 500 applications for withdrawals from the Federal Reserve System.

The main factors underlying withdrawal has to do with the fact that reserve requirements for members are more stringent than those pertaining to nonmember state chartered banks. These reserves are held in noninterest bearing accounts with the Federal System, whereas state banks have greater freedom in determining the manner in which reserves can be held. Some states allow banks to hold reserves in interest bearing instruments and in correspondent bank deposits. During periods of sustained and rising inflation, the costs of holding noninterest bearing deposits with the Federal System are greatly exacerbated, more so when nonmembers of the Federal System are able to obtain identical services without assuming the costs of membership.

Declining Federal Reserve membership, it was felt, would further reduce the ability of the Federal Reserve Board to effectively control the nation's money supply. In an effort to eliminate the incentives for withdrawing from the Federal System, Congress in March of 1980 enacted legislation which made universal uniform reserve requirements mandatory on transaction accounts for all depository institutions. Thus, all financial institutions were brought under the umbrella of the Federal Reserve System. In addition, the Federal Reserve System was also instructed to begin charging for its services by September 1980. These and other provisions of the Depository Institutions Deregulation and Monetary Control Act of 1980 will be discussed more fully in later chapters.

BANK FAILURES AND THE GREAT DEPRESSION

During the 1920s, economic prosperity in the United States reached a peak position as the economic welfare of an increasing population attained new heights. Times were so good that the decade immediately after World War I is still called the "Roaring Twenties."

In line with the general ambience of prosperity pervasive throughout the economy, total assets of savings and loan associations demonstrated remarkable growth, moving from $2.9 billion in 1921 to approximately $8.7 billion in 1929. The number of associations increased from 8,633 in 1920 to 12,342 in 1929. Many, however, were wiped out by the events that were to follow.

Although by the 1900s most states had made some legislative provision for the regulation and supervision of savings and loan associations, by 1929 the economic chaos that followed the crash of that year led to the introduction of new laws governing the operations of these associations. Many historians and economists tend to attribute some of the underlying factors responsible for the difficulties of the 1930s on the excesses of the 1920s.

In the years after the stock market crash of 1929, there was a general decline in public confidence in business activity, unemployment increased, payrolls decreased, financial institutions failed and the value of the assets of investors fell significantly. It was widely believed that the basic cause of the stock market debacle was the fact that too many stock shares were purchased with loans on the assumption that stock prices would continue to rise. When prices plummeted drastically, several investors lost fortunes.

All of these developments had serious repercussions on the savings and loan industry. Associations were deluged with demands for withdrawals, and by 1930, the member of associations in operation had fallen to 11,777 and to 8,957 in 1938. Withdrawals continued largely because of public distrust of financial institutions and the necessity for individuals to use past savings accumulated to meet expenditures during a period of declining incomes.

Cash supply in the savings and loan associations was further reduced by the freezing of credit lines available from commercial banks and the retention of deposits of savings and loan associations held in commercial banks. Of the 2,826 associations which went out of business during this time, more than half were voluntarily liquidated, many merging with other associations. In almost every area where a savings and loan association closed, one or more commercial banks in the area had previously closed. Where the commercial banks remained in operation, it was also generally the case that the savings and loan associations in the area also survived.

Naturally, the business climate within the economy during the period was further weakened by the collapse of the commercial banking system. Commercial banks in great numbers failed, not because of a lack of assets, but rather the inability to meet cash withdrawals by the rapid conversion of assets held into cash. As a result, today both savings and loan associations and banks keep a stipulated proportion of their assets in cash or highly liquid assets readily convertible into cash.

BANK FAILURES

Bank failures were frequent, particularly among state chartered banks all through the 1920s and culminated in the virtual breakdown of the banking system during the Great Depression of the 1930s.

Between 1920 and 1920, bank failures averaged about 550 per year with nonmembers of the Federal Reserve System accounting for the majority of failures. Many were small rural banks affected by the decline in agricultural production during those years. By 1930, in that year alone, 1300 banks suspended operations. Farm area banks were particularly hit by weakening farm prices and declining incomes during the depression.

On December 11, 1930, The Bank of the United States in New York, with over $200 million in deposits, suspended operations—the largest bank to do so up to that time. The failure of this bank severely damaged public confidence, more so since the bank was a member of the Federal Reserve System.

By 1931, the atmosphere of financial panic intensified; and in that year, over 2,000 U.S. banks with over $1.7 billion in deposits were forced to suspend their operations.

The effects of this financial melée reverberated throughout the entire United States economy as Gross National Product and employment levels declined drastically.

In 1932, the Reconstruction Finance Corporation (RFC) was created by Congress to render assistance to distressed banks. Public disclosure, however, of assistance by the Reconstruction Finance Corporation made depositors acutely aware of weak banks and signalled impending failure, as in many instances, an RFC loan often was followed by a run and ultimate suspension. By March of 1933, all states imposed bank holidays, mandating the closure of banks to protect themselves and borrowers.

BANKING ACT OF 1933

The Banking Acts of 1933 and 1935 and many state laws enacted about the same time were designed to reduce and prevent the high rate of failure which had characterized American banking history. The Banking Act of 1933 did not diminish nor abolish the powers of the existing governmental machinery relating to banking. Rather, the main provisions simply superimposed the establishment of a deposit insurance agency, the Federal Deposit Insurance Corporation (FDIC) on the existing structure.

All bank members of the Federal Reserve System were required to have their deposits insured by the FDIC. The original capital of the institution—$289,000,000—was provided by the Treasury and the Federal Reserve banks. Insurance coverage by the FDIC was optional for state chartered banks. The FDIC was also granted powers of supervision and regular examination that served to maintain the soundness and viability of member institutions. The Federal Deposit Insurance Corporation was designed to prevent bank failures, not primarily to repay depositors after failure takes place. Depositors were insured up to $2,500 which has been intermittently increased over the years to the present level of $100,000.

Another noteworthy reform enacted in 1933 was a law prohibiting banks from paying interest on demand deposits and the imposition of a ceiling on interest rates paid on time and savings deposits. These restrictions were introduced to deter excessive competition among banks for deposits which would lead to unsound lending and investment practices. Membership in the Federal Reserve System was also granted to mutual savings banks.

The Securities Exchange Act of 1934 authorized the Federal Reserve System to establish margin requirements on security purchases. Such a provision in the 1920s, in retrospect, might have averted the stock market crash of 1929.

HOME OWNERS LOAN ACT AND
FEDERAL HOME LOAN BANK ACT

As a means of remedying weaknesses in the operational structure of the savings and loan industry, the Federal Home Loan Bank System was established. Although the idea of a "central bank" for savings associations was conceived of earlier in 1919—largely to provide parity with the commercial banking system—its actual implementation was not forthcoming until after the events of the Great Depression of 1930.

In 1932, President Hoover recommended the establishment of a Federal Home Loan Bank system. The bill was introduced and passed by Congress in 1932. The system was to be a permanent mechanism within the nation's home financing industry, in spite of the fact that it was created during a period of economic emergency. Such a system was a central reserve credit agency for savings institutions engaged in home mortgage finance. The heavy withdrawals of savings during the Depression period had almost exhausted the supply of home mortgage funds. By advancing funds to its member savings and loan associations, the Federal Home Loan Bank system not only made new funds available for home loans, but also provided the mechanism whereby funds were available to meet withdrawals readily. This served to foster renewed confidence in member savings institutions and stimulated the attraction of new flows of savings.

The Federal Home Loan Bank system is virtually identical in organizational structure with that of the Federal Reserve System. The system is similarly divided into 12 regions or districts, with each district headed by a regional bank. Each regional bank is owned by the member institutions of the region. Chart II-1 illustrates the geographical delineation of the 12 districts. All of the Federal Home Loan Banks are governed by their particular Board of Directors. The Federal Home Loan Bank Board is the central governing body of the entire system. The Board located in Washington, D.C. is comprised of three members appointed for four-year terms by the President with the consent of the Senate. Only two members of the Board may belong to the same political party. The Federal Home Loan Bank Board is responsible for the supervision and regulation of the national Home Loan Bank system. It appoints six of the directors of each of the 12 regional banks. The total number of directors appointed for each regional bank is dependent on the aggregate assets of its mem-

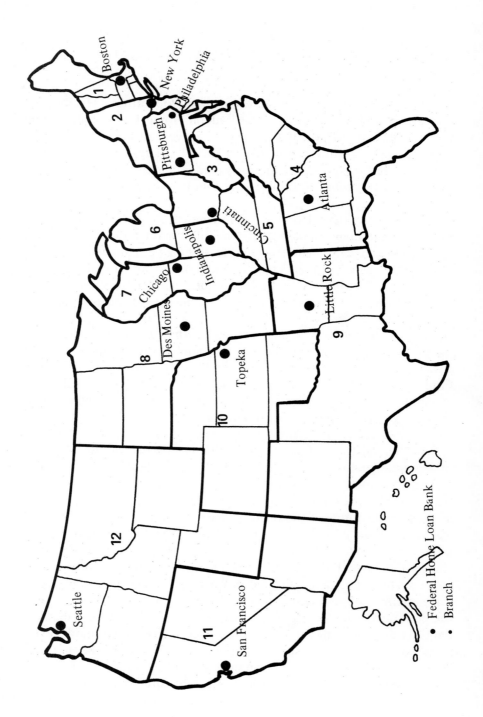

Boston

New York

Philadelphia

1

2

Pittsburgh

3

4

Atlanta

Cincinnati

6

Indianapolis

5

7

Chicago

Little Rock

Des Moines

9

8

Topeka

10

12

11

Seattle

San Francisco

• Federal Home Loan Bank

• Branch

Chart II-1 Federal Home Loan Bank Districts

District

1. **Federal Home Loan Bank of Boston**
   Raymond H. Elliott, President
   Post Office Box 2196
   Boston, Massachusetts 02106
   Connecticut, Maine, Massachusetts, New Hampshire,
   Rhode Island, and Vermont
   District Director-Examinations: Charles E. Seaman

2. **Federal Home Loan Bank of New York**
   Bryce Curry, President
   One World Trade Center, Floor 103
   New York, New York 10048
   New Jersey, New York, Puerto Rico, and Virgin Islands
   District Director-Examinations: Leonard Nightingale

3. **Federal Home Loan Bank of Pittsburgh***
   Louis J. Rub, President
   11 Stanwix St., 4th Floor, Gateway Center
   Pittsburgh, Pennsylvania 15222
   Delaware, Pennsylvania, and West Virginia
   District Director-Examinations: William C. Shone

4. **Federal Home Loan Bank of Atlanta**
   Carl O. Kamp, Jr., President
   Post Office Box 56627
   Atlanta, Georgia 30343
   Alabama, District of Columbia, Florida, Georgia, Maryland,
   North Carolina, South Carolina, and Virginia
   District Director-Examinations: Howard L. Caffrey

District

5. **Federal Home Loan Bank of Cincinnati**
   Charles Lee Thiemann, President
   Post Office Box 598
   Cincinnati, Ohio 45201
   Kentucky, Ohio, and Tennessee
   District Director-Examinations: Donald E. Ison

6. **Federal Home Loan Bank of Indianapolis**
   Freeman A. Goss, Interim Chief Administrative Officer
   2900 Indiana Tower, One Indiana Square
   Indianapolis, Indiana 46204
   Indiana and Michigan
   District Director-Examinations: Ervin Berlinger

7. **Federal Home Loan Bank of Chicago**
   H. Robert Bartell, Jr., President
   111 East Wacker Drive
   Chicago, Illinois 60601
   Illinois and Wisconsin
   District Director-Examinations: Victor S. Meller

8. **Federal Home Loan Bank of Des Moines**
   Dean R. Prichett, President
   907 Walnut Street
   Des Moines, Iowa 50309
   Iowa, Minnesota, Missouri, North Dakota, and
   South Dakota
   District Director-Examinations: Bernard C. Zimmer

9. **Federal Home Loan Bank of Little Rock**
   Raymond F. Widmer, Acting Chief Administrative Officer
   1400 Tower Building
   Little Rock, Arkansas 72201
   Arkansas, Louisiana, Mississippi, New Mexico, and Texas
   District Director-Examinations: Richard J. Wick

District

10. **Federal Home Loan Bank of Topeka**
    Kermit Mowbray, Interim Chief Administrative Officer
    Post Office Box 176
    Topeka, Kansas 66601
    Colorado, Kansas, Nebraska, and Oklahoma
    District Director-Examinations: Raymond J. Gatti

11. **Federal Home Loan Bank of San Francisco**
    Milton Feinerman, President
    Post Office Box 7948
    San Francisco, California 94120
    Arizona, Nevada, and California
    District Director-Examinations: Joseph W. George

12. **Federal Home Loan Bank of Seattle**
    Donald R. Deever, Interim Chief Administrative Officer
    Seattle, Washington 98101
    Alaska, Hawaii and Guam, Idaho, Montana, Oregon,
    Utah, Washington, and Wyoming
    District Director-Examinations: James L. Braz

Source: Federal Home Loan Bank Board.
*Philadelphia Branch Office
3 Parkway Building
16th Street and Benjamin Franklin Parkway
Philadelphia, Pennsylvania 19102

ber associations. Directors are appointed by the Federal Home Loan Bank Board, however, for a term of four years, while those elected by the member institutions in each region are directors for only two years.

The Federal Home Loan Bank Board also is the chartering and regulatory authority for federal savings and loan associations and more recently for federal mutual savings banks. The Board also supervises the Federal Home Loan Mortgage Corporation and the Federal Savings and Loan Insurance Corporation. In its role as a supervisory and regulatory agency, the Board conducts regular examinations of member institutions operations and also adjudicates on matters relating to chartering, mergers and insurance of accounts.

It should be noted that all funds for settling expenses of the Board are derived from within the thrift industry, from examination fees, assessments on the Regional Banks and the Federal Savings and Loan Insurance Corporation. The Board submits an annual report to Congress as an independent agency, and its expenditures are also reviewed by the General Accounting Office.

Membership in the Federal Home Loan Bank system is mandatory for all federally chartered thrift institutions, while state chartered savings associations, mutual savings banks, and life insurance companies may join the system at their own discretion. All members are required to satisfy the requirements set by the Federal Home Loan Bank Board, and to purchase stock in its regional Federal Home Loan Bank in an amount equal to 1 percent of loans outstanding.

THE REGIONAL BANK SYSTEM

As mentioned previously, each regional bank is entirely owned by its member institutions, notwithstanding the fact that they are federal governmental agencies. The regional banks are responsible for effecting the policies of the System in its interaction with member institutions. Member institutions procure services through the particular Federal Home Loan Bank of their district. Each regional Federal Home Loan Bank, in essence, performs the function of a central credit bank, providing funds to members to meet seasonal fluctuations in demands for housing finance and in the pattern of savings inflows. The Regional Bank also functions to supplement housing funds when national policies and financial developments reduce the supply of mortgage finance. Hence, the major and fundamental role of the Regional Banks revolves around the provision of credit to member institutions from the system's pool of funds.

Funds required by the regional banks for undertaking this function and other operations are obtained from the deposits of member institutions, capital stock purchases by members and the sale of consolidated obligations. Surplus banks in the system may also provide additional funds when necessary to other banks via interbank deposits. Consolidated obligations, however, account for the bulk of bank funds averaging approximately 70 percent of total funds within the system.

Member institutions deposit funds in their particular regional banks either in the form of demand deposits or time deposits. The former deposits are used for meeting day-to-day operations, while the latter deposits are held in varying maturities and interest rates.

As was previously mentioned, all members of the Federal Home Loan Bank system are required to hold stock in a Regional Federal Home Loan Bank. Up to 1962, such stock holdings were to be equal to 2 percent of total loans; but as of 1962, this requirement was reduced to 1 percent of total loans. Member institutions which borrow an amount in excess of 12 percent of its total loans must hold stock at least equal to 1/12 of the principal balance owed to the regional bank.

The Federal Home Loan Bank Act also stipulates that 20 percent of net earnings should accrue to the capital accounts of the banks at the end of each semi-annual period. Paid-in capital stock and retained earnings presently average approximately 20 percent of the total resources of the regional Federal Home Loan Banks.

The issuing of consolidated obligations by the Federal Home Loan Bank System represents the only incidence of direct contact with the general public. Federal Home Loan Bank (FHLB) Board consolidated obligations are issued by the FHLB Board and are bought by financial institutions, corporations, and individual investors. The Rate Control Act of 1969 also authorized the Treasury to purchase as much as $4 billion of FHLBB obligations. Previous to the 1969 Act, the Treasury was authorized to purchase $1 billion of these securities by a 1950 Act.

The Federal Home Loan Bank Board's borrowing through the issue of consolidated obligations varies directly with the demand for advances by members, which in turn is affected by the demand for housing finance, deposit flows and fluctuations in the nation's financial markets. In 1974, for example, 23 different issues of consolidated bonds were undertaken by the Board, yielding $11.6 billion in funds.

In contrast in 1976, only six issues totaling $2.8 billion were undertaken, largely a reflection of heavy deposit inflows at member institutions and, hence, a reduction in the demand for bank advances.

These examples illustrate the volatility in the provision of advances to members by the FHLB Board and is also indicative of the dynamic nature of the thrift industry. Generally, though, numerically approximately 50 percent of the FHLB members maintain loan balances. Apart from facilitating the provision of home financing by members during periods of monetary stringency, the FHLB system also provides stability to the savings and loan industry by allowing members to meet heavy withdrawals rapidly and smoothly.

On a broader level, it is also possible for the system to be a net contributor of funds to national capital markets as, for example, when the amount on deposit in the FHLB system and the amount of paid-in stock exceeds the amount borrowed by FHLB members.

In terms of official lending policy, the maximum amount of borrowing by each member of the FHLB system was restricted by law to 50 percent of its total savings balance. The FHLB Board, however, as of January 1982 increased the percentage to 100 percent of total savings. In practice, each regional Federal Home Loan Bank usually stipulates the extent of credit provision to each member. The FHLB Board also limits borrowing in practice to an amount not to exceed 25 percent of the association's total withdrawable savings balances unless the funds are required to meet withdrawals.

The interest charged on borrowings by members provides each regional bank with sufficient funds to meet Bank expenses and dividend payments to members. There is some autonomy and diversity in interest rate policy instituted by each regional bank, and the interest rate charged by each regional bank can vary widely across districts. Interest rate policy for each Regional Bank is dictated by local financial conditions and the needs of member institutions in the particular district.

The Federal Home Loan Banks also provide other services in addition to the provision of deposit facilities and advances. Each regional bank also provides security facilities for the holding of securities by members and acts as an agent in the purchase and sale of securities. Several of the regional Home Loan Banks provide advisory and consulting services to members and furnish statistical and research material regarding local financial conditions to member institutions.

HOMEOWNER'S LOAN ACT AND THE
HOMEOWNER'S LOAN CORPORATION

Congress in 1933, a year after the Federal Home Loan Bank Act, authorized the establishment of the Home Owner's Loan Corporation under the general direction of the Federal Home Loan Bank Board. Through this agency, about 12 percent of urban home mortgage debt was transferred from private lending organizations, including savings and loan associations, to the Home Owner's Loan Corporation during the years 1933-1936. The principal aim of the HOLC was to refinance these mortgage loans on easier terms, so that families threatened with losing their homes could retain possession by arranging for smaller payments on their mortgage liability. Between 1933 to 1936, the Homeowner's Loan Corporation refinanced $3.1 billion of home mortgages. The Corporation also purchased over $770 million of mortgage held by savings and loan associations and invested over $200 million in accounts at savings and loan associations. It also provided assistance for renegotiating loans, closing costs and assessments.

The records of the Homeowner's Loan Corporation indicate that the total losses in the mortgage business was in the region of 18 percent. When associations sold bonds to the Corporation, additional losses were also incurred. These bonds were not guaranteed by the United States Treasury as to principal nor interest and had a market value less than par. The Homeowner's Loan Act also authorized the federal chartering of Savings and Loan Associations under the direction of the Federal Home Loan Bank Board. Confidence in the savings and loan association business was further enhanced by the creation of the Federal Savings and Loan Insurance Corporation in 1934. This agency afforded similar protection to savings and loan associations as that provided to commercial banks by the Federal Deposit Insurance Corporation. In 1934, the use of mortgage insurance through the Federal Housing Administration was also authorized. FHA insured loans would, it was hoped, stimulate the home construction industry. These and other more recently established federal agencies engaged in the housing industry will be discussed more fully in later chapters.

PART TWO

REGULATORY
DEVELOPMENTS

Chapter III

Chartering—Dual—
State/Federal

State supervision and regulation of banking was the dominant form of regulation for 80 years after the ratification of the United States Constitution. During this period, federal involvement in banking was confined to two banks; the First and Second Bank of the United States each chartered for 20 years from 1791-1811, and 1816-1836 respectively. The "free banking" laws preceding 1838 were accompanied by further development of state supervisory and regulatory controls. The National Bank Act of 1864 ushered in another period of national federally chartered banks. "Free-banking" was, in effect, ratified at the national level, and a federal regulatory agency, the office of the Comptroller of the Currency was also established.

Bank chartering by either federal or state government, the "dual-banking" system was in operation from as early as 1863, though the 1864 Act formalized what has emerged as a peculiarly American banking phenomenon. The 1913 Act superimposed on the existing banking system the authority of a new federal agency, the Federal Reserve Board, with the principal objective of encouraging state banks within its arena of regulation. Such a transition was, however, voluntary and many state-chartered banks did not join the Federal Reserve System. It was not until the creation of the Federal Deposit Insurance Corporation in 1933 that all banks, in general, were under some federal regulation. Banks that were members of the Federal Reserve System, whether national or state chartered, were required to have their deposits insured with the Federal Deposit Insurance Corporation, and all other banks could of their own volition participate in the federal insurance program.

Most state banks found it prudent to join the Federal Deposit Insurance Corporation and, thus, de facto, became subject to the regulatory authority of a federal agency—the FDIC. The Bank Holding Company Act of 1956 granted the Federal Reserve Board full regulatory authority over multi-bank holding companies. The Act was further extended in 1970 to cover all bank holding companies, whether one bank or multi-bank. By 1973, 98.4 percent of 13, 976 commercial banks were under some form of federal regulation. However, of that number, under 6000 were actually members of the Federal Reserve System. Currently, there are 14,600 commercial banks in operation, 5,480 of which are members of the Federal Reserve System. Federal Reserve member banks account for approximately 70 percent of total bank deposits nationwide of $720 billion, while over 9,900 state-chartered, nonmember banks are responsible for the remaining 30 percent.

The "dual system" is thus that uniquely American arrangement whereby commercial banks, savings and loan associations, credit unions and, more recently, mutual banks are chartered by both state and federal governments. This system of bank regulation has proved effective in providing financial institutions with the flexibility to meet changing economic and consumer needs. Such flexibility has largely been achieved by removing the necessity for a financial institution to be subject to anachronistic and restraining laws at either the federal or state level. If a state, for example, is reluctant to introduce innovations in response to changing needs, financial institutions can resort to the procurement of federal or national charters. Conversely, if Congress is vacillatory in effecting change, a state legislature may respond by amending and improving the charter under its jurisdiction.

The dual system thus provides a mechanism of checks and balances that serves to foster some degree of equitability and moderation in regulatory activities, together with increased incentive for innovation and improvement of supervisory and regulatory techniques. Often, too, the system generates a certain degree of parallelism in action, in the sense that a realized gain or concession in one regulatory arena usually stimulates similar action in the other. The recent federal override of state interest ceilings on loans and the subsequent passage of similar legislation by the state of New York is a case in point. To this end, the dual system may be highly beneficial in preserving and maintaining some harmony and stability between the two competing segments and the banking sector in general.

On the other hand, the dual system is often adversely viewed as encouraging competition in laxity, since financial institutions have the option of operating by the easier alternative where standards are less stringent. Others argue that the duplication of regulatory authority is inefficient, complicated, and only serves to confuse and burden the nation's financial institutions. Nevertheless, most industry analysts would tend to agree that the dual system, both conceptionally and operationally, does offer definite advantages.

BANK CHARTERING

As was previously mentioned, prior to the free banking laws of 1837 and the National Currency Act of 1863, banks could only be established in the United States by Special state or federal legislative action. With the emergence of "free banking," bank chartering activities mushroomed given the more liberal chartering policies, reaching a peak of 31,076 in 1921. Notwithstanding the entry of new banks into the industry, however, a net increase in the number of banks in existence has only been evident for relatively few years, during the period since 1921, due largely to failures, mergers, and liquidation of previously existing institutions. With the onslaught of the Great Depression, by 1933, there were only 14,771 banks in operation. Currently, the number of banks in operation is approximately 14,600.

The Office of the Comptroller is the sole federal agency charged with the responsibility for chartering a bank. The process of obtaining a national bank charter involves the satisfaction of several requirements as stipulated by the National Bank Act. The formal procedure requires that the group seeking a bank charter file an "Application to Organize a National Bank" with the relevant Regional Administrator of National Banks. Based on the information provided in the application, the Comptroller of the Currency undertakes an investigation of the proposed bank.

In evaluating the application, the examination department of the office of the Comptroller of the Currency adopts certain criteria in determining the viability of the proposed institution. These include the capital adequacy of the proposed bank, the potential future earnings of the proposed institution, the convenience and needs of the community in which the bank will operate, the quality, expertise and experience of proposed banking personnel, and the social standing and character of the principal proponents, prospective officers, directors, and employees. Analysis is, of course, circumscribed by the extent to which the data furnished are consistent with and conform to the norm for national banks as stipulated by the National Bank Act. Comments on the proposed bank are also solicited from existing area banks.

Assuming that all the provisions for chartering have been satisfied by the proposed bank, the Comptroller of the Currency is empowered to issue a tentative approval of the application, pending the submission of the required documents for the incorporation of a national banking association. Subsequent to the filing of the above documents by the Comptroller, a charter certificate is issued which authorizes the institution to engage in the business of banking. It should be mentioned in passing that the Comptroller of the Currency is likely to view negatively any application for a bank charter where the proposed original capital funds are less than $250,000. The agency is of the opinion that unless the proposed bank is able to develop in the near future to a position where bank funds are in the region of $2.5 million, the prognosis for success and viability would be poor. A capital outlay of $250,000 in the above scenario would give the bank a 10 percent margin of safety. Such guidelines, however, are not inflexible and are subject to revision as dictated by changes in the current banking environment.

All nationally chartered banks are ipso facto members of both the Federal Reserve System and the Federal Deposit Insurance Corporation.

STATE CHARTERING REQUIREMENTS FOR BANKS

Chartering regulations, on the other hand, vary from state to state and reflect very little uniformity in terms of requirements and activities in which the proposed bank may engage. However, owing to the fact that virtually all state departments are unwilling to approve an application unless the bank has obtained federal deposit insurance, the Federal Deposit Insurance Corporation, in a sense, provides some degree of uniformity in state-chartering requirements. The Federal Deposit Corporation in ruling on an application for insured status is required by statute to consider several pertinent factors. These include conformity of the banks' corporate powers to the objectives of the Federal Deposit Insurance Act, capital adequacy, the convenience and needs of the community in which the bank is to be located, potential earnings outlook, and an assessment of the character of the banks' management and staff. The standards adopted by the Corporation, for example, those pertaining to capital requirements are similar to those utilized by the Office of the Comptroller of the Currency.

State-chartered banks have the option, too, of applying for membership in the Federal Reserve System in which case approval by the Federal Reserve Board bestows insured status certification on state-chartered institutions. The procedures and requirements for joining the Federal Reserve System are also similar to those adopted by the Comptroller of the Currency, in the processing of national charter applications.

Although the procurement of Federal Deposit Insurance greatly enhances an application for a state charter, it does not preclude the particular bank from satisfying other state provisions. Such requirements may include the number of directors and the length of time each director may serve before re-election, minimum capital outlay and the location of its business. Because of the potential juxtaposition and overlap of state chartering procedures with those pertaining to Federal Reserve System membership or Federal Deposit Insurance coverage, the processing of chartering applications is usually undertaken with the participation and co-operation of the relevant state and federal agencies involved.

FEDERAL CHARTERING OF SAVINGS AND LOAN ASSOCIATIONS

The chartering and supervisory framework within which the savings and loan association business is conducted does not differ in structure from that of the commercial banking industry as just described. Savings and loan associations are established and operate under a similar system of duality; that is, chartering and supervision by either state or federal authorities. While state chartering and supervision of savings and loan associations was the sole form of industry organization for over a century up to 1933, because of the heterogenous nature of state chartering provisions and the wide diversity in permissible association activities, federal charter provisions are more convenient to describe. Moreover, analysis of state charters is further compounded by the fact that state chartered associations may be of the permanent stock or the mutual-type organization, while all federally chartered savings and loan associations must be mutual organizations.[1] For purposes of exposition, and in order to present a generally uniform view of chartering procedures, the federal chartering system will be discussed primarily and then followed by an overview of state chartering provisions.

In order for an association to commence operation, it must first obtain a charter. A charter is simply a statutory authorization to engage in business and is usually granted by the relevant regulatory authority. Sandberg[2] defines a charter as "the birth certificate of a particular association." It is "simply a license to conduct business as a corporation." The establishment of federal savings and loan associations was authorized by the Home Owners Loan Act of 1933, which granted such authority to the Federal Home Loan Bank Board. Section 5(a) of this Act amended by the 1982 Depository Institutions Act states: "In order to provide thrift institutions for the deposit or investment of funds and for the extension of credit for homes and other goods and services, the Board is authorized under such rules and regulations as it may prescribe to provide for the organization, incorporation, examination, operation and regulation of associations to be known as Federal Savings and Loan Associations or Federal Savings Banks, and to issue charters, therefore, giving primary consideration to the best practices of thrift institutions in the United States. The lending and investment authorities are conferred by this section to provide such institutions the flexibility necessary to maintain their role of providing credit for housing."[3]

The original regulations, including charter form (Charter E), were promulgated in that year. Charter E provided for four separate types of accounts retained certain undesirable withdrawal penalties and in general was drafted in confusing jargon and terminology. Though a considerable improvement on state charters, there were still shortcomings. In 1936, Charter K was introduced and was soon adopted by many associations previously chartered under Charter E. In 1949, in response to a changing environment, Charter N was drafted and replaced Charter K. While Charter K did not make specific reference to provisions for withdrawals, Section 6 of the Charter N regulations provided a framework for withdrawals to be dealt with "in accordance

---

[1] The 1982 Garn-St Germain Act removed this restriction.

[2] Richard T. Sandberg, *Introduction to the Savings Association Business* 2nd Ed., American Savings and Loan Institute, p. 149.

[3] Prior to the 1982 Depository Institutions Act Section 5 (a) of HOLA stated: "In order

with such methods and procedures . . . .made by the Federal Home
Loan Bank Board in effect at the date of the request for withdrawal."
In 1953, Charter K was revised and was virtually a duplicate of Charter N, with the exception that withdrawal provisions were made more
specific in terms of a rotational timing procedure and prescribed
dollar magnitudes. It should however, be pointed out that while withdrawal procedures are not explicitly delineated in the Charter N provisions, Section 545.4 of the federal regulations governing operations
specifically details the required procedures which are identical to the
provisions contained in Section 6 of Charter K (Rev.)

As can be seen if Charter K provisions are reviewed carefully,
Section 3 of these regulations stipulates what are the object and
powers of the association, including the right to raise unlimited
capital by accepting payments on savings accounts, to lend and otherwise invest its funds and to mortgage and lease any real and personal
estate. Other provisions of the charter define the rights of members
including voting rights, the power to borrow, make loans and investments, the structure of its directorate and other operational matters
pertaining to reserves, surplus, and the distribution of earnings.

The issuance of a charter thus in essence constitutes the incorporation of a federal association by the Board, the charter document
providing legal evidence of the corporate existence of the particular
federal association.

Federal regulations governing charter applications require that an
application for federal chartering must be submitted by at least
seven persons on the prescribed forms. In addition, all applicants
must provide supporting information as directed by authority of
the Board which attests to the following criteria; (1) that the applicants are citizens of the United States and are of good character
and responsibility; (2) there is a necessity for the proposed association in the community to be served by it; (3) there is a reasonable
probability of usefulness and success of the proposed association;
and (4) establishment of the proposed association can be undertaken
without undue injury to existing soundly managed local thrift and
home financing institutions. The Board is also empowered to take
into consideration all communications in favor of or against the
particular application and may also hold oral hearings in arriving at
a decision regarding the application.

Preliminary approval of the application as determined by the
Board is, however, not binding and does not guarantee the final
issuance of a federal charter. The issuance of the charter is contingent on the satisfaction of certain requirements as stipulated by

TITLE XII—CHARTERS FOR THRIFT INSTITUTIONS

Sec.12.01. Section 2(d) of the Home Owners' Loan Act of 1933 (12 U.S.C. 1462(d)) is amended to read as follows:

"(d) The term 'association' means a Federal savings and loan association or a Federal mutual savings bank chartered by the Board under section 5, and any reference in any other law to a Federal savings and loan association shall be deemed to be also a reference to a Federal mutual savings bank, unless the context indicates otherwise."

Sec. 1202. Section 5(a) of the Home Owners' Loan Act of 1933 (12 U.S.C. 1464(a)) is amended to read as follows:

"Sec. 5. (a) In order to provide local mutual thrift institutions in which people may invest their funds and in order to provide for the financing of homes, the Board is authorized, under such rules and regulations as it may prescribe, to provide for the organization, incorporation, examination, operation, and regulation of associations to be known as 'Federal Savings and Loan Associations', or 'Federal mutual savings banks' (but only in the case of institutions which, prior to conversion, were State mutual savings banks located in States which authorize the chartering of State mutual savings banks, provided such conversion is not in contravention of State law), and to issue charters therefor, giving primary consideration to the best practices of local mutual thrift and home-financing institutions in the United States. An association which was formerly organized as a savings bank under State law may not convert from the mutual to the stock form of ownership. An association which was formerly organized as a savings bank under State law may not convert from the mutual to the stock form of ownership." An association which was formally organized as a savings bank under State law may, to the extent authorized by the Board, continue to carry on any activities it was engaged in on December 31, 1977, and to retain or make any investment of a type it held on that date, except that its equity, corporate bond, and consumer loan investments may not exceed the average ratio of such investments to total assets for the five-year period immediately preceding the filing of an application for conversion and such an association which was formerly organized as a savings bank under State law shall only be permitted to establish branch offices and other facilities in accordance with the limitations imposed by State law controlling applications of a savings bank organized under such State law, provided that such an association: (1) shall be exempt from any numerical limitations of State law on the establishment of branch offices and other facilities, and (2) may, in any case, subject to the approval of the Board, establish branch offices and other facilities in its own Standard Metropolitan Statistical Area, its own county or within thirty-five miles of its home office, but only in its State of domicile. An association which was formerly organized as a savings bank under State law shall be subject to the requirements of State law (including any regulations promulgated thereunder and any sanction for the violation of any such law or regulation) in effect at the time of conversion, in the State of its original charter—

"(1) pertaining to discrimination in the extension of home mortgage loans or adjustment in the terms of mortgage instruments based on neighborhood or geographical area,

"(2) pertaining to requirements imposed under the Consumer Credit Protection Act, if the Board determines that State law and regulations impose more stringent requirements than Federal law and regulations."

Sec. 1203. Section 403(a) of the National Housing Act (12 U.S.C. 1726(a)) is amended by inserting after "Federal savings and loan associations" the following: "and Federal mutual savings banks".

Sec. 1204. The first paragraph of section 5(i) of the Home Owners' Loan Act of 1933 (12 U.S.C. 1404(i)) is amended by inserting "(including a savings bank)" after "member of a Federal Home Loan Bank".

Sec. 1205. The Federal Deposit Insurance Act is amended by adding at the end thereof the following new section:

"CONVERSION OF MUTUAL SAVINGS BANKS

"Sec. 26. With respect to any State-chartered insured mutual savings bank which converts into a Federal savings bank or merges or consolidates into a Federal savings bank or a savings bank which is (or within sixty days after the merger of consolidation becomes) an insured institution within the meaning of section 401 of the National Housing Act, the Corporation shall indemnify the Federal Savings and Loan Insurance Corporation against any losses incurred by it which arise out of losses incurred by the converting bank prior to conversion as follows: One hundred per centum of such losses incurred by the Federal Savings and Loan Insurance Corporation during the first two years after conversion. 75 per centum during the third year, 50 per centum during the fourth year, and 25 per centum during the fifth year. The Corporation and the Federal Savings and Loan Insurance Corporation shall, within six months after enactment hereof, mutually agree on what shall be treated as 'losses incurred by it which arise out of losses incurred by the converting bank prior to conversion' for purposes hereof and, failing such agreement, the General Accounting Office shall prescribe the meaning of those terms. Any conversion, merger, or consolidation covered by this section shall not be deemed a termination of insured status under section 3(a) of this Act."

---

the Board. These include a minimum number of subscribers to the association's capital, minimum amount of capital to be paid into the saving accounts of the association at the time of receiving the charter, and any other provisions as required by the Board. Capital requirements are not fixed, but are discretionarily set and vary in response to the Board's interpretation of local economic and geographic conditions. However, with regard to reserve capital funds, both the Federal Home Loan Bank Board and the Federal Savings and Loan Insurance Corporation require initial reserves to be 10 percent of the savings accounts subscribed to prior to the commencement of business of a new association.

The granting of a federal charter automatically qualifies the new association for membership in a Federal Home Loan Bank, as well as the provision of insurance for its accounts by the Federal Savings and Loan Insurance Corporation. State chartered associations that are members of the Federal Home Loan Bank system may also convert into a federal association, and nonmembers of the Home Loan Bank system may file simultaneously for membership and conversion to a federal charter. In these cases, requirements and procedures are similar to those governing applications for federal charters by do novo institutions.

STATE CHARTERING

There is no uniform state chartering policy, rather each of the fifty states has developed separate chartering requirements and procedures. Moreover, twenty-nine states charter only mutual-type associations, while the remaining twenty-one states charter both mutual as well as permanent-stock associations. This bifurcation in ownership characteristics makes even more difficult a standardized description of state chartering regulations.

Several of the state charters are similar in content and terminology to federal charters, and many state charters with deficient requirements have revised their chartering provisions in accordance with their federal chartering blueprint. In other states, the chartering provisos and format are entirely distinct from the federal model and from each other. However, most state charters generally make some reference to the purpose of the association, its corporate name, its capital structure, the number of directors the association has, its principal business location, its full ownership, and its membership voting rights. Others may include permissable investments and operational regulations.

An industry-wide numerical analysis of state and federally chartered associations illustrates that over the years, although the total number has declined, the rate of attrition has been more pronounced in the case of state-chartered associations. As Table III-1 reveals, the number of state associations has declined by 2,341 since 1960, while over the corresponding period, federal associations recorded a net decrease of 146.

The decrease in the number of associations, particularly state savings and loan association, is largely reflective of increased merger activity, voluntary liquidations, and conversions to federal charters. Given the present economic scenario of high and volatile interest rates, declining savings flows, formidable and widespread competition from nonbank financial intermediaries and consequent attenuation of association earnings, a continuation of the shrinkage in the number of associations can be anticipated as the smaller and less secure institutions consolidate and merge with the more resilient and efficient associations.

Another observation from the data presented in the table relates to the fact that over the years the percentage distribution of associations between state and federal charters has virtually remained stable since 1969. As of December 1982, state-chartered associations accounted for 55 percent of all associations, with federally chartered associations comprising the remaining 45 percent. The fact that the dichotomy between state or federal chartering has not been significantly skewed towards one system attests to the efficacy of the dual chartering system, more so against the background of the enormous growth in assets of savings associations since 1950. Geographically, Pennsylvania has continued to be the location for the largest number of associations followed by Ohio, Illinois, and Texas. While a savings and loan association may be found in every state, the growth of savings and loan associations both numerically and in terms of assets has varied markedly from state to state. Several factors have been responsible for this uneven growth pattern, including the earlier domination of financial services in some states by savings and loan associations, population patterns and growth, income disparities, regional developments, level and pattern of urbanization, and difference in regulatory provisions.

As Table III-1 reveals, assets of federally chartered associations up to 1980 represented almost 56 percent of total assets, with the remaining 44 percent held by state-chartered associations. This distribution has more or less remained constant over the years since 1950, notwithstanding the fact that from the latter year to 1980, total assets of the industry had increased to over 30 times their former level. It is significant that inspite of the enormous growth in assets, the distribution of asset shares between state and federally chartered institutions had demonstrated remarkable consistency as if guided by an invisible regulatory hand. Currently, the distribution of assets between federal and state associations is approximately 69 percent and 21 percent due largely to state conversions.

Geographically, the Pacific region accounts for the largest share of industry assets; namely, 21.7 percent while at the state level, California dominates the asset distribution, representing 18.2 percent of total assets, followed by Florida with 17.8 percent and Illinois with 17.5 percent. As alluded to before, several factors including income growth and distribution, population level, degree of urbanization and so on, are relevant factors influencing the national pattern of dispersion of the assets of the savings and loan industry.

In terms of association size, at the end of 1978, 57.7 percent or 2,723 savings associations held assets of at least $10 million but less than $100 million. The average asset size for the industry in 1980 was, however, $136.5 million. Table III-2 provides some indication of the distribution of savings associations by asset size for the year 1980. As shown, associations with assets under $10 million numbered 790 or 17.1 percent of the total, with assets of $3.14 billion or 0.5 percent of total assets.

Although associations with assets of over $500 million account for

Table III-1   Number and Assets of Savings Associations, by Charter

Year-end	Federally Chartered†	State-chartered Total	FSLIC-insured	Noninsured‡	Grand Total
1960	1,873	4,447	2,225	2,222	6,320
1965	2,011	4,174	2,497	1,677	6,185
1970	2,067	3,602	2,298	1,304	5,669
1971	2,049	3,425	2,222	1,203	5,474
1972	2,044	3,254	2,147	1,107	5,298
1973	2,040	3,130	2,123	1,007	5,170
1974	2,060	2,963	2,081	882	5,023
1975	2,048	2,883	2,030	853	4,931
1976	2,019	2,802	2,025	777	4,821
1977	2,012	2,749	2,053	696	4,761
1978	2,000	2,725	2,053	672	4,725
1979	1,989	2,695	2,050	645	4,684
1982	1,727	2,106	1,616	490	3,833
		Millions of Dollars			
1960	$ 38,511	$ 32,965	$ 26,919	$ 4,046	$ 71,476
1965	66,715	62,865	57,861	5,004	129,580
1970	96,259	79,924	74,386	5,538	176,183
1971	114,229	91,794	85,755	6,032	206,023
1972	139,925	107,202	100,424	6,778	243,127
1973	152,240	119,665	112,557	7,108	271,905
1974	167,671	127,874	120,552	7,322	295,545
1975	195,410	142,823	134,849	7,974	338,233
1976	225,763	166,144	157,409	8,735	391,907
1977	261,920	197,321	188,078	9,243	459,241
1978	298,195	225,347	215,115	10,232	523,542
1979	323,058	255,904	245,049	10,855	578,962
1982	483,898	222,147	208,765	13,382	706,045

*Preliminary.

† All federally chartered associations are insured by the Federal Savings and Loan Insurance Corporation.

‡ Includes the assets of institutions insured by the Co-operative Central Bank of Massachusetts, the Maryland Savings-Share Insurance Corporation, the North Carolina Savings Guaranty Corporation, the Ohio Deposit Guarantee Fund and the Pennsylvania Savings Association Insurance Corporation.

Sources: Federal Home Loan Bank Board; United States League of Savings Associations.

only 4.8 percent of the total number of associations, in relation to asset distribution such associations represent over 46 percent of the aggregate assets of the industry. The bulk of savings associations's assets are, however, held by associations with assets of over $100 million. Numerically, they total 1,246 institutions and are responsible for 81.1 percent of total assets. At the end of 1983, the American Savings and Loan Association; Stockton, California was the largest

Table III-2   Distribution of Savings Associations, by Asset Size, December 31, 1980

Asset Size (Millions)	Number of Associations	Percentage of Total	Assets (Millions)	Percentage of Total
Under $1.	225	4.9%	$ 100	†
$1 and under $5.	280	6.1	808	0.1%
$5 and under $10.	285	6.2	2,234	0.4
$10 and under $25	788	17.1	14,338	2.3
$25 and under $50	898	19.5	34,698	5.5
$50 and under $100	891	19.3	67,019	10.6
$100 and under $150.	396	8.6	50,250	8.0
$150 and under $250.	359	7.8	71,004	11.3
$250 and under $500.	270	5.9	94,242	15.0
$500 and under $1,000	124	2.7	84,604	13.4
$1,000 and over.	97	2.1	210,532	33.4
Total	4,613	100.0%	$629,829	100.0%

Note: Components may not add to totals due to rounding.
† Less than 0.05%.
Sources: Federal Home Loan Band Board; United States League of Savings Associations.

savings and loan association, surpassing Home Savings of America, Los Angeles which had been the largest savings and loan for the previous 28 years. American Savings was ranked first both in terms of assets and deposits and also in terms of net income for 1983. Assets and deposits held by American Savings at the end of 1983 were $18.3 and $22.5 billion, respectively. It is interesting to note that the five largest and most profitable thrifts using 1983 data are all located in the State of California.

FEDERAL CHARTERING OF SAVINGS BANKS

History and Present Legislation

Against the background of the unrivaled and remarkable safety and liquidity position of the mutual banking industry during the depression years of the 1930s, it was not surprising that interest in acquiring the ability to obtain federal charters was virtually nonexistent at the time. Thus, while the savings and loan industry, commercial banks, and other financial institutions which suffered massive attrition together with deterioration in prestige and public confidence envisioned distinct restorative advantages to be derived from federal support, there was no parallel sentiment on the part of the mutual banking industry. Rather, the latter institutions viewed federal regulation and supervision as lacking a positive quid pro quo.

However, with the rapidly changing operational evnironment in a dynamic industry and the re-alignment of competitive positions vis-a-vis other industry participants, the mutual banking industry group gradually began to discern tangible benefits and advantages from being able to legally, but voluntarily, play the game on the same turf as other related financial institutions. Mutual bank growth and expansion was in many instances severely circumscribed by the particular state statutes.

Such regulations often were not revised to reflect changes in fedderal statutes and the financial environment, and hence many mutual banks found themselves incapable of responding to competitive pressures. Moreover, with the volatile interest rates and inflationary pressures of the last decade, particularly the later years, astute pragmatism on the part of the mutual banking industry dictated that future growth and stability would to some degree be influenced by having the option to operate under a federal charter. That alternative finally became a reality on October 15, 1978 with the passage of the Financial Institutions Regulatory Act and Interest Rate Control Act of 1978, twenty-one years after the first legal quest.

The following analysis details the events leading up to the ultimate granting of dual chartering parity for the mutual banking industry. Numerous bills, consolidations, deletions, recommendations, and cooperative thrift efforts characterized the lengthy passage of this dual chartering effort culminating in what the chairman of the National Association of Mutual Savings Banks, Saul B. Klaman, has described as holding "broad implications for the future and may well prove to be the single most important piece of legislation in the history of savings banking."[4]

The first legislative attempt at federal chartering for mutual savings banks was spearheaded by Representative Abraham J. Multer, a New York democrat who introduced HR.4296 in the 85th Congress

---

[3] Prior to the 1982 Depository Institutions Act Section 5 (a) of HOLA stated: "In order to provide local mutual thrift institutions in which people may invest their funds and in order to provide for the financing of homes, the Board is authorized under such rules and regulations as it may prescribe to provide for the organization, incorporation, examination, operation and regulation of associations to be known as 'Federal Savings and Loan Asssociations', and to issue charters, therefore, giving primary consideration to the best practices of local mutual thrift and home financing institutions in the United States."

[4] Saul B. Klaman, *Savings Bank Journal*, October 1978, p. 9.

on February 4, 1957. That bill sought to authorize the creation of a national system of federal mutual savings banks, chartered and regulated by the Comptroller of the Currency. Such federal mutual savings banks would be insured by the Federal Deposit Insurance Corporation. However, the bill was not a reflection of prevailing attitudes within the banking community in general nor within the mutual savings bank industry in particular. Rather, the bill was endorsed by a group of mutual savings bankers in New York State who advocated federal charters for savings banks as a means of circumventing the restrictive laws governing savings bank branching in the State of New York.

The quest for federal chartering of mutual savings banks was not sanctioned at the national level by the industry until almost a year after the introduction of the Multer bill. On March 28, the industry's national forum and mouthpiece, the National Association of Mutual Savings Banks, promulgated a Board of Directors policy statement endorsing federal chartering for the industry. Through the Federal Legislative Committee of the National Association, efforts were consolidated in drafting various federal charter bills during the late fifties and early sixties. On July 1, 1960, during the 86th Congress, the first National Association of Mutual Bankers federal charter bill was tabled in the Senate by Democratic Senator John Sparkman and simultaneously in the House by the original protagonist Representative Abraham Multer. These bills were introduced to generate "study and discussion" within legislative and financial circles, with more vigorous efforts for passage directed at the 7th Congress in 1961.

It should be mentioned that while the original federal chartering bill in 1957 was a reflection of attempts to overcome New York State branching laws, the 1960 bills were introduced to provide for the expansion of the mutual banking industry nationwide. Such shifts of rationale behind the introduction of federal charter bill would become an inherent part of the mutual banking industry's drive for federal chartering. The 1960 bill provided for the federal chartering and supervision of federal mutual banks by a Federal Mutual Savings Bank Commission, authorized the conversion of Savings and Loan Associations to federal mutual banks and for the insurance of accounts by the Federal Deposit Insurance Corporation. The 1960 bill produced considerable interest in the chartering of federal mutual savings banks by members of the financial industry and federal departments. Indeed, the 1961 Report by the Commission on money and credit endorsed federal charters for mutual savings banks. The same view was expressed by several federal agencies, including the FHA, VA, and HUD.

Continued discussion on the federal chartering proposals and future courses of action dominated the scene in 1969, but it was not until early 1970 with the appointment by President Nixon of the Commission on Financial Structure and Regulation, more popularly known as the Hunt Commission and the subsequent release of its report in December 1971, that renewed efforts for drafting an acceptable federal chartering bill were undertaken. The Hunt Report recommended the granting of federal charters to the mutual banks pointing out the inadequacies and inefficiencies occasioned by a lack of dual chartering powers, such as undue restrictions on entry and expansion, and reduced interest in stimulating innovation and change pro bono publico.

After a hiatus of some eighteen months, the Financial Institutions Act of 1973 was drafted with the endorsement of the administration; the mutual bankers and other co-sponsors. The FIA bill was similar in content to the previous federal chartering legislative efforts. In spite of an easy passage of the bill in the Senate in December 1975, the bill made no further advance in the legislative process, largely due to opposition from the commercial banking, labor, and housing sectors. The Financial Institutions and the National Economy, (FINE) study by the House was also in progress at the same time, and the resulting legislative proposal, the Financial Reform Act, because of its massive scope and opposition from commercial banks, labor and housing lobbyists was short-lived.

HR9600 was introduced to the full committee as HR13088, the Financial Institutions Regulatory Act of 1978. After committee action, a new bill HR13471 was dispatched to the full House in July. Cleared by the House Rules Committee, the bill was tabled for floor consideration, a lengthy process, as the bill HR13471 contained 19 other titles in addition to Title 12.

Rhetorical warfare, nonetheless, continued from opposition lobbyists and several amendments to Title 12 were introduced by Representative Hanley and adopted by the House on October 5th in an attempt to mediate the controversy. These included the provision that federal savings mutual banks were to be prohibited from converting to stock form, the nonpre-emption of state laws requiring state approval of conversion applications and also of state consumer credit protection laws which were more stringent than federal law. On October 5th, HR 13471 was tabled in the House and the first 12 titles were approved, including Title 12 with the Hanley amendments. After a recess and assembly again on October 12, it was improbable that the House have sufficient time to deliberate on HR 13471's remaining titles, with adjournment scheduled for October 14th.

One bill that had to be considered was a Senate approved bill extending Regulation Q provisions also containing a federal charter amendment. The House quickly passed the Regulation Q extensions for two years and for expediency opted to include other legislative items previously approved by the House and/or Senate. The House finally adopted the two-year Regulation Q extensions and the retirement insurance accounts amendments together with NOW account authorization for New York State. The twelve titles of HR13471 previously approved by the House on October 5 were also added. The revised bill HR14279 was passed on October 15 by the House and sent to the Senate where it was approved. The federal chartering of mutual savings banks had become a legislative reality under Title 12 of the Financial Institutions Regulatory Act and Interest Rate Control Act of 1978, with the Federal Home Loan Bank authorized to issue federal savings bank charters six months after the President signs the bill.

The federal chartering alternative for mutual savings banks has broadened the industry's position and "federal clout" in Washington. No doubt, too, a number of mutual banks would find it prudent to convert to take advantage of less restrictive branching laws, and to take advantage of the benefits of being part of the Federal Home Loan Bank system. It can also be projected that more equality of competitive structures between the Savings and Loan Associations and mutual savings banks, that is greater structural and functional convergence, will emerge as the Federal Home Loan Bank regulates the thrift industry.

Title 12 of the Financial Institutions Regulatory and Interest Rate Control Act authorizes the conversion of state-chartered mutual savings banks to federal mutual charters if the relevant state laws permit such conversion. Activities which the federal mutual bank was engaged in on December 31, 1977 are grandfathered subject to the discretion of the bank board, with the exception that equity, corporate bond, and consumer loan investments may not exceed the average ratio of such investments to total assets for the five-year period immediately preceding the filing of the conversion application.

Although federal mutual savings banks will be regulated and supervised by the Federal Home Loan Bank Board, state laws relating to branching will still be in effect. However, there shall be no numerical limitations and with the authorization of the Bank Board, a federal mutual bank may establish branch offices and other facilities in its own standard metropolitan statistical area, county, or within 35 miles of its home office subject, of course, to the provision that such offices or facilities are located within the bank's state of location. Title 12 also stipulates that if at the time of conversion state laws governing discrimination in the extension of home mortgage laws or which pertain to the Consumer Credit Protection Act are more stringent than federal laws, then the converted bank will be required to comply with the requirements of state law. Figure III-1 details the specific provisions of Title 12. In actuality, Title 12 amends the Home Owners Loan Act of 1933 which is the statute under which the Bank Board charters Federal Savings and Loan Associations. Section 1201 of the Title redefines the term "association" for purposes of the Act to include federal mutual savings banks under the jurisdiction of any other law applicable to a federal savings and loan association unless exceptions are indicated. Section 1201 of the Title amends Section 5 (a) of the 1933 Act to include provisions specifically applicable only to federal mutual savings banks, while Sections 1203, 1204 and 1205 relate to insurance by the Federal Savings and Loan Insurance Corporation, membership in a Federal Home Loan Bank, and the indemnification by the Federal Deposit Insurance Corporation of the Federal Savings and Loan Insurance Corporation against losses incurred by a mutual savings bank prior to conversion to a Federal Charter.

Only existing mutual savings banks located in states which permit the chartering of mutual savings banks and where conversion to federal charter would not contravene state law are eligible to acquire federal charters. Federal mutual savings banks could not be chartered de novo.

The Depository Institutions Act of 1982 removed these restrictions and also rescinded the prohibition against the establishment of or conversion to federal stock institutions in states where stock associations do not exist. Specifically, Section 312 of Title III of the new bill authorizes the Federal Home Loan Bank Board for the first time to organize, de novo, federal stock savings and loan associations or federal mutual or stock savings banks. The 1982 Act, thus, accords thrift institutions flexibility in determining the type of

CHARTER B

Section 1. Corporate Title. The full corporate title of the bank is _____ .

Section 2. Office. The home office of the bank shall be located in the County of _____ , State (Territory, possession or District) of _____ .

Section 3. General Objects and Powers. The bank is a mutual thrift institution established for the primary purpose of providing people with a convenient and safe place to invest their funds and to provide for the financing of homes, and is chartered under Section 5 of the Home Owners' Loan Act of 1933, as amended, and has and may exercise all the express, implied and incidental powers conferred thereby and by all acts amendatory thereof and supplemental thereto, subject to the Constitution and laws of the United States as they are now in effect, or as they may hereafter be amended, and subject to all lawful and applicable rules, regulations, and orders of the Federal Home Loan Bank Board ("Bank Board").

Section 4. Duration. The duration of the Bank is perpetual.

Section 5. Capital. The bank may raise capital by accepting payments on deposit savings accounts (and on deposit checking accounts) and by any other means (except capital stock) as may be authorized by the Bank Board.

Section 6. Members. All holders of the bank's savings accounts and all borrowers therefrom are members. In consideration of all questions requiring action by the members of the bank each holder of a savings account shall be permitted to cast one vote for each $100 or fraction thereof, of the withdrawal value of his or her account. A borrowing member shall be permitted, as a borrower, to cast one vote, and to cast the number of votes to which he or she may be entitled as the holder of a savings account. No member, however, shall cast more than 400 votes. Voting may be by proxy. Any number of membes present at a regular or special meeting of the members shall constitute a quorum. Except as otherwise provided by this charter or required by the Bank Board, a majority of all votes cast at any meeting of members shall determine any question.

The members who shall be entitled to vote at any meeting of the members shall be those owning savings accounts and borrowing members of record on the books of the bank at a date set by the board of trustees not less than 20 days and not more than 50 days prior to the date of such meeting. The number of votes which each member shall be entitled to cast at any meeting of the members shall be determined from the books of the bank as of such record date. Any member at such record date who ceases to be a member prior to such meeting shall not be entitled to vote thereas.

Section 7. Trustees. The bank shall be under the direction of a board of trustees of not less than 7, as fixed in the bank's bylaws or, in the absence of any such bylaw provision, as from time to time expressly determined by resolution of the bank's members. Each trustee of the bank shall be a member of the bank, and a trustee shall cease to be a trustee when he ceases to be a member. Trustees of the bank shall be elected by its members by ballot; Provided, That in the event of a vacancy in the board of trustees, including vacancies created by an increase in the number of trustees, the board of trustees may fill such vacancy by electing a trustee to serve until the next annual meeting of the members. Trustees shall be elected for periods of 3 years and until their successors are elected and qualified, but provision shall be made for the election of approximately one-third of the board of trustees each year.

Section 8. Withdrawals. Each withdrawal from a savings account shall be governed by this section except to the extent that a member's account book or other written evidence of the member's savings account contains additional requirements in accordance with regulations made by the Bank Board. The bank shall have the right to pay the withdrawal value of its savings accounts at any time upon application therefor and to pay the holders thereof the withdrawal value thereof. Upon receipt of a written request from any holder of a savings account of the bank for the withdrawal value thereof, the bank shall within 30 days pay the amount requested;

Provided, That if the bank is unable to pay all withdrawals requested at the end of 30 days from the date of such requests, it shall then proceed in the following manner while any withdrawal request remains unpaid for more than 30 days:

Withdrawal requests shall be paid in the order received and if any holder of a savings account or accounts has requested the withdrawal of more than $1,000, he or she shall be paid $1,000 in order when reached and his or her withdrawal request shall be charged with such amount as paid and shall be renumbered and placed at the end of the list of withdrawal requests, and thereafter, upon again being reached, shall be paid a like amount, but not exceeding the withdrawal value of his or her savings account, and until such withdrawal request shall have been paid in full, shall continue to be so paid, renumbered, and replaced at the end of the withdrawal requests on file: Provided, That when any such request is reached for payment, the bank shall so advise the holder of such savings account by registered or certified mail to his or her last address as recorded on the books of the bank and unless such holder shall apply in person or in writing for the payment of such withdrawal request within 30 days from the date of the mailing of such notice, no payment on account of such withdrawal request shall be made and such request shall be cancelled: And provided further, That the board of trustees shall have the absolute right to pay on an equitable basis an amount not exceeding $200 to any holder of a savings account or accounts in any calendar month and without regard to any other provision of this section.

When the bank is unable to pay all withdrawal requests within a period not exceeding 30 days from the date of receipt of written request therefor it shall allot to the payment of such requests the remainder of the bank's receipts from all sources after deducting from total receipts appropriate amounts for expenses, required payments on indebtedness, earnings distributable in cash to holders of savings accounts, and a fund for general corporate purposes equivalent to not more than 20 percent of the bank's receipts from holders of its savings (and of its checking accounts) and from its borrowers.

Section. 9. Redemption. At any time sufficient funds are on hand, the bank shall have the right to redeem, by lot or other non-discriminatory manner as the board of trustees may determine, all or any part of any of its savings accounts, except fixed rate-fixed term certificates of deposit, by giving 30 days' notice of such redemption by registered mail addressed to the holder of each such savings account at his or her last address as recorded on the books of the bank. The bank may not redeem any of its savings accounts when there is an impairment of its capital or when it has any request for withdrawal which has been on file and unpaid for more than 30 days. The redemption price of each savings account redeemed shall be the full value thereof, as determined by the board of trustees, but in no event shall the redemption price be less than the withdrawal amount of such savings account. If a savings account which is redeemed is entitled to participate in any reserve for bonus, the amount in such reserve for bonus which is properly allocable to such savings account shall not be paid as part of the redemption price thereof. If any notice of redemption shall have been duly given, and if the funds necessary for such redemption shall have been set aside so as to be and to continue to be available for that purpose, earnings upon such account shall cease to accrue from and after the date specified as the redemption date and all rights with respect to each such account shall forthwith, after such redemption date, terminate, except only the right of the holder of record of such savings account to receive the redemption price thereof without earnings.

Section 10. Loans, Investments, other Activities. The bank may make any loan or investment and engage in such other activities (including offering savings bank life insurance) authorized by the Bank Board provided, that the bank's equity, corporate bond, and consumer loan investments may in no event exceed _____ percent of its total assets.

Section 11. Reserves, Distribution of Earnings, and Liquidation. The bank shall maintain general reserves for the sole purpose of meeting losses in at least such amounts as may be required by the Bank Board; such reserves shall include the reserve required for insurance of accounts. Any losses may be charged against general reerves.

The bank shall distribute net earnings on its savings deposits on such basis and in accordance with such terms and conditions as may from time to time be authorized by the Bank Board, provided, however, that the bank shall not be required to distribute earnings on short-term savings accounts or on accounts of ten dollars or less.

All holders of savings (and checking) accounts of the bank shall be entitled to equal distribution of assets, pro rata to the value of their accounts, in the event of voluntary or involuntary liquidation, dissolution, or winding up of the bank. Moreover, in any such event or in any other situation in which the priority of such savings (and checking) accounts is in controversy, all such accounts shall, to the extent of their withdrawal value, be debts of the bank having the same priority as the claims of general creditors of the bank not having priority (other than any priority arising or resulting from consensual subordination) over other general creditors of the association.

Section 12. <u>Amendment of Charter.</u> No amendment, addition, alteration, change, or repeal of this charter chall be made, unless such is first proposed by the board of trustees of the bank, approved by the Bank Board, and thereafter approved by the members by a majority of the votes cast at a legal meeting. Any amendment, addition, alteration, change, or repeal so acted upon shall be filed with the Bank Board and shall be effective as of the date approved by the bank's membership.

Federal Home Loan Bank Board

By _____
(Chairman)

Attest

_____
(Secretary)

———————

ownership and form of incorporation under which they may operate.

In applying for a federal charter, the relevant application form and supporting documents must be filed with the Supervisory Agent of the Federal Home Loan Bank district in which the applicant is located and transmitted to the Bank Board for processing. The procedures for the processing and examination of application are basically similar to those governing federal savings and loan charter applications.

In ruling on an application, the Board will be primarily concerned with the best operations of local mutual thrift and home financing institutions in the United States. More to the point, the Board will consider the financial history and condition of the applicant banks, capital structure and adequacy, future potential earnings outlook, the general character and ability of management, home financing record and policy, indicated commitment to home financing and performance in helping to meet the credit needs of their local communities.

Upon approval of the charter application, the Bank Board will issue a charter to the converted federal mutual savings that constitutes its incorporation by the Board. An indication of the charter document, Charter B is provided in Figure III-2 and is comparatively similar, though not identical in structure and terminology to the Charter K stipulations governing federal savings and loan associations.

One major difference arising from the historical structure of mutual bank management and succession is the fact that mutual banks are directed by the board of trustees which elects its own successors or are elected by a separate group of corporators. As Section 7 of the charter document states, trustees will be elected by members of the bank, each holder of a savings account being entitled to one vote for each $100 or fraction thereof of the withdrawal value of the account. A phase-in plan for membership election of trustees is, however, permissible with at least one-fifth of a converted banks's trustees being elected by membership vote either in person or by proxy within two years after conversion. An additional one-fifth of the trustees should be elected by membership vote within each of the next four years.

More recently, amendments to the former charter provisions in Figure III-2 were adopted by the Federal Home Loan Bank Board. These included a 5 percent leeway investment authority and corporate demand deposit account authority for federal mutual savings banks and the reconciliation of inconsistent investment limitations for federal mutual savings banks in corporate bonds and corporate loans as provided in the 1978 law and the recent *Depository Institutions Deregulations and Monetary Control Act.* In addition, the amendments define terms and conditions relating to the Board's authority to grandfather a mutual savings bank's activities and investments, and also permits the Board's reserve account regulations to include types of investments generally undertaken by mutual savings banks. In relation to grandfathering activities, the Board has decided that it will not grandfather any activity or investment which might deter a strong orientation toward home financing and community development.

To date, up to January 1984, there has been considerable attention focused on the federal conversion issue, as several of the nation's largest mutual banks have opted for federal charters, more so in the light of the expanded powers granted federal thrifts institutions under the *Depository Institutions Deregulation and Monetary Control Act of 1982.*

In January 1980, Newport Savings Bank of New Hampshire filed the application for a federal charter more than ten months after the ability to acquire a federal charter became law on March 11, 1979. The Newport application was approved by the Federal Home Loan Bank Board on September 11, 1980 and on December 1, the Newport Savings officially adopted the new name "Newport Mutual Savings Bank, fsb.", the nation's first federal mutual savings bank. Shortly after, two more federal charters were granted by the Board to the Anchor Savings Bank of New York City and the Citizens Savings Bank in upstate Ithaca, New York. Sixteen other New York Savings Banks had federal charter applications pending, one from Minnesota and one from Pennsylvania, the nation's largest savings bank, the $6.9 billion assets, Philadelphia Savings Fund Society.

Newport Savings, the nation's first federal savings bank, has operated under a state charter since 1868. The principal reason for undertaking the charter conversion was the ability under federal charter to branch into the New London area in a shorter time than permitted under state law.

John Kiernan, President and Chief Executive Officer of Newport, viewed the federal charter as providing " . . . .more convenience and broader service." Most of the federal charter applications are reflective of the above sentiment. For example, Albert B. Hooke, President of the Community Savings Bank and Chairman of the National Association of Mutual Savings Banks, saw a federal charter for the bank as providing expanded service powers and new markets, reflective of the "general liberal attitude of the Federal Government which recognizes that we need more powers to compete in a Reg-Q-less environment." The enactment of the *Depository Institutions Deregulation and Monetary Control Act of 1980*, too, further authorizes federal savings banks to issue credit cards, corporate and consumer loans, accept corporate business deposits, trust services and wider investments.

As was alluded to before, the majority of charter conversions so far have originated in New York State. Notwithstanding the passage of a State Omnibus Banking Bill in late November, most of the charter applicants have remained committed to obtaining federal charters. One major overriding factor influencing this decision is the concern of thrift officials for the apparent lethargy and unresponsiveness of the state legislature to the needs of the thrift industry. Many view the recent parity bill as action taken to reduce the current conversion problem devoid of any change in the future attitude of the state legislature reflecting a genuine commitment to the thrift industry.

The chairman of the United Mutual Savings Bank, New York City, Edward J. Maude, whose application for a federal charter was then awaiting Board approval inferred that "We want to get to Washington . . . to have one regulator rather than two, and to have one that's basically interested in thrifts." Kenneth H. Myers, Citizens Savings Bank's President and Chief Executive Officer surmised that the "Federal Home Loan Bank Board has been the leader in broadening powers for thrifts; the State has only been reacting. We anticipate this pattern will continue in the future and we'd rather be six months to two to three years ahead in terms of new powers."

One other industry official asserted that "there are many aspects of a federal charter which go beyond what the state could do."

While the New York State Parity Bill encompasses significant new powers for thrifts comparable to the *1980 Monetary Control Act*, there are still several shortcomings. The state law does not provide for the authorization to charge fees on checking accounts, to make out-of-state loans for housing and also contains lower state borrowing limitations in compairson to federal guidelines. Moreover, the state law does not permit, as under federal law, commercial and savings banks to share electronic banking facilities.

In Pennsylvania a situation similar to that in New York before the passage of a Parity Bill developed and threatened the existence of all nine mutual banks as state chartered institutions. Already two mutual banks, the Philadelphia Savings Funds Society, the nation's largest, and the Eastern Savings Fund Society had initiated federal charter application procedures. While both institutions would like to see the required comparable state legislation enacted, the uncertainty surrounding the passage of such legislation necessitated alternative action in the form of a federal charter bid.

It can, therefore, be expected that conversions to federal charters will continue to increase unless state legislatures adopt a more innovative and active profile in response to the new competitive environment of the thrift industry. The Federal Home Loan Bank has adopted regulations to date which reflect the commitment of the Board that federal savings banks will continue to be "savings banks" and not savings and loan associations. The Board has and will exercise its discretion in ruling on grandfathering issues and the housing commitment of savings banks in an attempt to allow converting savings banks to continue to operate in their traditional manner. While the federal requirement that converting savings banks must phase in the depositor election of savings bank trustees may deter some potential charter conversion applicants, most industry analysts view the factor of negligible influence on federal chartering decisions. No doubt, as long as there remains an imbalance of competitive powers, attempts will be made to correct this inequitable situation and enhance the viability of the mutual banking industry. The federal charter alternative is certainly one potential palliatory strategy.

While the mechanism has been put in place to foster the application for federal charters by state chartered savings banks, few applications for federal charters by state chartered savings banks, had been approved prior to 1982. As a result of extraordinary disintermediation, many savings banks had sought entry into the Federal Home Loan Bank system to secure the credit available to members of the system. While without conversion mutual banks may become stockholders of and acquire membership in the Federal Home Loan Bank, many have felt that conversion offered greater advantages. Since savings banks are insured by the Federal Deposit Insurance Corporation, their change to a federal charter would remove them from the coverage of that agency and bring them under the umbrella of the Federal Savings and Loan Insurance Corporation.

Consequently, the new status placed an additional responsibility upon the FSLIC in the insurance of additional deposits held by the converting institution. In normal times, this new burden would have no effect upon the Insurance Corporation. Since the *Banking Act of 1933*, neither corporations were ever concerned with the depletion of their own capital to any extent to bolster failing institutions. However, with the onset of high money costs and the extraordinary erosion of net worth of the thrifts, both the FDIC and the FSLIC have become increasingly concerned with the condition of their own net worth. A conversion of a distressed thrift to a federal charter would, in effect, act to impair the net worth of the FSLIC. Unsettled negotiations, in an effort to secure indemnification from the agency which had insured the converting institution to the new agency, reduced the likelihood that many federal savings bank charters were granted. In rare instances, a few institutions with more than adequate net worth have been brought into the Home Loan Bank System.

However, the *1982 Depository Institutions Act* authorized the Bank Board, if state law permits, to approve the conversion of a state-chartered savings bank to federal charter without requiring the converted institution to be insured by the FSLIC. FDIC-insured federal savings banks will operate with the same investment powers as FSLIC-insured federal institutions. The FDIC would, however, be empowered to conduct special examinations of these federal savings banks, approve mergers of such associations with institutions not insured by the FDIC and to act as receiver in cases of failure. The FDIC would also have the authority, as an emergency measure, to request the Bank Board to approve a federal stock charter to a distressed state-chartered savings bank. Such authority would, however, be repealed three years after passage of the 1982 Act.

STATE CHARTERING OF MUTUAL SAVINGS BANKS

In terms of geographic distribution, the mutual banking industry does not conform to the familiar nationwide dispersion of its thrift counterpart, the savings and loan association. In fact, mutual banks exist in only seventeen states on the continent and in the associate state of Puerto Rico. At the end of 1982, mutual savings banks numbered 424 in the United States with total assets of over $174 billion.

The relatively limited territorial dispersion of the mutual banking industry is largely the result of legal restrictions which prohibit the operation of mutual savings banks in the remaining states. Another factor influencing this limited distribution is partially historical, with savings and loan associations developing rapidly in the Western states and hence there being no necessity for establishing mutual banks in these states.

The majority of mutual savings banks are located in the New England and Mid-Atlantic regions as Table III-3 illustrates. Massachusetts accounted for the largest number of savings banks, 155 followed by New York, Connecticut, Maine, New Hampshire and

Table III-3   Distribution of Savings Banks According to Size, by States,
December 31, 1982

State	Total Number of Savings Banks	Deposits (in millions of dollars)					
		Less than 50.0	50.0 to 99.9	100.0 to 249.9	250.0 to 499.9	500.0 to 999.9	1,000.0 and over
Massachusetts	155	36	44	59	9	5	2
New York	95	1	14	28	12	17	23
Connecticut	62	6	17	21	11	5	2
New Hampshire	25	3	14	6	2	–	–
Maine	24	7	10	3	3	1	–
New Jersey	19	2	2	5	6	2	2
Washington	9	–	2	4	2	–	1
Pennsylvania	8	1	1	2	–	–	4
Rhode Island	6	–	–	3	2	1	–
Vermont	5	1	1	2	1	–	–
Indiana	4	1	3	–	–	–	–
Maryland	3	–	–	1	–	1	1
Wisconsin	3	2	1	–	–	–	–
Alaska	2	2	1	–	–	–	–
Delaware	2	–	–	1	–	1	–
Oregon	2	–	–	2	–	–	–
Total	424	60	109	138	49	33	35

Source: NAMSB.

New Jersey. In terms of deposit distribution, however, mutual savings banks in the State of New York are responsible for over 50 percent of the total deposits of the mutual banking industry (See Table III-4). Seventy-five percent of the deposits of the mutual banking industry are insured by the Federal Deposit Insurance Corporation as of 1982, with the remaining 25 percent being insured by state funds such as the Mutual Savings Central Fund Inc. of Massachusetts. Thirty-one percent or 130 mutual banks were members of the Federal Home Loan Bank system, but with insurance coverage by the Federal Deposit Insurance Corporation as of 1982.

In spite of the limited geographic extension of the mutual banking industry, each state has its own chartering provisions which, while containing some similar features to other state charters, are often quite distinct and unique. In Indiana, for example, where four mutual banks are in operation, no new savings banks can be established. Indiana also was one of the few states in which savings banks were allowed to accept checking accounts prior to recent legislation. Generally, though, most mutual savings bank charters stipulate that

Table III-4 Deposits, Number of Accounts and Average Size of Accounts in Savings Banks, by States, December 31, 1982

State	Deposits (in millions of dollars)					Number of Accounts (in thousands)		Average Size of accounts (in dollars)	
	Total	Regular Deposits				Total	Regular	Total	Regular
		Total	Savings	Time	Other				
New York	78,287	77,062	27,802	49,260	1,225	15,964	13,754	4,904	6,603
Massachusetts	22,196	22,080	9,711	12,368	116	5,829	5,454	3,808	4,049
Connecticut	15,710	15,463	5,807	9,656	247	3,494	2,990	4,497	5,172
Pennsylvania	13,281	13,098	3,909	9,189	184	2,829	2,538	4,695	5,161
New Jersey	9,745	9,404	3,254	6,150	341	2,098	1,588	4,645	5,923
Washington	3,594	3,548	1,283	2,265	47	684	678	5,258	5,232
Maine	2,765	2,723	1,129	1,595	41	752	641	3,678	4,250
New Hampshire	2,694	2,673	1,101	1,572	21	695	653	3,874	4,096
Maryland	1,934	1,862	843	1,019	72	435	351	4,447	5,309
Rhode Island	1,918	1,912	702	1,210	6	466	423	4,114	4,523
Delaware	978	929	353	576	49	309	232	3,167	4,005
Vermont	781	761	242	519	19	190	155	4,107	4,915
Alaska	514	488	65	423	26	28	27	18,692	17,932
Oregon	425	417	106	311	8	83	76	5,111	5,480
Indiana	282	268	72	195	15	89	53	3,159	5,025
Wisconsin	91	89	29	60	2	22	20	4,164	4,356
Total	155,196	152,777	56,408	96,369	2,419	33,966	29,632	4,569	5,156

Note: Regular deposits include savings, time and transaction deposits. Savings deposits refer to all ordinary passbook or statement type savings accounts and interest-bearing NOW accounts. Time deposits consist of certificates, special notice accounts, term and other time deposits. "Other" deposits include all school, club, checking, non-interest-bearing NOW accounts and certain other accounts. Deposit data exclude mortgagors' escrow accounts.

Source: NAMSB.

these institutions are basically established to accept savings deposits guaranteeing their safety and to make appropriate investments. All mutual banks are governed by a board of trustees who are elected from among themselves and not by depositors. All mutual banks are self-perpetuating and thus operate with the right to a continued existence. Most charters also stipulate what investments mutual banks are permitted to undertake. In Massachusetts, New York, and Connecticut, mutual banks are permitted to sell life insurance. Given the fact that mutual banks historically occupied a fiduciary position in that they solicit the public to submit to them personal property, the public is primarily entitled to protection. It is against this background that most of the laws governing investments by mutual banks have been formulated. Most are highly restrictive, but in Maryland and Delaware, investment of savings bank funds is left to the discretion of the officers of the bank, though such activities are carefully monitored by the state banking departments.

With the passage of the Depository Institutions Deregulation and Monetary Control Act of 1980 which broadens the lending and branching powers of federally chartered savings banks, most state legislatures had of necessity to enact comparable "parity" legislation in order to place state chartered savings banks on a more equal competitive footing vis-a-vis other financial intermediaries. As was discussed earlier, a number of mutual savings banks are actively considering converting to federal charters in order to procure expanded powers, more so with the passage of the 1982 Garn Act.

STOCK CHARTERS VERSUS MUTUAL CHARTERS

As was previously mentioned, savings and loan associations may also be chartered as permanent stock or capital stock associations. Geographically, however, the development of permanent stock associations has been restricted due to the fact that only twenty one states charter or permit the operation of stock associations.

California, Texas, Ohio and Illinois account for over 60 percent of the total number of stock associations operating nationwide. Of 195 associations in operation in California during 1980, 122 or approximately 63 percent were organized under permanent stock ownership, representing over 60 percent of total assets of associations within the state. Nationally, the assets of stock associations in California accounted by 47 percent of all stock association holdings at the end of 1980. Table III-5 provides some indication of the number and total assets of stock associations for the years 1981 and 1982.

Quantitatively on a national industry-wide basis, stock associations accounted for by 21.6 percent of all associations in operation in 1982. In terms of asset share, these stock associations held 31.1 percent of the total assets of the savings and loan industry in 1982.

While the 1948 amendment to the Home Owners Loan Act authorized the conversion of federal mutual to state chartered mutual to stock association, it was not until October 28, 1974 that an amendment to the National Housing Act permitted the conversion of federal mutual associations to federal stock associations in states where stock associations are authorized. Notwithstanding the vigorous efforts of various interest groups to prevent such conversions and the promulgation of a number of moratoriums on stock conversions, recent litigation has supported the validity of the authority of the Federal Home Loan Bank to undertake such activities.

Since 1974, a number of federal mutual associations have converted to a federal stock association, and the number of applications for conversions have been steadily increasing over the past year. The whole subject of conversions from mutual to stock associations will be discussed more fully in the following chapter, but a principal reason for the increase in the number of conversions is that stock associations can raise additional funds to expand net worth by the sale of shares, while for mutual associations substantial additions to net worth can only be generated from after-tax income. Moreover, given the current volatile and high interest rate scenario and the

Table III-5   Permanent Stock Savings Associations
(dollar amounts in millions)

State	December 31, 1981		December 31, 1982*	
	Number of Associations	Total Assets	Number of Associations	Total Assets
California	129	$ 194,346	125	$100,293
Texas.	218	25,982	208	31,951
Ohio	78	15,465	76	15,841
Florida	32	11,956	35	12,761
Other States	413	53,545	386	58,856
Total	870	$194,346	830	$219,702

Source: U.S. League of Savings Institutions.

consequent outflow of deposits into higher yielding instruments, the ability to raise additional capital can be of assistance in cushioning such destabilizing developments. More recently, too, the scope for acquiring federal stock charters has been considerably expanded with the enactment of HR4986 and FHLB Board resolution No. 80-529 dated 8/21/80 which permits federal stock conversion of state associations in existence four years prior to the enactment of HR4986. Before the above amendments, only mutual associations could convert to federal stock charters. The 1982 Depository Institutions Act, as was mentioned earlier, further extended the ability of thrift institutions to operate under federal stock charters.

Chapter IV

Conversion

MUTUAL TO STOCK CHARTERS—PROS AND CONS

Pro stock proponents cite many advantages to be derived from stock ownership of savings and loan associations. Former chairman of the Federal Home Loan Bank during 1978, Robert McKinney, endorsed the conversion of mutual savings associations to stock form in the following extract:

> In the savings and loan industry, equity capital is critical because of its capacity to provide leverage for increased savings growth. The new equity capital infused through conversions has been used to support dramatic increases in savings growth and branching, thereby enabling converted associations to expand significantly their mortgage lending and service to the community.[1]

Moreover, new injections of capital via stock issues would potentially provide a source of capital in capital deficit areas. Because of the well-known "multiplier effect," the ultimate effects of the additional funds are considerably expanded, a small increase in reserves having the potential to cushion a significantly larger increase in deposits. Such possibilities are even more useful as a means of

---

[1] Letter from Chairman McKinney to Senator Proxmire and Representative St Germain dated 6/9/1978.

ameliorating the effects of disintermediation during periods of volatile and high interest rates.

Another argument in support of stock conversions hinges on the "equitability notion" that savings and loan associations should have the ability to operate under the stock form of corporate organization which is the normal and traditional method of business organization for the majority of private industrial and financial enterprises. The efficacy of this method of organization and its supporting structures has also been well documented over the years and would augment the structure and stability of the savings and loan industry.

A more beneficial juxtaposition of liability portfolios can also be undertaken with conversion. A lengthening of liability maturities will enable a more efficient matching of long-term mortgage investments. This would ideally serve to reduce the cost of external borrowing to the association and also moderate the impact of saving deposit flows on association activity.

Managerial recruitment and retention can also be enhanced by stock option or purchase incentives. This remunerative provision could conceivably provide a more useful index for evaluating and compensating management performance as reflected by the price of the stock of the association. Moreover, potential managerial personnel might be more receptive to such an incentive scheme because of the more attractive tax advantages. At the same time, the association's cash outflow in the form of salary disbursements would be reduced and such benefits could be channeled into other growth inducing activities.

Other supporters of stock conversions assert that the original need for mutual organizations has been obviated over the years, and that stock organizations are the more familiar and easily understood method of incorporation. Stock associations, it is also suggested, facilitate the process of merging, providing opportunities for merger activity which otherwise might not exist. The use of stock holding companies, too, potentially can effect desirable geographic and investment diversification. In addition, economies of scale may accrue to associations organized in this manner. This aspect will be discussed more fully later.

Conversion to stock form thus provides the association with increased operating flexibility which may reduce the necessity for overt supervisory action if the particular association is experiencing net worth and operational problems. The power to raise equity capital may be an effective means of overcoming these problems.[2]

On the other hand, advocates of the mutual form of organization make reference to the historical derivation of the savings and loan association movement in the United States. It is argued that maximum benefits to the public in terms of affordable interest rates and the availability of mortgage funds are generated by institutions which operate entirely for the benefit of depositors and the general community, and not for the profit motives of a group of stockholders.

Other proponents of the mutual form of association express concern that the conversion of mutual associations to stock form will facilitate the takeover of mutual thrift institutions by commercial banks. Furthermore, inherent in the conversion process is the possibility of insiders securing large windfall profits from the conversion of the association. The costs of conversion, too, may be quite onerous and could dilute significantly the benefits to be derived from converting to the stock form. Indeed, a classic example of this problem was the demise of the First Savings and Loan Association of Del Rio, Texas, a $15 million state chartered mutual which instituted conversion procedures in September 1976, spending over $70,000 in order to obtain approximately $325,000 from stock offers. This particular case was further compounded by an almost concurrent outside tender offer to purchase all existing shares at a price considerably higher than the stock subscription price and focuses on the problems involved in preserving the integrity of the conversion process. Much controversy has centered around the fact that reserves of mutual thrifts have been accumulated over decades, and it would not be equitable to allocate these reserves as windfall gains to individuals who have a vested interest in the association at the particular point in time when the conversion process is effective.

The Council of Mutual Savings Institutions has also argued that conversion into stock savings and loan companies would result in reduced independence of the thrift and home-mortgage industry via holding company acquisitions. This would tend to increase the concentration of economic power within the industry. The mutual organization also facilitates the promotion of thrift and homeowner-

---

[2] Subject to the market acceptance and perceptability of the particular association, its operations, performance and future growth prospects. Given the recent plight of most thrifts vis-a-vis net worth adequacy and earning attrition, new issues of equity capital by S&Ls were virtually at a standstill and several large S&L holding companies have had their ratings lowered by the traditional ratings agencies.

ship, since its prime objective is fulfilling the needs of its members. This type of organization is thus capable of providing a more meaningful balance between the needs of the community, the market place, mutual savers and borrowers and social welfare. It is further asserted that the greatest community need is housing; and in this regard, the mutual thrifts have a better operational record than capital stock commercial banks.

Supporters of the mutual form of savings and loan associations declare that it is not necessary for mutual associations to convert to stock form in order to raise capital rather an effective alternative is the use of subordinated debentures.

Having briefly reviewed the principal arguments for and against the conversion of mutual thrift organizations to stock form, or the "why" component of the analysis, what follows, therefore, is an examination of the legal framework and provisions which govern conversions; that is, the "how" aspects of the conversion process.

A 1948 amendment to the Homeowners Loan Act of 1933 authorized the conversion of federal mutual savings and loan associations to State chartered associations to stock associations. Conversion provisions and regulations were further revised in 1955 to 1957. In 1973, the Federal Home Loan Bank Board enforced an administrative moratorium on conversion of any federally insured (FSLIC) savings and loan association to stock form. The moratorium would be effective from December 5, 1972 until 30 days after approval of Public Law 93-100 on August 16, 1973. (The exception was the San Francisco case in 1972.) The statutory moratorium imposed by Public Law 93-100, as to all except supervisory cases would last until June 30, 1974. During this one-year period, Congress authorized the conversion of a maximum of eight associations on an experimental supervisory basis.

On October 28, 1974, an amendment to Section 402 of the National Housing Act permitted the conversion to federal stock associations in states where stock associations are permitted. Previously, all federally chartered mutual associations converting to stock form were required to relinquish their federal charter and operate under state incorporation. However, the October 1974 amendment also imposed a moratorium on conversions until June 30, 1976, but in the interim allowed up to 51 conversions for purposes of assessing whether such conversions were in the public interest. Up to February 15, 1976, the Federal Home Loan Bank Board had received 43 "experimental" mutual-to-stock conversion applications. Since 1975, revised conversion regulations have deleted the earlier give-away or "free distribution" approach to conversions which had resulted in numerous questionable practices during the conversion process. Rather, a sale of stock approach has been adopted which involves full public disclosure, independent valuation of pro forma market values and pre-emptive purchasing rights by savings account members. Of the 43 applications received up to February 1976, 7 were approved, with the remainder in various stages of the conversion process.

With the expiration of the moratorium on "experimental" conversions on June 30, 1976, the Federal Home Loan Bank Board adopted the interpretation that its authority to approve conversions did not expire with the moratorium. The Comptroller General, however, was of the opinion that the Board's authority to approve conversions with the limitations expired along with the limitations on June 30, 1976. The Council of Mutual Savings Institutions in late August 1978 brought suit in the U.S. District Court of Washington D. C. questioning the authority of the Board to authorize the conversion of federal mutual associations to federal stock organizations. In January 1980, the U.S. District Court, District of Columbia ruled that the Bank Board's authority to authorize conversions to federal stock associations is permanent. In July 1980, the Appellate Court also ruled that under the National Housing Act, the Board's authority to permit conversions is "designed to be permanent," a ruling which was later upheld by the Supreme Court.

As of May 1977, 73 applications for conversions were filed, 25 of which were approved. By April 1978, there were 97 conversion applications, of which 32 had been approved. By September 15, 1980, the number of conversion applications filed had risen to 183. From 1974 to 1981, 214 applications for conversion had been filed, with 103 being approved—46 in 1980 alone. Up to May 1983, 180 conversions were approved, with over $700 million in new capital issued. In 1983, the total number of stock conversions approved by the Federal Home Loan Bank Board was 101. With the current highly competitive and volatile interest rate scenario, many associations are opting for stock charters in order to augment their capital structure and reserve base. Several analysts, including regulators and investment bankers, are of the opinion that conversion activity will escalate over the next year or two with over $1 billion in stock offerings being placed on the market.

Several studies have been undertaken by various interest groups which have brought into question whether the process of conversion can be completed on an equitable basis. Permeating these discussions was a common concern for the ability of existing management and other insiders to secure profitably large amounts of stock in converting institutions, which did not attest to an equitable situation. Controversy surrounding the valuation of stock was also evident.

In May 1977, the General Accounting Office released a report in which an audit was undertaken of eight of the twenty-two associations that had converted within the last two years.[3] Despite the small representation of the sample, the survey brought to the foreground certain discrepancies which have since necessitated further amendments to the regulations governing conversions. The GAO report to the Senate Committee on Banking Housing and Urban Affairs dated May 26, 1977 inferred that the Board did not adequately monitor conversion activities in order to ascertain whether converting associations complied with the regulations.

More to the point, the GAO found that members of management and associates substantially increased their holdings through stock transfers shortly after conversion. This development suggested inequities in stock distribution in contravention of the Board's intentions and guidelines. In several instances, management and associates increased their savings account balances before the eligibility record date of conversion. Such action enabled members of management to expand their subscription rights and obtain additional stock to which they otherwise were not entitled.

Moreover, with Board regulations permitting an association to act as its own stock transfer agent, this further facilitates "insider" activities for personal managerial objectives. Information obtained concerning potential transfers was in several cases used by management to acquire the majority of shares traded in the secondary market.

In one case, for example, management increased its initial percentage of total shares of 5 percent to 39 percent through secondary market acquisitions. The GAO also recommended that the Board regulations on rights pertaining to subsequent stock issues, stock transfer agents and acquisitions of converted associations be revised in order to effectively allow a wider participation of subscribers and a curtailment of activities generating insider benefits. The Federal Home Loan Bank Board was in general agreement with the GAO's findings and recommendations. Revisions in existing conversion regu-

---

[3] "Changing Ownership of Mutual Savings and Loan Association—An Evaluation." Report to the Senate Committee on Bankings, Housing and Urban Affairs, By the Comptroller General of the United States.

lations were studied with a view to preventing the inequitable activities discussed above.

In April 1978, the Council of Mutual Savings Institutions in New York, an avid opponent of mutual to stock conversions, published a study on conversion of mutual to stock associations.[4] The study was based on an analysis of 29 mutual to stock savings and loan conversions that were completed between June 30, 1974 and December 31, 1977. The salient conclusions of the study were:

- Conversion on a fair and equitable basis and without a windfall to some one is a technical impossibility given the inherent problem of distributing the mutual savings and loan associations' net worth and reserve values.

- Only about 3.5 percent of the 29 converting savings and loan associations member-savers actually purchased stock in the converting savings and loan associations, indicative, therefore, of little member-saver participation.

- Approximately 40 percent of the stock issued in 28 sale of stock conversions were purchased by management, directors, syndicates or insiders, with the percentage rising as high as 72 percent, suggesting concentration of control.

- Control of and beneficial interest in approximately $107 million in net worth and some $3 billion in assets of the converted associations was transferred from many mutual association members to a few new stockholders.

- The converted associations were vulnerable to tender offers and corporate raiding by Savings and Loan Holding Companies and other entities, as was the case with some recently converted associations. On the other hand, mutual associations are not prone to such activities.

- In at least 21 of the sale of stock conversions, management, directors and other insiders purchased control with loan commitments from commercial banks with the savings and loan stock pledged as collateral in most cases. One other case in-

[4] Council of Mutual Savings Institutions, Survey, March 17, 1978.

volved a loan commitment from a credit union. There is thus
the significant question as to whether insiders are buying
control by means of the associations' own funds.

- Directors of the converting associations were also directors
  and/or stockholders of the commercial banks providing the
  loan commitments to "insiders" in at least six conversions,
  suggesting a conflict of interest.

- Only five of the 29 converted associations were below Federal
  Insurance Reserve requirements prior to the conversion, imply-
  ing that the need for additions to capital to margin growth is
  not usually the real reason for conversion.

- Conversion is expensive accounting for approximately $9
  million in costs for the 28 sale of stock conversions or over
  10 percent of the gross proceeds. Expenses ranged from 4.5
  percent to 20.3 percent of the capital raised.

- The number of mutual to stock association conversions or even
  the number of conversion applications does not reflect a strong
  conversion movement on the part of the nation's 4,000 federal
  and state mutual associations.

The lengthy arguments against conversion just outlined are representative of the traditional opposition to conversions by the Council
of Mutual Savings Institutions. Most of the arguments have already
been discussed and deemed without merit by the Federal Home Loan
Bank Board. In particular, the Council's view on the net worth and
windfall problem has been cited by former FHLB Board Chairman
Bomar as being incorrect in the sense that a stock is sold in an amount
equal to the pro forma market value of the association and with
proper pricing of the stock, there is no windfall gain.

Nonetheless, the controversy surrounding conversion activities has
further stimulated the FHLB Board to institute more stringent regulations in an attempt to overcome previous criticisms and discrepancies involving the conversion process.

In March 1979, the Federal Home Loan Bank Board issued new
regulations governing conversion applications which would greatly
reduce the likelihood of "insider abuses" and other inequities.

Specifically, the revised regulations stipulate the following:

- Stock purchases by any individual, including officers and directors were limited to 5 percent of the total stock offering. The total purchases by all officers and directors were also limited to 25 percent of the total stock offering.

- Stock rights of officers and directors based on increased deposits in the one-year period prior to the record date were subordinated to the purchases of other eligible account holders.

- Subscription rights of account holders were further increased by adding a supplemental eligibility or second, more current record date. This provision was designed to foster a wider distribution of stock among members and the general public.

- Officers and directors were prohibited from obtaining any stock rights which were based on the more current supplemental record date.

- Officers and directors were also restricted from transferring purchased stock for a period of three years following conversion.

- Stock purchased by officers and directors subsequent to the conversion must be obtained through an SEC-registered brocker-dealer, with the exception of negotiated transactions involving more than 1 percent of outstanding stock.

- While under previous regulations, officers and directors usually purchased unsubscribed shares, the new regulations now required the public offering of any remaining shares and limited officer and director participation to one-tenth of 1 percent of the total offering.

- For the first ten years after the conversion, dividends were also limited to 50 percent of net income.

The main objective of the above amendments was to foster a wider degree of participation in conversions by accountholders and the public in general and reduce the potential for concentration and control of stock among officers and directors. Bank Board Chairman at the time, Robert H. McKinney, stated that these "regulations provide strict safeguards which will assure the integrity of the conversion process. Any reasonable concerns over so-called 'insider abuses' and 'windfall profits' have been addressed by these regulations. In addition, they provide benefits to the consumer and the community at large."[5]

Recent evidence on savings and loan associations that converted during the period June 1979 to September 1980 reveal that the net worth of these institutions increased from 4.6 percent before conversion to 8.4 percent after conversion. The average percentage increase in the net worth of these converting institutions was 82.5 percent. Of the 50 associations which converted to stock form during the period June 1979 to September 1980, the average percentage stock holdings of officers and directors was 18.37 percent which was substantially less that the comparable figure of 36.6 percent for the 35 associations which converted during the earlier period April 1978 to June 1979. The Federal Home Loan Bank Board rules in 1979 appear to have had a solutary effect in this regard in reducing concentration of stock ownership by management.

A study published by the Federal Home Loan Bank Board[6] in July 1980 also concluded that converted stock associations were in general more aggressive, more profitable and exhibited a higher degree of risk exposure than mutual associations.

Given the weak performance of the thrift industry over 1981-82, it was unlikely that any major offering of stock by savings and loan associations would have received wide public acceptance. In late 1982—with the decline in interest rates and enactment of the Garn-St. Germain Act—the market for thrift stocks displayed renewed vigor with 31 conversions yielding over $110 million in new capital. Several large thrift institutions have initiated plans to undertake conversion to stock form in the near future. The conversion process has also been facilitated by a number of regulatory amendments by the Federal Home Loan Bank Board designed to simplify and render less costly the conversion process. In February 1983, for example, the size of the proxy statements that must be sent to customers of a converting thrift was reduced by over 100 pages. Whether or not the mutual form of ownership will continue to be the dominant form of organization vis-a-vis the changes in competitive pressures and structure of the fi-

[5] Savings and Loan Reporter, Vol. 3, No. 47. March 23, 1979, p. 3.

[6] "An Investigation of the Impact of Savings and Loan Associations' Conversions from Mutual to Stock form of Ownership," Federal Home Loan Bank Board, July 1980.

nancial industry remains to be seen. At present, over 80% of the $800 billion thrift industry operate under the mutual form of ownership.

As was mentioned in Chapter III, under the provisions of the 1982 Garn-St Germain Depository Institutions Act federal thrift institutions now have a liberalized option of a stock or mutual form of ownership. Prior to the 1982 Act, existing statutes prohibited the chartering of federal stock associations in states that did not permit the establishment of state stock institutions.

CONVERSION PROCESS

In obtaining approval from the FSLIC and the Bank Board, a converting mutual association must first of all solicit approval by a vote of a majority of eligible association members. Secondly, at least two-thirds of the associations' Board of Directors must approve the plan of conversion. In addition to the plan of conversion, the conversion application includes the proposed stock charter and by-laws, proxy statement, and an independent valuation of the stock price which should be equal to its estimated pro forma market value. The application is filed concurrently with the Federal Home Loan Bank and the Federal Deposit Insurance Corporation. The plan of conversion, charter and by-laws, and non-financial statements of the proxy document are reviewed by the Office of the General Counsel. The Office of Examinations and Supervision reviews the financial statements. Federal Deposit Insurance regulations of the FSLIC require that all stock to be issued in the conversion must be sold prior to completion of the conversion process and such stock be offered in a serier of priorities to savers, borrowers and management as of a determined record date. Savers who are members subsequent to the above record date are also allowed to obtain stock as stipulated in the regulations.

After the FSLIC has approved the preliminary application, the members of the association are required to approve the plan. If a state-chartered association is converting or a federal mutual association is converting to a state stock charter, endorsement of the State Commissioner is also required. With the public offering and pricing of the stock, unsubscribed shares after member entitlements have been completed are sold in an underwritten placement or in a community offering. All federally chartered stock associations are issued a federal stock charter, Charter S (Figure IV-1). The Charter S document contains basic provisions as to directors, capitalization, preemp-

FIGURE IV-1

CHARTER S

_____ Federal Savings and Loan Association _____.

SECTION 1. *Corporate Title.* The full corporate title of the association is "_____ Federal Savings and Loan Association _____.

SECTION 2. *Office.* The home office of the association shall be located in the County of _____, State (Territory, Possession or District) of _____.

SECTION 3. *Powers.* The association is a capital stock association chartered under Section 5 of the Home Owners' Loan Act and has and may exercise all the express, implied and incidental powers confered thereby and by all acts amendatory thereof and supplemental thereto, subject to the Constitution and laws of the United States as they are now in effect, or as they may hereafter be amended, and subject to all lawful and applicable rules, regulations, and orders of the Federal Home Loan Bank Board.

SECTION 4. *Duration.* The duration of the association is perpetual.

SECTION 5. *Capital Stock.* The total number of shares of capital stock which the association has authority to issue is _____, all of which are to be shares of common stock, _____ dollar(s) par value per share (or if no par value, a stated value of _____ dollar(s) per share). The shares may be issued by the association from time to time as approved by its board of directors without the approval of its stockholders except as otherwise provided in this Section 5. The consideration for the issuance of the shares shall be paid in full before their issuance and shall not be less than the par value [stated value] per share. Neither promissory notes nor future services shall constitute payment or part payment for the issuance of shares of the association. The consideration for the shares shall be cash, tangible or intangible property, labor or services actually performed for the association or any combination of the foregoing. In the absence of actual fraud in the transaction, the value of such property, labor, or services, as determined by the board of directors of the association, shall be conclusive. Upon payment of such consideration such shares shall be deemed to be fully paid and non-assessable. In the case of a stock dividend, that part of the surplus of the association which is transferred to stated capital upon the issuance of shares as a share dividend shall be deemed to be the consideration for their issuance.

Except for shares issuable in connection with the conversion of the association from the mutual to the stock form of capitalization (not of other securities) shall be issued in the following cases unless their issuance or the plan under which they would be issued has been approved by a majority of the total votes eligible to be cast at a legal meeting: (i) shares of common stock to be issued, directly or indirectly, to officers, directors or controlling persons of the association other than as part of a general public offering or as qualifying shares to a director; or (ii) shares of common stock exceeding 15 percent of the total number of shares of common stock then outstanding.

The holders of the common stock shall exclusively possess all voting power. Each holder of shares of common stock shall be entitled to one vote for each share held by such holder, except as to the cumulation of votes for the election of directors. Subject to Section 7 of this charter, in the event of any liquidation, dissolution or winding up of the association, the holders of the common stock shall be entitled, after payment or provision for payment of all debts and liabilities of the association, to receive all assets of the association available for distribution, in cash or in kind. Each share of common stock shall have the same relative rights as and be identical in all respects with all the other shares of common stock.

SECTION 6.   *Preemptive Rights.*   Holders of the capital stock of the association shall not be entitled to preemptive rights with respect to any shares of the association which may be issued.

SECTION 7.   *Liquidation Account.*   Pursuant to the requirements of the Rules and Regulations for Issuance of Accounts of the Federal Savings and Loan Insurance Corporation, the association shall establish and maintain a liquidation account for the benefit of its savings account holders as of _____ ("eligible savers"). In the event of a complete liquidation of the association, it shall comply with such Rules and Regulations with respect to the amount and the priorities on liquidation of each of the association's eligible saver's inchoate interest in the liquidation account, to the extent it is still in existence. Provided, however, that an eligible saver's inchoate interest in the liquidation account shall not entitle such eligible saver to any voting rights at meetings of the association's stockholders.

SECTION 8.   *Directors.*   The association shall be under the direction of a board of directors. The number of directors, as stated in the association's bylaws, shall not be less than seven.

SECTION 9.   *Amendment of Charter.*   No amendment, addition, alteration, change, or repeal of this charter shall be made unless such is first proposed by the board of directors of the association, then preliminarily approved by the Federal Home Loan Bank Board, and thereafter approved by the stockholders by a majority of the total votes eligible to be cast at a legal meeting. Any amendment, addition, alteration, change, or repeal so acted upon shall be effective on the date it receives the final approval of the Federal Home Loan Bank Board or on such other date as such Board may specify in its approval.

[as added eff. 6-16-75]

tive rights, liquidation account, and regulations governing amendments. The By-laws of the connected association which are modeled after the Model Business Corporation Code form, governs procedural administrative and substantive matters such as voting rights, meetings and the election of directors. Section 5 of the Charter provisions also permit the subsequent issuance of shares not exceeding 15 percent of those outstanding without the approval of the Bank Board or stockholders. In addition, associations may also issue preferred stock under an optional charter provision. While the FHLB Board previously denied requests by associations to issue preferred stock for satisfying net worth regulations and reserve requirements, it recently approved the issuance of preferred stock by Biscayne Federal to bolster the future growth of the association. Parenthetically, it should be noted that the public offering of common stock of savings and loan associations is exempt from registration requirements of the Securities Act of 1933 with respect to disclosure and prospectus requirements.

The FHLB Board also has jurisdiction to administer and enforce certain sections of the Securities Exchange Act of 1934 "with respect to institutions, the accounts of which are insured by the Federal Savings and Loan Insurance Corporation." However, the Securities Exchange Commission has retained jurisdiction under antifraud provision; for example, Section 12(2) and 17(a) of the 1933 Act and Rule 106(5) promulgated under the Exchange Act of 1934. Section 17(a) prohibits the use of false or misleading information by any person in the offer or sale of any securities. Rule 106-5 makes it illegal for any person to utilize false and misleading information in connection with the purchase or sale of any security. The Bank Board would, however, have joint jurisdiction with the SEC in actions brought under Rule 106-5.

The FHLB Board also monitors acquisitions of control after initial conversion of more than 25 percent of voting shares, as well as the activities of savings and loan holding companies owning more than 25 percent of stock. Any such transactions involving more than 25 percent of voting shares requires prior Bank Board approval. A mandatory agreement between the Federal Savings and Loan Insurance Corporation and the converted association places a prohibition for a duration of three years after conversion on the acquisition of control of the association by any company significantly engaged in unrelated business activity. This provision, however, does not apply to acquisitions of control by holding companies and individuals not significantly engaged in unrelated business activities. The converted association is also restricted from repurchasing its capital stock for a period of 10 years except under circumstances provided in the regulations. The fledgling stock association also is required to register the securities under the Securities Act and be subject to the periodic public disclosure and filing requirements of the Exchange Act for three years following conversion.

In order to reduce the likelihood of takeovers, the FHLB Board has endorsed several stringent optional charter provisions which prohibit offers for and acquisitions of more than 10 percent of voting stock.

The Board also amended its regulations on mergers between federally chartered capital stock and other institutions insured by the Federal Insurance and Loan Insurance Corporation to permit a supervisory exception codifying the Board's authority to allow the association resulting from a merger of a stock and mutual to be a stock association. Previously, the product of such combinations were required to be mutual. This amendment was effective February 9, 1981 and provides the Board with additional latitude and flexibility in the area of supervisory activity.

CONVERSION OF A STATE OR FEDERAL SAVINGS AND LOAN ASSOCIATION INTO A SAVINGS BANK

Any savings and loan association, federal or state where permitted, may convert into a savings bank upon receiving the approval of its shareholders and the particular superintendent of banking. Approval by the superintendent will be conditional on the insurance by the Federal Deposit Insurance Corporation of deposit accounts of the resulting bank to the extent permitted by federal law. The plan of conversion to a savings bank must also specify, by type and amount, all nonconforming deposits, loans and borrowings; that is, those items which are legal for an association by illegal for a savings bank and indicate the method by which they will be disposed of by the resulting savings bank.

Over the period 1974 to 1978, there were two conversions of savings and loan associations to savings banks. The Catskill Savings and Loan converted to a savings bank under the name Green County Savings Bank on May 18, 1974. In January 1978, the Niagara Permanent Savings and Loan Association converted to the Permanent

Savings Bank. Conversion by savings and loan associations had, therefore, not been very widespread nor popular. Generally, in the few cases where conversion had been undertaken, the main objective was to obtain the ability to offer expanded services and engage in investment activities not legal for a savings and loan association.

The newly enacted Depository Institutions Act of 1982 states that "subject to the rules and regulation of the Board, any federal association may convert itself from the mutual form to the stock form of organization or from the stock form to the mutual form but such conversion shall be subject to the rules and regulations as the Board shall prescribe, and thereafter the converted association may change its designation from a federal savings and loan association to a federal savings bank, or the reverse." Federal thrift institutions, thus, have complete leeway in this regard.

With the passage of the 1982 Garn Act, there has been an unprecedented flurry of savings and loan conversions to savings banks. During 1983, more than 100 savings and loans have converted to savings bank charters with 15 former savings and loan associations now ranking in the top 100 largest savings banks. The Garn Act simplified the conversion procedure and some applications were approved in one week by the Federal Home Loan District Bank. While the ease with which the conversion process could be undertaken was a factor favoring the conversion decision, the majority of converting savings and loans cited the desire to change the institution's image by having "bank" in its name and the more favorable tax treatment for savings banks. Savings banks qualify for the maximum bad debt deduction if 72 percent of their assets are in home mortgages, in comparison to the 82 percent of assets for savings and loan associations. For many savings and loan associations, the name "bank" was synonymous with the change in business philosophy, increased commercial lending activity and the perception of customers that these institutions were now offering an expanded array of "bank-like" services.

Several state savings and loans have also converted to state savings banks. In New Mexico, for example, where savings banks were nonexistent, state regulators approved amendments allowing savings and loans to adopt savings bank charters.

State chartered savings banks have also been converting to federal charters, particularly in Connecticut, Maine and Massachussetts. By grandfathering state powers and being able to use the new powers provided by the Garn-St. Germain Act, many of these converting state banks viewed themselves as being able to take advantage of the "best of both worlds." It can be predicted that many more savings and loan associations in the near future will adopt savings bank charters, if only for purposes of public image and perception. Empire of America FSA, for example, originally was chartered as a savings bank, Erie Savings Bank of Buffalo, which converted to a federal savings and loan association in August 1982, and in November 1983 in seeking a stock charter opted for conversion back to a savings bank. The president of Empire noted that "bank" in the name of the institution may provide a competitve edge given the trend toward diversification of services by commercial banks.

Indeed, the quest for the notion of bank image is also evident in the first conversion of a savings and loan association into a national bank in June 1983, when approval was granted by the Comptroller of the Currency for Arkansas Federal Savings and Loan Association in Little Rock, to become First American Bank/Little Rock N.A.

CONVERSION OF MUTUAL SAVINGS BANKS
TO STOCK FORM

In January 1982, Puget Sound Mutual Savings Bank of Seattle, Washington, became the first savings bank in the nation to convert to stock ownership. 2.5 million shares of stock were offered priced between $11.75 and $15.90 per share with net proceeds estimated at $32 million. The stock sale would double the net worth of the bank. One officer of the $379.9 million asset bank which was parenthetically, the most profitable savings bank in 1980, viewed increased flexibility and additional strength and capital as the principal factors influencing the conversion decision. Washington state changed the relevant banking laws in 1981 to permit conversion of savings banks from mutual to stock form. At that time, seven states allowed savings banks to convert from mutual to stock form; namely, Alaska, Maine, New Hampshire, Oregon, Rhode Island, Washington and Wisconsin. The conversion of Puget Sound Mutual Savings Bank to stock form represented a pioneer development in an industry which had been mutually owned for over 150 years. It is perhaps indicative of the continuing process of adaptation and adjustment required in the currently rapidly changing financial environment.

Moreover, Section 314 of the 1982 Depository Institutions Act eliminates the prohibition against the organization of or conversion to federal stock institutions in states where stock associations do not exist. Whether state legislatures will adopt parity legislation in this regard remains to be seen. In New York, for example, a constitutional amendment authorizing stock savings and loans and savings banks was approved in November 1983 and the necessary legislation to implement the amendement is expected to be enacted during 1984. Several of the larger New York state-chartered savings banks have initiated plans to convert to stock form, as too, have other savings banks nationwide. With declining interest rates in late 1982 and early 1983, the market for thrift stocks has improved markedly and many thrifts will no doubt seek new capital injections through the stock conversion alternative in the near future. Given that the demand for thrift stocks is a function of earnings and hence of interest rates, a rapid escalation of interest rates could easily render market acceptance of these stocks nonexistent. In such a tenuous situation, the timing of the stock conversion and potential market saturation are factors of importance in planning and effecting the conversion.

Chapter V

Mergers and Acquisitions—
Voluntary and Involuntary

Recently, there has been a resurgence in the number of mergers between savings and loan associations, as well as between mutual savings banks. Indeed, the present mushrooming merger activity has been matched by a similar trend in the early 1970s, when voluntary mergers peaked at 136 in 1974. Nor has such activity been confined to the thrift industry; rather, it extends throughout the financial community in general and the economy at large. In a setting of high and volatile interest rates, destabilizing inflation, declining savings flows and intensified competition, many financial concerns have opted for consolidation via mergers in order to expand and strengthen their competitive niche in the marketplace.

The American financial industry is undergoing a rapid transformation and synthesis which will necessitate re-alignment and perhaps disappearance of many of its participants as the competitive pressures and innovations shift the balance of market strengths to the more aggressive and astute opportunists. No doubt, too, a concomitant reshaping of the regulatory environment, as it affects major financial institutions, will be necessary. The recent acquisition by Prudential of the Bache group, together with the American Express/Shearson Loeb Rhoades merger and the consequent excoriations of such developments by the banking community clearly focuses on the regulatory problem and competitive equality.

It was, therefore, not surprising that given the general climate of financial upheavels and adjustments, merger activity among savings and loan associations should have been so rampant. While in 1978 there were only 44 voluntary mergers, the number of these mergers increased to 108 at the end of 1980. By the end of 1981, mergers of Federal Home Loan Bank member associations totaled 217 (Table V-1). Along with the 217 mergers in 1981, there were 30 assisted mergers requiring $188 million in Federal Savings and Loan Insurance Corporation funds. For 1982, there were 215 voluntary mergers from a total of 425, approved by the Federal Home Loan Bank Board. The Federal Savings and Loan Insurance Corporation had estimated that the number of its assisted mergers would be about 100 for 1983 in comparison to 77 for 1982, costing the agency $1.1 billion. As of August 1983, there were 95 mergers approved by the Federal Home Loan Bank, of which 61 were voluntary.

Mergers of savings and loan associations were relatively unimportant in determining the structure of the industry before the late 1960s. From 1966 to 1970, 357 mergers of Federal Home Loan Bank member associations were undertaken with the total amount increasing to 606 over the period 1970-1975. Since the latter year, there has been a decline in merger activity, more so in 1978 and 1979 among savings and loan associations, until in 1980, when the level of merger activity again demonstrated significant growth.

Some understanding of the reasons underlying the increase in merger activity is fundamental to evaluating the impact of mergers on the organization of the industry. In general, there are two prime motivations, higher profits or smaller losses. Many smaller associations are of the opinion that as part of a larger organization, they can compete more effectively and enhance their services in the market area. Mergers may, therefore, take place to improve management of an institution, to gain control of the lending market, to gain control of

Table V-1   Voluntary Mergers of
FHLB Associations

Year	Mergers	Year	Mergers
1960	23	1976	88
1965	32	1977	43
1970	118	1978	46
1971	132	1979	38
1972	107	1980	109
1973	128	1981	217
1974	136	1982	215
1975	119		

Source: 1983 Savings and Loan Sourcebook.

the supply of savings in the area, to lower costs of operations, to obtain branch offices or for other reasons related to the prime effort of increasing earnings or minimizing losses. Mergers may also be undertaken voluntarily or involuntarily to avoid liquidation. Recently, the number of supervisory or involuntary mergers has been increasing rapidly under the direction of the Federal Savings and Loan Insurance Corporation.

The attenuation of savings and loan earnings positions, occasioned by the high interest rate environment over 1980-82 and the consequent erosion of the capital base of several associations, may have been the principal factor responsible for the increase in merger activity. Mergers have also been undertaken as a less costly method of expanding operations, compared to the expenses involved in establishing de novo facilities. Often, two or more small savings and loan associations may merge for defensive or survival purposes in order to bolster their competitive position against a larger association. The four-way savings and loan association merger in Ohio announced in January 1981 is a case in point. An official of the Federal Home Loan Bank of Cincinnati suggested that this merger reflected a trend among small and medium-sized thrifts here and elsewhere in the country who are merging to increase their efficiency as they prepare to compete with commercial banks to offer credit cards, NOW account, and trust services. The first vice president of the Cincinnati Federal Home Loan Bank further asserted "I guess you'd call a merger like this a sign of the times and a recognition by S and L's that through merger they feel they can take advantage of their new lending powers." It is interesting to note that the net worth of the combined Ohio State Savings and Loan Association was over 7.3 percent of total assets of $270 million, which was higher than the national average for the industry.

Similar observations are also echoed by the Illinois Savings and Loan Commissioner who stated recently that "We are seeing any number of institutions discussing friendly mergers, because on their own, they lack the capability to provide the services required in this competitive market." Parenthetically, too, many small associations may perceive a merger as a viable means of procuring more technologically advanced support services in areas such as marketing, data processing, accounting and loan servicing.

The rise in merger activity, however, has not been limited only to small savings and loan associations. Rather, extensive merger activity has also been observable among the largest savings and loan associations. At the end of December 1982, total deposits of the industry's

300 largest institutions increased by 19.8 percent or $54.5 billion, in comparison to an increase of 7.7 percent for the industry as a whole. Of the $54.5 billion increase in deposits among the largest associations, merger activity was responsible for approximately $33 billion or 60.5 percent of the total deposit gain. The growth in merger activity among the largest associations resulted in the number of associations with assets over $1 billion increasing to 126 from 108 a year ago.

Among the largest mergers were the acquisition by the sixth-ranked Talman Home Federal Savings and Loan Association formerly ranked thirteenth, of the $1.3 billion North West Federal Savings and Loan Association and the $297 million asset Alliance Savings and Loan Association, both located in Chicago; the acquisition by eighth ranked World Savings Federal Savings and Loan Association of Oakland, California of two Colorado based thrifts with assets of $1.94 billion as well as the $134 million asset Commerce Savings Federal Savings and Loan Association of Shawnee, Kansas.

Several other interstate mergers also resulted in changes in the structure of the savings and loan industry with previously non-existent associations assuming importance in terms of size and merger activity. These included the seventeenth-ranked Empire of America FSA, Buffalo, New York, formerly the Erie Savings Bank, Buffalo, which was involved in several interstate mergers: and the twenty-fourth ranked Northeast Savings FA, Hartford, Connecticut, which previously operated as Schenectady Savings Bank of New York. These and other interstate mergers will be discussed in greater detail in another section of this chapter.

California has historically accounted for the largest share of mergers and acquisitions within the savings and loan industry. In fact, about one out of every three savings and loan associations chartered in the State of California has been involved in a merger at one time or another. More mergers, too, have occurred in California since 1950 than in any other state, with the exception of Pennsylvania and New Jersey where special conditions prevailed.

Mergers of savings and loan associations are, of course related to the organizational and legal structure of such institutions. California, the "leader" state in this area, as in most states, has federally chartered, as well as state-chartered associations. The federal associations operate under the same regulations and laws as all such associations throughout the nation, while the great majority of state-chartered associations in California are organized with guaranteed capital stock. Without the capital stock form of association ownership which makes profit-taking easier than in mutual operations, there probably would be fewer mergers of savings and loan associations in California.

When mutual associations combine, there is no capital stock advantage. Most of the mutual mergers in recent years were associated with management situations, economies of scale or expansion via the procurement of branches. There is strong evidence that in New Jersey and Pennsylvania, the peculiarities of the law have contributed to mergers. Pennsylvania permitted the establishment of branch offices since 1952, but because the assets of an association after the establishment of a branch office must be at least $1 million with a 5 percent reserve fund, it has been more feasible to merge with another association rather than to establish branch offices. In New Jersey, a similar situation was evident. The law categorically stipulates that no association may establish more than one branch office if its capital is less than $5 million, no more than two, if capital is between $5 and $10 million and no more than three as a maximum. Therefore, an association desirous of expansion would opt for a merger with another association because of the legal obstacles to branch expansion.

Recently, savings and loan merger activity has been accelerating in the Midwest, particularly in Illinois and Indiana. Most of these mergers have been undertaken in response to the comtemporary high interest rates, the pressure from intensified competition, and the desire to effectively provide new and expanded services permitted under the 1980 Depository Institutions Deregulation and Monetary Control Act.

Industry-wide, too, a fear of the future and a much publicized prognosis of mass attrition in thrift organizations and financial institutions in general has exerted some influence on the spate of merger activity. Mergers are, of course, not a panacea in themselves, as acquisitions devoid of some fundamental benefits only serve to increase size without providing operational advantages. Concern about the likelihood of business being "gobbled up" by the giant money center banks and the potential impact of interstate branching has motivated many regional and community banks to consolidate operations while it is opportune to do so. There are undoubtedly, however, several independent community associations and other financial institutions that could remain viable as autonomous entities without recourse to merger activity. It should also be noted that despite the growth in merger activity over the past few years, the thrift industry remains highly unconcentrated. As thrift institutions recover from the debilitating financial upheavals of the early 1980s, there may be a new surge in consolidations, as these institutions focus on expansion; moreso, given the increased flexibility in acquisition methods.

Since most merger proponents cite the advantages to be derived from economies of scale, it is useful to analyze the documented evidence available in support of such economies. Economies of scale may be interpreted as denoting the situation where increasing size results in more efficient operations at lower average costs. It has generally been assumed that larger associations can function more efficiently than comparatively smaller organizations. Most studies that have been done about economies of scale in the savings and loan industry infer that economies of scale do exist in the industry. By estimating the elasticity of cost with respect to output, an indication of the degree to which operating costs increase as the size or output of the association rises can be obtained. The cost elasticity co-efficient is computed by dividing the percentage increase in costs by the percentage increase in output, usually total assets in the case of the savings and loan industry. If the elasticity co-efficient is less than unitary, then economies of scale exist within the industry. For example, if a $200 million asset association has operating expenses of roughly $2 million, and a $400 million asset association has operating expenses of $3.7 million, then the elasticity estimate would be 0.85 calculated as the percent change in cost/per change in assets = $(1.7/2) \times 100 / (200/200) \times 100$. The closer the elasticity estimate approaches one, the less is the significance of the gains from economies of scale. In the above example, a one dollar increase in assets resulted in an 85 cent increase in costs, as output was doubled.

Most of the studies that have been conducted have derived elasticity estimates ranging from .84 to .94, indicating the existence of economies of scale in the savings and loan industry. A study by Benston in 1969 using 1963-1966 data on over 3,000 savings associations and using the number of loans made a measure of output, estimate the elasticity to be within a range of 0.91 to 0.94. More recent studies completed by Morris in 1978 using 1976 data on 187 associations in Arizona, California, and Nevada computed an elasticity estimate of 0.90, using total number of loans closed as an approximation for association output. Atkinson in 1977 and in 1979, using total assets as the measure of association output and a national sample of association, calculated the elasticity co-efficient to be 0.86 and 0.84 to 0.91 respectively. A perusal of the available literature thus indicates the existence of economies of scale in the savings and loan industry but not of a sufficient magnitude to support mass consolidation of the industry as a solution to the present problems confronting the industry.

All such previous studies used average data, hence it was not possible to isolate those ranges in asset size where economies of scale would tend to be more marked and significant. A more recent study undertaken by J. E. McNulty of the Federal Home Loan Bank of Atlanta, while not conclusive, attempted to estimate the elasticity of cost co-efficient and the operating cost ratio for associations of varying degrees of asset size. The sample areas chosen were the Fourth Federal Home Loan Bank District, South Florida, Baltimore SMSA, Washington SMSA, Atlanta SMSA, and California.

For the Fourth District in total, the results provided no evidence of economies of scale with an estimated elasticity of 0.98. For the other five area samples, Atlanta SMSA also demonstrated negligible evidence of economies of scale, perhaps due to the relatively small size of the sample. Baltimore, Washington, and South Florida samples yielded more positive results. In the Baltimore and Washington areas, the results were particularly outstanding for associations with assets less than $650 million. The reduction in operating costs achieved as a result of doubling the asset size of a $250 million asset association in the Baltimore and Washington areas was estimated to be 18 basis points and 24 basis points, respectively. However, the gains were much lower in the case of doubling the size of a $50 million asset association (7 and 11 basis points, respectively), perhaps supporting the notion that economies of scale vary markedly with asset size.

The results for the California area sample were markedly significant with an elasticity estimate of 0.82. What this latter figure conveys is that a doubling of assets would only increase costs by 82 percent. In fact, the results suggest that operating cost ratios would tend to decrease with increasing asset size until assets exceeded approximately $9.7 billion. The operating cost ratios for associations in California with assets of 5 billion and 10 billion were estimated to be 0.86 and 0.76 respectively, which would suggest a high degree of efficiency. The fact that diseconomies of scale were evident in the Baltimore and Washington samples, as asset size approached $1 billion, and $3 billion in the case of South Florida, indicates that other factors in addition to size, perhaps peculiarly related to the various market areas, exert strong influence on the degree to which economies of scale exist. Notwithstanding the diverse results, the California findings would tend to support the historically widespread incidence of merger activity in that state. While the results of the above study are not conclusive, given the fact that even in the case of California, only 28 percent of the variation in operating costs can be explained by association size, the analysis does provide useful insights for association executives and highlights some pertinent areas for further research and study.

In summary, mergers and acquisitions do provide positive benefits and advantages, and consolidation may be inevitable for many banks and thrift institutions. Indeed, from 1980 to year end 1982, the savings and loan industry recorded a decrease of 768 associations. Many more small regional and local banks—according to one analyst—would be more comfortable, however, if they were reminded of the old story of the sergeant who declared, "You hundred men are going into battle and only one of you is coming out alive." Each soldier says to himself: "Gee, I am going to miss the other fellows." Against the background of intensified competition and the spirit of deregulation, this story may be instructive.

MERGER PROCEDURES—VOLUNTARY MERGERS AND ACQUISITIONS

In a merger, the old corporation is merged into an existing or newly created corporation. The old corporation's shareholders receive either cash or stock in the new corporation. In a mutual association, however, there are no shareholders; the federal statutes require the approval of a plan of merger by at least two thirds of the Board of Directors of each association. Associations that are not federally chartered must be insured by the Federal Savings and Loan Insurance Corporation and comply with the merger requirements of the laws of the jurisdiction in which the associations were organized. The merger agreement between the associations in question must state that it is effective only when approved by the Board. In addition, the agreement should also specify which of the associations is to be the resulting association, the name to be used by the resulting or surviving institution, and the location of the home office and any branch offices of the resulting association. The method of issuing saving accounts by the resulting association must also be indicated in the merger agreement, as well as the number of directors, their names and addresses and the term of office for each director of the resulting association.

The attached application for merger form provides some notion of the administrative procedures involved in nonsupervisory merger activities. Two copies of the preliminary merger agreement must also be submitted with the application.

The term "merger," as defined by the Federal Home Loan Bank Board, also includes bulk purchases of assets in exchange for assumption of savings accounts and other liabilities, as well as consolidations. Mergers are viewed by the Board as chiefly business decisions to be exercised by the management of the participating institutions, and hence such activities are not overtly encouraged or discouraged by Board policy.

In ruling on a merger proposal, the Federal Home Loan Bank Board will evaluate the equitability of the merger plan and the existence of full disclosure of all relevant information. The Board also reviews the managerial and financial resources of the resulting association, in addition to the impact that the proposed merger will have on the needs and convenience of the community in terms of loan availability and the provision of savings facilities.

All merger proposals are also governed by the Clayton Act, the Sherman Anti-trust Act, and the Hart-Scott Rodino Anti-trust Improvement Act of 1976. In evaluating the competitive aspects of the merger application, the Board examines each pertinent geographical savings and mortgage market and submarket. Analysis of the impact on the competitive structure of the market by the proposed merger involves the derivation of several economic indices of market structure and performance. Assessment of the competitive positions of other savings and home financing institutions with regard to the proposed merger will also be undertaken.

Some of the more important indices include market concentration and ranking of the resulting and of other competing institutions, the number and size distribution of competitors, actual or potential competition notably curtailed by the merger, trends towards concentration due to mergers, overlap of branch systems when two or more branch networks are combined, and the degree to which the merger will influence the future competitive determination of interest rates both on savings and mortgages given statutory and regulatory constraints.

In mergers involving thrift institutions, merger proponents generally advocate a wide product line which includes savings and time deposits of commercial banks. Others argue for a narrowly defined market of thrift deposits. The U.S. Supreme Court, however, in four significant

FEDERAL HOME LOAN BANK BOARD
OFFICE OF INDUSTRY DEVELOPMENT
WASHINGTON, D.C. 20552

APPLICATION FOR MERGER

(Follow carefully the instructions concerning the preparation and submission of this application and its supporting documents)

SAVINGS AND LOAN INSTITUTION CODE:

"A" – ACQUIRING INSTITUTION
"B-1" – DISAPPEARING INSTITUTION
"B-2" – DISAPPEARING INSTITUTION (if more than one)
"C" – PROPOSED RESULTING INSTITUTION

TO: (Name and address of Federal Home Loan Bank of which you are a member)

FILING DATE	DOCKET NO.

ACQUIRING INSTITUTION "A" (Name and Home Office Address)

The above named institution hereby makes this application for merger, as provided in Section 546.1 thru 546.2 and 556.2 of the Regulations for the Federal Savings and Loan System.

DISAPPEARING INSTITUTION "B-1"	DISAPPEARING INSTITUTION "B-2"
NAME	NAME
CITY, STATE AND ZIP CODE	CITY, STATE AND ZIP CODE
LOCATION	LOCATION
DOCKET NO.	DOCKET NO.

As the duly elected officials of the above associations we certify that at legally held meetings of the Boards of Directors resolutions were passed which approved an agreement respecting the proposed transaction and directed the officers of the applicant association to apply for merger by preparing and filing an application with supporting information as required by the Federal Home Loan Bank Board.

The undersigned officials of the associations hereby attest to the adoption of the necessary resolutions and certify to the correctness of all information submitted in support of this application.

In submitting this application the applicant understands and agrees that appropriate actions will be taken by the respective Boards of Directors of the contracting institutions in conformity with the requirements of applicable Federal and State statutes and regulations.

_____
Acquiring Institution

_____
President

_____
Secretary

_____
Disappearing Institution*

_____
President

_____
Secretary

*If there is more than one, add signature lines to the left as required.

cases under the Clayton Act addressed the issue on a product line basis involving only bank services. The Federal Home Loan Bank Board in evaluating the competitive structures uses both thrift and commercial bank savings as a product market. Geographically, the Home Loan Board has adopted an anti-competitive posture in mergers or acquisitions where offices of the acquiring and acquired associations are within three miles of each other.

The Federal Deposit Insurance Corporation, on the other hand, argued that the decisive line of commerce for assessing mergers of mutual banks is "thrift institution banking" as provided by savings banks and savings and loan associations. The Federal Deposit Insurance Corporation thus does not focus on product lines such as savings accounts and mortgages, rather uses an approach that emphasizes a set of institutions that offer a similar cluster of services. This approach is analogous to the single line of commerce theory applied by the Courts to commercial banking. Analyses of market structures thus tend to be somewhat arbitrary and inconsistent among the various regulatory and supervisory agencies.

Mergers between federally chartered associations are usually effected through a pooling-of-interest approach where the assets, liabilities, and reserves of the merging associations are merged together by aggregating at their existing book values. With a purchase form of acquisition, the purchase price is usually allocated to the assets acquired and the liabilities assumed on the basis of fair value at the date of acquisition. The excess of the purchase price over the fair value is treated as goodwill arising from the acquisition and usually amortized in future years.

Mergers involving federal mutual associations and state stock associations often involve complicated accounting transactions, as under federal regulations, the resulting or surviving association was required to be mutual. Recently, however, with the increase in merger activity, the Federal Home Loan Bank Board amended its regulations in order to provide greater latitude in resolving merger cases involving problem institutions. The amended regulations adopted in February 1981 authorized the agency to allow the surviving institution to be a stock association in order to avert the insolvency or imminent failure of an association.

In anticipation of a large increase in the number of voluntary mergers during 1981, the Federal Home Loan Bank in February 1981 also expanded the authority of the Principal Supervisory Agent of the District Banks to approve mergers among federally insured thrift institutions. The new regulation authorizes the Principal Supervisory Agent to approve merger applications of associations with assets of $30 million or less and where the resulting association has assets of $250 million or less.

Under the original federal statutes governing mergers, the Principal Supervisory Agent at the district level had authority as designated by the Board to approve mergers involving associations with assets of less than $10 million where the resulting institution would have assets of less than $40 million. In July 1980, in order to facilitate the processing of merger applications but at the same time ensuring that mergers involving significant issues of competition are reviewed by the Board, the limitations on the authority of the Principal Supervisory Agent were further relaxed. Under the 1980 amendments, approval of merger applications involving associations with assets of less than $10 million where the surviving institution had assets of less than $150 million could be granted by the Principal Supervisory Agent at the District level.

It is estimated that as much as 60 to 70 percent of all merger applications would be handled at the District level under the amended regulations. In December 1982, the Federal Home Loan Bank Board, in a continuing effort to simplify the merger process, approved a three-tiered procedure that granted automatic approval by regional banks within thirty days of application to unprotested merger applications. Regional banks were also authorized to approve any application that did not qualify for automatic ratification. All the mergers not eligible for approval under the above tiers were forwarded to the Federal Home Loan Bank Board for action. Local offices were also authorized to approve some mergers requiring assistance from the Federal Savings and Loan Insurance Corporation, under the Voluntary Assisted Merger Program, initiated in June 1983.

Comparatively, in relation to the other financial regulatory agencies, the revised Federal Home Loan Bank procedures governing merger application are more in line with the procedures regulating mergers by commercial banks. Regional administrators of the Federal Deposit Insurance Corporation are permitted to approve routine mergers regardless of the asset size of the uniting banks. The Federal Reserve Board, too, also entrusts merger approval authority to its regional banks, except in cases involving anti-trust or Community Reinvestment Act Issues. The Office of the Comptroller of the Currency, however, is solely responsible for action on all merger activity undertaken by banks within its supervisory jurisdiction.

It should also be mentioned that the 1977 Community Reinvestment Act, effective November 1978, stipulates that the Federal Home Loan Bank Board in ruling on an application for merger, consolidation or acquisition of assets should consider the record of each association in satisfying the credit needs of its community, including the low and moderate income localities within the community. Merger applicants are required to submit a copy of the Community Reinvestment Act statement adopted by the Board of Directors of each applicant institution.

Supervisory Mergers

The Federal Savings and Loan Insurance Corporation has recently been favoring or advocating a policy of merger or acquisition as a means of assisting an insolvent or "distressed" savings and loan association. Smaller savings and loan associations in trouble have been forced for supervisory reasons by the Corporation to merge with a larger and more financially secure association in order to avoid ultimate receivership and liquidation which may be more costly to the Corporation in the long run.

The National Housing Act, Section 406, empowers the Corporation to make loans, to purchase the assets of, or to make a contribution to an insured institution in order to prevent a default or for purposes of restoring an insured institution in default to viable operation as a normal going concern. The statutes further declare that whenever an institution is in default or in the judgement of the Corporation is near default, the Corporation, in order to enhance the merger prospects or consolidation of the association with another insured institution, may purchase any such assets or assume any liabilities or guarantee the other insured association against loss due to its merging or consolidating with an association in default or in danger of default. Such action hinges on the discretionary authority of the Federal Savings and Loan Insurance Corporation subject to the proviso that it should provide contributions or guarantees "reasonably necessary to save the cost of liquidating the insured association." However, if the Corporation determines that guarantees or commitment of funds greater than that which is "reasonably necessary" is required in order to ensure the continuation of the association—because the services of the latter are vital to the provision of adequate savings and home financing services to the community—the limitations are not applicable. In cases involving state-chartered associations, mutual cooperation and consultation is, of course, required between the Corporation and the relevant state department administrators.

The following tables detail the activities of the Federal Savings and Loan Insurance Corporation in salvaging or rehabilitating distressed associations and also presents data on the reserve fund standing of the Corporation over the years.

As shown in Table V-2, contributions have accounted for over 54 percent of all settlements by the FSLIC with only ten associations or approximately 7 percent of total settlements involved in outright receivership. The FSLIC, since its inception, has dealth with an average of about one association failure per year.

The settlement method used in failures involved either liquidation and reimbursing depositors or paying another association to acquire all or part of the failing institution. Often in a supervisory merger, the FSLIC would purchase the loan assets of a failed association if the spread between yields and current market rates was so wide as to render their disposal only at exorbitant losses to the FSLIC.

The recent sustained bout of domestic inflation, declining savings flows and the ensuing earnings squeeze and consequent plunge in the net worth position of several associations, exerted considerable pressure on the resources of the FSLIC and generated concern over its ability to absorb or adequately deal with the rising number of distressed associations in a manner that would foster continued public confidence in the operation of the thrift industry. Table V-3 presents data on the reserve fund position of the FSLIC from 1962 to Decem-

Table V-2   Summary of Insurance Settlement Actions by the FSLIC
(Cumulative through March 31, 1981)

Method of Settlement	Number	Percentage of Total
Acquisition of assets	13	9
Acquisition of assets and contributions	18	13
Contribution	74	54
Contribution and loan	5	4
Contribution, loan, and acquisition of assets	4	3
Loan	5	4
Loan and acquisition of assets	1	0.7
Purchase and assumption	5	4
Receivership and acquisition of assets	3	2
Receivership	10	7
TOTAL:	138	100.0*

*Figures may not total 100 due to rounding.

ber 1982. At present, the fund is over \$6.5 billion or about equivalent to 1.3 percent of the total amount of all accounts of insured institutions. In 1980, the Federal Savings and Loan Insurance Corporation disbursed \$1 billion of its \$6 billion fund to purchase the assets of only three failing savings and loan associations. This raised questions concerning the FSLIC's ability to handle a potentially massive onslaught of financially strapped associations seeking assistance or ultimate reimbursement to its insured members. In March of 1981 alone, the Federal Savings and Loan Insurance Corporation added 114 associations to its problem list which then totaled 246. The additional 114 associations represented an increase of over 86 percent in the number of problem associations under the scrutiny of the FSLIC. In 1980, the FSLIC spent an unprecedented \$1.3 billion to assist 11 mergers and to render aid to 20 other savings and loan associations experiencing financial difficulty. In 1979, the FSLIC had disbursed only \$72.5 million. In 1981, there were 30 assisted mergers requiring \$988 million in FSLIC assistance. For 1982, the insurance agency provided assistance to the mergers of 77 savings and loan associations at a cost of \$1.1 billion.

Table V-3   Aggregate of Primary and Secondary Reserve of FSLIC

Year	Amount ($ Billion)	Percent to Total Amount of All Accounts of Insured Members of All Insured Institutions
1962	0.677	0.838
1963	0.944	1.011
1964	1,248	1.196
1965	1,537	1.353
1966	1,803	1.526
1967	2,049	1.622
1968	2,409	1.813
1969	2,801	2.138
1970	2,902	2.048
1971	2,986	1.767
1972	3,142	1.564
1973	3,453	1.563
1974	3,791	1.602
1975	4,119	1.478
1976	4,480	1.365
1977	4,872	1.286
1978	5,328	1.262
1979	5,848	1.269
1980	6,462	1.289
1981	6,156	1.198
1982	6,308	1.137

In May 1981, the FSLIC reimbursed the depositors of a Chicago savings and loan association that was the first liquidation in over a decade. Given the huge losses to the thrift industry during 1981 and 1982, the insurance agency was hard pressed to meet the needs of distressed associations.

Awareness of potential problems was undoubtedly reflected in the thrust by the FSLIC to introduce plans to alleviate the potential financial burden of failing associations on the Agency. The Agency has been experiencing difficulty in finding suitable merger partners for ailing associations in states such as New York, for example, where the search for a merger partner for one association extended over six months. In New York, too, one savings bank was involved in mergers with two different troubled savings and loan associations in just six weeks. To offset this difficulty and to further strengthen the capabilities of federal regulators, a bill was introduced to Congress in May by these agencies which sought to permit interstate mergers between banks and/or savings and loan associations. In addition, the Federal Savings and Loan Insurance Corporation petitioned for an increase in its line of credit with the Treasury from the present $750 million to $3 billion.

The rationale behind the request for Congressional sanctioning of these interstate activities was the belief that banks and other financial institutions may be willing to pay more for failing thrift institutions because the incentive of interstate branching increases the value of the association to the acquiring institution. The highly controversial bill was, however, rejected by the Reagan Administration, not because of its interstate banking implications, but because of the administration's reluctance to provide government bailouts to specific industries or individual enterprises. The line of credit increase to the FSLIC would have cost the Treasury Department $2.25 billion.

Instead, the Treasury Department proposed a program under which Federal insuring agencies would issue temporary letters of credit to those institutions whose net worth falls below 4 percent of assets. These letters of credit or demand notes could be added to capital totals by the thrifts. They would essentially be "paper transactions" not involving real capital infusions, but rather bolstering net worth figures on the books of thrift institutions and thus public confidence in troubled institutions. Some industry analysts viewed the Treasury proposal as a compromise appeasement ot the clamoring for government bailout of the ailing thrift industry, however limited its effect may be.

Massive government assistance to the thrift industry, as embodied in the FSLIC bill, thus appeared to be anathema to the present administration which favored bolstering the mechanisms of the private free marketplace to generate solutions. Other industry analysts also viewed the proposed bill as a "back-door approach to interindustry acquisitions and nationwide banking."

Nevertheless, for the thrift industry, the Federal Home Loan Bank Board policy change governing interstate acquisitions would, on a limited basis, foster interstate mergers between savings and loan associations. In March 1981, the Federal Home Loan Bank Board ruled that if the latter body determines that an interstate merger is required to prevent a failure and reduce the risk or insurance liability to the Federal Savings and Loan Insurance Corporation, the Board will consider approval of the interstate merger. Attempts will, however, be made to find suitable merger partners in the same state before any interstate mergers are approved. Such approval, too, will be on a very limited basis.

In one preliminary test case, several District of Columbia associations offered bids for a failing Maryland association at prices significantly higher than in-state Maryland associations. There was widespread belief among industry analysts that a bill to provide interstate and interindustry acquisitions would in all likelihood receive the support of the present administration as a solution by the private market to the current difficulties facing the savings and loan industry.

In September 1981, the Federal Home Loan Bank Board approved the first supervisory interstate merger involving savings and loan associations from California, New York, and Florida. West Side Federal Savings and Loan Association of New York City, and Washington Savings and Loan Association of Miami Beach were merged in Citizens Savings and Loan Association of San Francisco, California. The parent company of Citizens Savings, National Steel Corporation, made an agreement to infuse $75 million in additional capital to the newly merged institution. The funds from the parent company would be provided in three annual installments beginning in September 1982. The Federal Savings and Loan Insurance Corporation also undertook to provide financial assistance to the new association for a period of 10 years in order to compensate for any losses on the existing portfolios of West Side Federal and Washington Federal Savings and Loan Associations.

In order to effect the merger procedure, Citizens and Washington Savings converted to federal charters. West Side Federal then acquired

Washington Federal; Citizens then acquired the combined entity. The Bank Board estimated that the tri-state merger would save the public approximately $750 million. Citizens, Federal, subsequently, changed its name to First Nationwide Savings.

In its efforts to utilize the least costly method in dealing with problem associations, the FSLIC has approved several other inter-state mergers. The troubled First Federal Savings and Loan of Broward County, Florida, was acquired by Glendale Savings and Loan of California. The Glendate merger involved the use of purchase accounting whereby losses are amortized over a longer period of perhaps 40 years, while income and payments from discounted mort-gages are recognized over a shorter period of 10-12 years. Earnings are, thus, substantially improved in early years. Home Savings of America, Los Angeles, has under supervisory mergers, also acquired five savings and loan associations in Texas, Illinois, Missouri, and Florida.

During 1982, the FSLIC approved 16 interstate mergers. Note-worthy mergers included, in March, Schenectady Savings Bank of New York acquired Hartford Federal Savings and Loan Association, Connecticut. Schenectady converted to a savings and loan charter after the merger and became North East Savings FA, Hartford, Connecticut. In October, North East Savings acquired First Federal Savings and Loan Association Boston, and Freedom Federal Savings and Loan Association of Worcester, Massachusetts.

In August, Erie Savings Bank of Buffalo, New York merged with American Federal Savings and Loan Association of Southfield, Michigan; First Federal Savings of Mid-Florida, Deland; and Harris County Federal Savings and Loan Association, Baytown, Texas. After the merger, Erie Savings changed to a savings and loan charter and became Empire Savings of America FSA, Buffalo, New York. First Federal and Harris County Federal became part of Empire of America FSA, Deland, Florida, a divisional subsidiary to Empire of America FSA, Buffalo. In November, Empire of America FSA, Deland, Florida, acquired Island Federal Savings and Loan, Hempstead, New York, and South Shore Federal Savings and Loan, Massapequa, New York. Empire of America acquired in December a savings and loan in Kingston, New York and another in Fort Worth, Texas, without FSLIC assistance. Subsequent to these mergers, Empire of America acquired with $15 million in FSLIC assistance, the Metropolitan Savings Association of Farmington Hills, Michigan. After the merger in February 1983, Empire had assets of over $6.3 billion, with corporate offices in Southfield, Michigan and administrative offices in Buffalo, New York. Offices of the Empire conglomorate numbered 119 geographically spread over Michigan, New York, Texas, and Florida.

Another noteworthy interstate/interindustry merger was Citicorp's acquisition in September 1982, of the $2.9 billion asset Fidelity Savings and Loan Association of San Francisco, California, with an 80 branch network. Several stipulations, however, were imposed by the Board in granting approval of the cross-industry interstate merger. Citicorp was required to operate Fidelity as a savings and loan association, with emphasis on residential housing credit. Fidelity was also prohibited from operating a remote service unit outside of California, and from establishing or operating branches at locations not authorized for national or state banks in California. In addition, the acquired thrift had to be operated as a separate, autonomous profit-oriented corporate entity and not in tandem with any other Citicorp subsidiary. These restrictions placed on the operation of Citicorp Savings, as Fidelity was known after the acquisition, were lifted by the Federal Reserve Board in June 1983.

While the $800 billion industry was undergoing unprecedented earnings pressure over the last two years and, perhaps, as many as 60 percent of all federally insured associations were operating in the red, several strong associations had reserves large enough to withstand losses at current rates for at least a decade. A loss of public confidence could trigger a run on the cash reserves of several institutions, particularly withdrawals of uninsured deposits over $100,000 and ultimately lead to failure. Consolidations and merger activity will continue and many of the smaller associations will be forced to seek suitable merger partners. Whatever solutions are devised, an allaying of public uneasiness must be a factor of prime consideration.

The FSLIC in its continuing efforts to reduce the costs of assistance to troubled associations has also resorted to the consolidation of problem institutions with other distressed or federally supported thrifts via interim mergers. One such institution involved in these consolidations is the First Federal Savings and Loan Association of Rochester, New York, which is being dubbed a "phoenix" institution, analogous to the mythical bird that is consumed by fire and re-emerges again from the ashes. First Federal was involved in consolidations of five New York associations up to March 1982. Another New York thrift Suffolk County Federal Savings and Loan Association, Centereach, became a "phoenix" in April 1982 when the distressed association was merged with the troubled County Federal Savings and Loan Association of Rockville Centre. The FSLIC, to date, has created five such "phoenixes" around the country, providing assistance to the total entity rather than individually, when assisted mergers with healthy institutions have not been available or involve too great a financial outlay by the Corporation.

Recently, the FSLIC has begun divesting itself of these "phoenixes" given the improved state of the thrift industry, seeking healthy thrifts as acquirors of these government-supported consolidations. Suffolk County, for example, was acquired in May 1983 by Long Island Savings Bank, and approval was granted in late November by the Federal Home Loan Bank Board for Citicorp to acquire another phoenix, the First Federal Savings and Loan Association of Chicago.

The Federal Home Loan Bank Board, in April 1983, closed the Biscayne Federal Savings and Loan Association of Miami, and chartered and established a new federal mutual association, New Biscayne FS&LA of Miami. The failed Biscayne was a stock association with about 1.9 million shares outstanding to 1,500 stockholders. These stockholders would share pro rata in the disposition of the assets of the association, after creditors and the FSLIC have been reimbursed, which, in effect, could result in losses to the majority of shareholders. The shareholders brought suit against the Federal Home Loan Bank Board, and in September, the U.S. District Court ruled that the association be returned to its stockholders on the grounds that the Board acted in a manner that was "arbitrary and capricious and purposely misleading." The Bank Board appealed the District Court ruling, and in November, the Federal Appeals Court in Atlanta overturned the District Court ruling and upheld the takeover of Biscayne by the Federal Home Loan Bank Board. The latter agency declared that it was "extremely pleased" that the court upheld its authority to deal "decisively with insolvency cases." The Biscayne case, no doubt, effected revised guidelines by the Board in dealing with problem associations and negotiations with stockholders. Biscayne was subsequently acquired by Citicorp.

MUTUAL BANKS

Merger activity among mutual savings banks has also been quite pronounced, particularly in the New England states and New York. Two of New York's largest thrift institutions, the Metropolitan Savings Bank and the Brooklyn Savings Bank, announced plans to merge in April, 1981. The consolidation became the fourth largest mutual savings bank in the United States with combined assets of over $3.9 billion. The Chairman of Metropolitan noted that "The combined resources of both banks will better position us to compete on an equal footing with commercial banks and other major thrifts." This statement echoes similar sentiments expressed by many other merging institutions.

Merger applications by the mutual banks require both the approval of the Federal Deposit Insurance Corporation and the particular State Banking Department. The procedures involved are similar to those governing merging applications processed by the Federal Home Loan Bank Board and the Federal Savings and Loan Insurance Corporation.

Legislative requirements for mergers among state-chartered savings and loan associations and/or mutual banks have never been overly stringent. State laws differ, but a look at the California situation is instructive, since the largest proportion of mergers have occurred in California. The laws there require the affirmative vote of at least a majority of the directors of the associations involved, and ratification of the vote by the shareholders holding more than two-thirds of investment certificates or stock. Since 1931, there has been no major change in this legislation. At no time in California has there ever been legislation restricting the number of associations which may be merged into one organization. The statutes regulating mergers of state-chartered thrifts in New York State require the approval of the Superintendent of Banking. A plan of the merger also must be submitted that has the approval of the relevant boards of directors.

Given the current state of the thrift industry, an increasing number of supervisory mergers have also been negotiated by the relevant state banking departments and the FDIC. Some of these mergers have included cross-industry arrangements between commercial banks and savings banks. In February 1982, for example, Farmers and Mechanics Savings Bank, the only savings bank in the state, was merged into Marquette National Bank, both of Minneapolis, Minnesota. In March 1982, Fidelity Mutual Savings Bank of Spokane, Washington, was merged into First Interstate Bank of Seattle, Washington. The Mechanics and the First Interstate merger jointy cost the FDIC approximately a total of $140 million in assistance.

In March 1982, after 163 years of operation, the New York Bank for Savings in New York, the nation's second oldest mutual savings bank, was merged into the Buffalo Savings Bank of Buffalo, New York. Buffalo Savings became the largest savings bank in the nation with assets of $8.1 billion. That distinction, however, was short-lived when in April 1982, Western Savings Bank of Philadelphia was merged with Philadelphia Savings Fund Society for combined assets of $9.5 billion thus enabling Philadelphia Savings to regain its position as the nation's largest savings bank. The merger was undertaken at an estimated cost of $294 million to the FDIC. Both the Buffalo and the Philadelphia mergers were affected through the use by the FDIC of capital infusion notes to compensate these institutions for the negative spreads on their acquired associations' portfolios under the Corporation's "income maintenance" and capital infusion program. In dealing with distressed institutions, the FDIC has sought to apply whatever methods it deems to be cost-effective, including granting financial assistance to facilitate voluntary mergers of savings banks.

COMMERCIAL BANKS

For commercial banks, Section 5 of the Bank Merger Act of 1966 stipulates that the responsible agency should not approve any proposed merger transaction which would be in "furtherance of any combination of conspiracy to monopolize or to attempt to monopolize the business of banking in any part of the United States." Furthermore, the Act states that approval should also be denied if the proposed merger may substantially "lessen competition" or tend to create a monopoly, unless the supervisory agency involved believes that the anti-competitive effects of the proposed arrangement are strongly outweighed in the public interest by the potential effect of the proposed merger in meeting the needs and convenience of the community to be served. Bank mergers are also subject to the Sherman and Clayton Acts, following the 1963 Supreme Court decision involving two Philadelphia banks. In April, in the largest bank merger in U. S. history, Bank America Corporation of California acquired the ailing Seafirst Corporation of Seattle, Washington. The agreement required passage of legislation in Washington State that would allow out-of-state banking organizations to buy distressed Washington State financial institutions. The consolidation made the $9.6 billion asset

Seafirst and its principal Seattle First Natinal Bank, an independent subsidiary of the $119.7 billion asset Bank America. Seafirst had been experiencing heavy losses as a result of writedowns on energy loans.

Recently, there has been renewed interest in cross-industry mergers and acquisitions, in particular between banks and thrift institutions. Congress has traditionally opposed such mergers and, in fact, a specific bill prohibiting banks, bank-holding companies and their subsidiaries from acquiring thrift institutions was passed in the Senate in September 1980, but was subsequently not ruled on by the House. The possibility of a multi-billion dollar subsidy effort to bail out troubled thrifts may, however, assist in overcoming resistance to cross-industry mergers and acquisitions, more so since the present administration appears more favorable to the latter course of action rather than the former which would involve committing federal funds to rescue private interests.

One interesting development was the recent merger in March 1982 of a healthy savings and loan association into a commercial bank in California. Commonwealth Bank of Hawthorne acquired Equality Savings and Loan Association of San Diego. In this cross-industry merger, however, there was a common bond between the two institutions. The Chairman and Chief Executive Officer of the Hawthorne Bank is also Chairman of Equality Savings and Loan. California banking law is silent on bank-thrift mergers, and regulators have interpreted the lack of an explicit statute as either permitting the action or prohibiting such arrangements, depending on which regulator, thrift, or bank is involved. The savings and loan department in California has generally opposed bank-thrift mergers except in supervisory cases where no alternative partner could be found. Approval is usually given on the proviso that the saving and loan acquired by a bank-holding company continue to operate as a thrift institution. In the Commonwealth Bank case, Equality Savings and Loan would cease to operate as a thrift and would be absorbed as a subsidiary of the acquiring bank. While the action was approved by the Banking Department of California, it was not sanctioned by the Department of Savings and Loans. Currently, legislation that would explicitly permit bank thrift acquisitions and, vice versa, is being debated by the California legislature.

The 1982 Garn-St Germain Depository Institutions Act authorized the FSLIC/FDIC to approve emergency acquisitions according to a tiered bidding process. After soliciting offers from any qualified prospective purchaser, if the bid that generates the lowest cost to the FSLIC is not from an in-state same-type institution, all tenders within 15 percent of $15 million of the lowest cost, first bid may submit new bids. After the second round of bidding, the FSLIC is directed to give consideration to the following priorities: in-state, same type institution, in-state, different type institution; out-of-state, same type institution; and out-of-state, different type institution. The FSLIC is further required to give preference to minority controlled bidders in the case of ailing minority institutions, and to institutions in adjacent states, if the FSLIC goes outside the in-state bidding tier.

The number of supervisory mergers is, however, expected to decline during 1983, as a result of the net worth guarantee program mandated by the 1982 Act, which will bolster the net worth of financially weakened institutions. For institutions, however, with net worth of less than ½ of 1 percent of assets, merger activity may be the most feasible means of restoring solvency to these problem associations.

HOLDING COMPANIES

A holding company is a corporation that controls one or more banks. It represents one method of circumventing branching restrictions. Texas, Florida, and Illinois do not permit multi-bank holding companies. In 1956, the Bank Holding Company Act gave the federal system full regulatory authority over multi-bank holding companies. By 1970, all such corporations were under the umbrella of federal regulation and supervision when one-bank holding companies were no longer exempt from the Act.

A savings and loan holding company is a company which directly or indirectly controls a FSLIC insured institution or federally chartered savings bank insured by the FDIC, or controls any other company that is a savings and loan holding company. Savings and loan holding companies are subject to the provisions of the Savings and Loan Holding Company Act (SLHCA). The SLHCA was enacted to control the "creation of . . . . new unitary or multiple holding company systems" and requires the prior written approval of the FSLIC for the acquisition of 25 percent or more of the voting shares of a

FSLIC insured savings and loan by a company or savings and loan holding company.

A savings and loan holding company that is "unitary" controlling only one association rather than "multiple," where there are two or more associations, is not subject to geographic restrictions on the operations of subsidiaries, if the association it owns qualifies as a "domestic building and loan association" under the Internal Revenue Code. There are also no restrictions on the activities in which the savings and loan holding company's other affiliates may engage. A unitary holding company may, therefore, undertake activities authorized for savings and loan associations on an interstate basis, as well as engage in other activities not allowed for savings associations. On the other hand, multiple holding companies are limited to activities pertaining to the operation of a savings and loan association and other ancillary activities which are deemed to be a proper incident to the operation of a savings and loan association.

It should be mentioned that legislation in late 1983 has been introduced in Congress which would *inter alia* limit the type of companies that would be allowed to own insured savings and loan associations. Savings and loan holding companies have grown from 44 with 93 capital stock savings and loan subsidiaries with assets of 4.3 billion in 1960 to 122 such holding companies with 131 capital stock association subsidiaries and assets of $33 billion in 1972. While in 1972, there were 605 capital stock savings and loan associations that could be acquired, by 1980, the number had increased to over 850.

It is interesting to note that as of December 31, 1983, the largest savings and loan holding company was Sears, Roebuck and Co., Chicago, which controlled the Allstate Savings and Loan Association, Los Angeles, California with assets of over $5 billion. Thirty-seven of the largest savings and loan holding companies controlled one savings and loan association, three companies controlled two associations, two controlled four associations, and one—Financial Federal Inc. of Los Angeles, California—controlled eleven savings and loan associations.

In California, which has the largest number of stock associations, holding companies control approximately 50 percent of all stock associations and about 85 percent of their assets. Seven of the ten largest holding companies are located in California, as are eighteen of the largest forty-two savings and loan holding companies. Holding companies are, thus, a significant part of the savings and loan scene, as well as the banking industry in general where multi-bank holding companies control over 65 percent of total bank deposits.

CONCLUSION

While merger activity may be less intense than in 1981 and 1982, some mergers will continue, particularly where net worth falls below ½ of 1 percent and assistance under the 1982 Garn Act cannot be obtained.

The recent spate of *ad hoc* supervisory mergers, interstate and interindustry, placed in the foreground the need for Congressional action and uniformity on a subject which, no doubt, would shape the nature and structure of the financial industry in the future. It appeared that the traditional barriers to interstate and cross-industry activities were being slowly eroded, plausibly to the point where given the lengthy Congressional gestation period, ultimate Congressional decree gave legal sanction to what was de facto a practical reality.

Chapter VI
Branching

OVERVIEW

Globally, the majority of banking systems consist of a relatively small number of banks, each with a large network of branch offices. There are only nine banks in Canada and less than twenty in England. The Bank of England, the central bank in that country, oversees the scope of branching activity, which is permitted on a nationwide basis. There are no legislative restrictions on the establishment of a branch operation by any of the major joint-stock banks in England.

On the other hand, the United States is the only major country to have a unit-banking system; that is, a system in which most banks do not have branch subsidiaries. There are over 14,600 banks currently in operation in the United States of which 5,800 are located in eleven unit-banking states. As of December 1960, the comparable figures were a total of 13,480 banks of which 11,025 were unit banks. It has been suggested that perhaps one reason for the tendency toward unit banking in the United States related to a fear of banking monopoly. Historically, the majority of states did not allow banks to establish branches, and as late as 1910, only twelve states permitted local banks to undertake branching. There was no provision regarding branching in the National Bank Act of 1863 and its amendments of 1865; and in 1911, in a ruling by the Attorney General, this lack of authorization was interpreted as a prohibition of branch banking activity. In 1922, the Comptroller of the Currency, then Crissinger, declared that national banks could operate additional branches in the same city as the head office, in order to provide certain types of routine services. Such branches were, however, not authorized to grant loans independently of the head office. The Comptroller of the Currency thus issued permits allowing national banks to establish branches, but only in cities where state banks were already operating branches. During the next five years, over 200 branch permits were issued.

Such ad hoc permission was formally and generally legalized in the McFadden-Pepper Act of 1927, which allowed national banks to establish full service branches within the cities in which they were located, provided that state banks possessed similar authority.

The Banking Act of 1933 liberalized these laws for national banks by further allowing these banks to establish branches on the same applicable terms as those pertaining to state banks in the various regions. Thus, in a state permitting state-wide branching, national banks can establish branches anywhere in that state, in a state where branching is restricted to the head office city or county, national banks are subject to the same restrictions. The 1933 Act also defined a branch as an office of a bank which lends money, receives deposits and provides check cashing facilities.

The McFadden-Pepper Act and the Banking Act of 1933 are two examples of the continuing controversy over state's rights in the area of banking. National banking law is blatantly inconsistent, it is argued, since if branch banking is desirable, national banks should be allowed to establish branches independently of the particular state statutes regulating branching. If branching is undesirable, then no national banks should be permitted to establish branches. This branching issue is still unresolved and remains one of the most vigorously debated issues in American banking. With the substantial technological advances that have been attained recently in the provision of banking services, new competitive pressures and a rapidly changing financial environment, it appears that a relaxation of anachronistic geographical constraints on banking may be inevitable. The issue of inter-state branching will be discussed more fully later.

The Banking Act of 1933 thus established state boundaries as the ultimate limits for the geographic expansion of a bank through branching. There were, however, certain "grandfathered" exceptions, in particular branches operated by the Bank of California in Oregon and Washington. In essence, the Act relegated to the state authorities the responsibility for determining the type of branch banking structure each state would ratify.

Geographic expansion of banking operations, however, where restricted, was achieved through the formation of bank holding companies. Such expansion both state-wide in some unit banking states and inter-state flourished in a largely unfettered environment until the introduction of the Bank Holding Company Act in 1956. Section 3(d) of the Act, more commonly referred to as the Douglas Amendment, prohibited multi-bank holding companies from acquiring banks in a state other than its home state, unless such out-of-state acquisitions were permitted by the state in which the bank to be acquired was located. An amendment to the Bank Holding Company Act in 1970 extended the restrictions on inter-state acquisitions to one-bank holding companies.

Holding companies are, nevertheless, able to perform many banking functions across state lines. The Bank Holding Company Act in strictly defining a bank as an institution which accepts demand deposits and provides commercial loans, fostered the development of nonbank subsidiaries that can undertake several banking functions across state boundaries. A popular inter-state function has been the establishment of loan production offices in several states for the purpose of soliciting loan business both at the commercial and retail level. Currently, there are approximately 350 loan production offices operating in twenty states. Other bank holding companies have established inter-state operations in the area of consumer finance such as credit cards, for example, mortgage banking, leasing, and other banking functions. Moreover, in the area of international banking, Edge Act Corporations are able to offer full banking services on an inter-state basis as defined by the 1970 Holding Company Act to customers involved in international trade activities.

The International Banking Act of 1978 further expanded the branching and operational capabilities of Edge Act Corporations and also sought to re-align the competitive inequality of foreign banks vis-a-vis domestic banks with regard to branching. Foreign banks were required to declare which state would be designated as the head or home-office location and would only be allowed to branch in that particular state. Previously, foreign banks could operate branches on a multi-state basis and the 1978 Act grandfathered thirty-six foreign banking organizations with banking operations on an inter-state basis.

Thus, in summary, bank operations—in spite of the restrictions governing inter-state branches—have developed a significant network of multi-state operations. The contemporary banking and financial system, together with the increased competition from nonbank financial institutions and the trend towards nationwide provision of banking services occasioned by technological advances, will, no doubt, reduce the segmentation of financial markets along geographic lines. The regulatory and statutory structure governing the operation of the banking industry will have to undergo reorganization and change if banks and thrift institutions are to effectively meet the challenges of the market place.

STATE BRANCHING PROVISIONS FOR BANKS

The extent of branch banking in the United States has been sharply constrained by the prohibition of inter-state branching. State branching laws run the gamut from outright prohibition of any branch banking to the privilege of state-wide branching. As Figure VI-1 illustrates, twenty-two states permit state-wide branching, seventeen permit limited branching such as within a city, a county or within contiguous counties, while eleven states prohibit branching altogether. Geographically, states in the west and along the eastern seaboard typically permit state-wide branching, whereas the majority of the unit banking states are located in the midwest.

For several years, however, the trend has been consistently toward more liberal branching laws, and there is little doubt that liberalization of branching restrictions will continue. While in 1960 only 16 states permitted state-wide branching, and 18 allowed no branching at all, by 1974, the number of states authorizing state-wide branching increased to 20, while the number of unit banking states declined to 13. By 1981, the comparable figures were 22 and 11 for state-wide and unit banking states respectively. The number of branches in operation has increased rapidly over the years from less than 4000 at the end of 1945 to over 28,000 at the end of 1973.

Some evaluation of the reasons underlying the trend toward more extensive branching over the years is perhaps useful. Several advantages may be derived from the establishment of branch operations. These include the ability of larger banks to generate economies of scale that permit more efficient, lower cost operation. Branches can also offer small communities, customer services that self-sufficient unit banks cannot afford. Diversification permitted by branching, too, further enhances the safety of the bank. In addition, more extensive branch banking may lead to more loans per dollar of deposits. Experience with the failure rate of very small unit banks also provides persuasive evidence in support of "large" branch banks.

The advantage of size must, however, be distinguished from that of branch structure. There is the dilemma faced by the antitrust

Unit Banking

Limited Branching

Statewide Branching

Data from the Conference of State Bank Supervisors

authorities in determining how far the system should go in sacrificing the advantages of size and diversity in order to combat the disadvantages of concentration. Given the highly competitive market place of the present decade, and the growth of the financial and banking industry toward an inter-state orientation, a phased liberalization of existing geographic restraints would serve to provide legal ratification to a de facto development over recent years. Geographic and product segmentation of the American financial industry has been rapidly eroded, particularly in recent years, and it has been argued that current restrictions inter alia "impede the efficient allocation of resources, retard the development and application of new technologies and restrict the ability of bank management to compete with other nonbank financial institutions playing under a different set of rules."[1]

The bank regulatory agency in each state thus exercises authority over branching policy. Not surprisingly, there is wide variance with respect to requirements which must be satisfied by state-chartered banks and in the procedures that are adopted by the various state regulatory authorities. All state banks with deposits insured by the Federal Deposit Insurance Corporation are subject to federal control over branching. For state banks that are members of the Federal Reserve system, the Federal Reserve Act requires that the approval of the Board of Governors "shall be obtained before any state member bank may hereafter establish any branch."

State-chartered banks who are not members of the Federal Reserve system but are insured by the Federal Deposit Insurance Corporation are subject to the stipulations of the Insurance Act that states that no bank shall "establish and operate any new branches unless it shall have the written consent of the Corporation." The Federal Reserve and the Federal Deposit Insurance Corporation thus de facto have what amounts to veto power over the actions of state authorities in authorizing branches for state-chartered banks. In practice, however, due to the close collusion between federal and state regulatory agencies in processing and assessing applications, such veto power is rarely exercised. In ruling on a branch application, most state authorities take into consideration the need and convenience of the proposed branch, probability of success, "undue injury" to other financial institutions, performance under the Community Reinvestment Act, and the safety and general financial condition of the particular insti-

---

[1] Carter Report on Geographic Restrictions on Commercial Banking in the United States, page 2.

tution. Some states also require that specific population levels be satisfied in approving branch facilities for certain locations.

On the other hand, applications for branches by national banks are regulated and processed by the Comptroller of the Currency, federal authority is, however, limited by the McFadden Act which is juxtaposed with state statutes. One such controversial limitation has to do with whether national bank branches may only undertake those functions which branches of state-chartered banks are authorized to perform. Such problems are prominent in states which do not Permit branches to provide all banking services but only limited banking functions such as the cashing of checks or the collection of deposits. The Office of the Comptroller of the Currency has been of the opinion that as long as branches of state banks are permitted to provide any of the branching services as defined in the National Bank Act, offices of national banks may operate as full-service branches.

Most states, as mentioned, also restrict branching to designated geographic areas, such as city limits, counties, contiguous counties or regions. Branches of national banks are also bound by minimum capital requirements pertaining to the establishment of out-of-town branches by state banks. State provisions, with respect to "need" and "solvency of the branch" criteria are also applicable to national banks.

To the extent that savings banks and savings and loans are state chartered, their ability to branch is regulated by the banking laws of that state. They are, therefore, subject to the same provisions covering state chartered banks in their branching applications. Also similar to state banks, both institutions need approval of either their appropriate insurance corporation in order to open a new branch facility. Consequently, in the case of savings banks, consent was also required of the FDIC and for state savings and loans, the FSLIC.

Federal chartered savings and loans and savings banks have a status in branching that frees them from the limits of state statutes.

MUTUAL SAVINGS BANKS—BRANCHING

Nationally, the mutual savings banking industry is numerically and geographically restricted. Essentially, the industry is concentrated in the 17 states that comprise the middle Atlantic region and New England. State laws and/or supervisory requirements of the Federal Deposit Insurance Corporation for the initial advances for reserves by organizers continue to make it extremely difficult to establish mutual savings banks de novo, even in those states which do permit their operation. Because the formation of new mutual savings banks has been so difficult, the need for increased savings facilities in newer neighborhoods and communities has been partially met through the establishment of savings bank branches.

Between 1945 and 1960, the number of mutual savings banks having branches increased from 85 to 195, while the number of branches more than tripled from 143 to 487. Presently, nearly 90 percent of all mutual savings banks have branches compared with approximately 16 percent in 1945, and branches account for about 50 percent of all mutual savings bank offices compared with 20 percent of all offices at the start of the post-war period. At the end of 1982, there were 2,777 branches of mutual savings banks with the state of New York accounting for over 40 percent of the total number of branch facilities. While some of the additional branches were acquired through mergers, most were de novo established branch offices.

The diversity among the states in savings bank branch operations reflects in part differences in state laws. In Wisconsin, the three mutual banks in operation there do not have branch facilities due to statutory prohibition. In Minnesota, where there is no specific statute authorizing branches for mutual savings banks, the savings bank located there has acquired one branch by way of merger. Connecticut, Rhode Island, Vermont, Maryland, Washington, and New York permit with certain stipulations statewide branching systems. Maine and Pennsylvania permit branches to be established in counties contiguous to the head office county, as well as with the head office county. In New Jersey and in Massachusetts, branches may be established within the head office county subject to certain restrictions.

With the passage of Omnibus Banking "parity" Bill in New York during November 1980, mutual savings banks were permitted unlimited branching authority with the repeal of the restriction of one new branch per year. In line with regulations pertaining to federal mutual savings banks, a state savings bank in New York may establish branches in its own Standard Metropolitan Statistical Area, its own county, or within 35 miles of its home office without numerical limitations.

For the mutual banking industry as a whole, some indication of branching structure on a comparative basis with commercial banks and savings and loan associations can be obtained from Table VI-1.

Of a total number of offices (25,569) operated by these three financial intermediaries in the 17 states in which mutual banks operate, mutual savings banks accounted for 3,201 or 12.5 percent while

Table VI-1 Number of Offices of Selected Types of Financial Institutions in Mutual Savings Bank States, December 31, 1979

State	Mutual Savings Banks			Commercial Banks			Savings and Loan Associations		
	Banks	Branches	Total Offices	Banks	Branches	Total Offices	Assns.	Branches	Total Offices
Massachusetts	155	521	676	143	994	1,137	133	244	377
New York	95	952	1,047	347	3,269	3,616	89	539	628
Connecticut	62	390	452	54	618	672	38	150	188
Maine	24	108	132	35	316	351	17	27	44
New Hampshire	25	59	84	72	184	256	13	26	39
New Jersey	19	230	249	148	1,648	1,796	170	844	1,014
Washington	9	113	122	113	856	969	45	348	393
Pennsylvania	8	194	202	1 355	2,630	2,985	288	811	1,099
Rhode Island	6	73	79	18	232	250	4	26	30
Vermont	5	23	28	28	180	208	5	9	14
Indiana	4	3	7	402	1,193	1,595	131	273	404
Maryland	3	66	69	91	1,036	1,127	159	377	536
Wisconsin	3	–	3	630	462	1,092	88	467	555
Alaska	2	3	5	14	115	129	5	12	17
Delaware	2	24	26	30	150	180	15	12	27
Oregon	2	18	20	99	604	703	22	315	337
Total	424	2,777	3,201	2,579	14,487	17,066	1,222	4,480	5,702

Note: Figures for commercial banks include stock savings banks and non-deposit trust companies.
Source: FDIC and USLSA.

savings and loan associations were responsible for 5,702 offices or 22.3 percent and commercial banks for 17,066 or 66.7 percent of the total.

BRANCHING PROVISIONS FOR
SAVINGS AND LOAN ASSOCIATIONS

Limitations on the establishment of branches by savings and loan associations are determined by state laws for state-chartered savings and loan associations. Branch powers of federal savings and loan associations are authorized by the Federal Home Loan Bank Board. Before examining the various state-branching statutes and federal regulations, reference should be made to the very rapid increase in association facilities over the past decade and the current trend towards greater utilization of automated teller machines and other electronic banking devices. No doubt, the proliferation of association offices contributed to the rapid ascent of the savings and loan industry in 1972 to become the second largest type of financial intermediary in the United States. At that time, too, the number of branch offices (5,851) surpassed for the first time the number of associations (5,298). As Table VI-2 illustrates, while in 1955 there were only 601 association branches, by 1973, the number had increased to over 7,000. With the increasing urbanization of the nation and the accompanying rise in the demand for mortgage credit, together with competition from other financial intermediaries, the establishment of branch facilities extended savings and loan services to greater numbers of individuals.

By 1975, the number of branches reached a figure of over 10,500 increasing by 1,743, the largest annual increase. As of December 31, 1982, the number of branches of associations totaled 18,712 with over 1,000 branches added during that year. As Table VI-3 reveals, using 1977 data, California accounted for the largest number of branch facilities followed by Texas, Ohio, and Florida. California continues to dominate the branching arena, accounting for over 3,000 branch offices at the end of 1982.

The 1977 data also illustrates the substantial role of branch facilities in the expansion of savings flows. Home offices nationwide held $165 billion in savings, while full branches, limited facilities and satellite offices generated over $203 billion in savings deposits.

Table VI-2   Number of Savings Association Offices

Year-end	Number of Associations	Number of Branches	Number of Offices
1955	6,071	601	6,672
1960	6,320	1,611	7,931
1965	6,185	2,994	9,179
1966	6,112	3,206	9,318
1967	6,036	3,357	9,393
1968	5,947	3,667	9,614
1969	5,835	3,938	9,773
1970	5,669	4,318	9,987
1971	5,474	4,961	10,425
1972	5,298	5,851	11,149
1973	5,170	7,036	12,206
1974	5,023	8,775	13,798
1975	4,931	10,518	15,449
1976	4,821	11,908	16,729
1977	4,761	13,087	17,848
1978	4,725	14,250	18,975
1979	4,684	15,508	20,192
1980	4,613	16,733	21,346
1981	4,292	17,495	21,787
1982	3,833	18,712	22,545

Source: Federal Home Loan Bank Board; U.S. League of Savings Associations.

For several states, too, in particular California, Florida and New York, the dollar amount of savings held by branch operations is quite significant.

There has, thus been a rapid and pervasive expansion in the number of savings and loan association branch offices over the past decade. The trend toward more extensive branching is further reflected in the streamlining of procedures and in the rapidly evolving powers granted by the Federal Home Loan Bank Board to federal associations to operate various types of facilities. Over 50 percent of all branch offices are operated by federal savings and loan associations. At the state level also, legislative enactments and amendments have further extended branching powers and introduced new branching statutes where they were previously non-existent. In 1958, 16 states prohibited savings association branching and by 1972, only 2—West Virginia and Montana—prohibited branch operations. Currently, in the 1980s, savings and loan association branches are located in every state in the nation.

Facilities of FSLIC-Insured Savings and Loan Associations, by State—September 30, 1977

	Number by type of facility						Savings (dollar amounts in millions) by type of facility					
	All facilities	Home offices	Full branches	Limited branches	Satellite offices	Mobile Units	All facilities	Home offices	Full branches	Limited facilities	Satellite offices	Mobile units
UNITED STATES	16,524	4,061	11,353	773	292	85	$369,225	$165,774	$198,279	$4,158	$926	$88
Alabama	216	60	136	17	3	0	3,246	1,786	1,344	101	15	0
Alaska	17	4	13	0	0	0	222	122	100	0	0	0
Arizona	186	16	163	5	2	0	3,598	606	2,979	11	2	0
Arkansas	174	71	97	0	0	3	2,770	2,057	701	0	7	5
California	2,171	164	1,694	267	24	22	65,545	13,039	50,636	1,694	147	29
Colorado	273	46	209	17	1	0	5,161	1,648	3,384	127	2	0
Connecticut	160	36	114	6	4	0	2,937	1,698	1,215	20	4	0
Delaware	15	5	10	0	0	0	195	121	74	0	0	0
District of Columbia	91	16	74	1	0	0	3,075	1,183	1,892	*	0	0
Florida	974	121	681	80	87	5	29,379	9,255	19,343	390	383	8
Georgia	375	97	262	10	6	0	7,047	3,643	3,364	31	9	0
Hawaii	117	8	107	0	2	0	2,007	519	1,484	0	4	0
Idaho	46	11	35	0	0	0	738	405	333	0	0	0
Illinois	869	393	429	32	15	0	27,978	21,367	6,422	154	35	0
Indiana	340	152	168	20	0	0	7,016	4,795	2,088	133	0	0
Iowa	249	70	159	18	2	0	4,697	3,287	1,347	59	4	0
Kansas	222	83	132	6	1	0	4,471	2,751	1,698	21	1	0
Kentucky	237	107	120	7	3	0	4,059	2,854	1,185	17	3	0
Louisiana	267	117	147	3	3	0	5,202	3,507	1,684	11	0	0
Maine	41	21	18	2	0	0	466	347	114	5	0	0
Maryland	307	70	227	1	9	0	5,994	2,450	3,514	7	23	0
Massachusetts	130	30	91	3	6	0	2,779	1,657	1,103	10	9	0
Michigan	478	65	398	13	2	0	11,452	3,254	8,131	48	19	0
Minnesota	257	55	177	18	7	0	6,769	3,162	3,563	37	7	0
Mississippi	192	58	129	0	1	4	1,863	1,064	805	0	3	1

Missouri	441	112	300	7	1	21	9,726	4,277	5,385	49	2	13
Montana	43	12	28	1	2	0	834	521	311	1	1	0
Nebraska	171	40	91	26	14	0	3,028	1,530	1,411	71	16	0
Nevada	63	7	45	9	2	0	1,179	437	650	92	*	0
New Hampshire	25	17	7	1	0	0	759	701	56	2	0	0
New Jersey	724	126	527	12	9	0	14,918	6,884	7,972	41	21	0
New Mexico	80	32	48	0	0	0	1,423	813	610	0	0	0
New York	641	131	488	8	14	0	19,655	7,259	12,284	75	37	0
North Carolina	393	160	225	5	3	0	7,391	5,158	2,217	13	3	0
North Dakota	77	11	56	9	1	0	1,329	688	628	13	*	0
Ohio	1,123	306	746	32	37	2	23,861	11,221	12,424	92	120	4
Oklahoma	150	53	93	4	0	0	3,393	1,721	1,667	6	0	0
Oregon	275	28	237	2	1	7	4,579	1,054	3,514	6	3	2
Pennsylvania	858	263	566	17	12	0	15,805	8,045	7,652	85	23	0
Rhode Island	30	6	24	0	0	0	565	188	377	0	0	0
South Carolina	220	72	138	0	3	7	4,071	2,536	1,526	0	2	7
South Dakota	34	16	15	3	0	0	684	621	57	6	0	0
Tennessee	229	96	128	3	2	0	4,563	2,469	2,086	5	3	0
Texas	1,170	325	805	35	2	3	19,744	11,170	7,971	590	3	10
Utah	74	13	57	0	0	4	1,166	665	496	0	0	5
Vermont	10	7	3	0	0	0	177	148	29	0	0	0
Virginia	381	80	293	5	1	2	5,675	2,513	3,133	28	*	1
Washington	310	49	254	4	3	0	5,303	2,361	2,889	44	9	0
West Virginia	62	30	26	5	1	0	964	810	130	22	2	0
Wisconsin	407	116	268	17	6	0	8,097	4,623	3,426	43	5	0
Wyoming	33	13	18	0	0	2	530	374	155	0	0	1
Guam	5	2	3	0	0	0	34	16	18	0	0	0
Puerto Rico	87	12	70	2	0	3	1,064	394	664	5	0	1
Virgin Islands	2	0	2	0	0	0	37	0	37	0	0	0
Pacific Islands	2	0	2	0	0	0	5	0	5	0	0	0

*Less than $0.5 million.

BRANCHING PROVISIONS FOR
FEDERAL SAVINGS AND LOAN ASSOCIATIONS

The Home Owner's Act of 1933 contained no specific statute relating to branching. Thus, federal branching regulations governing association branching—as promulgated by the Federal Home Loan Bank Board—had no specific statutory foundation. In ruling on a 1951 case of the North Arlington National Bank vs Kearney Federal Savings and Loan Association, the court, however, held that the Federal Home Loan Bank Board's statutes governing regulation was broad enough to include the power to authorize branches.

In a subsequent ruling on another case in 1952, pre-emptory power over state authorities was given to the Federal Home Loan Bank Board in regulating branching by Federal Associations under the supremacy doctrine. State Law was viewed as being not applicable to federal associations. The Federal Home Loan Bank Board, however, adopted a policy of not permitting branches in states where they have been prohibited to state chartered savings associations and banks. Over the years, in spite of branching restrictions/prohibitions in certain states, the Federal Home Loan Bank Board where the need is officially recognized, due to economic and social developments, has permitted the establishment of branches. The Federal Home Loan Bank Board thus historically has exercised discretionary power as to the granting of branching permission to federal associations. In fact, a federal district court ruled in 1957, specifically and emphatically that the competitive equality principle of the National Bank Act and cases enforcing it were inapplicable to the ability of federal associations to undertake branching. It has also been argued that the "supervisory discretion" approach with regard to the Bank Board's regulation of savings and loan association branching enhances the dual chartering system.

By making the processing of applications for additional facilities easier and lessening the restrictions on the type and functioning of such facilities, the Federal Home Loan Bank Board has endeavored to encourage the expansion and development of the savings and loan business through branching. In 1965, data processing offices and centers were authorized, and mobile facilities were permitted in 1966. Further liberalization of regulations governing these types of facilities were also undertaken, and in 1972, the establishment of "satellite offices" and automated teller facilities were authorized. Point of sale of business funds transfer system or remote service units were authorized in 1974, permitting customers to make deposits or withdrawals at a terminal located in a place of business such as a retail store or shopping center. Decentralization of branching authorization was also affected in 1974, when local Bank Board supervisory agents were permitted to approve branch applications where no "substantial protest" had been lodged. In June 1979, the Bank Board issued proposals for the consolidation and simplification of the branch office application process. The Board's rules and regulations, up to this time, consisted of six separate sections dealing with branching, branch office, drive-in facility, mobile facility, satellite office, agency and change office location, respectively. The 1979 proposals consolidated the requirements governing the above facilities into one set of branch regulations with similar requirements and procedures. Such consolidation would foster the expansion of services to wider areas of population and enhance the ability of savings and loan associations to serve all areas of their local communities.

Federal associations would, however, be permitted, exclusive of the new regulations, to establish drive-in and pedestrian offices within 500 feet of an association office. Regulations concerning data processing service centers and agency offices were also separated from branching provisions. Arbitrary limits on size, location, cost, and hours of operation of customer service facilities were also removed in keeping with the Board's thinking that such limits "may unnecessarily stifle development of innovative means of providing savings and loan services." A satellite facility would no longer be required to be within 5 miles of the nearest branch, and the restrictions on a mobile facility operating only on certain days for a given number of hours were also removed.

In line with the Board's philosophy that "branching should be a business decision of the management of an association," the evaluation criteria governing branch applications were also streamlined. The principal criteria for evaluating branch applications were reduced to the "undue injury" test, and the performance of the applicant under the Community Reinvestment Act. The "need" and the "probability of success" requirements were eliminated. The Board in its supervisory capacity, however, would continue to assess the viability and safety characteristics of each application.

The Federal Home Loan Bank Board has generally over the years adopted an increasingly liberal posture with regard to branching operations of savings and loan associations. In line with such an approach, the Board issued as a final rule effective January 1980, the elimination of the 100-mile limit which applied in the states of

Illinois, Pennsylvania, Minnesota, Louisiana and Indiana, thus permitting state-wide branching authority to federal savings and loan associations in all fifty states regardless of state law.

The foregoing discussion for analytical purposes has considered facilities which are not classified as "branches" in the statutes. An agency, for example, may only service loans and contracts or perform real estate management functions, while a data processing service office is involved strictly with only data processing services. Perhaps the most important and controversial of these extended facilities has been the remote service unit or point-of-sale funds transfer system.

A remote service unit performs only one function—funds transfer—and as such is not considered by the Federal Home Loan Bank Board to be a branch or an additional office, but rather an extension of a savings function performed by the principal office of the association. Regulations pertaining to the operation of remote service units are not grouped with branching regulations but are included in those regulations relating to withdrawals, third party payments and other activities involving savings transactions.

Board rules define a remote unit ": . . as an information processing device, including associated equipment, structures and systems, by means of which information relating to financial services rendered to the public is stored and transmitted whether instantaneously or otherwise to a financial institution and which for activation and account or deposit access is dependent upon the use of a machine readable instrument in the possession and control of the holder of such account or deposit. The term 'remote service unit' includes without limitation both 'on-line' computer terminals and 'off-line' cash dispensing machines, but does not include terminals or teller machines using passbooks regardless of whether the passbooks are machine readable."

Basically, RSUs are computer terminals which permit members of savings associations to undertake transactions on their accounts without having to be present at an office of the association. These remote service units may be located away from the association's offices in places such as shopping centers, office buildings, transportation depots and retail sales enterprises. They may be completely automated or require the services of personnel at the particular location where the unit is established. The electronic transfers of funds via RSUs of savings associations are in essence technological improvements on the traditional methods by which savings customers may have access to their accounts and conforms with the purposes and past practices of savings and loan associations.

It should be reiterated that for federal savings and loan associations, a remote service unit is not a branch office, satellite office or other type of facility or agency of a federal association within the meaning of applicable federal statutes. For banks and other financial institutions in many states, such facilities are considered the equivalent of a branch office. The original federal regulations issued on June 26, 1974, permitted a federal savings and loan association to establish a remote service unit after an application to and subsequent approval by the Federal Home Loan Bank Board. Types of transactions which may be effected through a RSU are clearly delineated. These include a deposit of funds to a savings account, a transfer of funds between accounts, a withdrawal of funds not in excess of the depositors' balance from a savings account, a payment or a loan and such other financial services as the Board may approve. A savings account or loan application may not be initiated or approved at a remote service unit. Remote service units were also to be located within the state in which the home office of such association is located, or within the primary service area as determined by the Board of any branch office of an association located outside the state.

In January 1981, the Federal Home Loan Bank Board eliminated the application process for the establishment of remote service units by federal savings and loan associations. Associations were permitted to establish such facilities without applying and obtaining permission from the Home Loan Bank Board. Elimination of the application procedure was prompted by the paperwork costs and the inability of associations to provide these services on a competitive basis vis-a-vis other financial institutions.

On August 6, 1981, the Federal Home Loan Bank Board, in continuation of its policy of liberalization in matters relating to branching, authorized the establishment by federal savings and loan associations and mutual banks of remote service units on a nationwide basis. Reference was made by the Board in its comments to the pre-existing competitive imbalance whereby national banks and credit unions, several state chartered banks and thrift institutions were permitted to undertake RSU operations on an interstate basis. In addition, several non-banking institutions, such as investment firms, money market funds, provide banking-type services on an interstate basis, which further increases the competitive disadvantage of federal thrift institutions. While the regulations governing national banks and credit unions permit these institutions to use remote service units across state lines on a fee-per transaction basis, these institutions are prohibited from renting or owning these operations in other states by the McFadden Act. The new regulations applicable to federal thrift institutions authorizes the rental and/or ownership of these facilities in other states. The Board has, however, argued that such a technical advantage will only indirectly affect the competition for customers. On a broader level, the recent removal of geographic restrictions on these facilities may be viewed as a harbinger of the inevitable erosion of barriers to full interstate banking.

The National Bank Act defines the word "branch" as any "office at which deposits are received, or checks paid or money lent." Recent litigation with regard to electronic funds transfer systems have been primarily focused on the use of remotely located terminals by financial institutions to undertake transactions for customers. One of the well-known cases involving RSUs is the Hinkey Dinky case. First Federal Savings and Loan Association of Lincoln, Nebraska, established an on-line RSU in each of two Hinkey Dinky stores operated by American Community Stores Corporation. The two stores were located in Lincoln, Nebraska and were staffed by employees of the parent company, American Community Stores. Depositors of First Federal could make deposits and withdrawals through the use of the RSU. Deposits were collected by the employee of American Community Stores. Through the use of a store card and the depositor's card, the RSU was activated and the amount of the deposit was transferred by a computer located at First Federal's main office from the account of American Community Stores with First Federal to the depositor's account with First Federal. A withdrawal was effected through a reversal of the above procedure.

The Nebraska state authorities brought action against American Community Stores on the grounds that it was engaged in the banking business, but the Supreme Court ruled that it was First Federal and not American Community Stores that was responsible for the deposit and withdrawal transactions which were undertaken at the RSU.

Other Federal Savings and Loan Associations, such as Bloomfield Federal Savings and Loan Association, challenged the authority of the Federal Home Loan Bank Board to issue its remote service unit regulation. The court, however, dismissed the motion on the grounds that Congress left it to the discretion of the Board to determine by regulation what constitutes a branch of a Federal Savings and Loan association. The court also ruled that the Federal Home Loan Bank Board acted properly within this discretion in adopting the RSU regulation.

Another case settled on June 30, 1978 concerned the suit by the Independent Bankers Association of America filed on January 19,

1976 challenging the legality of the RSU regulations ". . . on the grounds that RSUs were inconsistent with the purposes and practices of savings and loan associations contemplated in the statute granting the Federal Home Loan Bank Board authority to regulate such institutions and as the functional equivalent of checking activity in violation of the statute prohibiting savings accounts from being subject to check or withdrawal or transfer on negotiable or transferable authorization."

The Court ruled that the Federal Home Loan Bank Board had not surpassed the scope of its statutory authority under Section 5(A) of the Home Owner's Loan Act. The most salient aspect of the decision, however, concerns the ruling of the Court that "RSU transactions within the meaning of the language of 12 USC Section 1464 (b) (1), either as a technical matter under Uniform Commercial Code considerations, or as a matter of substance as suggested by the plaintiff's 'functional equivalent' argument, do not constitute checking transactions."

Electronic banking networks, no doubt, have greatly reduced the efficacy of restrictions on interstate banking. Customers traveling outside their home states, for example, in Wisconsin and Michigan, are capable of making cash withdrawals from either checking or savings accounts through the use of electronic terminals operated by Tyme system with a 250 institution network of electronic teller machines and point-of-sale terminals. First Interstate Bank, formerly Western Bankcorp, Los Angeles, operates an 11 state, 900 branch system with hundreds of automatic teller machines accessible to customers in all eleven states. In Iowa, South Dakota, California, Oregon and Washington, interstate banking transactions are being undertaken by customers through the use of electronic banking devices. However, it should be pointed out that in most instances, customers are only capable of making cash withdrawals from out-of-state terminals. Full interstate banking, the making of deposits, payments and loans on a nationwide basis, as defined by the McFadden Act, remains entangled in a web of federal and state regulations that many analysts have argued have no relevance to the realities of the rapidly changing financial environment.

The 1982 Depository Institutions Act prohibits the establishment of a branch by a federal association outside of its home state unless the association qualifies as a domestic building and loan association by satisfying the requirements of the "bad debt deduction" under the Internal Revenue Code, which requires at least 60 percent of an association's assets to be held in mortgages and mortgage related instruments. Section 334 of the Act also states that no out-of-state branch so established shall be retained unless the total assets of the branches in the particular foreign state also satisfy the asset composition criteria of the Internal Revenue Code's "bad debt deduction." Existing interstate branches of federal associations are grandfathered, and state associations with out-of-state branches converting to federal charter will be permitted to continue operating these branches. Federal associations will also be authorized to operate out-of-state branches in any state which allows branching by out-of-state thrift institutions.

In spite of McFadden and other state regulations, the setting for nationwide branching has been provided by the economic pressures of the 80's and the need of the Insurance Corporations to address the problem of large losses within the industry. As discussed in later chapters, the traditional method by which both the FDIC and FSLIC have resolved failures of the thrifts has been through the merger process. Due to the extraordinary amount of institutions approaching failure in 1981, the FSLIC found it progressively difficult to resolve all problems by merger within state lines. Consequently, in order to prevent the failure of a New York and Florida thrift, the FSLIC permitted the merger of Citizens Savings and Loan of California with West Side Federal of New York and Washington Federal of Florida. This was accomplished by the conversion of Citizens to a federal charter and its acquisition of the Florida and New York institutions. The new entity renamed First Nationwide Federal is now branched within three states.

Similar cross-state mergers have been permitted with reference to other failing institutions, the most salient of which was the September 1982 acquisition of the failing Fidelity Savings and Loan Association of San Francisco by Citicorp of New York. The Citicorp/Fidelity acquisition also marked the first acquisition of a savings and loan by a bank holding company across state lines, and has been viewed by many as further evidence of the gradual erosion of restrictions on interstate banking. Many banking analysts, however, are of the opinion that interstate banking should, if permitted, be on a nationwide basis and not on piecemeal authorizations. Pressure is certainly building for elimination of barriers in non-supervisory cases.

The 1982 Garn-St Germain Bill stipulates that if an insured thrift institution is acquired by a bank or a banking holding company under emergency thrift acquisition regulations, the insured thrift thereafter will be limited by the national bank branching requirements in that it may branch in the manner that a state bank may branch. Branches resulting from action under the emergency thrift acquisition powers are not affected by the Section 334 limitations of the Act discussed previously.

SURVEY OF STATE BRANCHING STATUTES FOR SAVINGS AND LOAN ASSOCIATIONS

While as late as 1967 there were no branches of savings and loan associations in Vermont, West Virginia, Illinois, New Hampshire and South Dakota, by 1977 there was at least one branch office of a savings and loan association in each state in the nation. State regulations governing branches of savings and loan associations are not uniform and vary, for example, by geographical limitations, population criteria or according to the discretionary authority of the state supervisory agency. A brief survey of the various state statutes pertaining to association branching is presented below.[1] Some statutes define the term "branch", while others are not as specific and delegate discretionary power to the state banking department. Several states, including New York, New Jersey, California, permit state-wide branching, and there are indications that there is a gradual trend towards more liberal branching policies in the less permissive states.

SURVEY OF STATE SAVINGS ASSOCIATION BRANCH STATUTES

ALABAMA   General prohibition against savings association branches (5 Ala. Code Sec. 247) but later statutes of exception authorize branching in certain named counties and in counties having specified range of population of 47,000 to 49,000.

ALASKA   Commissioner may approve branch office application if there will be no undue injury to existing associations in community. "Branch office" is the legally established place of business other than home office; "agency" is place of business stationary or mobile other than home office or branch. Branches and agencies are subject to direction from home office. Alaska Stats., Sec. 06.30.340.

ARIZONA   Superintendent may approve application for branch if he finds it advisable and in public interest. "Branch office" is legally established place of business of association other than home office. Arizona Rev. Stats., Sec. 6-475.

[1] Adopted from *Legal Bulletin*, May 1977.

ARKANSAS No association shall, without the prior approval of the Board, establish any office other than the principal office stated in its articles of incorporation. Home office may not be moved from county in which originally located. Arkansas Stats. 1947 Ann., Sec. 67-1829.

CALIFORNIA If the commissioner is satisfied that proposed branch is in interest of the association, that the proposed location is not adequately served by one or more associations or federal associations, that association's financial program is sound, and public advantage is served, he may issue license for proposed branch. Financial Code, Sec. 6000, et seq.

"Branch" means any office or other place of business in this state owned and operated by an association other than its principal office in this state. Under this provision, mobile facilities are authorized by regulation. Financial Code, Sec. 5056.

COLORADO "Branch" means any office or other place of business in this state where subscriptions are sold, taken or solicited for shares. Col. Rev. Stats. 1963, Sec. 122-1-3(7).

If satisfied, branch is in the interest of the association and public convenience and advantage will be served, the commissioner shall issue his license, *Ibid*, Sec. 122-2-20.

CONNECTICUT With commissioner's approval, association meeting stated reserve requirements may establish (a) one or more branches within the town where it is located; (b) one or more branches in any town or towns within the state in which, at the time such branch is established, the main office of no savings association is located; and (c) continue to operate as a branch the business of another association acquired by purchase, consolidation or merger. Conn. Gen. Stats. Ann., Sec. 36-180.

DELAWARE Any building and loan association incorporated under the laws of this State may open a branch office upon application approved by the State Bank Commissioner. If in public interest and for good and sufficient reason, he shall issue certificate. Delaware Code Ann., Sec. 2011.

DISTRICT OF COLUMBIA No building association shall maintain any office in the District of Columbia until it shall have secured the approval and consent of the Federal Home Loan Bank Board, District of Columbia Code 1967 Edition, Sec. 26-103(c). FHLBB has issued regulations which parallel federal association regulations. 12 CFR Part 581.

FLORIDA Commissioner may approve branch upon proper application if no undue injury to existing associations. "Branch office" is legally established place of business other than home office at which savings accounts and loan payments may be accepted, loan applications received, account books and membership certificates issued and loans closed. Fla. Stats., Sec. 665,441.

GEORGIA Georgia statute (formerly silent while regulations authorized branching) amended in 1973 to add new section prohibiting associations from accepting deposits except on premises of place of business (principal or branch office). Branch office is any office intended to be permanently established in fixed location and to be operated at such location on substantially full time basis. Georgia Building and Loan Act, Sec. 6A; Rules of Commissioner, Sec. 590-3.13 set standards of probable success, no undue injury.

GUAM Existing locally chartered association has a branch.

HAWAII No association may establish a branch office or agency without the prior written approval of the bank examiner who determines if branch office will unduly injure existing association in community or in neighboring community. Revised Laws of Hawaii Sec. 407-41.

"A branch office is a legally established place of business of the association other than the home office or any agency. . . ." *Ibid*, Sec. 407-42.

IDAHO   "Branch office" means office which is a legally established place of business other than the home office . . ." Idaho Code, Sec. 26-1802(4).

No association may establish or maintain a branch office without the prior written approval of the commissioner upon showing if no undue economic injury to an existing, properly managed association in the community where it is proposed. *Ibid*, Sec. 26-1815.

ILLINOIS   Commissioner may provide by regulation for establishment of "facility" in case of supervisory merger, consolidation or bulk sale, or single facility in case of relocation. Facility may do no business except receive deposits, cash and issue checks, drafts and money orders, change money and process loans. 32 Ill. Rev. Stats. Sec. 709, (Ill. Savings and Loan Act, Sec. 1-9); Article X, Savings and Loan Regs. Secs. 1-5.

INDIANA   Any association may open or establish one or more branch offices within the limits of the county in which the principal office of the association is located or within 100 miles of the principal office, at which any business association may be transacted. In a merger or consolidation, resulting association may continue as branch office any principal and branch offices of merged association subject to stated reserve requirements and the prior written approval of the department. Burn's Indiana Stats. Ann., Sec. 18-2160.

"Association" as used in Sec. 18-2160 means any savings association organized and operating under the laws of the state of Indiana. *Ibid*, Sec. 18-2159.

IOWA   Attorney general has interpreted "silent" statute to permit branching based on references to "home office" and "principal place of business." May 1966 *Legal Bulletin 197*. Later ruling, November 5, 1973, holds that branches are not necessarily confined to a distance within 100 miles of home office.

KANSAS   No branch may be established, opened, moved or relocated without prior approval of savings and loan board; prescribed standards of usefulness, no undue injury must be met; branch office is place of business other than home office; any business of association may be transacted at any branch office. Kansas Stats. Sec. 17-5225.

KENTUCKY   A branch office is a legally established place of business of the association other than the home office of the association where savings accounts and loan payments may be accepted, applications for loans received, and account books and certificates issued. No association may establish a branch office without the prior written approval of the commissioner. Standards of no undue injury and advisability applicable. No branch shall be established in any county other than the county in which is located the principal office of the association. Kentucky Rev. Stats., Sec. 289.061.

LOUISIANA   Associations organized prior to noon 7/7/32 which are domiciled in New Orleans may continue to operate one or more branch offices as then existing. Otherwise, no branch offices shall be established by any association either in the parish of its domicile or in any other parish where it may be authorized to make loans, without the written approval and permission of the commissioner. Louisiana Rev. Stats., Sec. 6:733. See Sec. 6:732 for territorial restrictions on loans based on parish where home office is located.

MAINE   No association shall establish or operate a branch until it shall have received a warrant to do so from the commissioner who shall do so when satisfied that public convenience and advantage will be promoted thereby. No branch may be established except within the county of the association's main office or a county adjoining that of its main office. (Section is inapplicable to branches authorized and in existence on Sept. 16, 1961.) Maine Rev. Stats. Ann., Title 9, Sec. 1595.

MARYLAND No domestic federally or state chartered association shall establish any branch office without filing an application therefor with the director and securing his prior approval thereof. If public interest, convenience and advantage will be served, he may approve application. Ann. Code of Maryland 1957, Art. 23, Sec. 161V. Branch office is any office of association open to public for acceptance of share payments or where loan payments are regularly made. Regulation 100.13.

MASSACHUSETTS Cooperative bank may establish and maintain one or more branch offices (a) in the town wherein its main office is located, or (b) in other towns within the same county having no main office or branch office of a cooperative bank or in which, in the opinion of the commissioner, the public convenience and advantage would be served by the establishment of additional cooperative bank facilities. Offices of cooperative bank consolidated or merged, under C. 170, Sec. 48, or substantially all of the assets and liabilities of which have been acquired under Sec. 47, may be maintained as branch offices by surviving cooperative bank, subject to commissioner's approval and if town in which offices are situated are within county wherein the main office of surviving association is located. Ann. Laws of Mass., C. 170, Sec. 12.

Mobile branch banking may be authorized by commissioner in the county in which main office of bank is located subject to such conditions and regulations as he may approve. Ch. 167, Sec. 60.

Maintenance of remote, unmanned, automated facilities either above or by sharing with another bank or savings and loan association subject to certain restrictions as to number and percentage of ownership and to regulations issued by commissioner. Ch. 167, Sec. 64, added by H. B. 6591, Ch. 1147. Laws 1973, approved December 6, 1973.

Banks, including cooperative banks are authorized, with commissioner's approval, notwithstanding contrary provisions of law, to establish a branch on the grounds of any state community college, state college, university or institute in Massachusetts. H.B. 7462, Ch. 1089, Laws 1973 approved November 27, 1973.

MICHIGAN "Branch office" means a legally established place of business other than the home office at which savings accounts and loan payments may be accepted and loan applications received, account books issued and loans closed. Mich. Stats. Ann. Sec. 23.540(115). "Agency" limited to accepting savings accounts and loan payments for transmission to main or branch office. Sec. 411.

No association shall establish a branch office for the transaction of business until prior application has been made to and approved by the supervisory authority. Approval is subject to determination of reasonable probability of success, public interest and public need, reserve requirements, etc. *Ibid*, Sec. 23.540(412).

MINNESOTA Minnesota courts have interpreted "silent" savings association law as permitting branching. *Austin Savings and Loan Assn. v. First National Bank*, 133 NW 2d 505. The Minnesota Uniform Commercial Code provides by Section 336.1-102(6):

"Nothing in this chapter shall be construed to authorize the establishment of branch offices for banks, savings banks, trust companies, savings and loan associations, or building and loan associations."

MISSISSIPPI No branch office shall be established or operated without prior approval of the Board and procedure therefor shall be the same as for approval of a charter. Miss. Code 1942, Sec. 5288-12.

MISSOURI The commissioner shall approve establishment by associations of branch offices with consideration given to public convenience and advantage and whether there will be undue damage to existing associations establishment of "offices"; regulation #30-72 provides for establishment of tandem branch (satellite, either manned or automatic).

MONTANA   Agents may be licensed and employed to "solicit loans" and "sell stock." Rev. Code of Mont. Sec. 7-119.

NEBRASKA   No statutory prohibition and branching is permitted with supervisory approval evidenced by procedural regulations which have been subject of litigation (*First Federal Savings and Loan Assoc. v. Dept. of Banking*, 187 Neb. 562, 192 NW 2d 736).

NEVADA   No association may establish or maintain a branch office without prior written approval of the commissioner. Branch office is legally established where business of association may be conducted. Nevada Rev. Stats., Sec. 673.112.

NEW HAMPSHIRE   A cooperative bank or savings and loan association may establish or operate a branch upon receipt of a warrant to do so from the bank commissioner, who shall issue such warrant only when satisfied that public convenience and advantage will be promoted thereby and subject to other conditions. Such branch must be within a radius of 15 miles of the association's principal office. N.H. Rev. Stats., Sec. 393:60.

NEW JERSEY   A savings association may establish and operate one or more Sec. 25 branch offices (*de novo* branches) in (1) the same municipality in which it operates its principal office; (2) in any municipality where there is no office of any other association; (3) in any other municipality, where office or offices of other associations are located, subject to phase-in population schedule; or (4) in municipality where association itself operates a section 25 or section 27 branch office where there is no office of another association. New Jersey Code Secs. 17:12B-25,26.

Association surviving a merger or acquiring assets of another association may apply to operate its office as a section 27 branch. Sec. 17:12B-27. (Law previously divided state into three districts and restricted branch on basis of districts. This was amended by Assembly Bill 508, July 3, 1973 to abolish districts and to apply population schedule for home office protection, applicable to branches both newly created and resulting from merger.)

Principal and branch office may be interchanged; approval of commissioner required if different municipality involved. Sec. 17:12B-28.

Agencies (for receipt of payments on loans, obligations and savings accounts) and auxiliary offices within 1500 feet of office (for receipt of payments, paying withdrawals, cashing checks, issuing money orders) are authorized. Secs. 17:12B-29, 17:12B-37.

NEW MEXICO   An association authorized to transact business in the state may conduct a branch or branches. Branches may do business the same as parent, but must be located within a radius of 50 miles from the principal office of the parent association, within the State of New Mexico. Provisions not retroactive with respect to branches in existence prior to enactment of Savings and Loan Act. "Branch" includes any additional house, office or place of business at which deposits are received and money lent except where connected by underground or overhead passageways. Limits imposed based on net worth of association and population. N. Mex. Stats. 1953, Sec. 48-15-61.

NEW YORK   A savings association, in addition to a branch office not more than 50 miles from its principal office, may open branches as follows: Principal office in a city or village of more than 30,000 and not more than 100,000, one additional branch office within the county in which its principal office is located; principal office in a city or village of more than 100,000 and not more than 200,000, two accitional branch offices within such county; principal office in a city of more than 200,000 and not more than one million, three additional branch offices within such county; principal office in a city of more than one million, six additional branch offices at any place within such city. Further, an association (in addition to the foregoing authority), when the principal office is located in a county of more than 400,000 which does not comprise a part of or adjoin a city having a population of more than one million, may open one additional branch office at any place within such county, or, if its principal office is in a county of more than 700,000 population adjoining a city having a population of more than one million may open two additional branch offices within any place within such county, provided, however, that one of two such additional branch offices may be opened instead in such adjoining city. An association may not apply for a branch within a year after the date on which the Banking Board granted approval of another branch unless prior to the expiration of such period such branch has been abandoned for any reason. Banking Law, Sec. 396.

Note. Statute has been amended effective in 1976 to permit opening of branch offices at any location in the state with certain limitations relating to population and principal offices of unit banks.

NORTH CAROLINA   No statutory authorization. Term "where association has
                                        its principal office" appears in several sections of statute.
Branching is permitted with supervisory approval.

NORTH DAKOTA   No statutory provision, but offices maintained in separate
                                        locations are authorized by banking board regulations.

OHIO   No building and loan association shall establish more than
                                        one office, or maintain branches other than those established before July 3, 1923, nor relocate any branch, except with the approval of the superintendent of building and loan associations previously had in writing. Page's Ohio Revised Code Ann., Sec. 1151.05.

OKLAHOMA   Statute silent but Building and Loan Board has by regulation established procedures re applications and has authorized branches in city where home office located and in other cities.

OREGON   No savings and loan association doing business in this
                                        state shall establish a branch office in its own or in any other community in this state, without first securing a permit therefor from the commissioner. Same consideration and investigation as in the case of a permit for a new association. Oregon Rev. Stats., Sec. 722.115.

PENNSYLVANIA   "Branch" is an office or place of business other than the
                                        principal place of business of a savings association except an agency for collection of dues, interest premiums and fines.

An association may establish a branch after the effective date of this act only in the same county in which its principal place of business is located or in a county contiguous thereto. If the location of the proposed branch is outside of the city, incorporated town, borough or township in which the principal place of business of the association is located, the association shall give notice of the filing of the application by advertisement in the county in which the proposed branch is to be located. The branch shall be approved by the department. Upon a merger, consolidation or conversion of a federal savings and loan association into a state association the resulting association may with the prior written approval of the department maintain as branches, in addition to its principal place of business, every office which was maintained prior to the merger or consolidation by the parties thereto or prior to the conversion by the federal savings and loan association and which is located in the same county as the principal place of business of the resulting association or in a contiguous county. Purdon's Pa. Stats. Ann., Sec. 5403.

RHODE ISLAND   An association may establish a branch or branches within
                                        this state at any other place than its principal place of business upon obtaining the consent of the board of building-loan association's incorpora-

tion therefor. Public convenience and advantage are the criteria applied by the board. Gen. Laws of R. Island, 1956, Sec. 19-22-11.

SOUTH CAROLINA   No branch building and loan association shall be established without the approval in writing of the Board. Board makes investigation of compliance with law, qualifications of operators, whether public interest would be served. Code of Laws of South Carolina 1962, Sec. 3-57.

SOUTH DAKOTA   No association shall open, maintain, or conduct a branch without a license from the Superintendent. Criteria considered by Superintendent are best interests of association, whether area is adequately served by existing associations, and that institution's financial program is sound. H.B. 549, Ch. 13, Sec. 2, 1967 Laws.

TENNESSEE   Currently no statutory provision for branches. Proposed recodification provides for state-wide branching.

TEXAS   No association shall, without prior approval of the Commissioner establish any office other than the principal office stated in its articles of incorporation. Regulation 2.2 authorizes branches, loan offices and mobile facilities. Vernon's Ann. Civ. Stats., Art. 852a, Sec. 2.13.

UTAH   Application for authority to open branch must be filed with Commissioner. Granted if to public convenience and advantage served. No building and loan association or branch thereof shall be established at a location in such close proximity to an established association or branch as to unreasonably interfere with the business thereof. Utah Code Ann. 1933, Sec. 7-7-2.

VERMONT   Association may petition commissioner for permission to establish branch at any location of its choice, indicating location, need, functions, business volume, expense and mode of payment. After public hearing petition may be approved or disapproved based on standards of "good of the state" and no undue injury to competition. Vermont Stats., Title 8, Ch. 67. Sec. 1891.

VIRGINIA   No savings and loan association may establish a branch office nor may it engage in business in more than one place, except that the Commissioner, when satisfied that the public convenience and necessity will be served may authorize an association to establish a branch or branches including mobile branches. Code of Virginia, Sec. 6.1-195.48.

WASHINGTON   An association with the written approval of the supervisor, may establish and operate branches in any county of the state. Criteria of fitness, reserves, public convenience and probability of successful operation. Branch may not be established where supervisor would not permit proposed new association to engage in business. Rev. Code of Washington, Sec. 33.08-110.

WEST VIRGINIA   No association shall establish more than one office nor maintain branches other than those already established. West Virginia Savings and Loan Code, Sec. 7.

WISCONSIN   Subject to the approval of the commissioner, any savings and loan association in a county may establish and maintain one or more branch offices within the normal lending area of its home office. When associations are absorbed or consolidated a branch office may be maintained at that location if within home office lending area. Wisconsin Stats, Sec. 215.13(39), (40).

WYOMING   No statutory authorization but state-chartered and federal associations in the state have branches.

OVERVIEW—INTERSTATE BRANCHING

While significant developments have occurred in the area of interstate branching through the use of electronic banking devices, full branch banking on an interstate basis is still restricted by provisions of the McFadden Act.

A study of the 1927 McFadden Act, as stipulated by the International Banking Act of 1978 and released in January 1981 as the McFadden Act Report, concluded that the present limitations on branch banking are "increasingly ineffective, inequitable, inefficient and anachronistic and recommended a phased relaxation of geographic restraints." The report further states "Unrestricted branching would increase the actual or potential competition of most banking markets nationwide at least initially. The convenience and needs of the public would be better met and bank performance in terms of more services and lower prices would be advanced. Capital markets would benefit to some extent from the more efficient transfer of funds from surplus to deficit areas. Conceptually at least, unrestricted nationwide branching is the preferred way of achieving the benefits of freer market competition most rapidly."

The Carter Report further concludes that liberalization of the branching framework can be achieved either by modification of the McFadden Act or through revision of Section 3(d) of the Bank Holding Company Act, the Douglas Amendment. The report favors the latter strategy, arguing that a "modification of the Douglas Amendment would have a less intrusive impact upon many institutions and the existing regulatory structure." Interstate expansion through Bank Holding Company acquisitions is recommended on a gradual basis. For example, regionally or by limiting the local market share percentage of a local bank to be acquired by an out-of-state holding company.

The Report also proposes greater deployment of electronic funds transfer terminals, initially on a state-wide basis and within SMSAs which converge across state lines ultimately leading to nationwide electronic banking facilities. The acquisition of "failing banks" by out-of-state banks is also recommended.

In conclusion, the Carter McFadden Act Report strongly urged states to liberalize branch banking restrictions and proposed liberalization of the limitations on bank holding company ownership. It does not, however, propose any immediate modification of the

McFadden Act, citing the need to preserve the efficacy of the dual banking system, without impinging on the prerogatives and activities of state banking regulators. The Report delegates to Congress the responsibility for considering the necessary changes to the McFadden Act in the long run, suggesting that Congress might "consider permitting unlimited intra-state branching or interstate branching within 'natural market areas' such as SMSAs for federally chartered institutions."

In the evolutionary process of the thrifts, branch banking has become a method to meet the needs of the changing and more mobile society. Initially, as inner cities expanded and population moved to the suburbs, banks needed to develop additional customer facilities to service this expanding population. Most of these facilities were not cost effective; but because of the extent of new deposits they generated, the large overheads were well covered. With the development of electronic facilities and the entry of credit card companies into the debit card market, consumer banking is taking on a new face. Since most depositor needs can be provided at remote units, large branch buildings begin to lose their effectiveness. Thus, the need to apply for and build branch locations is supplanted by the use of automated teller machines and small remote units in other locations. For the future, the development of debit card and its full utilization will greatly reduce the need for fully staffed buildings.

Chapter VII

Bank Failures and Insurance of Accounts

What does the term "bank failure" denote? A bank has failed when it does not open on a business day because of its inability to satisfy the demands of its depositors. This ultimate condition of failure usually is preceded by an extended process beginning when a bank runs into financial difficulties. However, it should be noted that the criteria and tests applied to a particular bank situation before it is deemed to have "failed" are complicated, and failure usually results only after attempts to avert the failure have been unsuccessful.

Prior to 1933, bank failures were numerous and regular. Between 1890 and 1899, 1,084 banks failed or suspended operations. Even during the boom years of the "roaring 20s," an average of about 600 banks annually suspended operations.

In 1929 alone, 659 banks failed. During the following year, 1,350 banks suspended operations. For the four years from 1930 to 1933, over 9,000 banks closed their doors. Between December 1929 and December 1933, the number of banks declined from 24,026 to 14,440.

The major cause of the collapse of the banking industry during the 1930s was the rapid reduction of the money supply commencing about March 1929. With a decline of over 25 percent in the money supply, many bankers had difficulty in selling their assets quickly to provide depositors with the currency they demanded.

Most of the banks that failed were unit banks. California, the principal statewide branching state at the time, experienced few failures. From 1921 to 1931, only seven failures were recorded for banks with more than ten branches. Unlike branch banks, unit banks cannot meet deposit claims and losses in one area with funds and offsetting profitable loans from another area.

One Federal Reserve Committee study also found that a major cause of suspension was depreciation of bond and stock values, since many portfolios were financed by bank loans. Fraud was and still is a significant cause of bank failures. It has also been suggested that poor management has been and still may be a significant cause of bank failures.

Probably the most important structural change in the banking system as a result of the debacle in the early 30s was federal insurance of deposits in financial institutions. Although the creation of the Federal Deposit Insurance Corporation in 1933 appears to have made bank runs crises of the past, the Corporation cannot provide the entire banking system with liquidity. Only the Federal Reserve has that power and responsibility. The failure of a few banks is unlikely to produce a repetition of the situation in the 1930s, unless the Federal Reserve allows or is responsible for a decline in the money supply over a relatively short period. Moreover, since depositors are insured against loss, the probability of banking panics similar to past decades has been substantially reduced. Regional or industry-wide depressions may still cause bank failures, however, particularly in states with unit banking and poorly diversified economies.

From 1934 to 1973, 641 banks failed; 487 of those occurred during the first nine years of the period. After 1942, fewer than ten banks failed in any given year. The Federal Deposit Insurance Corporation analyzed the causes of the 436 insured bank failures during the period 1934-1957. Most of the failures during the first nine years of deposit insurance were primarily because of weaknesses in asset positions and management as a result of the Great Depression. According to the Federal Deposit Insurance Corporation, "in approximately one fourth of the banks, defalcation or losses attributable to other financial irregularities by officers or employees appear to have been the primary cause of failure. Such irregularities were responsible for most of the failures occurring since World War II."

The 56 banks that failed during the period 1959-1971 were also analyzed in some detail by the Federal Deposit Insurance Corporation. Thirty-seven or 66 percent were classified as failing because of fraud and irregularities, 15 or 27 percent because of brokered funds and loan losses and 4 or 7 percent as a result of inept management. The ten banks that went out of business during the April 1971 to December 1973 period were recorded in the Federal Deposit Insurance Corporation Annual Reports as exhibiting similar causes as those described previously. Of one of the more prominent failures, that of the United States National Bank (San Diego, California) in 1973, the second largest in the Corporation's history, the federal agency states, "There had existed self-serving, unsafe, and unsound loan practices and policies." The largest failure, in 1974, of the Franklin National Bank with deposits over $1.4 billion, was brought about by unsound management and losses on foreign exchange operations. Thus fraud and poor management appear to be the principal comtemporary causes of bank failure. This situation should be of some concern, particularly since current bank examination practices are not well designed to cope with and identify these problems. Approximately one year before they failed, 59 percent of the 56 banks that folded during the period 1959-1971 were rated by bank examiners as having "no problem." Over 5 percent of these were given the highest rating. Of the 41 percent rated as "problem" banks, only one half were considered serious. The recent embezzlement exposure at the Wells Fargo Bank in California and the disclosure of fraudulent loan operations at Chase Manhattan Bank, both in 1981, are current examples of the shortcomings of the bank examination system and the difficulty in dealing with unscrupulous employees.

During 1982, 42 banks failed, including eight mutual savings banks. This surpassed the previous post-war peak of 16 bank failures in 1976. The most prominent of the failures in 1982 was the July 5th receivership of the Penn Square National Bank of Oklahoma. The Penn Square failure resulted in the largest bank liquidation and payout in the history of the Federal Deposit Insurance Corporation. The demise of the $460 million deposit Penn Square was largely the result of poor, fraudulent, and in some cases, spurious energy loans, mainly to oil and gas wildcatters. Oil and gas loans constituted about 80 percent of Penn Square's loan portfolio, and over $2 billion in energy loans were sold "upstream" to larger banks, notably Continental Illinois and Seafirst Corp. of Seattle, Washington. Both of these institutions reported huge losses for 1982, and Seafirst eventually was merged with Bank America Corp. in July 1983 in order to bolster its sagging capital position.

In the Penn Square case, the FDIC resorted to the payout rather than the purchase and assumption method in dealing with the bank failure. Because Oklahoma is a unit-banking state where bank-holding company acquisitions are prohibited, it was virtually impossible for the FDIC to lure private investors to take over the stricken bank without excessive financial subsidies.

With a purchase and assumption arrangement, the obligations of the uninsured creditor are automatically assumed by the successor institution and, hence, creditors face no risk of asset loss. Stability and continuity of the banking system and market forces are maintained when failed banks are merged into healthy institutions, although usually at some cost to the insurance agency. With a payout method, uninsured creditors may suffer considerable loss on their obligations in receiving on a pro-rata basis the proceeds from the liquidation of the banks' assets by the FDIC.

For 1983, there were 48 bank failures, including three savings banks. Among the commercial bank failures were two large institutions, the First National Bank of Midland, Texas, with assets of $1.4 billion, and the United American Bank of Knoxville, Tennessee, with assets of $838 million. In the case of the Midland bank, the failure was largely because of poor energy loans, and in the case of the Knoxville bank, failure was attributable to large and unusual loan losses, particularly to now bankrupt real estate enterprises involved in the 1982 Knoxville World's Fair. Of the 48 banks that failed during 1983, 12 were located in Tennessee with eight having direct links with the United American Bank of Knoxville. Chart VII-1 shows in detail the ten largest commercial bank failures in the United States since the inception of the Federal Deposit Insurance Corporation and the action taken by the Corporation in dealing with each failure.

Thrift Failures

Mutual savings banks have an impeccable safety record unrivalled by any other deposit-receiving financial institution. There were no mutual bank failures during the 1930s; and although asset values declined substantially, they were not passed on to depositors. The principal contributing factor underlying the stability of mutual banks was the comparatively conservative investment policies undertaken by them during the 1920s. By maintaining sufficient cash and secondary liquidity to meet almost all their withdrawal demands, mutual banks continued to generate such confidence among savers that the result was a net savings inflow almost every year of the depression decade. The inflow of savings facilitated the meeting of withdrawal

Chart VII-1   Ten Largest Commercial Bank Failures by Deposit Size
(up to January 1, 1984)

1. Franklin National Bank, New York, N.Y. Deposits of $1.445 billion. Assets of $3.656 billion. Ceased operation October 8, 1974. Deposit assumption by European American Bank, N.Y.

2. United States National Bank, San Diego, California. Deposits of $932 million. Assets of $1.26 billion. Ceased operation October 18, 1973. Deposit assumption by Crocker National Bank, San Francisco, California.

3. United American Bank, Knoxville, Tennessee. Deposits of $794 million. Assets of $838 million. Ceased operation February 15, 1983. Purchased by First Tennessee Bank, Knoxville, Tennessee.

4. First National Bank of Midland, Midland, Texas. Deposits and liabilities of $620 million. Assets of $1.4 billion. Ceased operation October 14, 1983. Deposit assumption by Republic Bank First National Midland, Midland, Texas, a subsidiary of Republic Bank Corp., Dallas, Texas.

5. Banco Credito y Ahorro Poncino, Ponce, Puerto Rico. Deposits of $608 million. Assets of $713 million. Ceased operation March 23, 1978. Deposit assumption by Banco de Santander, Puerto Rico and Banco Popular de Puerto Rico.

6. Penn Square Bank NA, Oklahoma City, Oklahoma. Deposit of $470 million. Assets of $517 million. Ceased operation on July 5, 1982. The FDIC formed the Deposit Insurance National Bank of Oklahoma City in order to assume the insured deposits of Penn Square and pay off these depositors.

7. Hamilton National Bank of Chattanooga, Chattanooga, Tennessee. Deposits of $336 million. Assets of $412 million. Ceased operation February 16, 1976. Deposit assumption by First Tennessee National Corp., Chattanooga, Tennessee.

8. Abilene National Bank, Abilene, Texas. Deposits of $310 million. Assets of $446 million. Ceased operation on August 6, 1982. Abilene National was merged into Mercantile Texas Corp., Dallas, Texas.

9. American City Bank, Los Angeles, California. Deposits of $266 million. Assets of $272 million. Ceased operation on February 27, 1983. Deposit assumption by five banks: Central Bank, Oakland; American Asian Bank, San Francisco; Bank of Los Angeles; Valley State Bank, Los Angeles and Bank of San Redio, California.

10. City and County Bank of Knox County, Knoxville, Tennessee. Deposits of $253 million. Assets of $244 million. Ceased operation on May 27, 1983. City and County was acquired by the Bank of Knoxville, Knoxville, Tennessee.

demands while reducing the necessity for an immediate liquidation of assets.

On the other hand, there were significant failures among savings and loan associations during the 1930s. Over the years 1930-38, approximately 3,825 institutions went out of business, considerably more than half being voluntarily liquidated and many merging with other institutions. Losses passed on to savers have been estimated at $200.4 million. Savings accounts were also sold at a discount by individuals with a strong desire for immediate cash. This further added to the losses sustained by members.

In 1934, Congress provided for the creation of the Federal Savings and Loan Insurance Corporation to give similar protection to savings and loan associations as that afforded to commercial banks by insuring the safety of accounts. The establishment of the Federal Savings and Loan Insurance Corporation in 1934 provided insurance protection to individuals investing funds in savings and loan associations and thus stimulated the flow of private funds for home financing.

From 1934 to 1980, the Corporation rendered assistance to over 124 institutions. Twenty one times during its 50-year history the Federal Savings and Loan Insurance Corporation has declared a savings and loan association to be in default. Legally, default denotes a situation in which a receiver has been appointed for the purpose of liquidation. Seven of these cases occurred between January 1940 and September 1941, six between 1966 and 1971, one in 1981 and 1982, and six in 1983. In these cases, the associations involved went into receivership, and insured account holders were reimbursed for their deposits by the insurance agency. The FSLIC then undertook to liquidate the remaining assets in order to recover its disbursements as well as the uninsured portions of savings accounts. In this 50-year history, no insured saver has ever lost a cent of his savings. During the period up to 1980, cash requirements for rendering assistance to 124 institutions totaled $815 million, with losses of approximately $252.9 million being absorbed by the Corporation. In 1980, however, the Agency disbursed almost $1.3 billion in assistance to eleven savings and loan associations experiencing or on the verge of default. It is estimated that the net cost to the Corporation after recovery from assets acquired will be approximately $163 million. Because of the recent earnings and net worth deficiencies of the savings and loan industry, there has been a substantial increase in the need for FSLIC assistance in bailing out distressed associations, largely through merger arrangements. As of June 1981, the Agency had assisted seven supervisory mergers of problem savings and loan associations. By the end of October 1982, the FSLIC had approved 39 federally assisted mergers in comparison to 23 for all of 1981. Table VII-1 presents data on the failures of commercial banks, mutual savings banks and savings and loan associations for the years 1979-1983. During 1983, there was a 45 percent decline in savings and loan failures, largely attributable to declining interest rates and capital assistance under the Garn Act of 1982.

FUNCTION AND OPERATION OF THE FDIC AND FSLIC

Background

The FDIC is an independent and permanent agency of the Federal Government largely serving the banking industry while the FSLIC, a similar federal agency, services the insurance needs of savings and loan associations.

Deposit insurance plans were developed as a mechanism for overcoming a widespread lack of confidence in all financial institutions because of difficulty faced by one or a few financial institutions. A "run" on one bank tended to have a "domino effect" on other financial institutions, as the public perceived all other financial institutions to be insecure and, thus, unnecessarily instigated the default of financially solvent institutions. An insurance organization which provides security against losses to depositors in any particular institution will indubitably foster confidence in all other financial institutions and hence reduce the probability of pervasive and widespread withdrawals from sound financial institutions.

Table VII-1   Failures of Commercial Banks, Savings Banks, and
Savings and Loan Associations, 1979-1983

	Commercial Banks	Mutual Banks	Savings & Loan Associations
1979	10	–	–
1980	10	–	11
1981	10	–	28
1982	34	8	72
1983	45	3	52

Source: FDIC, FSLIC.

Before the establishment of the FDIC and FSLIC, eight states during the early 1900s attempted to insure or guarantee commercial banks in their jurisdictions. Such action was taken because the years between 1908 and 1917 were generally ones of depression and recovery, a period in which the "depression psychology" prevailed and it was thought desirable to stimulate and promote public confidence in the economy. Most of the state plans were created in the West and in the South and were unable to cope with the depression of 1921. All these state plans were terminated as they were not capable of meeting the heavy flow of insurance disbursements required from an insufficient reserve fund accumulated through assessments over the preceding years.

The failures of these early insurance plans were largely attributable to a concentration of risks in a few banks and in states where the local economy was not diversified and in many cases totally dependent on one productive activity, such as agriculture. Furthermore, assessments were formulated using the experience of national banks rather than based on the conditions and past operations of local banks within the particular state.

FDIC

The Federal Deposit Insurance Corporation was created by the Banking Act of 1933. The FDIC is managed by a Board of Directors, one of whom is the Comptroller of the Currency who serves ex-officio. The Corporation operates 14 regional offices, each of which is headed by a regional director. The operations of the FDIC are financed by assessments made on all insured member banks. All members of the Federal Reserve System are required to have deposit insurance by the FDIC.

The principal functions of the FDIC are to insure deposits, originally up to a maximum of $5,000 but currently $100,000, to act as conservator or receiver for the insured banks that terminate operations; and finally to foster and maintain a strong banking system by the use of its regulatory authority. The regulatory authority was granted in order to allow the FDIC as an "insurer of bank deposits to inspect its risk," and to make certain that the FDIC operates within the limits of its available resources.

Given the historical experience of failed state plans, the Federal Government made certain that funds would be sufficient to absorb losses by providing for three sources of funds to augment the resources of the FDIC. These sources were an initial subscription by the Treasury of $150 million; the subscription to the FDIC's shares of stock by each regional reserve bank in an amount equal to one-half of its surplus on January 1, 1933, and annual premiums paid by each insured bank at a rate of one-twelfth of one percent of all deposits. The latter annual payment has been the major source of funds for the Corporation.

By the middle of 1947, legislation was enacted providing for stock retirement by the Treasury and the Federal Reserve Banks since, in previous years, the Corporation had accumulated a substantial surplus. By the end of 1948, all stock was retired. Presently, the FDIC operates without government subsidy on lines similar to that of a mutual insurance fund. The FDIC, however, has the authority to borrow up to $3 billion from the Treasury should the need arise. As of January 1984, the FDIC's insurance fund totaled approximately $15.2 billion.

FDIC regulations stipulate that "whenever an insured bank shall have been closed on account of inability to meet the demands of its depositors, payment of insured deposits in such bank shall be made by the Corporation as soon as possible . . . either (1) by cash, or (2) by making available to each depositor a transferred deposit in a new bank in the same community or in another insured bank in an amount equal to the insured deposit." At the present time, Federal Deposit Insurance protects each depositor up to $100,000 in each insured bank. It has been estimated that 60 percent of all deposits in insured banks is covered by insurance.

As mentioned before, the FDIC, after other actions are ineffective and the bank ceases operation, has two basic methods available for undertaking depositor protection. The cash payment method is the one most often used, and up to 1973 was used in settling the claims of depositors in 197 failed banks. Since the beginning of its operations in 1934 until the year 1973, the FDIC protected depositors in 502 bank failure cases using either of the described methods, 297 pay-offs in cash and 205 by assumptions of the distressed banks' liabilities by another insured bank.

A fundamental difference between the two procedures relates to the extent to which protection is provided individual depositors. In the pay-off method when a bank is placed in receivership and deposits are settled by the FDIC up to the insurance maximum, any depositor with deposits in excess of this stipulated limit must hope to recover the remaining portion from the liquidation of assets. Such proceeds may not fully compensate for the short fall in the original insurance receipts. In the case of settlement by assumption, all depositors receive full compensation regardless of the size of their deposits. The liabilities of the defaulting bank are assumed by another insured bank, and insurance pay-off ceilings are not relevant.

Of the 502 failures up to 1973 that were covered by FDIC insurance, there were 2,152,000 accounts with deposits totaling 2,055 million; and 99.6 percent of these depositors received the entire amount of their deposits, 98.8 percent of all deposits were paid or made available to depositors, and $1,934 million of deposits were paid or made available to depositors. In the pay-off cases, depositors with accounts aggregating $407 million recovered $285 million from FDIC, an additional $96 million from other sources, primarily proceeds from receivers, with approximately $25 million to be recovered at a later date. A substantial portion of the latter figure is involved in presently active cases and may subsequently be paid to depositors.

An amendment to the Federal Deposit Insurance Law in 1950, Section 13 (c), authorized the Corporation in certain circumstances to assist an insured bank when it is in danger of default, or to foster a reopening of the bank if it has closed. This power may be used, however, only if in the opinion of the Corporation's Board of Directors the continued existence of the closed or endangered bank is essential in order to provide adequate banking facilities to the community. The FDIC first exercised this authority in 1977, when a $1.5 million loan to a bank with $9.3 million of deposits serving a black community was made. The loan was subordinated to the claims of depositors and other creditors. In order to render assistance to the billion dollar Bank of the Commonwealth in Detroit, Michigan, the FDIC again invoked this section of the deposit insurance law. The FDIC lent the Bank of the Commonwealth up to $60 million in the form of senior capital over a five-year rehabilitation period. The funds were subordinated to the claims of depositors and general creditors but took precedence over the banks' existing capitalization. Failure of the Bank of Commonwealth, it was felt, would have triggered adverse repercussions, both locally and nationally.

Thus, available evidence appears to indicate that protection given to depositors of failing insured banks has been extremely satisfactory. Moreover, of a total of $904 million paid out by the FDIC up to 1973, the Agency has recovered $780 million and sustained losses of $124 million. These losses are equivalent to an average loss of approximately $3 million annually since establishment of the Corporation.

Losses sustained by the Corporation in providing insurance protection have been well within the Corporation's financial resources. For a single year, 1973, the net interest income of the Corporation from U.S. Government securities was over $310 million, substantially more than the accrued total losses of the Corporation since its inception. As an insurer, therefore, the FDIC has had a salutary financial record and experience. During 1983, for example, despite a large number of failures and problem banks, the amount of premiums paid in was larger than the sum of the Agency's losses and operating expenses. Given the recent demise of the thrift industry, the FDIC has sought to assist troubled savings banks without exerting too much pressure on its financial base. Such actions will be discussed in a later chapter.

Federal Savings and Loan Insurance Corporation (FSLIC)

The Federal Savings and Loan Insurance Corporation was created by Title IV of the National Housing Act, passed by Congress in June 1934. The Office of the FSLIC operates under the general direction and supervision of the Federal Home Loan Bank Board. The Board, through a general manager, plans, organizes, and directs the operations of the Corporation. The basic goal is to preserve the integrity of the insurance fund in order to effect prompt settlement of insurance obligations up to the statutory limit. The FSLIC advises the Board on Corporation affairs, works in liaison with other offices of the Board on Corporation matters, and manages the Corporation's assets acquired as a result of default and default prevention action. The Corporation also established for a brief period an examinations department in 1978 which subsequently was transferred to the Federal Home Loan Bank Board.

The Agency is responsible for the prevention of default and to restore an insured institution to normal operation. If an insured association is in default, the FSLIC initiates procedures for the prompt settlement of insurance claims. Membership in the Federal Savings and Loan Insurance Corporation is compulsory for federal savings and loans and optional for state chartered association, building and loan associations, homestead associations, and cooperative banks. Membership applications are processed through the Home Loan Bank Board. In order to qualify, an institution must have adequate capital and reserves and must operate under sound financial policies and management. An association applying for insurance coverage with the FSLIC also is required to establish reserves adequate to absorb losses. According to the rules and regulations of the Corporation, an insured association must make allocations from its earnings to its reserve fund at the rate of at least (3/10) three-tenths of one percent annually of its total insured accounts. This special reserve for absorbing losses is built up so that it equals from time to time a series of annual "bench marks," reaching at least 5 percent of all insured accounts within 20 years from the effective date of the insurance. At the end of 1979, net worth reserves totaled $31.7 billion or 6.9 percent of the total savings deposits of insured savings associations, declining to $25 million in 1982, a reflection of the earnings problems of these thrift institutions.

The Corporation also has the authority to borrow up to $750 million from the United States Treasury. Given the recent demise of the thrift industry, the Corporation recently sought to increase its line of credit with the Treasury to $3 billion from the current $750 million limit. The request, however, was not favorably received by the current administration. The FSLIC further may levy additional premium assessments against its members to cover its losses and expenses, and it can request members to make deposits equal to one percent of their total savings.

The rapid growth of insured associations in the 1950s resulted in a reduction of the FSLIC's reserves to its insured liabilities to a low of 0.62 percent. Some improvement in the situation was achieved by legislative action in 1961 which required institutions to prepay premiums and the agency to establish a secondary reserve. There was a subsequent recovery of the reserve ratio and in 1975, efforts were initiated to phase out the secondary reserve provisions.

At the end of 1957, the number of Federal Savings and Loan Insurance Corporation insured associations was approximately 3,772 with assets representing over 92 percent of total insured and uninsured assets. The number of insured associations rose to 4,039, accounting for over 98 percent of the total assets of the savings and loan industry in 1979, but declined largely through consolidations to 3,343 at the end of 1982.

Two types of premiums may be levied by the FSLIC, the regular premium and the additional premium. The former premium is paid annually and is computed as equal to 1/12 of 1 percent of all savings accounts at FSLIC member institutions. The FSLIC also has the authority to institute an additional premium up to the full amount of all its losses and expenses with the proviso that individual assessments in any one year may not exceed an amount equal to 1/8 of 1 percent of the savings of the member insitution. To date, however, additional premiums have never been levied cn member associations.

As a means of increasing FSLIC insurance reserves at a faster rate than could be accomplished by the regular premiums alone, associations as of 1962 were required to make an annual prepayment of the regular premium equal to 2 percent of the increase in withdrawable savings accounts for the preceding year less an amount equal to any required purchases of Federal Home Loan Bank stock. These pre-payments were credited directly to the secondary reserves and were not included in the income of the Corporation. At the close of each calendar year, the FSLIC determines the yield on the investment of its secondary reserve funds and credits a pro-rata amount to the pre-paid account of each insured institution.

Legislation enacted in August 1973 discontinued pre-payments to the secondary reserve, primarily in order to eliminate the ad-hoc pattern of FSLIC premium payments. The whole secondary reserve program was phased out by a 1974 Act, over a period of ten years beginning May 1973. Such liquidation was to be accomplished by per-mitting associations to pay part of their regular premium with a credit from the funds accumulated in the secondary reserve and through direct cash refunds to associations.

Since its inception in 1934, up to the beginning of 1980, the FSLIC has rendered assistance to 124 insured associations. Five received fi-nancial assistance and a restructuring of management, while in 13 cases the savings accounts were acquired by another institution. The remaining 93 cases involved mergers with other sound and viable asso-ciations.[1] Total cash disbursements for these activities totaled $815 million, with the Corporation absorbing approximately $252.9 million in losses up to December 31, 1979.

The FSLIC regulations state: "In the event of a default by an insured institution, payment of each insured account in such insured institu-tion which is surrendered and transferred to the Corporation shall be made by the Corporation as soon as possible either (1) by cash or (2) by making available to each insured member a transferred account in a new insured institution in the same community or in another insured institution in an amount equal to the insured acccount of such insured member." The Financial Institutions Regulatory and Interest

---

[1] For a more detailed analysis of FSLIC assistance in merger cases, see the section in Chapter V dealing with supervisory mergers.

rate Control Act of 1978 further authorized the FSLIC to use the "purchase and assumption" method in dealing with troubled associations. This technique was commonly used by the FDIC over the years in preventing defaults among its insured member banks.

Generally, the FSLIC will consider several alternative methods of dealing with defaulting institutions before resorting to insurance payouts. Payouts are more costly than other solutions and place more pressure on the liquidity of the insurance fund. Mergers and other default prevention methods are less costly and require smaller cash outlays spread over time and, thus, reduce the liquidity drain from the insurance fund. Insurance payout settlements, too, may detrimentally affect the level of public confidence in the savings and loan industry and engender considerable disruption in the provision of financial services in the community where the association is located.

The FSLIC, in order to estimate the costs of the various alternative methods in dealing with distressed associations, uses computerized financial modeling as an analytical tool in evaluating such decisions. The models used by the agency are the liquidation model, the financial assistance model and the purchase and assumption model. Another model, the viability model, simulates the potential results of the actions of the FSLIC on the surviving association. As mentioned previously, the FSLIC attempts to utilize the method least costly to the Corporation.

Data illustrating the comparative statement of condition of the FSLIC for the years 1981-1982 are provided in the following table:

FSLIC Comparative Statement of Condition, 1981-1982
(Thousands of Dollars)

Item	December 31, 1981	December 31, 1982
Assets:		
Cash	$ 2,436	$ 203
Receivables	22,709	22,941
Investments at amortized cost	5,803,556	6,354,939
Accrued interest on investments	86,934	82,422
Income capital and net worth certificates	84,000	271,900
Loans to insured institutions and accrued interest, net	389,991	346,423
Subrogated accounts in insured institutions in liquidation	68,231	98,448
Mortgage loans and other assets	434,097	334,977
Total Assets	$6,891,954	$7,512,254

Liabilities and Reserves:
  Miscellaneous accrued and other

liabilities	$ 39,370	$ 43,073
Notes payable to insured institutions. . . .	84,000	456,503
Allowance for estimated losses (contribution agreements)	612,517	705,358
Primary reserve	5,556,806	5,693,670
Secondary reserve.	599,261	613,650
Total Liabilities and Reserves	$6,891,954	$7,512,254

Note: Components may not add to totals due to rounding.
Source: United States League of Savings Institutions. 1983 Savings and Loan Sourcebook.

It is the provisions and procedures for implementation rather than the ultimate payment methods that differentiate the insurance provisions of the FSLIC and the FDIC. Default "involves adjudication or other official determination of a court of competent jurisdiction" for the FSLIC, while for the FDIC a bank is closed ". . . on account of inability to meet the demands of its depositors." Whether a bank in financial difficulties becomes identified as a failed institution depends upon the applicable laws, federal or state, and the facts of the particular case. For example, if a chartering authority arranges a distress merger between a failing bank and a sound bank with financial assistance from the FDIC, the bank receiving aid is deemed to have defaulted or closed due to financial difficulties. A bank that has been restored to a sound financial footing without FDIC assistance is not classified in this way. As stated by law, the FDIC must be appointed as receiver for an insolvent national bank.

The FSLIC is not as limited in its actions with regard to insured savings associations in default. A major function of the Corporation's activities is the institution of corrective action to prevent impairment of savings accounts or to alleviate financial difficulties which may be encountered. Through this activity, default or the institution of the rotation procedure may not be necessary.

The merger technique is the most popular method used by the FSLIC to assist distressed associations. The Corporation facilitates this operation by indemnifying the resulting association for certain agreed upon costs and losses associated with the acquisition of the problem institution. In extreme cases where the problems of an association are difficult to solve or appear to be insoluble, the institution is placed in receivership and the FSLIC begins settling insurance claims immediately. In some instances, the FSLIC can, if warranted, take over the assets of the association and continue its operation or organize a new federal savings and loan association to assume its assets. Normally, once default is declared, the FSLIC begins procedures to liquidate the association, and usually tries to settle all insurance claims within two weeks.

Participation of Other Agencies—FHLBB, State Banking Department, and the Federal Reserve

A wide variety of policy prescriptions are available to the FHLBB, State Banking Department, and the Federal Reserve, and the particular measure adopted usually depends on the individual bank or association. The State Authority and/or the Comptroller of the Currency may demand and obtain the immediate replacement of lost capital or a merger may be arranged with a sound bank without recourse to the FDIC for assistance. Moreover, if the chartering agency is vested with the authority to place a "failed" bank in receivership, such a course of action may be adopted. This means that an agency of the chartering authority is delegated the responsibility of conserving the assets of the bank by restricting withdrawals.

The Federal Reserve or State Banking Department may also "bail out" a distressed bank by offering loans to rehabilitate the bank. The Federal Reserve, for example, exercised such authority in the Franklin National Bank failure in 1974 to the tune of seven billion dollars.

In the case of the Federal Home Loan Bank Board, federal associations may borrow from the Bank system up to 100 percent of their total savings accounts. Borrowings from any source other than a Federal Home Loan Bank cannot exceed 10 percent of total savings accounts. From time to time, special situations or conditions may be in effect which influence the amount which a Federal Home Loan Bank will advance to a member.

Insurance of Accounts

An insured account denotes a savings and/or investment account held by an insured saver in an institution whose accounts are covered by insurance up to $100,000. The saver is insured against impairment of his savings up to the prescribed limit if the insured institution closes its doors. An insured institution includes any federal association, and those state chartered institutions whose accounts are insured by the FSLIC and the FDIC.

The applicable legislation stipulates that all types of savings accounts are insured whether passbook accounts, certificates or bonus accounts, installment or systematic savings accounts, or other types of savings accounts in any one insured association. In the case of commercial banks, demand deposits are insured as are NOW accounts. An insured depositor may be an individual, partnership, association, corporation, trust beneficiary, or a public official custodian. An account holder may be covered in more than one capacity.

A joint tenancy account is insured as a partnership and the joint tenants of such an account constitute one insured member wholly separate and distinct from a joint tenancy account, including a third party even though two of the names are the same on both accounts. Mere reversal of the order of names in a joint tenancy account, however, does not create a new partnership. When two or more individuals have a tenancy in common account; that is, the entire account does not pass to the survivors in the event of the death of one of the members, the account is not treated as a partnership account. Each tenant is entitled to individual insurance in the amount of his claim against the account up to the limit of $100,000.

A corporation is also treated as a separate entity apart from its stockholders. The same is true of other types of associations, fraternal orders, and churches. Trust beneficiaries are also entitled to the $100,000 insurance coverage. For example, if under a trust there are two beneficiaries each having one-half interest in a $200,000 account, each would be insured up to $100,000. If one of the beneficiaries is also a beneficiary under another trust in the same institution, he is entitled to an additional $100,000 coverage. This provision is applicable under any number of additional but separate and different trusts. Furthermore, a trust beneficiary is also entitled to coverage, separate and apart from the above, for any accounts held in other capacities as an individual, joint, or other account. An official of any governmental unit as custodian of its funds is an insured member and entitled to the prescribed limit of insurance. Both the FDIC and FSLIC provide their members with equal insurance protection. Both insure accounts to the same maximum amount, both have basically the same pay-out provisions and in the more than 50 years that both institutions have been in existence, no saver has lost a penny covered by either type of insurance.

At the inception of both the FSLIC and the FDIC, the maximum insurance for all accounts was $5,000. This was raised to $10,000 in 1950, to $15,000 in late 1966, to $20,000 in 1969 and to $40,000 for private funds and $100,000 for public funds in 1977. In March 1980, with the passage of the Depository Institutions Deregulation and Monetary Control Act, the maximum coverage for private deposits was increased to $100,000.

Recently, with the deregulation of interest rates, several analysts have questioned whether Federal Deposit Insurance will be unnecessary in the future. The Director of the Federal Savings and Loan Insurance Corporation, H. Brent Beesley, for example, noted the success of unregulated money market mutual funds as evidence that deposit insurance may not be absolutely essential. It was further suggested that savings and loan associations could be rated by Standard & Poors and depositors could decide on a particular institution or institutions based on the rating service's recommendations. The FSLIC director also argued that "To the saver in an FSLIC or FDIC insured institution, there is absolutely no risk, and it is, therefore, clear that savings will flow to the highest insured rate regardless of the risks the association may be taking with those funds. There will be no market discipline to control risk, and this absence of market place control violates the very cornerstone of deregulations."[2]

Various proposals for variable rate premiums based on risk have been made over the years. The 1982 Depository Institutions Act mandates the Federal Savings and Loan Corporation, the Federal Deposit Insurance Corporation, and the National Credit Union Administration to prepare separate studies on several specific deposit insurance issues. Specifically, Section 712 of the 1982 Act requires the deposit insurance agencies with six months from enactment to complete a study of:

1. the current system of deposit insurance and its impact on the structure and operations of depository institutions;
2. the feasibility of allowing depositories to purchase additional deposit insurance coverage in excess of the $100,000 statutory amount, and the ability of private insurers to provide this coverage;
3. the feasibility of a risk or size-based premium structure;
4. the impact of expanding insured deposit coverage on the oper-

---

[2] H. Brent Beesley, speech to stockholders of the Federal Home Loan Bank, April 1982.

ations of the insurance funds, including the possibility of increased or undue risk to the funds;

5. the feasibility of revising deposit insurance coverage to provide more protection to small savers and to foster a greater sense of discipline with regard to large depositors;
6. the adequacy of existing public disclosure regarding the condition and business practices of insured depositories with an assessment of changes which may be needed to assure adequate public disclosure; and
7. the feasibility of merging deposit insurance funds and other related insurance matters.

While many of these proposals have been discussed periodically over the past decade, the congressional mandate brings the insurance issue to the center stage once again, and it is expected that some improvements and revisions will be made in the near future.

Although there has been opposition to plans for consolidation of the insurance funds by federal regulations, as depository institutions become more "bank-like" and homogenous in a deregulated environment and once hallowed distinctions become nebulous in practice, there may be some validity on efficiency arguments for merging the insurance funds. Moreover, the recent spate of cross-industry mergers also raises questions concerning the desirability of merging the insurance funds.

The adequacy of the current $100,000 deposit coverage limit in the light of several failures and liquidations is also a topical issue. In the case of the Penn Square National failure, for example, several large depositors, in effect, absorbed huge losses on their deposits over the statutory insurable limit. The Penn Square debacle also brought to the foreground the issue of charging variable premiums based on risk exposure. Institutions less risk averse than other more conservatively operated institutions perhaps should be assessed premiums reflecting the greater exposure to risk.

The Federal Home Loan Bank Board in November 1982 announced tentative plans to charge pro-rated insurance premiums based on interest rate risk. Institutions would be analyzed using a simulation of a 500 basis point rise in interest rates and its effect on the association's assets and liabilities, net worth, and other bench marks. Premiums of up to one-eighth of 1 percent of insured accounts would be levied, the amount assessed being directly proportional to the interest rate risk at each thrift institution. These new charges would be in addition to the current premium of one-twelfth of 1 percent.

Associations with below average risk would receive above average rebates and vice versa for more risky thrifts.

Title II of the 1982 Garn-St Germain Act also established a capital assistance program to allow qualified institutions to bolster net worth levels by obtaining promissory notes in exchange for net worth certificates from the FSLIC and FDIC.

In order to qualify for assistance, each institution must:

1. have net worth equal to or less than 3 percent of its assets,
2. have incurred losses during each of the two previous quarters,
3. have not incurred losses due to speculative transactions in futures or forward contracts, management action designed solely for the purpose of qualifying for assistance or excessive operating expenses,
4. have net worth of not less than ½ of 1 percent after the granting of assistance,
5. have investments in residential mortgages or mortgage-backed securities aggregating 20 percent of loans, and
6. agree to comply with the terms and conditions established by the FSLIC/FDIC after receipt of assistance.

For institutions with net worth of 3 percent or less, the level of assistance will be 50 percent of period operating loss; with net worth of 2 percent or less, 60 percent of period operating loss; and with net worth of 1 percent or less, 70 percent of operating loss over the particular period. The capital assistance program will expire on October 15, 1985.

Chapter VIII
Capital Adequacy

RESERVE REQUIREMENTS

There are three main functions of bank capital: (a) protective, (b) operational, and (c) regulatory. The protective function denotes the ability of banks to safeguard depositors and to maintain solvency by providing a cushion of excess assets. The operational function has to do with the provision of funds for purchasing land, equipment, machinery, and other assets. The regulatory function deals with capital requirements for a bank to prevent losses to depositors and to the community in which the bank operates.

How to determine satisfactorily the adequacy of capital reserves is a question constantly debated in banking circles. There is no hard and fast rule for determining an adequate level of reserves. What constitutes an adequate level of reserves for a financial deposit institution is a function of several variables, some of which are not quantifiable. These include the ability of management to monitor effectively and evaluate risks in each investment decision, fluctuations in business, trade and housing construction cycles, and the general attitudes of investors and savers.

In recent years, the rapid expansion of bank deposits has required substantial reliance on external debt, largely because of the unwillingness of banks to undertake equity financing which probably would dilute earnings, and the attractive financial leverage provided by debt financing.

Bank capital is largely viewed by regulators as a "cushion" to absorb loan and security losses and, hence, to reduce the probability of insolvency and bank failure. Bank capital is comprised of common stock, preferred stock, and intermediate and long-term debt (subordinated debt). Accretions to capital can also be made from retained earnings. Debt financing, however, is more risky than equity financing and usually is not easily or regularly undertaken.

Regulators and bankers do not agree about what constitutes capital "adequacy." It has been suggested that if the FDIC were to set premiums according to risk associated with each institution, the effect would be that bankers could reduce capital as long as they were willing to pay the cost of insuring this higher risk. This substitution of deposit insurance for some bank capital is one attempt at addressing the problem without increasing the potential costs to society of bank failures.

It is difficult to arrive at or measure the correct capital requirements for a particular bank. The study of ratios, however, provides the analyst and the regulator with a tool to compare a bank with others in the industry or with its own past record.

Simple adequacy measures include the ratio of capital to assets and capital to deposits. The capital/assets ratio implies that a bank's risk lies in its holdings of assets. A greater capital relative to assets reduces the risk of bank insolvency. Similarly, the capital/deposits ratio measures the proportion of long-term vis-à-vis short-term funds being used by a bank. The greater the proportion of long-term funds, the lower the probability of losses to borrowers.

As bank assets changed in composition, regulators recognized that the composition of a bank's assets could be more important in terms of risk than the size of its assets. They began to use a new ratio, namely, capital to risk assets where risk assets denote total assets less cash, bank balances, and U.S. government securities.

The capital to risk assets ratio also acquired considerable refinement over the years. The Federal Reserve, for example, categorizes bank assets according to probable risk and assigns a hypothetical capital reserve for the various categories of assets. The aggregate of the hypothetical reserves provides a standard for evaluating the bank's capital adequacy.

Ratios have an important place in the regulator's analysis, but other factors such as profitability, quality of management, fixed costs, efficiency and the competitive environment in which the institution operates are also taken into account. The Federal Reserve

Board's adjusted risk assets/liquidity approach estimates the level of capital required to insure the viability of a bank under abnormal conditions. Nonbalance-sheet factors are also taken into account in determining how adequate capital holdings are for the banks.

The Federal Deposit Insurance Corporation uses as its principal measure a ratio of capital minus investments in fixed and substandard assets, to average total assets.

The Comptroller of the Currency relies less on static ratios and more on viewing the bank as a dynamic institution and attempts to evaluate management performance.

For state regulatory agencies and some Federal Reserve districts, the methods used to evaluate capital vary significantly, though in general they tend to be more similar to the procedures used by the Federal Reserve Board and the FDIC than those used by the Comptroller of the Currency.

Analysis of capital adequacy involves study of the dynamics of risk and loss in the banking industry. Suggested methods to incorporate these phenomena include an "earnings test," which measures the extent to which current earnings cover anticipated losses, using a historical loss trend experience and stable business conditions in order to project future losses. A proposed earnings test requires annualized current earnings to be equal to at least twice the amount of actual loss anticipated by management. Another suggested index of capital adequacy is the degree to which capital funds (capital, undivided profits, surplus accounts, and all other reserves except depreciation and amortization) cover unanticipated losses. Capital funds totaling forty times the average value of historical loss expectations are viewed as furnishing adequate protection against unexpected losses.

The issue of capital adequacy remains a controversial one and despite a plethora of analyses and discussions on the subject over the years, a generally accepted definition of what constitutes capital adequacy remains elusive.

Although capital adequacy is important for the soundness of any banking institution, too much reliance on the level of capital can impede bank growth and overshadow other factors which provide a more meaningful depiction of bank solvency than statistical ratios. Moreover, the historical record reveals no causal relationship between the levels of bank capitalization and the incidence of bank failure. Capital ratios for banks that have failed are not markedly different from those of banks that did not fail. Asset quality, management practices, and fraud have contributed more to the incidence of bank failures than inadequate capital levels.

Some analysts thus argue that the soundness of a bank rather than its level of capital should be the focal point in evaluating bank solvency. Bank examiners, for example, have adopted an evaluation system called CAMEL, which rates banks on Capital adequacy, Asset quality, Management ability, Earnings, and Liquidity.

Other analysts suggest variable insurance premiums as a more equitable method of distributing the risks associated with banking between the private sector (bank shareholders) and the public sector, the federal insurance agency. In this method, a rational fee structure that is actuarially sound would allocate higher premium rates to riskier banks. The decision-making process of banks would not be constrained by rigid capital requirements but would be dependent on whether the bank's evaluation of the benefits of a riskier capital structure would exceed the costs of higher insurance premiums. Higher premium rates from banks with a higher risk portfolio should cover the costs of failures. Moreover, such a variable system would be more just and rational than one which allows a highly conservative and liquid bank to pay the same insurance rate as a more risk-oriented bank.

Because banks occupy a fiduciary position in society, and the social costs of bank failures can have profound debilitating reverberations throughout the economy, a market valuation of soundness would be inappropriate. It is true that banks and other financial institutions are rated in terms of risk by stock analysts and brokerage agencies in a market sense, and levels of confidence are reflected in market indexes such as stock prices and interest on debt capital. But such analyses do not capture the social costs inherent in the failure of high-risk banks. A purely unfettered market determination of the soundness of capital levels thus is not adequate.

Recently there has been widespread concern about declining capital ratios of banks. John E. Ryan, Federal Reserve director of banking supervision and regulation, noted that "We see banking as a private endeavor, but at what point does the private entrepreneur's contribution to the business become so small and the size of the government guarantee get so large that the entrepreneur forfeits his right to participate in both profits and decision making."

The capital ratios of banks with over $5 billion in assets have declined by more than 20 percent since 1970. In 1970, equity capital as a percent of total assets was 5.34 percent for the largest group of banks, but by the end of 1980, the comparable figure was 4.12 percent. This decline in capital ratios cannot be easily rectified or restored. For example, raising the Bank of America's capital/asset ratio by one percentage point would require $1 billion in new equity capital. Such an amount is significantly larger than the total amount of equity capital raised by all banks over the past few years. Banks can, however, increase capital levels by issuing perpetual or limited-life preferred stock or convertible debentures. It should be noted that although the ratios of capital/assets for the nation's largest banks have been declining, the absolute levels of these capital accounts have been large enough to absorb total loan losses for the entire banking system during the mid-1970s when losses were at a peak. The fact that the absolute level of capital accounts held by large national banks is substantial is perhaps one factor accounting for the practice of allowing large banks to operate with lower capital ratios than smaller banks.

In June 1981, the Federal Financial Institutions Examination Council proposed a uniform definition of capital for bank supervision. The Council adopted the proposal in October 1981 and urged the three banks' regulatory agencies to endorse the new definition.

For purposes of evaluating adequacy under the Council definition, bank capital is divided between primary and secondary capital. Primary capital, which is permanent, includes common and perpetual preferred stock, surplus and undivided profits, contingency and other capital reserves, mandatory convertible instruments and 100 percent of the allowances for loan losses. Secondary capital consists of limited-life preferred stock and subordinated notes and debentures. These items are secondary because, while they exhibit certain features of capital, they are not permanent having specific redemption and maturity dates.

Total secondary capital could not exceed 50 percent of primary capital and should have an original weighted average maturity of at least seven years. As these secondary items approach maturity, they would be phased out of the banks' capital account. Capital would decline by a fifth each year when the maturity date is less than five years.

Each federal regulatory agency, however, would have the flexibility to vary conditions of the definition in individual cases and approve items not included in the definition. The new definition of capital was approved by the Federal Reserve Board, and accepted by the

Comptroller of the Currency to be used in regulations for national banks, but the Federal Deposit Insurance Corporation argued that subordinated debt and limited-life preferred stock should not be viewed as capital since they lack permanence.

It was reported in 1981 that the Federal Deposit Insurance Corporation was actively considering replacing the current fixed-rate deposit insurance premium with a variable premium adjusted for different levels of bank risk. The Corporation was also considering co-insurance of banks with private insurance companies. High risk-taking banks would pay larger premiums than more risk averse institutions or be required to improve its capital position.

It remains to be seen whether recent attempts at establishing a uniform definition of capital and dealing with the problems of capital adequacy will yield a generally accepted format for evaluating the relative safety and solvency of banks in the future.

RESERVE REQUIREMENTS FOR THRIFTS

The Federal Home Loan Bank Board regulations, as stipulated by the National Housing Act of 1934, require that each insured savings and loan association set up a Federal Insurance Reserve Account (FIR) to be used for absorbing unexpected losses. A state-chartered association which is also insured "may designate as part of its Federal Insurance Reserve all of any reserve account which under the provisions of state law is established for the sole purpose of absorbing losses." While most state laws require state-chartered associations to maintain general reserves to be used only for the purpose of absorbing losses, there are usually provisions that, if aggregate general reserves exceed a specified amount, the excess amount may be transferred from the general reserve to an association's profit account.

The general reserves of federal associations and the requirements for the Federal Insurance reserve are similar. However, transfers of excesses from the Federal Insurance Reserve to profit accounts are prohibited for federally chartered savings and loan associations. Reserves are generally held in cash and balances with the federal regulators, though some states allow reserves to be held as correspondent balances, U.S. government securities, and municipal bonds.

During the first fiscal year in which a savings and loan association receives a certificate of insurance, the amount of reserves credited to the Financial Insurance Reserve Account should at least be equal to 3/10 of 1 percent of all insurable accounts. For older institutions, Table VIII-1 provides benchmark guidelines for the percentage of the associations' checking and savings accounts (i.e., insured accounts) required to be held as reserves.

At the end of 20 years, reserves held in the FIR account should be at least equal to 5 percent of total insured accounts on that particular date. The dollar amount of such reserves on each anniversary date may be computed by multiplying the required percentage for that particular anniversary date by the aggregate of the association's insured accounts on that date, or the average of such balances on that particular date and up to four such balances on consecutive preceding closing dates. The 5 percent requirement was subsequently reduced to 4 percent, until January 14, 1982, when it was further lowered to 3 percent with a retroactive effective date of December 31, 1980.

Since virtually all savings and loan associations are insured by the Federal Savings and Loan Insurance Corporation, state-chartered savings and loan associations are subject to the same FIR regulations as federally chartered associations. State-chartered savings and loan

Table VIII-1　Bench-Mark Annual Reserve Percentages
(FIR)

Anniversary	Percentage
2.	0.50
3.	0.75
4.	1.00
5.	1.25
6.	1.50
7.	1.75
8.	2.00
9.	2.25
10.	2.50
11.	2.75
12.	3.00
13.	3.25
14.	3.50
15.	3.75
16.	4.00
17.	4.25
18.	4.50
19.	4.75
20 and thereafter	5.00

associations may also hold other general reserves which may or may not be designated as part of the FIR account. Such general reserves are not considered part of the FIR, unless they are held solely for the purpose of absorbing losses.

In addition to the Federal Insurance Reserve requirements, an insured association is subject to "net worth requirements." Net worth is the sum of all reserve accounts (except specific or valuation reserves), retained earnings, capital stock, and any other nonwithdrawable accounts of an insured institution. As association was required to maintain on each annual closing date a net worth level which is equal to the greater of the aggregate of the Federal Insurance Reserve requirement and 20 percent of scheduled items or an amount computed under the asset composition and net worth index as shown in Table VIII-2.

Scheduled items were largely composed of mortgage loans delinquent 90 days or more, real estate acquired by way of foreclosure or repossession. As Table VIII-2 illustrates, under the asset composition and net worth index, each particular asset is given a minimum net worth percentage reflecting the relative riskiness of the particular asset, the higher the risk, the larger the percentage and vice versa. What this net worth measurement tried to assess was the riskiness of an association's pool of assets, the rationale being that a relatively riskier pool of assets required a higher level of net worth to be maintained. In order to calculate the dollar amount of net worth required under this index, each asset category is multiplied by its minimum net worth percentage, and the amounts so obtained are then totaled.

An additional amount of net worth equal to 5 percent of the unpaid principal amount of all outstanding secured borrowings (with certain exceptions) with an original stated maturity longer than one year must also be maintained by each insured association.

The Federal Home Loan Bank, however, amended November 17, 1980, net worth requirements for all insured associations by replacing the then current net worth requirement of 5 percent of insurable accounts, plus 5 percent of secured borrowings with a requirement of 4 percent of liabilities. The asset composition and net worth index requirement was also eliminated. Associations that sell residential mortgages carrying an interest rate of 7½ percent or less were also given a temporary reprieve of up to 5 years from meeting net worth and reserve requirements. The Federal Insurance Reserve requirement was also lowered to 4 percent of insured accounts. Current reserve and net worth requirements are 3 percent of insured accounts and liabilities, respectively.

Table VIII-2   Asset Composition and Net Worth Index

Asset Category	Minimum Net Worth Percentage
First Mortgage Loans and Contracts:	
Insured or guaranteed mortgage loans	2
Mortgage loans, participations, and mortgage-backed certificates insured or guaranteed by an agency or instrumentality of the United States (except excluded assets)	2
Conventional mortgage loans	
Single-family dwellings.	3
Homes—2-4 dwelling units.	5
Multifamily—more than 4 dwelling units.	6
Other improved real estate—commercial and industrial.	7
Developed building lots and sites	6
Acquisition and development of land.	8
Undeveloped land.	8
Nonconforming mortgage loans and contracts to facilitate sale of real estate owned	8
Other loans:	
Property improvement, alternation, or repair	
Insured or guaranteed loans	3
Other than insured or guaranteed loans	5
Educational loans	
Insured or guaranteed loans	2
Other than insured or guaranteed loans	6
Mobile home chattel paper	
Insured or guaranteed	3
Other than insured or guaranteed.	6
Equipping and secured consumer loans.	6
Unsecured consumer loans.	15
Unsecured construction loans	10
Real estate:	
Foreclosed and in judgment	10
Held for development or investment	7
Office premises—	
Land and buildings	3
Leasehold and leasehold improvements	3
Investment securities—Non-liquid:	
Securities other than those that qualify as liquid assets under § 523.10(g) or would so quality except for maturity (except excluded assets).	3
Other assets:	
Furniture, fixtures, and equipment.	10
Investment in service corporations and other subsidiaries	5
All other (except excluded assets)	3
[Subdivision (i) revised eff. 6-18-75]	

Source: Annotated Manual, Federal Home Loan Bank Board, page 387.

The change to a total liabilities base for net worth calculations was a reflection of the trend for savings and loan associations to increase leverage and outside borrowing to meet mortgage loan demand in periods when the growth in savings deposit inflows was inadequate. Hence, total liabilities would be a more accurate indication of financial solvency and capital adequacy given the declining ratio of savings to total deposits. The regulations also provided for a reduction in net worth requirements proportionate to the amount of long-term debt, flexible yield mortgages and short-term liquid assets held. The dollar amount of net worth requirement would be decreased by three cents for every dollar of "qualified assets" held up to a 10 percent limit. The amendment of the net worth regulations to a simple percentage of liabilities requirement was also in accordance with the stipulations of the Depository Institutions Deregulation and Monetary Control Act of 1980 that regulations should minimize "compliance costs, paperwork, and other burdens on financial institutions, consumers, and the public. . . ."

The Federal Home Loan Bank Board also issued new regulations effective November 4, 1982 permitting FSLIC insured institutions to include "appraised equity capital" as a reserve item in satisfying regulatory requirements. Appraised equity capital is defined as "The arithmetical difference between the net book value and the appraised fair market value of office land, building and improvements, including leasehold improvements owned by the insured institution or any of its subsidiaries, or in some instances, the deferred profit from a sale with leaseback of formerly owned office property." Net worth was redefined by the Board as "regulatory net worth" in order to overcome the inconsistency under general accounting principles and allow insured institutions to include built-up equity in land, buildings and improvements in computing the statutory reserve and net worth requirements.

Appraised equity capital may be included in reserves and net worth calculations by insured institutions on a one-time basis only. An insured institution in computing the new reserve then is required to submit to the Principal Supervisory Agency appraisals of fair market value for owned office building properties, including land, improvements and leasebacks, and a statement of the net book value of each property at the date of appraisal by an independent third-party appraiser. The Board, however, noted that appraised equity capital for regulatory net worth purposes may not constitute part of a line item amount on a financial statement included in a filing under the Securities Exchange Act of 1934 until December 31, 1985. The appraised equity capital regulation carries a sunset date of December 31, 1985.

The Board also stated that an institution will be required to include appraised equity capital within net worth and reserves as a prerequisite for eligibility under the capital assistance program of the Garn-St Germain Act. The Board views the inclusion of appraised equity capital as an indication of the real financial condition of the insured institution and, hence, of the extent of assistance that should be made available to qualifying institutions.

As Table VIII-3 reveals, net worth levels for the industry have been declining over the years from 7.04 percent in relation to total assets in 1970 to approximately 3.9 percent at the end of 1983. Additions to net worth are largely contributed by net income after taxes, so declining profitability due to volatile interest rates is one explanation for the secular decline in capital levels, particularly over the years 1980-1983.

Moreover, with rapid growth in deposits and assets since 1970, the

Table VIII-3   Net Increase in Association Net Worth and Year-end Ratios

Year	Net Increase in Net Worth (Millions)	Ratio of Net Worth	
		Savings Deposits	Total Assets
1950	$ 174	9.15%	7.58%
1955	370	7.96	6.79
1960	590	8.02	6.97
1965	805	7.89	6.72
1966	602	8.29	7.05
1967	450	7.97	6.91
1968	775	8.12	6.99
1969	929	8.57	7.17
1970	781	8.47	7.04
1971	1,191	7.80	6.60
1972	1,648	7.37	6.27
1973	1,816	7.51	6.27
1974	1,386	7.59	6.24
1975	1,337	6.92	5.85
1976	2,219	6.55	5.61
1977	3,186	6.51	5.48
1978	3,873	6.74	5.55
1979	3,509	6.93	5.62
1980	681	6.52	5.29
1981	4,044	5.41	4.27
1982	2,235	4.61	3.70
1983	3,672	4.82	3.95

Source: Federal Home Loan Bank Board.

return on net worth, that is the percentage increase in net worth, has not kept pact with the average growth in assets, increasing at a much lower rate. Another influence on the declining capital ratios of the savings and loan industry has been increasing levels of taxation, following the phase-out of the bad debt deduction provided for in the Tax Reform Act of 1969. These increased tax payments further reduced the amount of funds available for addition to net worth. Savings and loan associations' pre-tax incomes were also taxed at an effective rate of 30.6 percent for federal, state, and local taxes. This is significantly higher than the effective tax rates for commercial banks and several other financial institutions. Table VIII-4 shows the ratio of retained earnings to total assets for commercial banks, savings and loan associations, and mutual savings banks.

Table VIII-4   Retained Earnings as Percent of Total Assets Held by Selected Types of Financial Institutions, 1962-1982

Year	Savings Banks	Commercial Banks	Savings and Loan Associations
1962	.41	.73	.97
1963	.44	.72	.69
1964	.44	.70	.72
1965	.46	.70	.67
1966	.33	.69	.50
1967	.20	.74	.46
1968	.37	.72	.60
1969	.35	.84	.68
1970	.27	.89	.57
1971	.48	.87	.71
1972	.60	.83	.77
1973	.54	.85	.76
1974	.35	.81	.54
1975	.38	.78	.47
1976	.45	.70	.64
1977	.55	.71	.79
1978	.58	.77	.84
1979	.46	.81	.68
1980	−.12	.80	.14
1981	−.82	.77	−.74
1982	−.73	.72	−.62

Note: Data represent retained earnings after all expenses, taxes, and dividends paid depositors as percent of average assets. Data for commercial banks are for FDIC-insured institutions and since 1976 are based on consolidated reports. Data for savings and loan associations are for all associations since 1976 and FSLIC-insured institutions for prior years.

Source: FDIC, FHLBB, NAMSB, and USLSI.

RESERVE REQUIREMENTS FOR
MUTUAL SAVINGS BANKS

For mutual banks, a survey of statutory reserve and/or liquidity requirements reveal great diversity. The gamut of requirements range from no statutory requirements in Alaska, Indiana, Maryland, Rhode Island, New York, and Washington to varied requirements in New Jersey, Vermont, Maine, and New Hampshire.

In Delaware, savings banks are required to maintain liquid reserves of cash and deposits in other banks equal to 7 percent of the aggregate of demand deposits and 3 percent of the aggregate of time deposits.

In Maine, "every savings bank shall establish and maintain a minimum cash reserve in an amount established by the superintendent for all savings banks with the following levels:

(a)   Between 1 percent and 4 percent of the banks' savings deposits;
(b)   between 2 and 5 percent of the banks' time deposits; and
(c)   between 6 and 12 percent of the banks' demand deposits, less treasury tax and loan account deposits and between 6 and 12 percent of the banks' NOW account deposits."

The reserves so designated may be held in the form of cash on hand, deposits in commercial banks, savings banks and savings and loan associations, federal funds sold to banks, the book value of U.S. government securities, and any other securities' issues by any agency or instrumentality of the United States.

In New Jersey, all savings banks are required to maintain cash balances of not less than 3 percent of its aggregate deposits other than capital deposits. Such reserves may be held in cash, demand deposits in a reserve depository or in the FHLB of which the savings bank is a member, or in any bank incorporated in the United States. U.S. government securities of less than one year's maturity may also be held as reserves, with the limitation that they do not exceed 1½ percent of aggregate deposits.

In Pennsylvania, savings banks are required to maintain reserves of not less than 3 percent nor more than 6 percent of total deposits, as fixed by the Banking Department. These percentages also apply to time deposits. Such reserves may consist of cash on hand or on deposit in an amount not less than 1 percent of the deposits of the sav-

Table VIII-5   Capital Position of the Thrift Institutions, 1960-83
Net Worth as a Percent of Assets

End of Year	Savings and Loan Associations	Mutual Savings Banks
1960	6.97	8.75
1965	6.72	8.01
1970	7.04	7.25
1971	6.60	7.07
1972	6.27	6.91
1973	6.27	7.12
1974	6.24	7.27
1975	5.85	6.96
1976	5.61	6.71
1977	5.48	6.77
1978	5.55	6.90
1979	5.64	7.05
1980	5.29	6.63
1981	4.30	5.68
1982	3.70	5.3
1983	3.92[a]	5.45[b]

Sources: National Association of Mutual Savings Banks and Federal
Home Loan Bank Board.
[a]October 1983.
[b]November 1983.

ings bank and U.S. government securities, Pennsylvania securities, or any other securities approved by the Banking Department.

Vermont statutes require that every bank maintain a reserve of 3 percent of its savings deposits. New loans are not to be made if the reserve level should fall below this requirement.

Deposits payable to the United States as a result of subscriptions for U.S. government liberty bonds are not subject to these reserve requirements. At least 2/5 of these reserves are to be held in cash on hand or in demand deposits in other banks or "in direct short-term obligations of the United States with a maturity of less than one year."

Of these demand deposits in other banks, at least half shall be in a bank not occupying the same banking room and up to 3/5 of the reserve may be in the direct obligations of the United States or in any agency thereof, and up to 1/3 of that 3/5 reserve may be in obligations of the State of Vermont, the Vermont Housing Finance Agency, and The Vermont Municipal Bond Bank.

Vermont laws also stipulate that the commissioner be empowered to increase these reserves to an amount not to exceed 30 percent of demand deposits and 8 percent on time deposits. Reserve requirements may also be decreased to not lower than 9 percent on demand deposits and 2 percent on savings deposits. Should an increase in reserves be authorized by the commissioner, no part of that increase should be held in cash.

In Wisconsin, mutual banks are required by law to maintain reserves of cash on hand or on deposit in approved banks of at least 5 percent of its total deposits. Up to 3-5 percent of such reserves may be held in U.S. government securities.

Capital ratios for mutual savings banks have also been declining but are still higher than the ratios for savings and loan associations, in absolute terms over the years, perhaps due to more conservative management practices by mutual savings banks. (See Table VIII-5.)

COMPARISON WITH COMMERCIAL BANKS

Reserve requirements of the Federal Reserve System are more costly to banks than to nonmember banks. Federal banks are required to hold more reserves.

Federal reserves may be held in two forms:

(a)   cash, coin, and currency, or
(b)   deposits with the Federal Reserve Banks.

The Deposit Base is defined as net demand deposits (which is total demand deposits minus cash items in the process of collection, minus dues from other bank) plus savings deposits and time deposits.

The demand deposit reserve requirement as of December 1, 1977 was:

0-2 million	7%
2-10 million	9½%
10-100 million	11¾%
100-400 million	12¾%
400+	16¼%

For time and savings deposits, the requirement is 3 percent for savings deposits and 5 percent for time deposits. For the latter, the higher the maturity level, the higher the reserve requirement varies between 1-6 percent.

As of March 1, 1980, before the adoption of regulations embodied in the Monetary Control Act of 1980, reserve requirements were:

Federal Reserve Requirement Ratios

Type of Deposit and Deposit Interval ($ millions)	*Ratios (%) in Effect March 1, 1980*
Net Demand	
$0 to $2	7
Over $2 to $10	9½
Over $10 to $100	11¾
Over $100 to $400	12¾
Over $400	16¼
Savings	3
Time—By Initial Maturity	
30 to 179 days	
$0 to $5	3
Over $5	6
180 days to 4 years	2½
4 years or more	1
Marginal Reserve Requirement (on managed liabilities in excess of the institution's managed liabilities base)	8

Marginal reserve requirements were established by the Federal Reserve Board on October 6, 1979 and modified on March 14, 1980. A special deposit requirement for commercial banks and other financial institutions that were not members of the Federal Reserve System was also imposed. Such requirements were, however, of a temporary nature and were eventually rescinded.

RESERVE REQUIREMENTS FOR STATE BANKS

There are, of course, given the nature of the dual banking system, different rules for every state. Some states allow reserves to be held in coin, correspondence balances, and cash items in the process of collection. Some states allow U.S. government securities and municipal bonds. Only two states have the same reserve requirements of the Federal Reserve—New York and Connecticut. Illinois has no specific reserves. All but four states require reserves against savings and time deposits. There is great diversity in rates. In Vermont, for example, the requirement for demand deposits is 27 percent, in Florida for savings and time deposits it is 20 percent.

UNIFORM RESERVE REQUIREMENTS FOR ALL DEPOSITORY INSTITUTIONS AS ESTABLISHED BY THE FEDERAL RESERVE

The House Banking Finance and Urban Affairs Committee tentatively agreed in September 1978 on a plan to revitalize falling membership in the Federal Reserve System. The main points of the plan were the exemption from reserve requirements of the first $50 million of demand negotiable order of withdrawal and savings accounts, as well as the first $50 million of time deposits held by commercial banks. Reserve ratios to be implemented by legislation would be set between 6 percent to 8 percent for demand, NOW, and savings accounts, and between 1 to 6 percent for time deposits maturing under 180 days and 1 to 3 percent for those deposits with longer maturities.

The American Bankers Association at the time adopted the posture that membership in the federal system should be voluntary, and there should be equal treatment to all financial institutions. An amendment to the bill by the Federal Reserve Board to apply reserve requirements to thrift institutions which offer transaction accounts was, however, rejected by the House Banking Committee in September. In February 1979, "consumer banking" representatives took the stand that federal system reserve requirements should be made universal for all types of deposits and for all depository institutions, including savings and loans, mutual savings banks and credit unions, as well as nonmember commercial banks. Continued debate in Congress on a plan for universal mandatory reserve requirements resulted in the passage of the Depository Institutions Deregulation and Monetary Control Act of 1980 (HR4986). Title I of the Act required all depository institutions to hold mandatory reserves against all transaction accounts and nonpersonal time deposits.

Under the 1980 Act, reserves' requirements for all depository institutions are grouped into three categories; namely, mandatory reserve requirements, supplemental reserve requirements, and reserve requirements in extraordinary circumstances. The reserve requirements are uniformly applied to all transaction accounts at all depository institutions. Transaction accounts comprise demand deposits, negotiable order of withdrawal (NOW) accounts, savings deposits subject to automatic transfers, and share draft accounts. Other accounts may be included as transaction accounts by federal authorities, provided that such accounts "may be used to provide funds directly or indirectly for the purpose of making payments or transfers to third persons or others." A "nonpersonal time deposit" denotes "a transferable time deposit or account or a time deposit or account representing funds deposited to the credit of or in which any beneficial interest is held by a depositor who is not a natural person."

For all depository institutions mandatory reserve requirements on transaction accounts are based on the following scale: effective September 1, 1980:

(a)   3 percent of the first $25 million in transaction accounts, or 3 percent of all transaction accounts if less than $25 million; and

(b)   12 percent of the amount above $25 million. This latter percentage may be varied by the Federal Reserve Board within a range of 8 to 14 percent.

The base figure of $25 million was tied to changes in the growth of total transaction accounts of all depository institutions, increasing or decreasing by 80 percent of the growth or decline in such accounts, beginning in 1981.

All depository institutions are required to maintain reserves equivalent to 3 percent of its nonpersonal time deposits. This percentage may be changed by the Federal Reserve Board within a range of 0 to 9 percent.

In order to effectively undertake monetary policy, the Act also empowered the Federal Reserve Board to impose supplementary reserves on transaction accounts up to a maximum of 4 percent. However, while mandatory reserves are noninterest bearing items, interest will be paid by the Federal Reserve Board on supplemental reserves. Such interest will be paid quarterly at a rate based on the rate earned on the securities' portfolio of the Federal Reserve system in the previous quarter.

The Act authorized the Federal Reserve Board to require additional reserves during extraordinary circumstances and in consultation with Congress.

Required reserves of all depository institutions may be held in the following forms:

(a)   vault cash,
(b)   balances with Federal Reserve banks,
(c)   balances with the Federal Home Loan Bank,
(d)   balances with the National Credit Union Central Liquidity Facility, and
(e)   balances held in another depository institution maintaining required reserve balances at a Federal Reserve Bank. The latter three balances (c), (d), (e), are required to be passed through on a dollar for dollar basis to the particular Federal Reserve Bank.

A phase-in plan was devised for depository institutions that were not members of the Federal Reserve system on or after July 1, 1979. Beginning September 1, 1980, the new reserve requirements would be phased in over an eight-year period for nonmember institutions. The latter institutions would be required to maintain reserves equal to one-eighth of the reserve requirements calculated under the provisions of the Monetary and Control Act of 1980 and Regulation D. Required reserves would then be increased by an additional one-eighth beginning on each of the following dates:

September 3, 1981
September 2, 1982
September 1, 1983
September 6, 1984
September 5, 1985
September 4, 1986
September 3, 1987

Reserve requirements (12 percent) for NOW accounts held by institutions located in all states except New York, New Jersey, and the New England States would, however, be effective immediately and not subject to the "phase-in regulations."

The reserve requirements for member banks will be phased in from the present requirements over a three and one-half-year period beginning on November 13, 1980. Under the plan, required reserves would be equal to the amount required under the old structure, less one-eighth of the difference between that amount and the required reserve amount under the new structure. Required reserve balances would be further reduced by an additional one-eighth of this difference every six months beginning March 5, 1981 up to March 1, 1984. The immediate impact of the new reserve requirements would, thus, tend to reduce reserve balances held by member banks.

It is interesting to note that since the passage of the 1980 Act, withdrawals from the Federal System appear to have declined by over 30 percent, if the six-month rate as of June 1981 is annualized. As of that date, only 21 commercial banks withdrew from the system, which compares with an average of 34 withdrawals per half a year for the five calendar years preceding enactment of uniform mandatory reserve regulations for all depository institutions. Twenty-six existing banks also converted from nonmember status as of June 1981. It is suggested that the uniform, universal reserve requirements will improve the capacity of the Federal Reserve Board to effectively manage the money supply.

LIQUIDITY AND CASH REQUIREMENTS

Liquidity denotes the ability of a financial entity to readily and easily convert its assets into cash. Liquid assets are those assets which are held in the form of cash or are readily convertible into cash. Banks, savings and loan associations, mutual savings banks, and other financial institutions, are particularly concerned with the degree of liquidity of their assets. To maintain and foster confidence, these institutions must be in a position to meet withdrawals by their customers and unforeseen contingencies. In addition to satisfying withdrawal requirements, savings and loan associations seek to maintain liquid assets in order to meet current operating expenses and also to cover cash commitments involved; for example, in loans-in-process and mortgage loans for which previous commitments have been made. Basically, the sources of liquidity in savings and loan associations are:

(a)   cash on hand and due from banks,
(b)   Treasury bills and other short-term government securities,

(c)   repayments of the principal balance on amortized mortgage loans,

(d)   interest payments on mortgage loans,

(e)   net flow of savings into the association,

(f)   the ability to procure loans from the Federal Home Loan Bank, and

(g)   sources of advances other than the Federal Home Loan Bank.

BORROWING LIMITATION AND AVAILABILITY

Savings and loan associations that are members of the FHLB system are able to obtain funds from the regional Home Bank to meet liquidity requirements if necessary. Federally chartered associations may borrow up to 100 percent of their total dollar volume of savings accounts from the regional Federal Home Loan Bank. With the state-chartered associations and mutual banks, the percentage of total savings which may be borrowed ranges from 25 to 50 percent. These percentages differ according to state statutes and regulations under which state-chartered savings and loan associations operate. No member of the Federal Home Loan Bank system may borrow more than 10 percent of their total savings accounts from a source other than the Federal Home Loan Bank.

LIQUIDITY REQUIREMENTS (FHLB)

"For each calendar month, each member shall maintain any average daily balance of liquid assets in an amount not less than 7 percent of the average daily balance of the members' liquidity base during the preceding calendar month." The average daily balance requirement is 3 percent of the liquidity base for short-term assets.

For savings and loan associations with assets under $25,000,000, the liquidity requirement, by resolution of its Board of Directors, may be an average daily balance of liquid assets and short-term liquid assets of not less than 7 percent. "Liquid assets" include the total of cash, accrued interest on unpledged assets which qualify as liquid assets and the book value of the following:

(a) time deposits in a FHLB or the Bank for Savings and Loan Associations, Chicago, Illinois;
(b) U.S. obligations of not more than 5 years' maturity;
(c) obligations with less than 5 year maturities issued by the FHLB, the FNMA, the GNMA, A Bank or Banks for Cooperatives, a Federal Land Bank, the FICB, the TVA, the Export-Import Bank of the United States, the Commodity Credit Corporation, or the Federal Financing Bank; and
(d) time deposits in an insured bank, bankers' acceptances, general obligations of any state, territory or possession of the United States, also qualify as liquid assets, with certain stipulations.

Short-term liquid assets include cash and the unpledged assets described above, but having less than 6 months' maturity, or in some instances, not more than 12 months. A precise definition of the various categories of liquid assets is given in the footnotes following Table VIII-6.

Table VIII-6   Minimum Ratio[1] of Liquid Assets[2] to Liquidity Base[3]
Required of Members of the Federal Home Loan Bank System

Effective Date	All Liquid Assets	Short-term Liquid Assets[4]
Dec. 1950	6	([6])
Mar. 1, 1961[5]	7	([6])
Aug. 1, 1968.	6½	([6])
June 12, 1969.	6	([6])
Dec. 1, 1969.	5½	([6])
Apr. 1, 1971.	6½	([6])
May 1, 1971.	7½	([6])
Aug. 1, 1971.	7	([6])
Jan. 1, 1972.	7	3
May 1, 1973.	6½	2½
Aug. 1, 1973[7].	5½	1½
Sept. 1, 1974[7].	5	1
Apr. 1, 1975.	5½	1½
June 1, 1975.	6	2
Sept. 1, 1975	6½	2½
Mar. 1, 1976.	7	3
May 1, 1978.	6½	2½
Jan. 1, 1979	6	2
Oct. 25, 1979	5½	1½
Apr. 1, 1980.	5	1

Source: Federal Home Loan Bank Board Journal, June 1981, Vol. 14, No. 6, pg. 57.

Table VIII-6 notes continued:

[1] Before Dec. 22, 1969, the indicated minimum was required on each day a member closed loans. Beginning Dec. 22, 1969, compliance has been monthly, on the basis of an average of daily liquid asset balances to an average of the liquidity base for the preceding month, or, in the case of members with less than $25 million in assets, to the liquidity base at the end of the preceding month. Special provision is made in the case of deficiencies resulting from the withdrawal of savings.

[2]

month. Special provision is made in the case of deficiencies resulting from the withdrawal of savings.

[2] Liquid assets are defined as: (a) cash and unpledged demand deposits beginning in 1950; (b) U.S. Government obligations—all maturities for the period 1950—March 31, 1975 (subject to some limitation on holdings of longer-term issues beginning 1972) and only those maturing in 5 years or less since (with phase-in), (b) certain Federal agency securities maturing in 5 years or less beginning June 11, 1969; (c) time and savings deposits maturing in 1 year or less, or with a notice period of 90 days or less, beginning December 22, 1969; (d) loans of unsecured days (Federal) funds maturing in 6 months or less beginning November 21, 1973; (e) bankers acceptances maturing in 6 months or less beginning December 22, 1969, and in 9 months or less beginning April 1, 1975; (f) high-grade general obligations of state and local governments (beginning December 22, 1969) and U.S. guaranteed public housing authority notes (beginning April 1, 1975) maturing in 2 years or less; (g) shares of open-end investment companies limiting their investment to the foregoing beginning August 27, 1980; (h) high-grade corporate debt obligations maturing in 3 years or less and commercial paper maturing in 270 days or less beginning December 31, 1980, and (i) liquid assets held subject to repurchase agreement and accrued interest on liquid assets, and on assets which would so qualify except for maturity, beginning January 1, 1972. Additional restrictions were effective for some assets and special provisions applicable to mutual savings banks for some periods.

[3] Before Nov. 1, 1970, the liquidity base consisted of a member's net withdrawable accounts (or the policy reserve required by State law, in the case of an insurance company). Beginning Nov. 1, 1970, borrowings payable on demand or due in 1 year or less were added.

[4] Short-term liquid assets are the liquid assets defined in footnote 2 except: (a) U.S. Government and Federal agency obligations must mature in 12 months or less beginning April 1, 1975 (in 18 months or less earlier) and (b) time deposits, bankers acceptances, state and local government and housing authority obligations, corporate debt and commercial paper must mature in 6 months or less. The short-term requirement is not applicable to member mutual savings banks or insurance companies.

[5] During the period June 27-Nov. 1, 1966, members were permitted to reduce liquid asset holdings below the requirement by an amount not exceeding the smaller of (a) actual net savings withdrawn, or (b) 1 percent of withdrawable savings.

[6] No separate requirement.

[7] Penalties for liquidity deficiencies caused by net savings withdrawals during August through December 1973 and April through October 1974 were waived.

Before November 1, 1970, the liquidity base consisted of a member's net withdrawable accounts. As of November 1, 1970, borrowings payable on demand or due in one year were added. Net withdrawable accounts consist of the total of all withdrawable accounts less the unpaid balance of all loans on the security of such accounts.

As can be observed from the table, the short-term liquid assets requirements have fallen over the years from 6 percent in 1950, when there was no separate requirement from the all liquid assets ratio, to 1 percent in 1980, while the all liquid assets ratio has risen from 6 percent in 1950 to 7 percent in 1976, declining to 5 percent in 1980. One plausible reason for the fall in the short-term liquid assets ratio has to do with increased insurance protection offered by the FSLIC and a wider choice of assets which qualify as acceptable liquid assets.

MUTUAL BANK MEMBERS OF THE
FHLB SYSTEM/FSLIC INSURANCE

Assuming that this resolution is adopted by the Board of Directors for mutual banks, the liquidity ratio requirement is 5 percent of the liquidity base, computed on similar lines to that of savings and loan associations.

The specifications with regard to liquid assets, short-term liquid assets, etc., are the same for the mutual banks as those pertaining to savings and loan associations. For mutual banks that do not opt for the 5 percent ratio, the S&L ratio also applies.

Mutual banks following the 5 percent ratio must also maintain federal funds and commercial paper in an amount not less than the difference between the 7 percent requirement and the actual amount of liquid assets maintained by the particular mutual bank. Requirements for federal savings banks chartered after the 1982 Garn Act are identical to those for savings and loan associations.

COMMON AND PREFERRED STOCK—
BONDS AND SUBORDINATED DEBENTURES

Traditionally, all federally chartered savings and loan associations were mutually owned and, hence, were not permitted to issue stock. With mutually owned and, hence, are not permitted to issue stock. With the recent conversion of some stock state-chartered associations, this has created some confusion in interpreting the FHLBB regulations.

Stock associations which are state-chartered may, with approval from the particular state banking department, issue additional common or preferred stock to bolster capital reserves. Federal mutual associations do not have this option. Mutual banks, being "mutual" by organizations are also unable to issue common or preferred stock.

With the approval of the FSLIC, federally chartered and state-chartered insured associations may issue subordinated debt securities with the FSLIC's approval. Such securities must have a maturity of at least seven years and should not exceed 50 percent of the savings and loan associations' net worth.

In order to satisfy the annual closing net worth requirements, insured associations may include up to a limit of 20 percent of net worth requirements, the principal amount of any subordinated debt. A mutual savings bank, however, may issue subordinated debt and include the total amount of such debt in net worth computations. Published financial statements of an insured institution may not, however, include its subordinated debentures as part of net worth.

In August 1982, the Federal Home Loan Bank Board amended net worth regulations, authorizing the inclusion of the full amount of subordinated debt securities, redeemable mutual capital certificates, and nonpermanent preferred stock with a remaining term to maturity or required redemption of not less than one year, in net worth and statutory reserve requirements.

MUTUAL CAPITAL CERTIFICATES

To provide an additional source of capital funds for mutual thrift institutions, the Depository Institutions Deregulation and Monetary Control Act of 1980 authorized the creation and issuance of mutual capital certificates. In November 1980, the Federal Home Loan Bank issued final regulations governing procedures for the issuance of mutual capital certificates by mutual savings banks and savings and loan associations. No specific percentage of net worth limitation was established, and the total amount of mutual capital certificates issued may be used to satisfy reserve and net worth requirements. Mutual capital certificates are, in essence, equivalent to preferred capital stock and, hence, provide a source of capital for mutual organizations akin to equity issues by stock institutions. The Board Regulations stipulate that mutual capital certificates will be:

(a) subordinate to all claims against a mutual association and charge-offs for losses against mutual capital certificates can only be undertaken after all other net worth accounts have been depleted; and

(b) pay dividends on a fixed, variable, cumulative, participating basis, or any combination of the above.

The certificates would also be redeemable in certain limited instances, provided that the redemption would not render the association incapable of meeting its statutory reserve and net worth requirements. If the latter reserve requirements are not met by the association at any time, the regulations also prohibit the payment of dividends. Failure to pay dividends could not be used as a reason for any claim or action of default.

In addition, the regulations also delineate procedures for application to the Bank Board for approval of the issuance of mutual capital certificates, procedures for membership approval authorization, proxy solicitations and pre-approved charter amendments for federal mutual associations and federal mutual savings banks.

Mutual capital certificates, to date, have not been very popular, largely because of the high initial cost of issuing these certificates. A modification to the regulations was effected in December 1981, which permitted the use of general proxies and require only the majority approved of voters present or by proxy rather than the previous requirement that the institutions proposing the issue hold a special proxy solicitation. This modification is expected to reduce the initial cost of issuing these certificates.

COMMERCIAL PAPER

The Federal Home Loan Bank Board in January 1979 authorized the issuance of commercial paper by savings and loan associations as an additional source of securing funds. Mortgage-backed notes, that is short-term notes secured by mortgage loans, were also approved as another source of financing for savings and loan associations.

Commercial paper is normally issued in denominations of $100,000. The maturity of these issues will range from 5 to 270 days, with the average maturity being within 30 to 90 days. Commercial paper issues are exempt from registration under the Securities and Exchange Act of 1933,[1] since the maturity date of these notes is less than nine months, and the funds so raised are usually disbursed to finance current transactions. While commercial paper issues can be rolled over and, hence, used as general funds, such actions are risky and highly dependent on the state of the market.

The placing of commercial paper issues is usually less costly if the issue has at least two ratings, either by Moodys Investors Service Inc., Standard & Poor, or Fitch Investor Services. Highly rated issuers can usually obtain a relatively stable source of financing. Ratings generally reflect considerations as to the certainty of payment and the ability to meet payments on time.

Commercial paper issues are an attractive alternative source of financing since the interest rate on these issues is usually lower than prime lending rates of commercial banks; for example, the disparity between these rates being as high as 100 basis points. Funds obtained from these issues provide savings and loan associations with a flexible source of financing to meet seasonal fluctuations in loan demand. Savings and loan associations can also use commercial paper to originate mortgages and then sell or pass through these loans to secondary market participants such as the Federal Home Loan Mortgage Corporation or private investors.

Prior to 1982, federal and state-chartered insured associations were required to comply with insurance regulations that limit outside borrowings from sources other than a Federal Home Loan Bank or a state-chartered central reserve institution to 25 percent of assets. Total borrowings could not exceed 50 percent of assets. Federal associations are required to obtain the approval of the Bank Board before issuing commercial paper, while state-chartered associations must also adhere to state laws governing the issuance of commercial paper.

Savings and loan associations are also permitted to issue a collateralized form of commercial paper known as mortgage backed notes. Mortgage backed notes are secured by mortgage loans and mortgage backed securities. Such collateral must be held by a trustee responsible for guaranteeing the indenture agreement. Mortgage backed notes are generally issued with a collateral ratio of 108 percent. The ratio is increased if on valuation the collateral pool is below the collateral maintenance ratio. Mortgage backed notes are different

---

[1] Savings and loan associations are also exempt from registration requirements under Section 3(a) 5 of the Securities and Exchange Act of 1933.

from mortgage backed bonds, the latter instruments usually having an average maturity of five years. On the other hand, the average maturity of mortgage backed notes is about 45 days. Mortgage backed bonds, too, usually have collateral ratios of approximately 150 percent.

In conclusion, commercial paper represents a viable source of raising additional funds for savings and loan associations. The extent to which such issues are utilized in the future will be dependent on the level of market acceptance of the issues of associations. Size of associations may, thus, inhibit the widespread use of this type of financing, more so given the usually high minimum volume placement requirements of many dealers.

MORTGAGE BACKED BONDS

Mortgage backed bonds provide savings and loan associations with an additional alternative opportunity for obtaining funds. In April 1975, the Federal Home Loan Bank Board issued regulations which authorized insured savings and loan associations to issue mortgage backed bonds. Bank Board criteria established certain eligibility requirements, including limitations on borrowing from sources other than the Federal Home Loan Bank Board System, the maintenance of net worth requirements after giving effect to the issuance of bonds and repayment out of proceeds of any outside borrowings with an original maturity in excess of one year. In addition, the ratio of scheduled items (problem loans) to specified assets of the issuing association should not be in excess of 2.5 percent. The indenture agreement governing the issue of the bnds must also provide for written notice of default on bonds to the Federal Savings & Loan Insurance Corporation which has 30 days to decide whether to repurchase the collateral.

Mortgage backed bonds are also required to be issued with an average effective maturity date of at least five years, maximum required principal repayment be not more than 20 percent of the original principal amount per year and each bond bear the legend: "This security is not a savings account or deposit and it is not insured by the Federal Savings and Loan Insurance Corporation."

In essence, a mortgage backed bond is a financial instrument with

a stated maturity issued as a general obligation of the particular institution and collateralized by a pool of mortgages. Mortgage backed
bonds are issued with a fixed rate of interest and payment of such
interest usually made semi-annually. These bonds, thus, have a
known, fixed cash flow characteristic unlike the pass-through security, from which the cash flow may vary from payment to payment.

As a general rule, mortgage backed bonds are usually issued in
minimum denominations of $100,000 though there is no required
minimum denomination if the issue is a private placement to institutional investors or represent borrowings from commercial banks. A
minimum denomination of $10,000 is required, however, by Board
regulations if the issue is offered or sold at any office of the association and is sold in private placement to not more than 35 persons. In
a public offering of bonds with a minimum denomination of less
than $100,000, filing and preclearance requirements of the Bank
Board must also be satisfied.

Most issues of mortgage backed bonds to date have been secured
with highly marketable primary collateral, FHA and VA mortgage
loans, conventional mortgage loans, and GNMA modified pass-through
certificates. While GNMA securities and FHA-VA mortgages are
preferred forms of mortgage collateral by the rating agencies, the use
of conventional mortgages as collateral has been increasing with
greater market acceptance recently. Such conventional mortgages
were generally secured by one family owner—occupied detached
residencies—had a given maturity of 25-30 years, had a loan-to-value
ratio less than 80 percent, were at least three months old and did
not exceed the dollar purchase limit of the Federal Home Loan
Mortgage Corporation. Some issues also have provisions for variable-
rate mortgage loans to be included and flexible "basket" arrangements for "nonconforming" conventional mortgage loans. In order
to obtain market acceptability and favorable interest rates, most
mortgage backed bonds are rated by the various investment rating
agencies. The quality and type of collateral and the value of the
collateral in relation to the amount of borrowing by the mortgage
backed bond issue are important factors influencing ratings and
ultimately the interest rate of the issue. Mortgage backed bonds
issued to date have received AAA or Aaa ratings.

As a savings and loan association receives scheduled payments of
principal and prepayments, mortgages are continuously decreasing in
value. Hence, overcollateralization of the mortgage backed bond issue is required in order to ensure that the market value of the collat-

eralized mortgages will be in excess of the outstanding principal value of the bond issue. The first issues of mortgage backed bonds had an initial collateral level of 175 percent and a collateral maintenance ratio of 135 percent. Currently, the initial and collateral maintenance level is 150 percent. Most rating agencies now also require quarterly valuation of the collateral pool. The bond indenture usually requires the association to pledge additional collateral, unless such action is prohibited by Board regulations. In such a situation, a partial redemption of the bond issue must be undertaken in order to achieve the 150 percent collateral maintenance level.

Mortgage backed bonds, thus, provide a feasible alternative to obtain liquidity from assets which, if sold in the secondary market, would incur substantial losses. Low yielding mortgages, hence, provide an attractive source of mortgage collateral and tend to be more stable as to prepayment than more current assets.

Because ratings are dependent to a certain degree on the size and financial condition of the issuing association, most of the early issues of mortgage backed bonds have been placed by associations in California with a strong demand for capital funds. The first issue of mortgage backed bonds was, in fact, undertaken by California Federal Savings and Loan Association.

That issue, made on September 25, 1975, was for $50 million. In 1976, there was one bond issue of $75 million, and in 1977, 12 public offerings totaling $1.2 billion and three private placements totaling $80 million. In 1978, $151 million was raised through eight public offerings placed by savings and loan associations. In 1979, the amount of mortgage-backed securities grew to $1.04 billion from 11 public offerings. In 1980, five public offerings totaling $290 million were placed by various savings and loan associations. Mortgage-backed bonds have, therefore, become a highly attractive means of achieving portfolio leveraging by savings and loan associations. Most of the issues since 1976 have been collateralized by pools of conventional mortgage loans. Mortgage-backed bonds have also tended to demonstrate higher yields than comparable corporate bonds and United States Treasury bonds with a seven- to ten-year maturity.

Mortgage-backed bonds have been a successful tool for attracting institutional portfolio investors and, hence, for augmenting the supply of funds available for housing finance. The desirability of issuing mortgage-backed bonds is, of course, dependent on the available alternative means of raising funds, such as FHLB borrowings, subordinated debt, sale of mortgage loans to the secondary market, vis-à-vis yield spreads between that of the mortgage pool collateral and the cost (interest, etc.) of the mortgage backed bond issue. The ability to meet regulatory requirements is also an important factor, as is the overall financial condition of the association, particularly its level of capitalization and potential investor perception of the credit worthiness of the institution.

Table VIII-7 illustrates some of the characteristics of the earlier issues of mortgage backed bonds up to 1978.

On January 15, 1982, the Federal Home Loan Bank Board amended its regulations governing borrowing by associations insured by the Federal Savings and Loan Insurance Corporation. The amendments were designed to increase the flexibility of insured associations to manage liabilities and undertake the sales of loans in the secondary market. Specifically, the salient points of the revised regulations include the removal of the then current 50 percent limitation on the aggregate borrowing of insured institutions. The Board noted that the rationale for historically limiting borrowing by insured associations was the desire to reduce the volatility of costs of funds and, hence, earnings to associations. Given the current high and volatile interest rate scenario and the dramatic decline in the percentage of deposits held in the form of fixed-rate passbook and other savings accounts, costs of deposits and of borrowing have largely moved in tandem and, thus, there was no justification for limiting the ability of associations to procure funds from nondeposit sources. Borrowing would now be a function of management discretion and the prevailing characteristics of the market place. In addition, the 25 percent of assets limitation of the aggregate book value of all collateral securing outside borrowing was also eliminated. This amendment significantly increases the potential ability of savings and loan associations to utilize mortgage backed bonds or notes to augment the pool of available funds. The Board, however, stipulated that the FSLIC right of purchase requirement, would apply to any secured outside borrowing with the exception of collateral consisting of certain defined liquid assets. The FSLIC right of purchase provision would ensure that collateral is not sold at levels substantially below market value in the event of default by an insured institution.

Restrictions on the distribution of maturities of liabilities were also removed. The requirement that institutions must meet net worth requirements after taking into consideration the effects of outside

Table VIII-7 Summary of Terms of Some Issues of Mortgage-Backed Bonds

Issuer	Effective Date	Amount	Rate	Minimum Denomination	Maturity	Right of Redemption	Initial Collateral	Initial Dis. Val. of Col.	Maintenance of Collateral
California Federal Savings & Loan Association	25 Sept. 75	50M	9.125%	10,000	15 July 85 (approx. 10 yrs.)	callable 15 July 82	4,600 FHA, VA 1-4 family mortgages 7%, 27 yrs. to maturity	87.5M (175%)	135%
Great Western Savings & Loan Association, California	18 Oct. 77	100M	7.8%	10,000 (1,000 increments)	1 Oct. 89 (approx. 12 yrs.)	Holder's repayment election 1 Oct. 84	13,000 conv. single family mortgages 7.26%, 8.7 yrs. since origination	220M (210%)	150%
American Savings & Loan Association, California	26 May 77	200M	7.25%	10,000 (1,000 increments)	1 June 82 (approx. 5 yrs.)	at maturity	15,000 FHA, VA 1-4 family mortgages 6¾-9%, 15-29 yrs. to maturity, 3+ yrs. since origination	300M (150%)	125%
Imperial Savings & Loan Association, California	16 June 77	100M	7.7%	10,000 (5,000 increments)	15 June 87 (10 yrs.)	callable 15 June 84	10,000 conv. single family mortgages 5.25-11%, 23 yrs. aver. to maturity	200M (200%)	150%

Institution	Date	Amount	Rate	Denomination	Maturity	Call	Collateral	Collateral Amount	%
Home Savings & Loan Association, California	23 June 77	200M	7.25%	10,000 (1,000 increments)	15 June 82 (approx. 5 yrs)	callable 15 Dec. 81	15,000 conv. single family mortgages 7.25-9%, 10-27 yrs. to maturity, 4+ yrs. since origination	350M (175%)	150%
Guarantee Savings & Loan Association, California	7 Mar. 78	50M	8.45%	10,000 (1,000 increments)	1 Mar. 84 (approx. 6 years)	callable 1 Mar. 84	3,900 Conventional 1-4 family mortgages 8%, 7+ years aver. since origination, largest $75,000	90M (180%)	150%
American Savings & Loan Association, California	13 Apr. 78	200M	8.5%	10,000	15 Apr. 84 (approx. 6 years)	callable 15 Apr. 83	9,100 Conventional 1-4 family mortgages, 8.5-8.75% at least one year old, after collateralization GNMA pass-throughs FHLMC participation certificates	350M (175%)	150%
Talman Federal Savings & Loan Association of Chicago	13 Apr. 78	40M	8.375%	10,000 (1,000 increments)	15 Apr. 83 (approx. 5 years)	callable 15 Oct. 82	GNMA modified pass-through securities	60M (150%)	125%

borrowing with an original maturity in excess of one year was also rescinded. Associations were also permitted to sell loans with recourse without limit but with the requirement that net worth levels of 2 percent of recourse liabilities be maintained. Documentation procedures governing purchase of participation interests in loan pools were also amended by removing the restrictions on eligible originators/ servicers of loans. The requirements that the loans be collateralized by first liens on real estate and the periodic reporting to participants regarding the principal balance of the loans in the pool was also eliminated. These amendments to the borrowing regulations governing savings and loan associations are largely a reflection of and a response to the fact that, under current market conditions, savings and loan associations will have to resort to greater financial leveraging through the use of nondeposit sources of funds.

Given the earnings demise of the thrift industry during 1979-82, concerns about the capital adequacy of current reserves and net worth positions have necessitated the regulatory authorities to devise means of bolstering the sagging capital position of the thrift industry. These measures, together with some of the salient proposals, will be discussed more fully in Chapter XIII.

Chapter IX

Supervisory Reports and Examinations

The FDIC, FSLIC, and State Banking Departments are all concerned with supervision, as well as regulation. The terms supervision and regulation, it should be noted parenthetically, are often used synonymously, but their meanings are quite distinct at times. Supervision, according to Crosse: "is primarily concerned with the soundness of a banking institution; its policies and practices which, while conforming strictly to law may still be so risky as to imperil the safety of the depositors." Regulation, on the other hand, "is a matter of law, its interpretation and enforcement."[1]

There is considerable overlapping of supervisory and regulatory authority among the various supervisory agencies. As a matter of practice, however, both the federal and state agencies have instituted procedures which clearly divide areas of responsibility and greatly reduce problems of overlapping authority inherent on the supervisors.

STRUCTURE

Savings and loan associations, federally chartered by the FHLBB, are supervised theoretically by the FHLBB and the FSLIC. State-chartered

[1] Crosse, Howard, "Bank Supervision—Quality and Quantity," *Bankers Magazine,* Spring 1975, page 62.

S&Ls are under the jurisdiction of the state banking department and
the FSLIC if they are insured by the latter. Those institutions which
are not covered by FSLIC are wholly supervised by the state banking
department. Previous to November 1978, mutual banks were state-
chartered and, hence, were also subject to supervison by state authorities. With regard to federal regulation, the latter institutions are under
the virtual exclusive domain of the FDIC, if they are insured by them.
Indeed, the statistics at the end of 1982 reveal that there were 109
mutual banks or approximately 24.4 percent of the savings banks not
under supervisory jurisdiction of any federal agency.

The principal role of the FDIC and FSLIC in the supervisory scenario is related to the indirect chartering of savings institutions, and
the supervisory and regulatory powers contained in the provision of
insurance protection to member institutions. As insurers of banks
and S&Ls, these two regulatory institutions were, as was necessary,
granted the power to "inspect their risk." Such authority was essential to ensure that the risks of these corporations were confined within
the magnitude of their financial resources. In 1979, for example, the
Division of Bank Supervision of the FDIC accounted for almost 75
percent of the Corporation's personnel.

An application for Federal Insurance coverage by the FSLIC and
FDIC requires an investigation by these institutions and the approval
of their respective Board of Directors. In evaluating an application,
the FDIC, for example, takes into consideration the financial history
and condition of the bank, the adequacy of its capital structure, future
earnings prospects, the general character of its management, the convenience and needs of the community to be served by the bank, and
whether or not its corporate powers are consistent with the purposes
of the Federal Deposit Insurance Act.

It is very unlikely that a state charter will be granted without FDIC
insurance certification. The FDIC Board is also required to determine
on the basis of an examination that the banks' assets in excess of its
capital requirements are adequate to meet all of its reported liabilities
to depositors and other creditors. The capital adequacy test may be
more severe than that stipulated by State Law or required by the
State Chartering Agency. Investigations by the FDIC and FSLIC are
usually undertaken in conjunction with the assistance of the state-
chartering agency.

The State Banking Department is largely responsible for the direct
chartering of banks and savings and loan associations which desire
such chartering and for their supervision and regulation in accordance
with state statutes delineating the powers and limitations applicable

to state banks. While chartering and certification for insurance qualification status may be viewed as the initial stage for supervision and regulation by the State Banking Departments and the FSLIC and FDIC, respectively, the greater proportion of supervisory activity lies in the day-to-day operations of banks and savings and loan associations. A monitoring of these operations is usually undertaken at specified time intervals.

REPORTS AND EXAMINATIONS

Vital information in preparing supervisory functions is acquired by the FDIC, FSLIC, and the State Banking Department from reports and examinations. The submission of balance sheets by banks and S&Ls at regular intervals is a fundamental requirement entrenched in the supervisory mechanism. Historically, however, it was soon found that such reports were not adequate in terms of comprehensiveness to enable the regulators and supervisors to effectively monitor bank activity. Hence, bank examiners were employed to make personal inspections of the banks, their records and operations by means of regular visits to these institutions as representatives of public authority. At the conclusion of each visit, the information obtained was condensed and presented in a form denoted as the Bank Examination Report.

For all supervisory agencies, both federal and state, the Report of Condition that is, the balance sheet of the bank, is the primary source of information. Basically, this report specifies the assets, the liabilities, the reserves and the capital accounts of the financial institution at a particular point in time. A similar report known as the Report of Income is also compiled by the supervisory agency and reflects information on income, expenses, changes in capital accounts, reserves, etc., over a given fiscal period, usually a year. Both these reports are further supported by ancillary documents which provide greater detailed information on various individual items in the summarized reports. For example, great attention is often paid in the Condition Reports to the types of loans that the particular bank or saving and loan association holds.

In order to facilitate comparison of data collected by the three supervisory agencies, the latter agencies work in conjunction on the design and format of the various forms and in the setting of dates on which the examinations are to be undertaken in order to offset "window-dressing" practices by reporting banks and saving and loan associations. These supervisory agencies have implemented a system of calling for condition reports as of a date prior to the normal time of the call and not at regular intervals, in order to arrive at a more accurate representation of the banks' condition.

Any evaluation of the banks' or S&Ls' financial condition can only be meaningful if the balance sheet information is typical of the banks' condition during the period of the report. If items have been adjusted for the purpose of "window-dressing," the report, in such a situation does not reflect the reality of the financial institution's condition. As a further deterrent to such "window-dressing," the supervisory agency also requires information relating to daily averages of total loans and total loans for a specified period terminating with the report date.

In recent years, the federal supervisory agencies have adopted the use of two surprise calls for a Report of Condition of each year in addition to obtaining mid-year and year-end reports. In this way, some sort of systematic statistical reporting is achieved and aids in the formulation of "benchmark" data.

The Condition Report has also been of significance in the computation of Federal Deposit Insurance Assessments. The format and manner in which deposits and other related items are reported in order to determine the "assessment base" is stipulated by the FDIC Act and the FSLIC Act. All insured institutions are required to provide these corporations with a signed copy of the Condition Report. Twice each year these institutions are also required to file with the FDIC/FSLIC a certified statement which illustrates the "average assessment base" and the amount of the semi-annual assessment due to the corporation for deposit insurance.

As a result of the information collected by the Report of Condition and Income, various statistical abstracts are published by the FDIC/FSLIC for analytical and comparative purposes. These abstracts enable the comparisons of banks, S&L operations in each state and also within smaller geographical boundaries.

Data relating to deposit structure, and so on, necessary for the conduct of supervisory activity are readily available from these statistical compilations published by the FDIC.

PURPOSE OF EXAMINATIONS

A bank examination is an attempt to appraise the quality of bank management in the total setting of its operations. The primary purpose is to ascertain whether banks are complying with the law and whether they are operating soundly and are in good financial condition. Each agency applies essentially the same standards, although they may be differently expressed as, for example, in matters relating to the determination of capital adequacy. In essence, examination is a fact-finding procedure. If serious problems are revealed in the course of an examination, they are generally referred to a higher authority for remedial action. Obtaining corrective action promptly is the heart of the supervisory function. The efficacy of the supervision function, however, is greatly dependent on the quality of bank examiners and senior supervisory personnel.

In the course of the examination, attention is focused on many different matters of a highly specific nature, such as ceilings on the amount of credit extended to an individual borrower, technical deficiencies in the documentation of loan, and so on.

As mentioned, the main source of reference from which the Bank Examination Report is developed is the particular bank's balance sheet. Initially, the examiners extract information on the liabilities of the bank, their nature, scope, and extent. "The examiner's act is knowing where and how far to carry any verification process, and often may involve the verification of balances due to individual depositors."[2] Auditing enables the supervisory agency to verify the accuracy of all accounts. An audit also allows the detection of any existing irregularities. Internal operations are also reviewed to determine whether acceptable safeguards are followed in the processing of work and in the distribution of responsibilities among employees.

Another major aspect of the bank/S&L examination process involves the determination of the magnitude and quality of the S&L or banks' assets. Cash counting, verification of the authenticity of securities are all part of this process. These assets are also appraised with regard to their ability to generate cash, in order to enable the examiner to arrive at some conclusion as to the strength/weakness of the banks' asset structure.

Assessment of the capital adequacy is the crucial test for appraising the financial condition of the institution under examination. The "capital margin" denotes the amount of funds held in reserve accounts and is determined by subtracting the total liabilites as ascertained by the examiner from the appraised value of the assets. Assuming the book values for these items are correct, then the capital margin is the sum of the capital stock, surplus, undivided profits and reserves.

[2] Golembe, *Federal Regulation of Banking.*

This margin is usually expressed as a percentage of total assets and its adequacy assessed by comparison with other institutions of similar size and characteristics.

Should the examination procedure disclose some likelihood of capital inadequacy, if the situation cannot be remedied or augmented by further capitalizations, the bank or S&L faces the possibility of failure. The examination report thus becomes a source of information regarding problems, as well as a guide for remedial actions. In general, most financial institutions measure up to an acceptable standard of operation in their daily activities. Supervision is thus largely confined to remedial efforts, introduced to correct a few special problems and to avoid potentially greater problems in the future. More recently, too, there has been a marked trend toward examination of policy and process, management techniques, objectives, and so on rather than emphasizing financial ratios, assets, and other numerical indices. While such undertakings are highly subjective, it affords the examination authorities a more balanced perspective of the general direction and thrust of the particular financial institutions.

FREQUENCY AND TIMING OF REPORTS

Mutual banks and savings and loan associations are usually examined on an ad-hoc time schedule rather than at some specified point in time. The act of bank examination calls for great ingenuity in timing in order to overcome the problem of banks "window-dressing" their operations before a known examination date.[3]

All supervisory authorities require at least one examination annually, though the frequency of such examinations may be increased if the bank or savings and loan association is deemed to be a problem one. Given the increase in the number of failures over 1981-83, examination's schedules have been further reinforced. The FDIC, as of January 1984, recorded 631 banks on its problem list in comparison to 369 in 1982. Banks on the problem list, have been assigned a rating of four or five on the FDIC's scale of one to five representing good or poor condition respectively. Banks with the greatest likelihood of failure are rated five, while those with serious financial/operational

---

[3] Ibid.

shortcomings are assigned a rating of four. Of the 14,674 banks insured by the FDIC as of January 1984, 86.6 percent were considered sound and in good condition by the FDIC.

Periodically, too, without advance notice, savings and loan associations are examined and audited at random either by the FSLIC or FHLB examiners.

Although over the years each state supervisory authority has developed its own supervisory procedures, at the present time there is considerable uniformity in supervisory procedures due largely to the fact that virtually all S&Ls or mutual banks are insured by the FSLIC and FDIC respectively and, hence, fall under the supervisory jurisdiction of these two agencies, as far as insurance regulations are concerned.

TRUSTEE EXAMINATIONS–SAVINGS BANKS

Although mutual savings banks are also supervised by the supervisory agencies described above, because of the nature of their organization and operational characteristics, the mutual savings bank industry has a "built-in" supervisory structure, inherent particularly in the "mutuality" characteristic and trustee management system.

In keeping with the trustee system on which these institutions operate, a Board of Trustees has responsibility for the formulation of bank policy and the supervision of all bank activities. The boards of trustees are in most states legally limited in terms of size and composition. Through the establishment of various committees, these "trustees" are able to monitor the internal operations of savings banks. Furthermore, by periodic examinations, these trustees are able to determine the solvency and financial standing of the bank and whether there are any foreseeable difficulties likely to develop. In this way through trustee supervision, an internal checking system is instituted to ensure and preserve the viability of the particular bank.

Apart from the internal auditing functions by the trustee, external auditing may also be performed by selected individuals from outside the banks' management system. Such individuals are usually of high public stature and integrity and are normally experienced in the essentials of bank management. In addition, external auditor functions further provide the opportunity for irregularities and problems to be identified and the necessary remedial action adopted.

These examinations may also be frequent, depending on the type of problem to be resolved and its potential effect on the financial community in general.

Membership in the FHLB System

The office of Examinations and Supervision is the agency within the FHLB system which is responsible for the periodic and (when necessary) ad hoc supervisory examinations of all federal savings and loan associations, state chartered associations with FSLIC account insurance coverage, and members of the Federal Home Loan Bank System.

Table IX-1 depicts the total membership in the FHLB System with a breakdown by type of institutions. As of December 31, 1982, 3,571 institutions were under the direct regulation and supervision of the Federal Home Loan Bank Board, declining from over 4,200 in 1981, largely as a result of mergers.

In essence, the Office of Examinations monitors the operations of savings and loan associations with a view to ensuring adherence to the statutes and regulations and that the particular savings and loan association is operating on "sound and safe banking standards." Recently, attention has also been directed to the areas of the protection

Table IX-1   Membership of the FHLB System at Year-End 1982

Bank District	Savings and Loan Associations Insured by FSLIC			Other State- chartered	Mutual Savings Banks	Life Insurance Companies	Total Member- ship
	Total Number	Federally- chartered	State- chartered				
Boston	141	62	41	38	77	—	218
New York	241	104	136	1	35	—	276
Pittsburgh	260	109	134	17	3	—	263
Atlanta	533	380	152	1	—	—	533
Cincinnati	430	236	172	22	—	1	431
Indianapolis	181	119	62	—	—	1	182
Chicago	388	160	228	—	3	—	391
Des Moines	217	123	93	1	—	—	217
Little Rock	541	187	354	—	—	—	541
Topeka	193	105	88	—	—	—	193
San Francisco	186	68	118	—	—	—	186
Seattle	127	77	50	—	—	—	140
Total	3,438	1,730	1,628	80	131	2	3,571

Source: Federal Home Loan Bank Board.

of consumer rights, such as nondiscrimination in lending, truth in lending and equal opportunity for the granting of credit.

Tables IX-2 and IX-3 provide some data on the examination activities of the FHLBB Supervisory Office for the years 1975, 1976, and 1977. The data reflects the fact that notwithstanding the substantial increase in dollar volume of assets examined, there was no noteworthy increase in the number of overdue examinations. The examination review system has also been upgraded to improve efficiency and to standardize examination procedures.

One noteworthy aspect of FHLBB Supervision recently has been the use of R-memos and whether their use constitutes "rulemaking or not."

According to the Annotated Manual published by the FHLBB, "As of July 4, 1967, this office (Examinations and Supervision) is adopting a new general memoranda series bearing the letter prefix "R." This series of memorando will cover instructions to the staff and Supervisory Agents relating to rules and regulations, interpreta-

Table IX-2   Supervisory Examinations: Number of Examinations and Asset Volume Examined, by Asset Size Class, Calendar Years 1975, 1976, and 1977

Asset size (in millions)	Number of examinations			Assets examined (in millions)		
	1975	1976	1977	1975	1976	1977
Federal and State-chartered, OES examined:						
Under $5	123	89	76	455	317	264
5-10	197	151	122	1,564	1,165	919
10-25	511	433	409	9,462	7,336	7,135
25-50	507	450	421	18,591	16,283	15,586
50-100	378	388	387	26,841	27,309	27,389
Over $100	408	437	504	116,691	128,951	160,405
Total	2,124	1,948	1,919	173,604	181,361	211,698
State-chartered, joint examined:						
Under $5	106	86	69	345	274	219
5-10	180	136	141	1,347	1,001	1,048
10-25	405	364	325	6,775	6,200	5,571
25-50	335	308	310	11,837	11,171	11,166
50-100	192	219	234	14,568	15,340	16,043
Over $100	188	209	258	64,709	69,429	82,603
Total	1,405	1,322	1,337	99,581	102,415	116,650
Total examinations	3,530	3,270	3,256	$273,185	$284,776	$328,348

Table IX-3 Supervisory Examinations: Average Time Per Examination and
Per $1 Million of Assets by Asset Size Class, Calendar Years 1975, 1976, and 1977

Asset size (in millions)	Working days per examination			Working days per $1 million of assets		
	1975	1976	1977	1975	1976	1977
Federal and State-chartered, OES examined:						
Under $5	13.8	13.8	15.6	3.7	3.9	4.5
5-10	14.0	15.0	15.6	1.8	1.9	2.1
10-25	19.0	19.6	20.2	1.0	1.2	1.2
25-50	27.6	26.5	27.6	0.8	0.7	0.8
50-100	37.5	36.1	37.8	0.5	0.5	0.5
Over $100	61.2	62.6	67.7	0.2	0.2	0.2
Average	31.7	33.5	37.4	0.4	0.4	0.3
State-chartered, joint examined:						
Under $5	8.6	9.7	9.2	2.6	3.1	2.9
5-10	10.6	10.7	11.8	1.4	1.5	1.6
10-25	13.7	14.8	15.3	0.8	0.9	0.9
25-50		20.2	20.4	0.6	0.6	0.6
50-100		27.7	27.3	0.4	0.4	0.4
Over $100		57.8	57.2	0.2	0.2	0.2
Average	22.3	24.2	26.0	0.3	0.3	0.3
Average of all	28.0	29.8	32.7	0.4	0.3	0.3

tions and opinions, statements of policy and other matters that will affect any member of the public. The new series will cover matters to be made available to members of the public under the Public Information Act of 1966, Part 505 of the Board's General Regulations and any future expression of Board Policy implementing the Act . . . ." Compliance with the Public Information Act of 1966 requires the government agency to inform the general public about agency ground rules, including areas which previously were not revealed.

However, one analyst (Business Lawyer 7/78) was of the opinion that the use of "R-Memos" as "law" is not authorized by Congressional sanction. As such, they should not be used by the FHLBB and its staff as a means of unofficial "rule-making." An R-Memo—according to the above writer—does not have the "force and effect of regulatory law."[4]

"The problem which results from R-Memos and similar pronounce-

[4] *Business Lawyer*, 7/78.

ments is that field examiners cite them and rely on them when indicating to savings and loan association officers what they should do or must do in order to comply with Bank Board regulations."[5]

Enforcement powers of the FHLBB and other regulatory agencies range from "moral suasion," and other precatory recommendations, to more stringent measures such as cease and desist orders, revocation of charters, termination of Federal Insurance coverage, penalties and fines.

Any bank regulatory authority has the basic power, if it is also a chartering body, to suspend the operations of a bank and revoke its charter. Such a step, though, is usually the last resort after previous recommendations have not been heeded or effective. The financial institutions under FHLBB control, thus, face this ultimate regulatory tool. Entry and exit into the savings and loan industry is, thus, controlled in this way. In relation to exit—apart from mergers—failure of a financial institution is usually the form of exit, commanding particular FHLBB attention.

A less stringent enforcement measure has to do with cease and desist orders. Such powers were granted by the Financial Institutions Supervisory Act of 1966. Cease and desist orders may be temporary or permanent and may be issued to remedy violations of laws, rules, regulations, written conditions or agreements or to correct activities which seriously affect the future viability of the financial institution. They may also be issued against officers and employees of savings and loan associations who have been found to be in breach of trust or engaging in fraudulent activities.

The Financial Institutions Regulatory and Interest Rate Control Act of 1978 provides increased supervisory authority to the FHLB Board, particularly in relation to enforcement powers. Cease and desist orders may now be issued against individual directors, officers, employees, agents and other individuals involved in the operation of an insured institution, service corporations, savings and loan holding companies and their uninsured affiliates. Cease and desist orders prior to the Financial Institutions Regulatory Act of 1978 could only have been issued against insured institutions. Temporary orders may also now be issued to correct activities "likely to weaken the condition of an insured institution." This broadens the powers of the FHLBB in this respect, as previously such temporary action could

[5] *Ibid.*

only be taken in situations where the problem was likely to result in insolvency or substantial reduction in earnings or assets.

Penalties of up to $1000 a day may be levied against persons or entities violating a final cease and desist order. This also applies to Savings and Loan Holding Companies.

The ability of the Federal Home Loan Bank Board to use the power of Suspension and Removal of individual officers and directors has also been extended.

In general, though, the problems encountered in the day-to-day operations of savings and loan associations do not require remedial action such as those previously described. Rather, the normal situation is one where the supervisory agency advises the savings and loan association of a particular problem and the necessary corrective action to be taken. Should the savings and loan association ignore the recommendations, the FHLBB may place the particular association on the "problem list." Such a possibility is usually in cases of minor problems, an adequate deterrent to a savings and loan association to adopt the suggested recommendations, as a "problem list" institution faces increased and more frequent examinations. Most institutions prefer not to have examiners constantly delving into their daily operations and activities.

Membership in the FHLBB system also procures the right or ability to borrow from the regional FHLB, should the necessity for such action arise.

Institutions which are not members of the FHLB system may also borrow from the Federal Home Loan Bank if they are in the home financing business and under the supervision of a governmental agency. Such loans are made on a secured basis, with FHA loans as the only acceptable collateral. As would be expected, the rate of interest charged on these advances is usually (½%-1%) higher than the rate charged to members.

Most of the FHLB regional banks establish lines of credit for their members, upon which associations may draw from time to time. Special approval is usually required for advances in excess of the established line of credit. The Federal Home Loan Bank may also, in response to monetary and home financing conditions in particular, impose special conditions governing the use and the volume of advances a member savings and loan may obtain. The Federal Home Loan Bank, thus, provides liquidity to members and nonmembers to meet seasonal demands or unusually heavy withdrawals and also provides an additional source of long-term funds for home-financing purposes.

OVERVIEW

Recently, there has been some concern about the lack of uniformity in regulatory practices by the various supervisory agencies and also suggestions that perhaps there is a need for consolidation of the whole regulatory process and structure. In fact, the FIRICA Act of 1978 established the Financial Institutions Examination Council to promote uniformity in the examination policies and procedures of regulatory agencies.

A report by the General Accounting Office released in January 1981[6] asserted that there was a need for greater uniformity in the examination practices of the five regulatory agencies. In addition, the report noted that "We have been unable to find any clear Congressional mandate stating that regulators should promote sound management practices. The law, instead, appears to stress a supervisory role that focuses on the correction of unsafe and unsound practices." The Report suggested that Congress should address the question as to the extent that an examiner should go in influencing management decision-making at financial institutions. While examinations assess an institution's condition based on traditional solvency and liquidity criteria, current procedures also involve evaluations of the adequacy of an institution's administration and operational policies, management decisions and various management controls. Emphasis on management policy appeared to be stressed more by the Bank Board, NCUA and the Comptroller's Office. The FDIC and FSLIC, however, while concerned with management issues in general, adopt the posture that the "money-making aspects of banking are essentially matters for bank management rather than bank supervisors. For the Bank Supervisor or Examiner to intrude into the details of this aspect of banking is to encroach seriously upon the prerogative of bank management."[7]

The report suggests that the Examination Council should consider in detail the benefits of the examination policies adopted by the Bank Board, NCUA, and the Comptroller. Given the scarcity of financial and personnel resources, a policy trend of increasing examination of areas traditionally within the domain of management must be assessed against the potential costs and benefits of such a posture.

[6] General Accounting Office, "Federal Examinations of Financial Institutions: Issues that Need to be Resolved."

[7] *Savings and Loan Reporter,* Volume 5, Number 39. 1/30/81, page 3.

As Table IX-4 illustrates, the cost of financial intermediary supervision has increased markedly since 1978, reaching over an estimated $1.5 billion in 1981. This figure, however, does not include the estimated $3.2 billion which federal regulators provided in support of troubled institutions, in particular the thrift industry in 1981-82. The estimated cost of supervision and regulation provided above, no doubt, raises questions about the cost effectiveness of the regulatory mechanism and whether ultimately these costs lead to higher payments by individuals for the services financial institutions provide.

Indeed, the effectiveness of financial intermediaries is dependent, in such a highly regulated environment, on the quality and efficiency of federal and state supervision. As financial institutions become increasingly homogenous in terms of services offered, it may be cost effective to undertake consolidation of the supervisory and regulatory apparatus, more so given the current "spirit of deregulation." These and other issues will, no doubt, be debated by Congress and will require cognizance of the need for flexibility in adjusting the regulatory framework to a rapidly changing and innovative financial system. The Task Group on Regulation of Financial Services headed by Vice President George Bush proposed in January 1984 definitive changes in supervisory responsibility for the banking industry. Specifically, the Plan would recommend the transferral of the supervisory authority of the FDIC to the Federal Reserve, thus giving the latter agency supervisory authority over the nation's state banks. The Plan also proposes the creation of a new Federal Banking Commission which

Table IX-4   The Cost of Financial Intermediary Supervision, 1978-1981
$000

Agency	1978	1980	1981*
State Supervisors	89,825	97,410	104,228
Comptroller of the Currency	91,119	113,122	127,046
Federal Reserve System	485,545	613,962	675,445
Federal Home Loan Bank System	102,392	107,100	141,419
National Credit Union Administration	42,757	75,028	134,020
FSLIC	70,191[1]	322,918	223,956
FDIC	104,893[2]	116,597	131,046
Total	1,021,260	1,422,137	1,530,352

Source: Adapted from *United States Banker,* July 1981, page 20.

[1] Does not include assets acquired and loans to insured institutions for 1980 and 1981.

[2] Excludes provision for loss on capital investments in insured banks, funded through the insurance fund.

*Estimated.

would replace the Office of the Comptroller which currently regulates national banks. State Bank regulatory agencies would also be required to obtain federal certification of supervisory activities. It remains to be seen whether Congressional action will be taken on the final recommendations of the Bush task force, given the recognized need for streamlining and restructuring the bank supervisory mechanism.

PART THREE

OPERATION

Chapter X

General Powers by Charter—
Corporate Organization

Basically, as promulgated by the FHLBB regulations, the objectives of a savings and loan association are to promote thrift by the provision of a convenient and safe method for individuals to save and invest money, as well as the provision of financing for home acquisition. These activities should be undertaken in such a manner as to provide for the solvency, safety, and security of the association and its members. The operation of an association along these guidelines is usually effected through the establishment of a Board of Directors responsible for the functioning of the association as a corporate entity and organization.

Before discussing the corporate organization of an association, some of the general powers by charter of a savings and loan association which are identical in many instances to the powers exercised by mutual savings banks are presented next.

Savings and loan associations have the authority to act as fiscal agents of the U.S. Treasury and any other instrumentality as designated. In the conduct of business, savings and loan associations may adopt bylaws and rules and regulations not inconsistent with the Constitution and general laws of the nations. Savings and loan associations may have a corporate seal, sue and be sued and partake in any legal matters in courts of law or equity.

Any association may raise capital which is unlimited in magnitude by accepting payments on savings accounts representing share interests in the association. An association may issue such passbooks, time certificates of deposit, or other savings accounts as authorized. Holders of savings accounts are ipso facto members of the association and have certain voting rights. Savings and loan associations may borrow money, lend and otherwise invest its funds, purchase, hold and convey real and personal estate consistent with its objectives, purposes, and powers. Associations may dissolve, wind up, merge, convert, consolidate, reorganize as stipulated by charter regulations. Savings and loan associations may issue notes, bonds, debentures, or other obligations or securities as authorized by the Federal Home Loan Bank Board. In addition to powers to mortgage, or lease any real and personal estate and to accept gifts, savings and loan associations are also empowered to undertake activities which are "reasonably incidental" to the achievement of its stipulated goals and objectives.

Having briefly examined the general powers by charter of an association/bank, such powers are divested through the formation of a Board of Directors.

An association, according to Board regulations, shall be under the direction of a Board of Directors of not less than 5 nor more than 15 as fixed in the association's bylaws, or in the absence of any such bylaw provision as determined by resolution of the association's members.

All directors of the association must be members of the association and shall cease to be director upon termination of his membership. Directors shall be elected by members by ballot. Directors are elected for terms of three years and until their successors are elected and qualified, but provision is made for the annual election of approximately one-third of the Board of Directors. In the event of a vacancy, including vacancies created by an increase by vote of the members of the association of the number of directors within the limits specified, the Board of Directors may fill the vacancy, if the members do not, by electing a director to serve until the next annual general meeting, at which time a director will be elected to fill the vacancy for the unexpired term.

The Board of Directors shall elect a president, one or more vice presidents, a secretary, and a treasurer. Additional officers may also be appointed as necessary from time to time. The offices of secretary and treasurer may be held by the same person and a vice president may also be either the secretary or the treasurer. All officers are elected for a period of one year or until their successors are elected and qualified. Any officer may be removed at any time by the Board of Directors.

The ultimate responsibility of a bank director is to direct the affairs of the bank for the benefit of its depositors, shareholders, and the general public in such a manner consonant to the preservation of the safe and sound conduct of such activities. A bank director in accepting such responsibility is bound by the existing laws, the bank's charter and its bylaws in the performance of his duties. Indeed, there is a whole gamut of laws, regulatory rulings, proceedings, and court decisions which define the legal responsibilities of bank directors. It has been argued that bank directors are primarily guided in the interpretation of these guidelines by "reasonable discretion."

A bank Board of Directors is charged with the overall responsibility for the selection and retention of an adept management team of competent executive officers.

The practical necessity of delegating operational responsibilities to an executive management does not, however, abrogate the Board of Directors' responsibility to retain and exercise general supervision over the affairs of the particular institution. It is the responsibility of the directors to oversee the performance of executive officers in order to ensure that the Board's policies are being undertaken in an efficient manner and to take corrective action if deemed necessary.

A bank director is also responsible for providing the operational mangement of the bank with a set of guidelines, objectives, and policies within which the management team is expected to operate. The Board should provide the bank management with clearly elucidated policies covering all areas of the banks' operation, in particular a precise lending policy governing risk levels and loan ceilings, supervision of pricing policy in a general sense to avoid favoritism, and the formulation and monitoring of an effective investment strategy. The key here is the adoption and construction of sound policies. Internal control and auditing policies are extremely important to the effective functioning of the Board of Directors. The banks' audit program, responsibility and authority of the auditor, job rotation and audits by independent outside auditors in addition to comprehensive verification programs are vital to the effective performance of the banks' internal control and monitoring systems.

In order to ensure and facilitate the smooth succession of management and personnel, the Directors should ensure that an adequate personnel policy is established which provides equal employment opportunities to all employees as dictated by law. Training and career advancement programs should be an integral part of personnel policy.

Because of the complex regulatory machinery under which banks and other financial institutions operate, bank directors should ensure the particular institution functions in full compliance with the laws and regulations governing banking. More recently, consumer legislation such as Truth in Lending, the Fair Credit Billing Practices Act, the Real Estate Settlement Practices Act, and State Truth in Savings legislation should be adhered to and publicized to all members of the bank.

A bank director's position requires regular attendance at Board meetings in order that the director may be aware of all noteworthy matters affecting the operation of the bank. The law requires that these meetings be held at least once per month. Such meetings provide the opportunity for the review and establishment of policy and the endorsement of actions undertaken by operating mangement given access to all the relevant information.

Several state banking laws, such as those of New York, require the examination by a committee of nonoffice directors assisted, if necessary, by qualified independent accountants. Such an examination is undertaken at least once a year for the purpose of determining the banks' financial condition and reviewing its loan, investment, audit and control policies. Special attention should be given to the loans made to officers of directors. The directors' report of examination should be presented to the Board of Directors at the next regular meeting after completion of the examination. Such a report should be sworn to by the directors and be placed on file in the bank and be available to bank regulatory agencies if required.

Every bank director should cooperate with bank regulatory authorities and be cognizant of pertinent suggestions by banking regulators on the operations of the particular bank. Personal liability for losses resulting from negligence may occur if directors do not take into consideration the recommendations of the supervisory authorities.

In view of the fact that since 1960, of 107 bank closings, abusive insider transactions were responsible for 62 of these failures; such transactions should not be tolerated by a bank's Board of Directors. Any transaction between a bank and an insider which results in a more favorable situation to the insider than a comparable transaction with a noninsider would, should be eschewed and is an unsound banking practice.

The Financial Institutions Regulatory and Interest Rate Control Act of 1978 limits loans to banks' insiders and prohibits preferential loans. Recently in October 1982, the Federal Home Loan Bank

Board proposed more flexible conflict of interest regulations. In general, the conflict of interest rules are designed to restrict transactions that might be overly beneficial for an affiliated person, but not in the best interests of the particular institutions. The Board proposals would liberalize the definition of "affiliated person" to exclude limited partnerships. The change would enable a loan to be made to a firm even if one of the savings and loan association's directors was engaged in a limited partnership that procured less than 10 percent of the partnership's profits.

In addition, the proposals include a prohibition on kickbacks and unearned fees to all services offered by an insured institution and not only to loan transactions. The aggregate loan limit for home improvement, education, overdraft, consumer and credit card loans made to affiliated persons would also be increased to $100,000. The current requirement that two-thirds of an association's directors should be from outside the institution would be changed instead to a regulatory ratio which requires only that the majority of the directors are from outside the association. Because of the recent increase in voluntary mergers, many associations have argued that the previous two-thirds requirement had the effect of making the boards unnecessarily large.

Finally, the proposals authorize supervisory agents to disapprove certain transactions involving affiliated persons where the supervisory agent determines that the transactions are "not fair to or not in the best interests of the insured institution."

Banks' directors are also responsible for the general overseeing of trust departments. A bank's Board of Directors is particularly responsible for supervising a trust department and ensuring that there exist sound trust policies and practices, given the existing legal framework. Negligence on the part of directors which results in losses to Trust beneficiaries can lead to personal liability on the part of the director, a surcharge to the bank and detrimental publicity.

Banks are chartered, in conclusion, to serve the needs of the community in which they operate and, hence, ultimately bank directors have a responsibility to ensure that the banking needs of the community are being adequately serviced. In the final analysis, the success of the Board of Directors will be reflected in the ability of the bank to nurture balanced, sustainable levels of economic activity through the effective provision of financial services and the allocation of credit resources. Such an undertaking effectively expedited can have significant effects on the community in particular and pervasive benefits to the economy in general.

SPECIFIC CUSTOMER TRANSACTIONS

Savings Bonds, Traveller's Checks, and Safe Deposit Boxes

Savings and loan associations, mutual savings banks and commercial banks are all authorized to act as agents of the government in the sale of savings bonds, to deal in traveller's checks and in the provision of safe deposit boxes.

As a means of fostering savings, these financial institutions offer United States Savings Bonds in various denominations which can be liquidated at the current yield, should a saver decide to do so. These instruments provide a stable return and there are virtually no risks involved in holding these securities.

Ancillary to its principal activities and for the convenience of its members and others, a federal association may provide for the sale of checks, including traveller's checks and money orders on which the drawee is a Federal Home Loan Bank, commercial bank or other financial institution engaged in the business of handling such instruments.

Banks also provide safe deposit facilities, renting vaults, safe deposit boxes and other receptacles upon premises occupied by the bank on terms and conditions stipulated by the particular institution. FHLBB guidelines in T-Memo No. 33 in 1968 states that there will be no objection to any program whereby any insured institution provides free or discount safe deposit facilities to its members.

Extended Powers—Life Insurance and Trust Activities

A federal savings and loan association has no power to engage in the insurance business or to present itself to the public as/or operate as a general insurance agent. However, in connection with savings accounts and loan prepayment plans, a federal savings and loan association may enter into a contract with an insurance company to insure the lives and health of its members and may charge the lawful premium rate from members participating in the plan. Savings and commercial banks also offer this type of insurance facility. In addition, federal savings banks and associations may procure these services through service corporations which are wholly owned subsidiaries of the particular financial institution. General and casualty insurance plans are usually offered through these service corporations.

Savings and loan associations, savings and commercial banks also offer a variety of trust accounts ranging from irrevocable trusts, testamentary accounts, to accounts of executor or administrators.

MISCELLANEOUS OTHER FUNCTIONS

Several other (recent) customer transactions have been undertaken by savings and loan associations and other financial institutions. These range from NOW accounts, telephone bill paying, telephone transfer, automated clearing house, remote service units, automated teller machines, credit cards, and debit cards.

NOW accounts were first popular in Massachusetts and New Hampshire, but a 1979 legislative ruling allowed banks, credit unions, and savings and loan associations nationwide to offer these interest-bearing checking accounts. Most banks have instituted minimum balance requirements or a monthly service charge in lieu of the former.

Telephone bill paying is now offered by several financial institutions. Operating costs and the capital outlay for devices to lower these costs are fostering the use of service bureaus to handle telephone bill paying operations.

Telephone transfer has been offered by associations to businesses as a way to earn interest on short-term excess funds. Associations usually specify minimum account balance and minimum transfer amounts, often charging no fee. Such accounts average about 2 percent of total deposits of associations offering this service. Banks, since 1973, have also been able to offer a similar service. The service is also offered to individuals with minimum balance, as well as transfer amount.

Automated clearing house facilities, while allowing national transfers to be more easily effected, have not been fully utilized by savings and loan associations. Clearing is done by electronic messages and not on pieces of paper. Initial studies indicate use of the service to be low, about 0.03 percent of the total check volume.

Remote service units and automated teller machines are more popular with banks than with savings and loan associations. Credit and debit card systems linked to savings accounts in associations are still in their formative period and may prove popular and profitable in the future. In fact, as of 7/10/80, legislative amendments adopted provide the authority for Federal Savings and Loan Associations and their subsidiaries to undertake credit card operations. Recently, too, savings and loan associations and mutual banks have gone into leasing operations and in the provision of brokerage/money market fund services.

Chapter XI

The Deposit Function

ACCOUNT REGULATION—SAVINGS ACCOUNTS AND TYPES

Historically, savings accounts of savings and loan associations were of the share type, whereby members contracted to deposit a certain amount of funds over a specified time period. With the increasing sophistication concomitant with the development of services in response to the community needs, the number and type of savings accounts have been significantly expanded.

Contemporarily, savings and loan associations offer a variety of savings accounts to meet the diverse needs of its customers, ranging from the traditional passbook savings account to the more sophisticated money market deposit account. A brief description of some types of accounts follows.

Types of Savings Accounts

The passbook savings account is the basic type of savings plan offered by S&Ls, mutual banks, and commercial banks. This type of account allows a depositor a significant degree of flexibility in making deposits and withdrawals at any time. A fixed rate of interest is paid on balances held in this account over a stipulated time period. It should be noted that while dejure, depositors are required to give at least 30 days' notice prior to a withdrawal, de facto this stipulation has never been evoked by savings and loan associations, mutual banks, or commercial banks. Hence, in practice, depositors have complete freedom in making withdrawals at their discretion. In terms of ownership characteristics, savings accounts may be individually held, jointly held, or held in trust for a specific beneficiary. Savings accounts may also be of the fiduciary type, opened in the name of an estate executor or administrator for a particular beneficiary. Accounts may also be opened by partnerships or corporations earning dividends from day of deposit to day of withdrawal.

Holiday Club Accounts are another variant of the basic savings account. In this instance, depositors contract to deposit sums ranging from $1.00 to $20.00 on a weekly basis with maturity at a specific time, such as Christmas, when the accumulated principal and dividends may be withdrawn. The six-month money market account introduced in May 1978 is a fixed rate certificate account with the interest rate payable tied to the average yield on six-month Treasury bills. Currently, there is no statutory minimum deposit requirement for this account; minimum balance requirements are at the sole discretion of the particular bank. The Small Saver Certificate was introduced in January, 1980, tied to the rate on 2½ year Treasury bills with no minimum balance requirement. Both the MMC and SSC have proved very popular with savers, accounting for over 50 percent of savings and loan association deposits. Accounts more recently authorized will be discussed more fully later in the chapter, particularly with reference to the actions of the Depository Institutions Deregulation Committee.

REGULATION Q—HISTORY, BACKGROUND, AND DEVELOPMENT

Against the background of the Great Depression of 1929-30 and the spectre of massive and widespread bank failures, the Banking Act of 1933 was introduced to foster and ensure the stable and secure growth of the American banking industry. It is necessary to be cognizant of these circumstances surrounding the introduction of the 1933 Act, not only in terms of its historical perspective but also in order to appreciate the rationale for the continued existence and survival of one of the most important pieces of legislation in the history of

American banking. That Regulation Q, one aspect of this legislation is now anachronistic and about to be phased out does not in any way detract from the likelihood that although the ceilings may be abolished, the underlying concept of administered rate structures may be very much a part of American banking life for some time in the future.

Under the provisions of the Banking Act of 1933, the Federal Reserve was granted the authority to regulate by imposition of ceilings the rates that could be paid by member banks on time and savings accounts. Interest payments on demand deposits were categorically prohibited. The 1933 Act was extended in 1935 to apply to the deposits of nonmember federally insured banks, whereby the Federal Deposit Insurance Corporation was empowered to set regulations synonymous with Regulation Q. Federally insured savings and loan associations were not governed by the rate ceilings until an amendment to the Federal Home Loan Bank Act was enacted in 1966.

One factor influencing the introduction of Regulation Q was the instability engendered by the volatility in "banker balances" at the time. New York "money center" banks would compete for demand balances from smaller banks in the hinterland, and these "banker's balances" would flow freely from bank to bank in response to fluctuations in interest rates being offered. The transmission of these banker's balances to the New York banks, it was felt, resulted in a depletion of funds to meet the credit needs of the local communities from which these balances emanated. Moreover, funds acquired by the New York banks in this way were being divested in loan allocations to stock and commodity speculators, activities believed to have been a contributory factor to the 1929 crash. Coupled with several liquidity crises at New York banks due to large withdrawals by local banks, there was general agreement that legal ceilings were required to control the rates that New York banks could pay for such balances.

The Federal Reserve, it should be noted, had resorted to "moral suasion" up to 1920 in trying to place informal ceilings on rates paid on these banker's balances. Another factor influencing the adoption of the 1933 Act was the rapid increase in the number of time and savings accounts relative to demand deposits. The acquisition of time accounts vis-a-vis demand deposits was more favored due to the lower reserve requirements on time and savings accounts. It was further argued that increased competition for time deposits would further inflate rates on time accounts, thus increasing the bank's cost of funds.

This latter development would result in the banks undertaking higher yield, riskier investments which could have a detrimental effect on the solvency of the particular bank and the banking system as a whole; hence the need for interest rate controls. For the next two decades, the Regulation Q limitations ostensibly fostered a steady growth in the banking system, both in terms of solvency and stability and was, in general, consonant with the banking scenario of the time. In fact, the deposit rate ceilings were little more than superfluous, when interest rates on time and savings accounts up to 1955 averaged 1.36 percent, well below the stipulated ceilings.

However, rising interest rates during the late 1950s generated widespread rethinking as to the validity of the Regulation Q ceilings. In fact, several analysts rejected as unsound the original basis for the imposition of the ceilings.

Benston in 1964 and Cox in 1966 independently examined the hypothesis that the payment of interest on demand deposits by banks resulted in the assumption of greater risks by banks than they would otherwise have undertaken and, hence, ultimately lead to failure. The statistical evidence presented by these studies does not support this contention. Moreover, the decline in the number of bank failures since 1933 cannot be attributed to the imposition of the interest rate ceilings. Available evidence demonstrates that the rate of failure of banks since 1945 was about equal for both periods when interest ceilings prevented banks from paying the higher market rates and when market rates were below the ceilings on interest rates. During the 1960s, the rapid growth in the money supply coupled with rising prices and spending resulted in higher interest rates which reflected these inflationary expectations. Market rates rose above the deposit rate ceilings and financial intermediaries were thus prohibited from paying competitive rates. The inflow of savings to these institutions declined as individuals sought investments for their savings that yielded higher returns in keeping with the general notion of capital seeking the most appropriate return in a competitive setting.

More to the point, heavy disintermediation occurred during periods of rising interest rates as individuals withdrew deposits from banks and acquired instead market instruments such as securities and later money market funds with yields above the limited deposit rates. It was not surprising that in such a situation, liquidity crises developed at some institutions and others suffered failures.

The thrift institutions were also more vulnerable to rapid increases in market interest rates. With most of their assets carried over from a lower interest period and held in long-term instruments such as mortgages, many of these institutions could not generate sufficient current earnings to pay competitive rates of interest on savings deposits. The cost of deposit funds rapidly surpassed the return to the thrifts' mortgage portfolios resulting in pressure on earnings.

It was against this financial background that the Regulation Q deposit ceilings were extended to include thrift institutions in 1966. Nevertheless, these ceilings contributed to thrift disintermediation in the late 1960s resulting in earnings and liquidity problems similar to the pre-1966 period. With the large withdrawals from the thrift institutions occasioned by rising interest rates, severe restrictions were placed on the disbursement of mortgage funds and, hence, on construction in the housing industry. Because of the limited type of assets, savings and loan associations were allowed to hold in comparison to commercial banks and the prohibition on S&Ls accepting demand deposits, Regulation Q provided for a differential of ½ percent which was later reduced to ¼ percent between the deposit rate which thrifts and commercial banks could offer respectively.

While it has been argued that a ¼ percent spread between rates offered by thrifts and commercial banks has been rendered inconsequential by current market rates and banking developments, most analysts were of the opinion that extension of thrift powers vis-a-vis commercial banks in offering demand deposits and in broader consumer loans is a sine qua non for the continued growth and viability of the thrift industry. It has long been the conventional wisdom that in order to assure the flow of low priced housing funds, Regulation Q was necessary and should be maintained. Indeed, even with the current gradual approach to the phasing out of Regulation Q ceilings, the United States Savings and Loan League remained the principal opponent of legislation to abolish the ceilings, though in 1982, this position had been somewhat mollified by suggestions of a trade-off between the elimination of the differential and extended "bank-like" powers for thrifts.

National policy, too, had largely dictated that mortgage credit should be available as cheaply as possible and, in effect, has provided some rationalization for the fact that home buyers, as well as builders, developers, and lenders were being subsidized by savers. But concerns about continued high inflation has given savers an entirely different perspective. Many are hedging against inflation, disintermediating in search of investments which yield higher returns, gold, commodity futures, money market funds, and so on. The contemporary thrifty are no longer willing to sit back and bear the inflationary burden. As Thomas W. Thompson asserts, "The consumer, better educated and more discerning, has come of age; he is rate-conscious,

he is treatment-conscious, he is a shopper in a buyer's market."[1]
More to the point, as Frederick Dean, Chairman and CEO of The
Bank of Virginia points out, "Equitability is the most pressing reason
for eliminating Regulation Q. In a financial environment characterized by double-digit inflation, it especially penalizes. In any environment, it is discriminatory. Today's more mature consumer, our customer, rightly insists on fair rates and fair treatment. Removing
Regulation Q restrictions on savings rates is a necessary response to
this demand. In the short run, the prospect of more expensive operating funds may make the banker's job more difficult. But giving
consumers a fair shake is how we will keep their loyalty in the long
run. Not to move in this direction is, once again, to misread the average American."[2]

Higher passbook and savings rates, no doubt, will have some salu-
tary effect in reducing the disintermediation of funds from savings
accounts into higher yielding and more risky investment opportunities.
The phasing out of Regulation Q, however, requires action in a spirit
of gradualism. Financial institutions in the new social and economic
milieu will need time to adjust their asset portfolios. In particular,
savings and loan associations and savings banks will of necessity require time to acquire broader financial operational powers, as well as
time to effectively implement them.

It can be argued that gradualism in the phasing out the Regulation
Q limitations has been evident in the activities of the American legislature. The Hunt Commission in 1971 recommended a phased withdrawal of the ceilings on time and savings account but favored retention of the prohibition on the payment of interest on checking accounts. The Financial Institutions Act of 1973 supported the removal
of the ceilings but was not adopted. Certificates of Deposits over
$100,000, however, were removed from Regulation Q limitations
and financial institutions were allowed to offer the going market rate
with maturities as short as 30 days. Such an action was taken with
the view to encouraging depositors to maintain their funds in financial institutions rather than seeking more lucrative investments. In
June of 1978, the issue of a $10,000 minimum, six-month certificate
of deposit where the interest rate was tied to the weekly rate on the
six-month Treasury Bill was authorized for financial institutions. In

[1] Thomas W. Thompson, "In a World Without Q." *Journal of Retail Banking*, Spring
1976. p. 8.
[2] Thomas W. Thompson, "The Lively Ghost of Regulation Q"—Commentary—*United
States Banker*, December 1978. p. 8.

March, 1980, however, compounding of interest and the differential over 9 percent on these certificates were removed.

Title XVI of the Financial Institutions Regulatory and Interest Rate Control Act of 1978, (H.R. 14279) extended Regulation Q restrictions until December 5, 1980. Regulation Q ceilings, thus, in effect, apply to savers with less than $10,000 who hold passbook accounts limited to 5 percent and ¼ for thrifts, and on a variety of other deposits with maturities ranging from one to eight or more years with interest rate ceilings of 6 to 8 percent.

Financial institutions were hard pressed to encourage these smaller savers to retain funds in these institutions and, hence, the abolishment of Regulation Q was seen as enabling these organizations to offer higher rates. In 1976, the six-month Treasury Bill rate was 5.25 percent, in effect, the same as Regulation Q ceilings. By 1978, the Treasury Bill rate had risen to over 7 percent and by April of 1980 was over 14 percent. It was not surprising, therefore, that many financial institutions developed innovative methods for overriding the 5.25 percent interest ceilings. While Citibank could only pay 5 percent in New York, a Citicorp industrial bank subsidiary in Utah offered 6 percent on daily passbook accounts. Several banks took advantage of state regulations governing industrial banks and thrift plans.

Rhode Island, Colorado, California, Iowa, Maryland, and Utah permit the establishment of such organizations, and some states even allow these institutions to accept deposits from other states. One plan developed by the Old Stone Corp. of Providence, Rhode Island used its subsidiary, the Guild Loan and Investment Company to offer passbook savings accounts and six-month money certificates at rates above those being offered on comparable deposits at other financial institutions. Another innovation in Rhode Island, the Commercial Credit Plan, Inc. offered a "super savings account" which paid 8.5 percent on savings accounts of $2000 or more and 6.5 percent on deposits of a minimum of $500.

Coupled with the rising attractiveness of money market mutual funds, Merrill Lynch's Cash Management Account and other commercial finance offerings, in order to enhance the competitive position of the banks and thrifts, the Federal Reserve Board adopted in May 1979 several regulatory actions effective July 1 which included:

1. A 25 basis point increase in the passbook deposit rate ceiling.
2. Removal of minimum deposit amount requirements on all ac-

counts with the exception of money market certificates.
3. A fluctuating ceiling CD with original maturity of four or more years with the ceiling tied to the 4-year Treasury constant maturity yield when the latter is above current maximum rates payable on these maturity categories.

Changes were also instituted in existing minimum premature withdrawal penalties to three months' forfeiture of interest on time accounts with maturities of one year or less, and six months' forfeiture of interest on all other time accounts.

Notwithstanding, calls for the phasing out of Regulation Q in order to provide for the continued growth and stability of the banking system continued in the face of new commercial competition. As Walter B. Wriston, Chairman of Citicorp, New York, argued "The biggest problem facing banking today is not the new competition but the old regulations."[3] It was, therefore, inevitable that legal recognition would be given to the general consensus of opinion that Regulation Q should be phased out.

In January 1980, Congress enacted legislation cited as the Depository Institutions Deregulation and Monetary Control Act of 1980 which authorized several activities to be undertaken by the financial community. The Act was designed "to facilitate the implementation of monetary policy, to provide for the gradual elimination of all limitations on the rates of interest which are payable on deposits and accounts, and to authorize interest-bearing transaction accounts and for other purposes." The Act created uniform reserve requirements for all transaction accounts held by all depository institutions, authorized the issuance of NOW accounts by thrifts and banks nationwide, raised insurance account coverage to $100,000, the overriding of state usury laws and providing FIR and other capital adequacy relief. The Act was signed into law by President Carter on March 31, 1980.

Title II of the Act, known as the Depository Institutions Deregulation Act of 1980 (DIDA 1980), provided for the elimination of interest rate controls and ceilings by April 1, 1986. It was expected that the ¼ percentage differential between commercial banks and thrifts would in all probability remain for the major part, if not all of the six-year period. However, the 1982 Garn-St Germain Depository Institutions Act repeals the law establishing the statutory differential and mandates the phase-out of the differential for all ac-

---

[3] Walter Wriston, *Bankers Magazine*, March 1979. p. 93.

counts "on or before" January 1, 1984. For all accounts already scheduled for phase-out at earlier dates by the Deregulation Committee, as will be discussed later, the differential will be phased out as soon as practicable, but no later than already scheduled. Regulation Q has existed since 1933, but embraced all institutions since 1966 and has been extended 13 times since 1966. Depository Institutions will now be in a position to offer competitive market interest rates with the termination of the Regulation Q ceilings in April 1986.

Specifically, the Depository Institutions Deregulation Act of 1980 (DIDA) stipulated that the systematic and orderly phase-out of the maximum rates of interest that depository institutions may offer on deposits is to be undertaken by a Deregulation Committee. The composition and voting members of the Committee are as follows:

1. The Secretary of the Treasury.
2. The Chairman of the Board of Governors of the Federal Reserve System.
3. The Chairman of the Board of Directors of the Federal Deposit Insurance Corporation.
4. The Chairman of the Federal Home Loan Bank Board and the National Credit Union Administration Board respectively.

The final and sixth member of the Committee who is a non-voting member is the Comptroller of the Currency.

Public meetings will be held by the Deregulation Committee at least quarterly. Whereas previously the Federal Reserve Board, The Federal Home Loan Bank Board and the Federal Deposit Insurance Corporation, each had responsibility for establishing rate changes in interest rate ceilings for those institutions under their respective jurisdictions, only the new Deregulation Committee acting by majority vote is charged with the responsibility for the maintenance, reduction or increase in the Regulation Q interest rate ceilings under the new regulations. By Congressional decree, deposit rate ceilings are to be increased along a specific time period, a ¼ percentage increase in passbook rates within 18 months of enactment and during the third, fourth, fifth, and sixth years of implementation an increase of a one-half percentage point.

The Committee, however, has the authority, if it deems necessary, to increase ceiling rates at a slower or faster rate than the stipulated guidelines or not to raise rates at all during the entire six-year period. At the inaugural meeting of the Depository Institutions Deregulation

Committee on May 6, 1980, two new regulations were promulgated which sought to equalize for all depository institutions rules governing the handling of interest earned in relation to the early withdrawal penalties and the payment of interest on certificates of deposit after maturity, respectively. In the former case, the Committee adopted the FHLBB regulations, permitting the withdrawal of interest earned without penalty at any time during the initial term of the deposit, and in addition, if on maturity the time deposit is automatically renewed on the same contract terms and conditions, both the interest earned in the initial term, as well as during the renewal term, may be withdrawn without penalty. In the latter case, all depository institutions were allowed to continue the payment of interest on time deposits for a period of seven days after the maturity date, at the original contract rate.

On May 28, 1980, the Depository Institutions Deregulation Committee (DIDA) adopted final rules in relation to the ceiling rates of interest payable on 26-week money market certificates which were tantamount to de facto eliminating the differential on money market certificates, given the current market rate scenario.

In addition, new rules relating to the interest ceilings on the 2½ year and longer small saver certificates, and on the penalty for early withdrawal of time deposit funds, were also promulgated. Specifically with respect to the 26-week money market certificate, the DIDA ruled that the maximum rate of interest payable on money market certificates by all depository institutions will be at least 25 basis points above the rate determined for six-month, United States Treasury bills, and that this maximum, regardless of how low the Treasury bill rate may fall, will not be less than 7¾ percent. The Committee, however, also pointed out that an institution could of its own volition pay a rate lower than the stipulated minimum ceiling.

Commercial banks and thrift institutions may both pay a rate of interest 25 basis points higher than the Treasury bill rate, when the latter rate is 8.75 percent or higher. The differential is, however, maintained when the Treasury bill rate is higher than 7.25 percent but lower than 8.75 percent, with thrifts being able to offer up to 25 basis points above the ceiling. The differential of 25 basis points was thus eliminated above 8.75 percent and below 7.25 percent.

The Committee also rules that effective May 29 through November 30, 1980, Commercial banks could renew maturing money market certificates with the same depositor at a rate of interest equal to the ceiling rate applicable on money market certificates issued by mutual banks and savings and loan associations.

The above ruling was designed to deter the potential drain on the commercial banking sector and, hence, to reduce intra-industry disintermediation occasioned by the re-allocation of money market certificate balances.

With the removal of the interest rate differential outlined before, the United States League of Savings Associations filed suit against the Depository Institutions Deregulation Committee. The National Association of Home Builders, The American Savings and Loan League, and the National Association of Realtors, supported the League action and each filed amicus curiae briefs, providing additional information to bolster the League's arguments concerning potential damage to housing construction and finance triggered by the DIDC rulings. Criticisms of the actions of the Depository Institutions Deregulation Committee has also resulted in renewed Congressional hearings on this controversial matter. As the then Chairman of the Federal Home Loan Bank Board asserted: "The mere fact that the necessary laws are on the books for federal savings associations does not mean that all thrifts suddenly are capable of competing with commercial banks in the absence of the differential."

While there was perhaps some justification for maintaining the ¼ percent differential when banks and thrifts were fundamentally different in operation, many of the former distinctions no longer exist and deregulation, no doubt, will foster a greater degree of homogeneity among financial institutions. The crucial point, however, at this time appears to be the extent to which a meaningful balance can be achieved between the rate at which the provisions of the Deregulation Act are implemented and the ability of the thrift industry to respond to the changing dynamics of a novel and highly competitive environment.

With regard to the Small Saver Certificates, a new maximum ceiling rate of interest was established for all depository institutions. Effective June 2, 1980, all depository institutions were able to offer rates that were generally 50 basis points higher than the previous ceilings on 30-month certificates. Under the old rules, the ceiling rate of interest on 30-month certificates issued by thrifts was ½ percent below the 2½ year Treasury bill rate, while the rate was ¾ percent below the Treasury rate for commercial banks, with the maximum allowable rate for thrifts and commercial banks, being 12 percent and 11¾ percent, respectively.

The new regulations provide that mutual banks and savings and loan associations may now pay the 2½ year Treasury bill rate, while commercial banks are authorized to offer rates ¼ percent below the

2½ year Treasury rate. In addition, a minimum ceiling rate of 9.50 percent was established for thrifts, and 9.25 percent for commercial banks regardless of how low the 2½ Treasury rate may be. The ceiling rate for the 2½ year Small Saver Certificates will be established bi-weekly instead of monthly as was previously done. Compounding of interest earned on these certificates is permitted.

In order to increase the efficacy of the penalties for premature withdrawal of time deposit funds, especially during the early weeks of the deposit contract, the Depository Institutions Deregulation Committee adopted revised penalties for early withdrawals of time deposit funds.

Effective June 2, 1980, the revised penalty rule mandates the forfeiture of three months' interest on funds withdrawn before maturity from a time deposit with a maturity of one year or less and six months' interest on funds withdrawn prematurely from a time deposit with an original maturity of more than one year, irrespective of how long the funds have been on deposit. The modified penalty rule allows for a reduction in the principal amount deposited, whereas under the previous rule, early withdrawal penalties were limited to interest accrued or interest already disbursed. For funds of less than three months' maturity, the required penalty is the forfeiture of an amount equal to the interest that could have been earned on such funds at maturity. All penalties are calculated at the nominal simple interest rate and are not compounded.

In October 1981, the DIDC amended its ruling pertaining to the setting of interest rate ceilings for $10,000 minimum denomination, 26-week money market certificates. The amended rule effective November 1, 1981, authorized banks and thrift institutions to offer rates indexed to the higher of either (1) the rate for 26-week Treasury bills established immediately prior to the date of deposit, (2) the average of the rates for 26-week Treasury bills for the four weeks immediately prior to the date of deposit. This alternative method of establishment of MMC interest rate ceilings, it was felt, would enhance the competitive position of banks and thrift institutions vis-a-vis money market mutual funds during periods of declining interest rates. Generally, money market funds have demonstrated rapid growth in assets during periods of declining interest rates, owing to the lag in adjustment of money market funds portfolios to reflect the downturn in interest rates. The moving average method for calculating interest rate ceilings on money market certificates would reduce or remove this competitive disadvantage to banks and thrift institutions.

At the March 22nd, 1982 meeting of the DIDC, a new 91-day savings account was approved. The short-term certificate is indexed to the 91-day Treasury bill rate, with a 25 basis points differential for thrift institutions. If, however, the Treasury rate bill is 9 percent or less for four consecutive weeks, the differential will not be applicable. The new certificate had a minimum denomination of $7,500 and was effective May 1, 1982.

The 1982 Depository Institutions Act also required the DIDC to create a new account with no interest rate ceiling that is directly equivalent to and competitive with money market mutual funds. The new account is not subject to transaction account reserve requirements unless more than three transfers to third parties and three pre-authorized automatic transfers are permitted monthly. The new account was created within 60 days of the enactment of the 1982 Act, which was signed into law by President Reagan on October 15, 1982. On November 15, it was announced that the new account would have a minimum denomination of $2,500 as recommended by the United States League of Savings Associations. Depository Institutions were permitted to begin offering the new account as of December 14th, 1982.

At the December 6th, 1982 meeting of the Depository Institutions Deregulation Committee, banks, thrifts, and credit unions were authorized to offer an unlimited transaction, ceiling free and fully reservable "Super NOW" account. The NOW account hybrid was similar to the money market account recently approved for depository institutions. The "NOW" account was available January 5th, 1983 and required a $2,500 minimum and maintenance balance. If the balance falls below $2,500, the NOW account ceiling of 5.25 percent is applicable. Individuals, governmental units, and specific nonprofit corporations are eligible to hold the new NOW accounts.

The DIDC, also at the December 6th meeting, limited telephone transfers to be included in the six transfers permitted per month on the money market fund competitive account. Previously, telephone transfers were unlimited and were not included in the six transfers allowed each depositor. The ceiling on the rate offered on the 7 to 31-day account which was indexed to the 91-day Treasury Bill discount rate was also removed, effective January 5th. The minimum denominations of the $10,000 six-month money market certificate, the $7,500 91-day account, and the $20,000 7-31 day account were reduced to $2,500, also effective January 5th. The DIDC further sought comment on a proposal to reduce the $2,500 minimum denominations on the short-term accounts to zero, over the next three years. Plans were also promulgated by the regulatory committee to accelerate the deregulation of interest rates. Under these proposals, all interest rate ceilings would be removed by October 1984, rather than by March 31, 1986, as stipulated by the Depository Institutions Deregulation and Monetary Control Act of 1980.

It is anticipated that with the money market insured account and the Super NOW account, banks and thrifts will be able to attract a significant portion of funds that were funneled over the years into money market funds. Available data show that with the offering of the December 14th money market competitive account as much as $30 billion flowed to banks and thrift institutions.

The Federal Reserve Board estimated that new deposit funds at banking institutions averaged $52 billion in the first two weeks of operations, while money market funds recorded a $13 billion decline in assets over the same period. For the first five weeks since the introduction of the new money market account by banks and thrifts, assets of money market funds declined by almost $25 billion, indicating that the account offered by banks and thrifts was in fact directly competitive with money market funds.

Theory and Reasoning of Non-Interest on Demand Deposits

As mentioned previously, the 1933 Banking Act explicitly prohibited the payment of interest on demand deposits. Bank regulators at the time were chiefly concerned that interest payments on these accounts would create excessive competition among banks and could result in potentially destabilizing effects on individual banks and the banking system as a whole. Moreover, it could be postulated that given the transient nature of these transaction balances, and the higher reserve requirements on these accounts, payment of interest on demand deposits would further increase operational costs and perhaps reduce the profitability and solvency of the banking system. Individuals at the time, too, were more interested in the safety, liquidity, and convenience which these deposits offered, rather than on their attractiveness in terms of explicit interest payments.

With the rapid development of innovative financial services through technological change and mushrooming commercial financial organizations, several groups favored the removal of Regulation Q ceilings, in particular the removal of the zero ceiling rate on demand deposits.

It was argued that the prohibition against interest payments on checking accounts has resulted in greater resources being utilized in the provision of checking accounts than a free-market oriented system would dictate. Banks are unable to effectively choose the mix of interest payments and non-price factors which would minimize the cost of demand deposit funds. Instead, in order to attract deposits, banks resort to implicit interest payments in the form of greater customer conveniences and increased services, "free checking" and so on. Obviously, management alternatives are restricted, for example, during an economic recession when reduction in costs would be facilitated by lowering deposit rates, rather than by the reduction in customer conveniences such as the closing of branches, the reduction of services via less business hours, and other related activities.

Moreover, the recent innovative financial offerings such as money market mutual funds, repurchase agreements, cash management accounts juxtaposed with high rates of inflation has, in effect, virtually made the non-payment of interest on demand deposits obsolete. The astute depositor is no longer content to maintain "idle" transactions' balances in non-revenue earning accounts. The authorization of automatic transfers from savings to checking accounts and the limited introduction of NOW accounts in the late 1970s, and more so nationwide in 1980, attests to this practical reality. The Depository Institutions Act of 1980 by authorizing nationwide interest-bearing negotiable order of withdrawal accounts, in effect, permitted financial institutions to offer interest on checking accounts, thus lifting the 47-year old prohibition on the payment of interest on demand deposits. Such a development was a natural response to the increasing sophistication, complexity, and transformation of the nation's financial system.

Current Plans for Phase-Out of Regulation Q

The DIDC, at its March 22nd, 1982 meeting, also approved a deregulation-schedule beginning with the creation of a new 3½ year "wild card" account effective May 1, 1982. The schedule would reduce the minimum maturity of this new deposit category by one year starting April 1, 1983, and each subsequent April until all time deposits are "deregulated" or interest ceiling free by 1986.

The deregulation schedule requires the establishment of a 2½ year "wild card" account beginning April 1, 1983. A 1½ year interest ceiling free account would be authorized on April 1, 1984. On April 1, 1985, the maturity schedule on these "wild card" accounts would

246 Savings Banking: An Industry in Change

be six months, and by March 31, 1986, any account of 14-day maturity or longer would be interest ceiling free.

Prior to the revised schedule, the DIDC was widely criticized for its action and the manner in which the deregulation process was handled. Earlier attempts to raise by 50 basis points, the passbook ceiling rate effective November 1, 1981, were postponed indefinitely in October. Attempts also to introduce a deregulation schedule which would have created a four-year "wild card" account were also rescinded.

In the latter case, the Federal District Court ruled that the regulation "is null and void insofar as it eliminates any differential in maximum interest rate limitation on any account in existence on December 10, 1975."[4]

In October 1981, 36 House Banking members requested that the DIDC delay its action in raising the passbook rate until the House Banking Committee undertakes a review of the effects of the actions of the DIDC on the viability of depository institutions and upon consumers. The United States League of Savings Associations also recommended that the DIDC be reconstituted to consist of the Chairman of the FHLBB, FDIC and Federal Reserve only thereby removing the Secretary of the Treasury and the NCUA representative. In addition, the League proposed the establishment of the opportunity for either House of Congress to exercise veto power over final DIDC regulations. In this way, Congress would have some control of the activities of the DIDC.

More to the point, in November 1981, in testimony before the House Oversight and Renegotiation Subcommittee, Savings and Loan Associations of New York, President Paul A. Schosberg, asserted that the phase-out of deposit interest rate ceilings has not been conducted in an orderly manner as directed by Congress. Moreover, the actions of the DIDC appeared to be contrary to the congressional directive that it act "with due regard to the safety and soundness of depository institutions." Concerns about the inequitability of its voting structure and the inadequacy of its reporting procedures to Congress were also voiced.

In December 1981, Congressman Patterson announced plans to introduce legislation to restructure the DIDC in order to restrain the Committee from instituting any proposals that would be detrimental to financial institutions. In conclusion, Congressional action is neces-

[4] United States League of Savings Association—*Washington Notes*. July 31, 1981. p. 1.

sary in the future in order to determine the efficacy of the DIDC in implementing its mandate to deregulate the liability side of the balance sheet of depository institutions and what remedial action may be needed to facilitate the Committee in the conduct of its activities. As the Committee is now structured, it appears that thrift institutions are outvoted on major proposals. The Chairman of the FHLBB, Richard Pratt, suggested that "the efficiency of the Committee would be enhanced if no action were able to be taken if the Federal Reserve Board and the Federal Home Loan Bank Board both disapproved the action. . . . . . The pace of deregulation should be carefully metered as to its cumulative effect and more complete attention be paid to an accommodation of the considerations inherent in deregulation."[5] The 1982 Depository Institutions Act, in effect, accelerated the deregulation of interest rate controls by requiring the phase-out of the differential no later than January 1984.

On June 30, 1983, the DIDC removed interest rate ceilings on time deposits entered into after September 30, 1983, with maturities of more than 31 days, and on time deposits of $2,500 or more with original maturities of 7-31 days. The opening deposit minimum for any account with a maturity of 31 days or less was set at $2,500. There was no minimum requirement for accounts of longer maturity, such as the six-month money market account. In addition, an early withdrawal penalty equal to 31 days' interest on deposits with maturities of one year or less than 90 days' interest on deposits with maturities over one year was also established. These rules were effective October 1, 1983.

In keeping with the stipulations of the 1982 Garn Act, the DIDC, on October 1, 1983, eliminated the thrift interest rate differential effective January 1, 1984. The interest rate ceiling on passbook accounts and on 7-31 day time deposits of less than $2,500 was, thus, increased from 5¼ percent to 5½ percent. The DIDC also established a phase-out schedule for minimum deposit requirements. Effective December 1, 1983, the $2,500 minimum deposit requirement for Individual Retirement Accounts or Keogh Trusts, funded by money market deposit accounts, Super NOWs, or 7-31 day accounts was eliminated. On January 1, 1985, the minimum deposit requirement for Super NOW, money market deposit, and 7-31 day accounts will be lowered to $1,000. On January 1, 1986, the remaining $1000 minimum deposit requirement will be eliminated. Banks, thus, will

[5] *Savings and Loan Reporter*. Vol. 6, #34. December 11, 1981. p. 3.

be permitted to operate in a virtually unregulated environment with regard to the denominations of deposits accepted and interest paid on these accounts.

PART FOUR

THE INVESTMENT FUNCTION

Chapter XII

The Investment Function

As discussed in earlier chapters, the bulk of the assets of savings and loan associations was historically invested in mortgage loans with a small percentage of assets held in the form of cash and government obligations. While mutual banks originally invested heavily in government securities, mortgage lending subsequently developed as the principal distribution of funds. The preponderance of mortgage instruments in the asset portfolios of savings institutions was further "institutionalized" and fostered by a series of legislative and regulatory provisos over the years.

Contemporarily, such asset specialization has continued to be the dominant modus operandi of these institutions with mortgage instruments representing up to 1980 over 80 percent of the assets of savings and loan associations and approximately 57 percent of the total assets of mutual savings banks. With the passage of the Garn Act in 1982, however, and the need to diversify asset portfolios, given the earnings problems over the years 1980-82, savings and loans and mutual savings banks have shifted funds into other permissible investments such as commercial loans, leasing, and real estate development.

SAVINGS AND LOANS ASSOCIATIONS

Table XII-1 presents data on the total assets of all savings and loan associations. While the pronounced asset specialization in mortgage instruments is evident from the magnitude of the figures for mortgage loans in comparison to total assets, there has been a declining trend since 1980. By 1982, mortgage loans accounted for 68.3 percent cash and liquid assets 12.0 percent, and other assets 18.3 percent of total assets respectively. Preliminary figures for 1983 show a further decline to 64 percent in the percentage of mortgage loans to total assets. Approximately 78.5 percent of all mortgage loans held by insured associations were collateralized by single family homes. The average loan balance of mortgages outstanding has been increasing steadily over the years from $15,175 in 1971, $30,090 in 1979, and $32,231 in 1981, partially a reflection of increasing housing costs in an inflationary environment. As can be seen from Table XII-2 as well, total mortgage loans outstanding were over $488 billion in 1983. Savings and loan associations provided financing for over 269,000 existing homes and for 237,000 new units in 1982. A breakdown of mortgage portfolios of insured associations by type of property is given in Table XII-3, with over 75 percent of the mortgages held on single-family units.

While there has been a marked emphasis towards the provision of loans for home purchase, particularly single-family units, savings and loan associations disbursed in 1982 over $9.1 billion or 16.8 percent of total loans in loans for home construction, in comparison to $20.4 billion or 37.6 percent of total mortgage loans for home purchase. The provision of such funds for housing acquisition reflects a positive correlation with the rising incidence of home ownership as depicted in Table XII-4. With the growth of the secondary mortgage market, savings and loan institutions have increased acquisitions of whole loans and participating interests in mortgage pools as alternative mortgage holdings. Although these holdings have shown marked variations from year to year, there was an absolute increase in the percentage of loans purchased from 5.8 percent in 1960 to 30.8 percent in 1982.

CONSUMER LOANS

Savings and loan associations were also authorized to invest in consumer loans, commercial paper, and corporate debt up to a limit of 20

Table XII-1   Total Assets of All Savings and Loan Associations
(millions of dollars)

Year-end	Mortgage Loans	Percent	Cash and Investment Securities	Percent	Real Estate Owned	Percent	FHLB Stock	Percent	Other Assets	Percent	Total Assets
1950	$ 13,657	80.4	$ 2,456	14.2	$ 21	0.12	$ 177	1.0	$ 582	3.4	$ 16,893
1955	31,408	83.5	4,549	11.9	33	0.08	507	1.3	1,159	3.0	37,656
1960	60,070	84.0	7,888	11.0	158	0.22	978	1.3	2,382	3.2	71,476
1965	110,306	85.1	12,123	9.3	1,065	0.81	1,2366	0.94	4,850	3.7	129,580
1966	114,427	85.4	12,049	8.9	1,271	0.94	1,313	0.97	4,873	3.5	133,933
1967	121,805	84.8	13,941	9.6	1,353	0.94	1,327	0.91	5,108	3.5	143,534
1968	130,802	85.5	14,078	9.2	1,026	0.66	1,328	0.86	5,656	3.6	152,890
1969	140,232	86.4	13,311	9.2	822	0.50	1,424	0.87	6,360	3.8	162,149
1970	150,331	85.3	16,526	9.3	746	0.42	1,539	0.86	7,041	3.9	176,183
1971	174,250	84.5	21,042	10.2	775	0.37	1,550	0.72	8,406	4.0	206,023
1972	206,182	84.7	24,355	9.9	777	0.32	1,675	0.68	10,138	4.1	243,127
1973	231,733	85.2	21,055	7.7	910	0.33	2,075	0.76	16,132	5.9	271,905
1974	249,301	84.3	23,251	7.8	1,211	0.49	2,575	0.84	19,207	6.4	295,545
1975	278,590	82.3	30,853	9.10	1,662	0.49	2,600	0.76	24,528	7.2	338,233
1976	323,005	82.4	35,724	9.10	1,928	0.49	2,800	0.71	28,450	7.2	391,907
1977	381,163	82.9	39,150	8.5	1,787	0.38	3,200	0.69	33,941	7.3	459,241
1978	432,808	82.6	44,884	8.5	1,714	0.32	4,000	0.76	40,136	7.6	523,542
1979	475,797	82.1	46,541	8.0	1,510	0.25	4,900	0.84	50,559	8.7	579,307
1980	502,812	79.8	57,572	9.1	1,900	0.30	4,900	0.68	62,645	9.9	629,829
1981	518,547	78.1	63,123	9.5	3,268	0.49	5,500	0.82	73,279	11.0	664,167
1982	482,234	68.3	84,767	12.0	3,600	0.50	5,900	0.83	129,544	18.3	706,045
1983	493,400		103,400		N/A		N/A		174,800		771,700

% of total assets.
Source: United States League of Savings Associations—1980 Fact Book.

Table XII-2   Mortgage Portfolio, Number, and Size of Loans
at all Savings Associations

Year-end	Loans Outstanding (millions)	Number of Loans (thousands)	Average Loan Balance
1950	$ 13,657	3,290	$ 4,151
1955	31,408	5,459	5,753
1960	60,070	7,567	7,938
1965	110,306	9,982	11,051
1966	114,427	10,079	11,353
1967	121,805	10,311	11,813
1968	130,802	10,536	12,415
1969	140,232	10,758	13,035
1970	150,331	19,951	13,728
1971	174,250	11,483	15,175
1972	206,182	12,223	16,869
1973	231,733	12,821	18,075
1974	249,301	12,912	19,308
1975	278,590	13,446	20,719
1976	323,005	13,933	23,183
1977	381,163	14,873	25,627
1978	432,808	15,480	27,960
1979	475,797	15,974	29,786
1980	502,812	16,592	30,302
1981	518,547	16,088	32,231

Sources: Federal Home Loan Bank Board; U.S. League of Savings Associations.

percent of assets as of 1980. Subsequently, the 1982 Depository Institutions Act empowered the Federal Home Loan Bank Board to authorize federal associations to invest up to 30 percent of assets in consumer loans without aggregation with investments made in commercial paper and corporate debt. As seen from Table XII-5, the greater proportion of consumer loans disbursed by associations are housing related, such as loans for the acquisition of mobile homes and for home improvement. Loans collateralized by passbook accounts also increased appreciably over the 1978-80 period from 26.8 percent of total consumer loans in 1974 to 40.0 percent of total consumer loans in 1980, but declining to 19.6 percent in 1982. It is expected that with the advent of expanded asset powers for thrift institutions, that short-term consumer and commercial loans will provide savings and loan associations with increased flexibility to ameliorate the problems associated with maturity intermediation, more so when long-term yields are below the yields on short-term instruments.

With the passage of the Depository Institutions Deregulation and Monetary Control Act of 1980, the asset composition structure of

Table XII-3   Mortgage Portfolio of Insured Associations, by Type of Property
(dollar amounts in billions)

Type of Property	1974	1975	1976	1977	1978	1979	1980	1981	1982
Single-family	$181.9	$202.9	$237.4	$283.2	$325.3	$360.9	$389.6	$397.7	$368.3
Two- to four-family	13.0	13.9	15.6	18.6	21.1	23.4	22.5	24.7	22.3
Multifamily	23.0	24.6	27.5	31.4	34.9	36.4	37.8	36.5	35.0
Commercial	21.3	25.3	29.5	32.9	35.1	37.5	38.0	40.6	40.5
Other	4.0	4.6	5.3	6.3	7.1	8.3	6.3	9.9	7.6
Total	$243.1	$271.3	$315.3	$372.4	$423.5	$476.5	$494.2	$509.4	$473.7
				Percentage Distribution					
Single-family	74.8%	74.8%	75.3%	76.0%	76.8%	77.4%	78.8%	78.0%	77.7%
Two- to four-family	5.3	5.1	4.9	5.0	5.0	5.0	4.6	4.8	4.7
Multifamily	9.5	9.1	8.7	8.4	8.2	7.8	7.6	7.1	7.4
Commercial	8.8	9.3	9.4	8.8	8.3	8.0	7.7	7.9	8.5
Other	1.6	1.7	1.7	1.7	1.7	1.8	1.3	1.9	1.6
Total	100.0%	100.0%	100.0%	100.0%	100.0%	100.0%	100.0%	100.0%	100.0%

Note: Components may not add to totals due to rounding.
Sources: Federal Home Loan Band Board/ United States League of Savings Association.

Table XII-4   Homeownership, 1890-1980

Year	Occupied Units	Owner-occupied Units	Renter-occupied Units	Percentage Owned	Percentage Owned
1890	12,690,000	6,066,000	6,624,000	47.8	52.2
1900	15,964,000	7,455,000	8,509,000	46.7	53.3
1910	20,256,000	9,301,000	10,955,000	45.9	54.1
1920	24,352,000	11,114,000	13,238,000	45.6	54.4
1930	29,905,000	14,280,000	15,625,000	47.8	52.2
1940	34,855,000	15,196,000	19,659,000	43.6	56.4
1950	42,826,000	23,560,000	19,266,000	55.0	45.0
1960	53,024,000	32,797,000	20,227,000	61.9	38.1
1970	63,445,000	39,886,000	23,559,000	62.9	37.1
1975	72,523,000	46,867,000	25,656,000	64.6	35.4
1976	74,005,000	47,904,000	26,101,000	64.7	35.3
1977	75,280,000	48,765,000	26,515,000	64.8	35.2
1978	77,167,000	50,283,000	26,884,000	65.2	34.8
1979	78,571,000	51,411,000	27,160,000	65.4	34.6
1980	80,076,000	52,516,000	27,560,000	65.6	34.4

Source: United League of Savings Associations—*Savings and Loan Source Book.* 1981-1983.

savings and loan associations was significantly expanded. Savings and loan associations were permitted to invest up to 20 percent of assets in consumer loans, commercial paper, and corporate debt securities. The total balances of all outstanding unsecured loans to a single borrower was limited to the lesser of one-fourth of 1 percent of an association's assets or 5 percent of its net worth. Regardless of this restriction, however, an unsecured loan up to $3000 can be made to any one borrower.

Investments in commercial paper and corporate debt securities must be within specified ratings and be dominated in dollars and the issuer domiciled in the United States. Savings and loan associations are also not permitted to hold more than 1 percent of assets in commercial paper and corporate debt securities of any one issuer. Associations were also authorized to invest in shares of any open-end management investment company registered with the Securities and Exchange Commission whose portfolio is limited to investments an association is authorized to invest in itself. Investments in any one such company however, should not exceed 5 percent of assets.

Savings and loan associations were also empowered to offer credit card services and to undertake trust and fiduciary activities. Such activities would further the consumer's potential perception of savings and loan associations as family-financial centers, capable of expanded cross-selling ability while capitalizing on traditional customer relation-

Table XII-5 Consumer Loans at Insured Associations
(dollar amounts in millions)

Type	1977	1978	1979	1980	1981	1982
Mobile Home Loans	$ 2,551	$ 2,157	$ 2,396	$ 2,608	$ 2,885	$ 3,222
Home Improvement Loans	3,545	3,653	4,391	4,960	5,254	5,429
Loans Secured by Savings Accounts	2,882	3,950	6,341	7,447	5,431	3,956
Education Loans	542	638	816	1,138	1,573	2,053
All Other Loans	718	1,071	1,855	2,579	3,471	5,495
Total:	$10,238	$11,469	$15,799	$18,732	$18,614	$20,155
			Percentage Distribution			
Mobile Home Loans	24.9%	18.8%	13.4%	13.9%	15.4%	16.0%
Home Improvement Loans	34.6	31.9	27.7	26.4	28.2	27.0
Loans Secured by Savings Accounts	28.2	34.4	40.1	39.7	29.2	19.6
Education Loans	5.3	5.6	5.1	6.1	8.5	10.2
All Other Loans	7.0	9.3	11.7	13.7	18.6	27.3
Total:	100.0%	100.0%	100.0%	100.0%	100.0%	100.0%

Note: Components may not add to totals due to rounding.
Sources: Federal Home Loan Bank Board; United States League of Savings Associations.

ships. In compliance with the stipulations of the 1980 Act, the Federal Home Loan Bank Board also liberalized regulations governing real estate loans provided by savings and loan associations. Specifically, the basic loan to value ratio was increased from 80 to 90 percent. All dollar restrictions on home loans were also eliminated. The loan to value ratio limit on multi-family loans was also raised from 80 to 90 percent and on commercial real estate loans from 75 percent with a 25-year term to 90 percent with a 30-year term. The requirement that loans be secured by first liens on property only was rescinded, thereby enabling associations to offer junior or second mortgages. The loan term for 1 to 4-family units was also extended to 40 years. In addition, geographic limitations on real estate loans were also eliminated. The former limit of $15,000 on home improvement loans was also removed, as was former percentage of assets limitations.

Further liberalization of asset powers for thrift institutions was achieved with the passage of the Garn-St Germain Depository Institutions Act of 1982. Specifically, the existing loan to value restrictions was rescinded, and the 20 percent of assets limitation on nonresidential real estate lending was increased to 40 percent of assets. The requirement that these commercial real estate loans be secured by first liens on other improved real estate was also eliminated.

In addition, the 1982 Act authorized federal associations to make secured or unsecured loans for commercial, corporate, business, and agricultural purposes. Loans to any one borrower, however, are constrained by the loan-to-one borrower limitations applicable to national banks; that is, 15 percent and 10 percent of unimpaired capital and surplus for unsecured and secured loans respectively. Federal associations may invest up to 5 percent of assets in these loans until January 1, 1984 when the percentage of assets limitation will be increased to 10 percent. Such loans may be disbursed through the provision of overdraft facilities.

SERVICE CORPORATIONS

Savings and loan associations are also authorized to undertake other housing related and ancillary investments through the use of service corporations. While federal savings and loan associations were able to invest in service corporations from as early as 1964, these investments were not very attractive due to the originally prohibitive regulations governing what activities could be undertaken. With the subsequent expansion in permissible activities during 1970, service corporations provided the mechanism whereby savings and loan associations could undertake investments such as real estate development, insurance brokerage, property management, and data processing services.

Service corporations are subsidiary enterprises of savings and loan associations, jointly owned by several associations or by only one institution. There are basically two types of service corporations, type A and B, respectively. The type A format is a statewide company and all qualifying associations of the state may invest in this corporation. Type B service corporations are either owned jointly by five or more associations, less than five, or individually owned. Approximately 95 percent of service corporations currently in operation are of the type B form.

In August 1980, the Federal Home Loan Bank increased the original 1 percent of total assets limitation on investments in service corporations to 3 percent of total assets. However, associations undertaking investments up to the maximum permitted are required to allocate 1 percent of their assets to projects that cater to the community; inner-city, or community development objectives.

MUTUAL SAVINGS BANKS

While early mutual savings banks invested primarily in United States Government securities, mutual savings banks, over the years in response to bouyant housing demand, have concentrated their investment orientation on mortgage lending activities. As Table XII-6 illustrates, mortgage loans increased from $858 million in 1900 to over $94 billion at the end of 1982. This represented a shift from 38 percent of total assets in 1900 to approximately 54 percent of aggregate assets in 1979, as shown in Chart XII-1.

Mortgage loans on residential property have traditionally accounted for the bulk of mortgage lending undertaken by mutual savings banks. Statistics presented in Table XII-7, indicate that residential mortgage loans comprised about 80 percent of total mortgage loans in 1945 and 83.7 percent of the total in 1982. Of the total residential mortgage loans in 1982 held by mutual savings banks, 81.0 percent were secured by one to four family homes, and 19.0 percent by multi-family properties. The growth of mortgage-backed securities

Table XII-6   Assets of Mutual Savings Banks, Selected Years, 1900-1983
(in millions of dollars)

Year	Mortgage Investments		Securities			Non-Mortgage Loans	Cash and Other Assets	Total Assets
	Mortgage	GNMA Mortgage Backed	U.S. Government	State and Local	Corporate and Other			
1900	858	—	105	567	462	169	167	2,328
1910	1,500	—	13	765	906	194	220	3,598
1920	2,291	—	783	650	1,213	336	313	5,586
1930	5,635	—	499	920	2,278	312	520	10,164
1940	4,836	—	3,193	612	1,429	82	1,764	11,916
1945	4,202	—	10,650	84	1,116	62	849	16,962
1950	8,039	—	19,877	96	2,260	127	1,047	22,446
1955	17,279	—	8,463	646	3,364	211	1,382	31,346
1960	26,702	—	6,243	672	5,076	416	1,463	40,571
1965	44,433	—	5,485	320	5,170	862	1,962	58,232
1970	57,775	85	3,151	197	12,791	2,255	2,741	78,995
1971	61,984	755	3,268	390	17,275	2,180	3,099	89,581
1972	67,563	1,384	3,510	873	20,522	2,979	3,762	100,593
1973	73,231	1,861	2,958	926	19,521	3,871	4,282	106,650
1974	74,891	2,230	2,555	930	20,320	3,812	4,812	109,550
1975	77,221	3,367	4,740	1,545	24,626	4,023	5,535	121,056
1976	81,630	5,808	5,840	2,417	27,985	5,183	5,948	134,812
1977	88,195	8,331	5,895	2,828	29,587	6,210	6,240	147,287
1978	95,157	10,021	4,959	3,333	29,711	7,195	7,796	158,174
1979	98,908	11,820	7,658	2,930	25,267	9,253	7,568	163,405
1980	99,865	13,849	8,949	2,390	25,433	11,733	9,344	171,564
1981	99,997	13,911	9,810	2,288	23,879	14,753	11,091	175,728
1982	94,091	14,055	9,743	2,470	22,106	16,957	14,774	174,197
1983	97,347	18,205	15,360	177	25,376	13,688	15,933	193,524

Note: Beginning in 1979, federal agency obligations are included in U.S. Government securities rather than in corporate and other securities; therefore, in this table, these two categories are not comparable with previous years. Data are end-of-year except for 1900 and 1930 which are as of mid-year. Balance sheet data are net of valuation reserves except for the period from December 31, 1971 to March 31, 1979. Annual and monthly changes in balance sheet items shown in subsequent tables of the National Fact Book are strictly comparable for all periods, reflecting adjustments made to take accounts of the shifts in reporting procedures as well as for conversions of different types of institutions.

Table XII-7 Mortgage Loans Held by Mutual Savings Banks, by Type of Property and Loan, Selected Year-End Dates, 1945-1980

(in millions of dollars)

Year-end	Total	Residential Total	Type of Property 1-to-4-Family	Type of Property Multi-family	Type of Loan FHA	Type of Loan VA	Type of Loan Conventional	Non-residential	Memoranda GNMA Mortgage-Backed Securities
1945	4,208	3,387	1,894	1,493	335	14	3,038	821	—
1950	8,262	7,054	4,326	2,728	1,615	1,457	3,982	1,208	—
1955	17,457	15,568	11,838	3,730	4,150	5,773	5,645	1,889	—
1960	26,935	24,306	20,575	3,731	7,074	8,986	8,246	2,629	—
1965	44,617	40,096	33,813	6,283	13,791	11,408	14,897	4,521	—
1966	47,336	42,242	35,644	6,598	14,500	11,471	16,271	5,094	—
1967	50,490	44,641	37,690	6,951	15,074	11,795	17,772	5,849	—
1968	53,457	46,748	39,493	7,255	15,569	12,033	19,146	6,709	—
1969	56,138	48,682	41,102	7,580	15,862	12,166	20,654	7,456	—
1970	57,948	49,937	42,149	7,788	16,087	12,008	21,842	8,011	85
1971	61,978	53,021	43,435	9,586	16,142	12,074	24,805	8,957	755
1972	67,556	57,139	46,229	10,910	16,013	12,622	28,504	10,417	1,384
1973	73,230	61,154	48,811	12,343	15,506	12,946	32,702	12,076	1,861
1974	74,920	62,136	49,213	12,923	14,808	12,703	34,625	12,784	2,230
1975	77,249	63,817	50,025	13,792	14,427	12,391	36,999	13,432	3,367
1976	81,639	67,266	53,089	14,177	14,596	12,317	40,353	14,373	5,808
1977	88,104	72,941	57,637	15,304	14,187	11,933	46,821	15,163	8,331
1978	95,157	78,781	62,252	16,529	14,203	11,824	52,754	16,376	10,021
1979	98,908	81,886	64,706	17,180	13,816	11,390	56,680	17,022	11,821
1980	99,827	82,647	65,307	17,340	13,308	10,855	58,484	17,150	13,849
1981	99,997	84,147	68,187	15,960	12,752	10,478	60,917	15,850	13,911
1982	94,452	79,132	64,095	15,037	11,730	9,400	58,002	15,320	14,055

Chart 1 Percentage Distribution of Assets of Mutual Savings Banks
Selected Years, 1900-1980

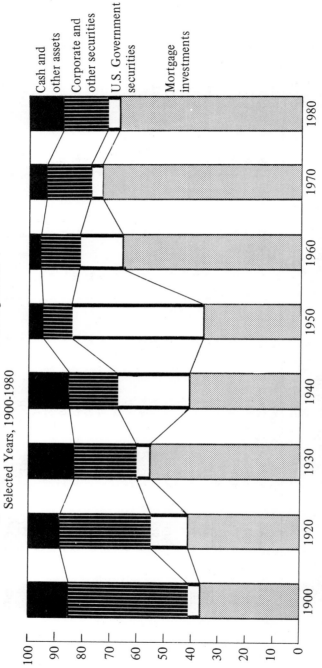

Note: End-of-year data except for 1900 to 1930 which are as of mid-year. Asset classifications are comparable to Table 1 except for corporate and other securities which include state and municipal obligations for all years shown and cash and other assets which include nonmortgage loans. Mortgage investments for 1980 include mortgage-backed securities. See note to Table 1.

Source: FRB NAMSB and state banking departments.

Source: National Association of Mutual Savings Banks. 1981 National Fact Book of Mutual Savings Banking, p. 10.

held by mutual savings banks since 1970 is also evident from the data presented.

Mortgage loans, it should be mentioned, may be either of the conventional, FHA, or VA form. Conventional mortgage loans are mortgage loans not insured or guaranteed by an agency of government, but usually by private mortgage insurance underwriters. Federal Housing Administration (FHA) loans are insured by this agency, while VA loans are guaranteed by the Veteran's Administration. Both these federal agencies stipulate certain requirements and provisions for the processing and granting of these residential loans by private lenders such as mutual savings banks.

Conventional loans represent over 73.3 percent of total residential loans made by mutual savings banks, with FHA and VA mortgage loans accounting for 14.8 and 11.9 percent, respectively, of total residential loans held by mutual savings banks in 1982. Conventional mortgages too, comprise the greater proportion of mortgage holdings held by savings and loan associations, commercial banks and life insurance companies, as can be seen from comparable data for 1982 given in Table XII-8. Conventional mortgage loans usually have higher down payment requirements and stipulate private mortgage

Table XII-8   Percentage Distribution of Mortgage Holdings of Main Types of Financial Institutions, by Type of Loan and Property, December 31, 1982 (in percent)

	Savings Banks	Commercial Banks	Savings and Loan Associations	Life Insurance Companies
By type of loan				
FHA	12.3	1.6	2.5	3.5
VA	9.9	.9	2.9	1.8
Conventional and other	76.0	82.1	89.9	93.9
Construction	1.8	15.4	4.7	.9
Total	100.0	100.0	100.0	100.0
By type of property				
Residential	83.0	57.0	87.8	25.0
1- to 4-family	68.8	54.4	80.1	11.8
Multifamily	14.2	2.6	7.7	13.2
Nonresidential	15.1	24.8	7.4	64.9
Farm	*	2.9	.1	9.3
Construction	1.8	15.4	4.7	.9
Total	100.0	100.0	100.0	100.0

*Less than .05%.
Source: HUD and NAMSB.

Table XII-9 Terms on Conventional Mortgage Loans

Item	Dec. 1977	Dec. 1978	Dec. 1979	Dec. 1980	Dec. 1981	Dec. 1982
New Single-family Homes:						
Interest Rate (%)	8.87	9.76	11.30	12.86	15.23	13.09
Loan Fees (%)	1.32	1.49	1.85	2.15	2.87	2.98
Maturity in Years	28.00	28.10	28.80	28.20	27.70	26.90
Loan-to-price Ratio (%)	75.50	75.10	72.90	72.90	75.30	75.20
Average Purchase Price	$57,700	$68,100	$79,400	$90,100	$88,700	$91,800
Existing Single-family Homes:						
Interest Rate (%)	8.93	9.85	11.59	13.15	15.53	13.44
Loan Fees (%)	1.17	1.32	1.64	2.12	2.30	2.47
Maturity in Years	26.10	27.00	26.90	26.50	25.30	24.80
Loan-to-price Ratio (%)	74.80	73.70	73.60	73.70	70.60	72.30
Average Purchase Price	$49,400	$61,500	$64,700	$65,300	$70,000	$71,600

Source: United States League of Savings Associations.

insurance for mortgages with a higher than 80 percent loan to value ratio, until that ratio falls to 75 percent. With regard to VA loans there are no set down payment requirements, VA loans having been written for 100 percent loan to value ratios. However, most savings and loan associations limit VA loan magnitudes to 95 percent of value of the property. Additional costs such as points are currently $6\frac{1}{2}$ percent for the seller and 1 percent for the purchaser. In the event of default, the Veterans Administration will reimburse the private lender up to 60 percent or $25,000, whichever is less, of the loan outstanding after foreclosure.

For FHA loans, thrift institutions usually require a down payment equivalent to 3 percent of the first $25,000 valuation of the property and 5 percent of the amount over $25,000. Loan fees or points on FHA mortgage loans are 6 percent for the seller and 1 percent of the purchase price for the buyer. In addition, the mortgage holder is required to pay to the FHA an insurance premium of $\frac{1}{2}$ of percent of the value of the mortgage loan. Tables XII-9 and XII-10 provide some comparable data on the terms on conventional mortgage loans at savings and loan associations from 1977-1980 and on FHA interest rate ceilings from 1970 to December 1982.

OTHER INVESTMENT ACTIVITIES

While investment powers of savings banks vary markedly from state to state, a general indication of balance sheet powers of mutual savings banks is presented in Chart XII-2.

In addition, the Federal Home Loan Bank Board adopted regulations which allow federal mutual savings banks to invest up to 5 percent of their assets in corporate commercial, or business loans, and to accept demand deposits in connection with such loans. Activities and investments of federal mutual savings banks, not permitted to federal savings and loan associations were also "grandfathered" by amendments to existing regulations. Many state regulators have since enacted corresponding parity legislation in order to equalize investment capabilities of federal and state-chartered mutual savings banks and reduce the desire for the conversion of state savings banks to federal charters.

Section 325 of the new Depository Institutions Act of 1982 also authorizes federal savings banks to invest up to $7\frac{1}{2}$ percent of assets in commercial, corporate business, and agricultural loans, with the percentage increasing to 10 percent after January 1, 1984.

Chart XII-2 Selected Balance Sheet Powers and Services of Mutual Savings Banks, by States

Item	Alaska*	Conn.	Del.	Ind.	Me.	Md.	Mass.	Minn.	N.H.	N.J.	New York	Ore.	Penn.	R.I.	Vt.	Wash.	Wis.
ASSETS																	
Mortgage loans																	
1- to 4-family	●	●	●	●	●	●	●	●	●	●	●	●	●	●	●	●	●
Multi-family	●	●	●	●	●	●	●	●	●	●	●	●	●	●	●	●	●
Non-residential	●	●	●	●	●	●	●	●	●	●	●	●	●	●	●	●	●
Unimproved (land) property	●	●	●	●	●	●	●	●	●	●	●	—	●		●	●	—
Other loans																	
Home improvement	●	●	●	●	●	●	●	●	●	●	●	●	●	●	●	●	●
Personal	●	●	—	●	●	●	●	●	●	●	●¹	●	●		●	●	●
Education	●	●	●	●	●	●	●	●	●	●	●	●	●	●	●	●	●
Securities and other investments																	
U.S. Government (including Federal agencies)	●	●	●	●	●	●	●	●	●	●	●	●	●		●	●	●
State and local government	●	●	●	●	●	●	●	●	●	●	●	●	●		●	●	●
Corporate bonds	●	●	●	●	●	●	●	●	●	●	●	●	●		●	●	●
Corporate stock (excluding bank)	●	●	●	●	●	●	●	●	●	●	●	—	●		●	●	—
Bank stock	●	●	●	—	●	●	●	●	●	●	—	—	●		●	●	—
Federal funds	●	●	●	—	●	●	●	●	●	●	●	—	●		●	●	—
Bankers acceptances	●	●	—	●	●	●	●	●	●	●	●	●	●		●	●	●
Investment "leeway provisions"	—	●	—	—	●	—	●	—	—	●	●	●	—	—	●	—	—

LIABILITIES

Deposits
Savings
NOW
Time
Demand
Debentures

OTHER FINANCIAL SERVICES

Savings Bank Life Insurance
General personal trust services

Note: Items marked "●" indicate that the power or service exists either by virtue of specific statutory provision, or a general "prudent man" or "leeway" investment authority, or through ownership of a commercial bank subsidiary. Information in this table refers to state statutes and regulations only. Federal chartering privileges are also available to savings banks under Title XII of the Financial Institutions Regulatory and Interest Rate Control Act. Informatioon on balance sheet powers and services for federally chartered savings banks is available from *A Savings Bankers' Introductory Guide to Federal Mutual Savings Banks*, published by NAMSB, June, 1980.

*Effective July 1, 1980, savings banks were authorized those powers granted to all state banks under the Alaska Banking Code.

[1]"Overdraft" loans.

[2]Noninterest bearing NOW accounts (NINOWs).

[3]The State Banking Department and FDIC approved the accessing of savings accounts by the VISA "debit card"; also noninterest-bearing NOW accounts upheld by State court.

Source: NAMSB.

Table XII-10   FHA Interest Rate Ceilings

Effective Date	One-Family Homes (%)	Apartments* (%)
January 5, 1970	$8\frac{1}{2}$	
December 2, 1970	8	
January 13, 1971	$7\frac{1}{2}$	
February 18, 1971	7	
August 10, 1973	$7\frac{3}{4}$	
August 25, 1973	$8\frac{1}{2}$	
January 22, 1974	$8\frac{1}{4}$	
April 15, 1974	$8\frac{1}{2}$	
May 13, 1974	$8\frac{3}{4}$	
July 8, 1974	9	
August 14, 1974	$9\frac{1}{2}$	
November 25, 1974	9	
January 21, 1975	$8\frac{1}{2}$	
March 3, 1975	8	
April 28, 1975	$8\frac{1}{2}$	
September 2, 1975	9	
January 5, 1976	$8\frac{3}{4}$	9
March 30, 1976	$8\frac{1}{2}$	9
October 18, 1976	8	9
May 31, 1977	$8\frac{1}{2}$	9
February 28, 1978	$8\frac{3}{4}$	9
May 23, 1978	9	9
June 29, 1978	$9\frac{1}{2}$	$9\frac{1}{2}$
April 23, 1979	10	$9\frac{1}{2}$
September 26, 1979	$10\frac{1}{2}$	$9\frac{1}{2}$
October 1, 1979	$10\frac{1}{2}$	10
October 26, 1979	$11\frac{1}{2}$	11
February 11, 1980	12	12
February 28, 1980	13	13
April 3, 1980	14	13
April 28, 1980	13	13
May 15, 1980	$11\frac{1}{2}$	13
July 7, 1980	$11\frac{1}{2}$	12
August 20, 1980	12**	12
September 22, 1980	13**	13
November 24, 1980	$13\frac{1}{2}$**	$13\frac{1}{2}$
December, 1981	$15\frac{1}{2}$	$15\frac{1}{2}$
March 2, 1982	$15\frac{1}{2}$	$16\frac{1}{2}$
November 15, 1982	12	13

*Excludes insurance premium.

**$\frac{1}{2}$ of 1 percent higher for graduated payment mortgages.

Source: United States League of Savings Associations—1981—*Savings and Loan Source Book*.

ALTERNATIVE MORTGAGE INSTRUMENTS

Alternative mortgage instruments to the traditional fixed rate and term mortgage have recently been widely introduced largely to provide mortgage lenders with alternatives for managing interest-rate risks particularly during periods of high and volative interest rates when fixed rate low-yielding long term mortgage loans produce severe earnings pressures, moreso for institutions holding a large portfolio of mortgage loans. Moreover, it was necessary to devise mortgage arrangements whereby the ability to acquire a loan for home financing purposes could be expanded to meet the needs of various individuals.

State chartered associations, particularly those located in California, have been utilizing variable rate mortgages with two associations offering these type of mortgages from as early as 1928. By the end of 1978, over $15 billion in variable rate mortgages had been offered in California. Variable rate mortgages were also offered in 1974 in New England States, Ohio, and Wisconsin. In 1977, the Housing and Urban Development Authority was authorized by Congress to insure graduated payment mortgages.

In 1979, the Federal Home Loan Bank Board authorized the nationwide use of variable rate mortgages by federally-chartered savings and loan associations. As part of the provision of the Depository Institutions Deregulation and Monetary Control Act of 1980, state usury ceilings were pre-empted, thus further relaxing impediments to the widespread use of alternative mortgage instruments available which has in essence served to shift the burden of interest/inflation risks to the buyer or consumer. A brief description of each type of instrument is presented next.

Graduated Payment Mortgage

Under the basic graduated payment mortgage authorized in 1977, the interest rate on the mortgage loan is fixed until maturity of the loan, but monthly payments initially are lower and gradually rise at a stipulated rate over the life of the loan. This instrument was designed to be attractive to young home buyers with using income over the life of the loan but lower initial incomes when the loan is closed. In the early years, the low monthly payments may not be sufficient to cover interest owed and there may be negative amortization. This instrument does not provide advantages over a fixed rate mortgage for institutions in terms of increasing yield when interest rates rise. In July 1981, the Bank Board authorized federal savings and loan associations and mutual savings banks to offer graduated payment adjustable mortgages (GPAM's). This type of mortgage has the same characteristics of the adjustable mortgage loans, but provide that in the early years payments need not be sufficient to fully amortize the loan. The payment amount is required to be adjusted within the first ten years and at least every five years subsequently, to a level adequate to amortize the loan. Amendments were also made to the GPM regulations which eliminated the requirement that payments could be adjusted no more than annually, as well as the prohibition against adjusting monthly payments and the provision that borrowers have the right to convert to a fixed rate mortgage.

Variable Rate Mortgages

Federal savings and loans were authorized to issue VRM loans in 1979. Under this type of loan, the interest rate may rise or fall in relation to some index such as the average cost of funds at all insured institutions as computed semi-anually by the Federal Home Loan Bank Board and is outside the control of the individual lender. Interest rate adjustments may not be made more than once a year with initial adjustment only after one year after the first regular monthly payments. Interest rates may vary by $\frac{1}{2}$ a point a year with a maximum increase of 2.5 percent over the life of the loan. Decreases of interest rates are mandatory while increases are optional. Borrowers may repay the loan without prepayment penalties when the interest rate is adjusted if he so desires. This is a type of an adjustable rate mortgage (ARM).

In April 1981, federal savings and loan associations and federal mutual savings banks were permitted to peg mortgage interest rates adjustments to any published public index of interest rates and raise or lower the loans monthly payments, principal, or terms to reflect fluctuation market conditions. No limits were set as to the extent to which interest rates or monthly payments could vary. Most savings and loan associations have tended to use FHLMC bid auction rate as the index for adjusting these mortgage loans. Most institutions now offer adjustable rate mortgages and it is expected that in future years over 40 percent or more mortgage portfolios will consist of adjustable rate mortgages.

Renegotiable Rate Mortgage

This type of mortgage loan was authorized in April 1980, and permits thrift institutions to undertake larger rate increases but at less frequent intervals than with variable rate or adjustable rate mortgages. The RRM composes a note with a term of 3, 4, or 5 years secured by a long term mortgage of up to 30 years, automatically renewable at equal intervals. The renewal interest rate may be adjusted according to changes in the FHLB monthly national average mortgage rate index, which is based on the contract rate of interest on previously occupied homes. Adjustments of interest rates are limited to the multiple of $\frac{1}{2}$ of 1 percent per year and the number of years in the renewal term with a maximum upward or lower adjustment of 5 percent over the life of the loan. The borrower has the right to repay the loan without penalty at the end of the first term. The borrower's interests are protected by a series of regulatory requirements.

Reverse Annuity Mortgages (RAMs)

Reverse annuity mortgages allow retired individuals to obtain a cash flow from the equity in their debt free home. Homeowners receive a monthly amount from the lending institution, which is secured by a gradually increasing mortgage on the residence. In October 1981, the Federal Home Loan Bank Board amended its regulations governing RAMs, by removing the requirement that such loan plans be submitted to the Board, that lenders offer refinancing of such loans at maturity and that such loans carry a fixed interest rate. Such changes would, according to the Board, enhance the marketability of RAM loans which have not been widely used by federal associations. Interest rate adjustments on RAM loans would be similar to the AML regulations governing implementation of rate changes, permissible indices, and pre-application disclosure.

Balloon Payment Mortgage

With the balloon payment loan, the mortgagor pays interest and perhaps principal over the term of the loan and repays the entire amount outstanding when the loan is due. In October 1981, regulations governing balloon loans were also amended by the Bank Board. Federally chartered thrift institutions were authorized to make non-amortized and partially amortized loans by increasing the maximum loan-to-value ratio from 60 to 95 percent, removing the existing five year maximum terms of such loans and allowing the interest rates on such loans to be also periodically adjusted. Balloon payment loans have been gaining popularity at some lending institutions in recent times.

Flip or Pledged Account Mortgage

The pledged account mortgage is a hybrid of the graduated payment mortgage loan. With a FLIP loan, the borrower's monthly mortgage payments are reduced during the first five years of the loan. Such a reduction is effected by using a portion of the borrower's down payment to fund a pledged savings account which is used to supplement monthly mortgage payments. Under this approach there is no negative amortization. Borrowers using this type of loan are able to obtain housing finance for which under normal circumstances they would not be qualified. FLIP, thus, provides a "head start" for individuals desiring to purchase homes earlier than otherwise would have been possible with a regular fixed rate mortgage.

SHARED APPRECIATION MORTGAGES

In October 1980, the Federal Home Loan Bank Board announced proposals for the authorization of federally chartered thrift institutions to offer shared appreciation mortgages. Lenders would receive a share in the equity profits when the house is sold, in return for charging borrowers below market interest rates on these mortgage loans. The lenders' share would be limited to 40 percent of the total appreciation over the life of the loan. Interest rate on these loans would be based on the lenders' evaluation of the future appreciation of the property. SAMs may be offered by certain service corporations of savings and loan associations. If the home is not sold within ten years, the proposed regulations would require that the borrower refinance the loan and pay the lender a lump sum defined as "contingent interest" which is equivalent to the agreed share of the appreciation less any home improvements. SAMs could provide potential tax benefits to both lenders and investors. Oppenheimer and Company and its subsidiary in August 1980 began offering the "Appreciation Participation Loan" to home buyers, with a conventional mortgage at an interest rate $\frac{1}{3}$ below the market rate. In return, the mortgagor gives to the lender $\frac{1}{3}$ of any profits when the house is sold. Such loans may be viewed as an inflation hedge for the lender, but expectations of appreciation may be overstated which increases yield risks. Cash inflow during the term of the loan would also be reduced.

With the rapidly changing financial environment and consequent innovation to meet changing needs and goals, federal savings and loan and other mortgage lenders were authorized to offer wraparound mortgages, although many states have been using these instruments prior to 1981.

A wraparound mortgage generally involves two lenders, a mortgage originator and a wraparound lender, in addition to a borrower desiring to purchase a home with an existing mortgage. If the borrower is unable to provide the downpayment necessary in order to assume the existing mortgage, the wraparound lender would provide the required funds. The wraparound lender would originate a loan for the amount desired for the down payment in addition to the amount of the existing mortgage. The lender would then average the rate on the existing loan; for example 9 percent, with the current market rate for the down payment, such as 15 percent and charge the borrower 12 percent on the entire loan. The wraparound lender would continue to service the 9 percent loan but obtain a 3 percent profit on the transaction. Wraparounds tend to extend the life of the low yielding loans, and could not be undertaken if due on sale clauses were applicable and enforced.

THE SECONDARY MARKET

Secondary market activity provide the machinery through which mortgage lenders are able to augment sources of funds whether by issuing mortgage backed bonds or pass-through certificates. The market also provides a channel of communications between mortgage originators and private investors desirous of holding mortgage assets without the associated costs of origination, servicing, and so on. In this way, funds not otherwise available for housing can be tapped and the level of housing credit raised beyond that generated by resources of lending institutions. A brief description of the various quasi-governmental agencies involved in the operation of the secondary is presented next.

Government National Mortgage Association

The Government National Mortgage Association (GNMA) created in 1968 is a wholly owned corporate instrumentality of the United States Government, functioning under the aegis of the Department of Housing and Urban Development. The Department of Housing through its secretary is responsible for making policy decisions concerning the operation of the association.

Through the Tandem Program of the Government National Mortgage Association, Ginnie Mae, as the association is commonly called, absorbes some of the interest rate risk when mortgages are sold at a discount, that is less than the face value. The program is called the Tandem Program because both the GNMA and the FNMA, the Federal National Mortgage Association, work in tandem on the purchases of these loans. Ginnie Mae issues a commitment to the seller to purchase the mortgage at a fixed price, the acquired loan being sold to Fannie Mae at current market prices. The discount on these loans is absorbed by the GNMA. A variation of the tandem program was developed for conventional loans in 1974, with the participation of the Federal National Mortgage Association and the Federal Home Loan Mortgage Corporation (FHLMC). The tandem programs have not been in operation recently, largely because of the limited resources of the GNMA.

Ginnie Mae plays a more vital role in the secondary market through the issuance of mortgage backed securities guaranteed or insured by the government. These issues are security instruments collateralized by a pool of mortgages with the cash flow from the pool being used to repay the security. The first GNMA pass-through security was issued in February, 1970 and has received wide market acceptance by private investors. There are basically two types of mortgage backed securities. The first, mentioned previously, the pass-through security, is composed of mortgages aggregated in pools, fractional participations in which are sold to investors. Mortgage payment receipts received by the issuer, the GNMA are "passed through" to the holders of these instruments. The investor is thus assured a minimum yield in monthly payments of interest and principal, which may fluctuate as a result of prepayments, or delinquent payments.

The second type of mortgage backed security is the mortgage-backed bond. This type of instrument is collateralized by a pool of mortgages, is a general obligation of the issuing authority, has a stated maturity, and is usually issued with a fixed interest rate payable semi-annually. Mortgage-backed bonds issued by the GNMA, thus, have fixed and certain cash flow similar to traditional corporate bond instruments. Pass-through securities are the more popular types of secondary market activity by the GNMA, as bond type instruments may be issued only by the federal secondary market agencies. The following tables provide data on the GNMA mortgage-backed security program for the years 1970-80, and on the holdings of GNMA mortgage-backed pass-through securities by selected types of investors for the years 1970-79. The phenomenal growth in the dollar volumes since 1970 is evident from the data given in Tables XII-11 and XII-12. In 1975, a futures market in GNMA pass-throughs was inaugurated on the Chicago Board of Trade, thus providing a hedge for secondary market participants against fluctuations in interest rates during the commitment period of the particular instrument held. Through the GNMA mortgage pass-through program, pension funds, state and municipal retirement funds, and other institutional investors have been attracted into the provision of housing finance through this medium. The GNMA guaranty which is presented on the face of each mortgage-backed security provides security to investors in the event that the issuer is unable to meet its obligations with respect to the payment of interest and principal, the GNMA will, through its guaranty, continue payments to holders of these instruments over the life of the pooled mortgages.

Federal National Mortgage Association

The Federal National Mortgage Association, Fannie Mae, as it is known in the industry, was chartered originally as a government corporation in 1938, rechartered as a federal agency in 1954, and then in 1968 was reorganized as a government-sponsored stock-holder corporation. The principal function of the FNMA is the creation of a secondary market in residential loans. Originally, this ability was limited to FHA and VA loans but was extended to conventional loans in 1970, by Fannie Mae or the largest purchaser of residential mortgages in the United States. As Table XII-13 illustrates, Fannie Mae, at the end of 1980, held a total mortgage loan portfolio of over $57 billion. Loans are

Table XII-11 Holdings of GNMA Mortgage-Backed Pass-Through Securities, by Selected Types of Investors, 1970–1980

End of Year	Total	Mutual Savings Banks	Commercial Banks	Savings and Loan Associations	Credit Unions	Retirement and Pension Funds	All Other Holders
(in millions of dollars)							
1970	452	86	10	248	—	67	41
1971	3,154	605	126	1,552	210	171	500
1972	5,816	1,216	301	2,426	354	291	1,228
1973	8,769	1,891	500	2,919	450	619	2,390
1974	13,321	2,402	789	4,505	534	1,028	4,518
1975	29,769	3,049	991	5,670	654	1,641	8,764
1976	34,533	4,496	1,844	6,775	895	3,446	17,077
1977	51,973	6,102	3,103	7,666	1,341	5,920	27,841
1978	67,331	7,406	3,966	9,204	1,602	7,743	37,410
1979	92,270	9,043	5,444	14,117	1,938	9,688	52,040
1980	112,920	10,953	5,985	19,422	2,258	10,389	63,913
(Percentage distribution)							
1970	100.0	19.0	2.2	54.9	—	14.8	9.1
1971	100.0	19.2	4.0	49.2	6.7	5.1	15.9
1972	100.0	20.9	5.2	41.7	6.1	5.0	21.1
1973	100.0	21.6	5.7	33.3	5.1	7.1	27.3
1974	100.0	18.0	5.9	30.4	4.0	7.7	33.9
1975	100.0	14.7	4.8	27.3	3.1	7.9	42.2
1976	100.0	13.0	5.3	19.6	2.6	10.0	49.5
1977	100.0	11.7	6.0	14.7	2.6	11.4	53.6
1978	100.0	11.0	5.9	13.7	2.4	11.5	55.6
1979	100.0	9.8	5.9	15.3	2.1	10.5	56.4
1980	100.0	9.7	5.3	17.2	2.0	9.2	56.6

Note: Data represent face amount of original issues, and differ from figures compiled by NAMSB which cover unpaid principal only. All other holders include mortgage bankers and investment bankers, corporations, life insurance companies, state and local governments, nominees and others.
Source: GNMA.
Source: National Association of Mutual Savings Banks—1981 Fact Book of Mutual Savings Banking.

Table XII-12   GNMA Mortgage-Backed Security Program
(millions of dollars)

| Year | Pass-through Securities | | Bonds Sold |
	Applications	Issues	
1970	$ 1,126	$ 452	$1,315
1971	4,374	2,702	300
1972	3,854	2,662	. . .
1973	5,529	3,249	. . .
1974	6,203	4,784	. . .
1975	10,449	7,366	. . .
1976	25,394	13,765	. . .
1977	31,076	16,230	. . .
1978	35,014	15,359	. . .
1979	53,820	24,592	. . .
1980	58,701	20,648	. . .
1981	36,915	14,253	. . .
1982	38,863	16,006	. . .

Source: U.S. League of Savings Institutions.

purchased by this agency under a system of competitive bids and on a
forward commitment plan. As the table reveals, loan sales by Fannie
Mae are very negligible in comparison to the volume of purchased
mortgages held, as thus characterizes the agency more as a permanent
holder of acquisitions rather than as a dynamic market-originating

Table XII-13   FNMA Activity
(millions of dollars)

Year	Loan Purchases	Loan Sales	Total Portfolio (Year-end)
1960	$ 980	$ 42	$ 2,903
1965	757	46	2,520
1970	5,078	. . .	15,502
1971	3,574	336	17,791
1972	3,699	211	19,791
1973	6,127	71	24,175
1974	6,953	4	29,578
1975	4,263	2	31,824
1976	3,606	86	32,904
1977	4,780	67	34,370
1978	12,303	5	43,311
1979	10,812	. . .	51,091
1980	8,099	. . .	57,327
1981	6,112	. . .	61,412
1982	15,116	. . .	71,814

Source: U.S. League of Savings Institutions.

institution, such as the Federal Home Loan Mortgage Corporation (FHLMC). Over the years, Fannie Mae has undertaken business primarily with mortgage bankers.

In November 1982, Fannie Mae announced an expanded program that could generate below market rate mortgages on two million homes. By offering resale and refinancing mortgage options to home owners whose current mortgage is owned by Fannie Mae and to buyers of these homes, the agency hopes to make some contribution to a housing recovery through the lowering of effective rates. Under the program, three below market refinancing alternatives will be available; namely, adjustable rate mortgages (ARMs), graduated payment adjustable rate mortgages (GPARMs), and a 30-year fixed rate loan. In the case of the first two options, there is no interest rate floor, while with the fixed rate alternative the interest will not be less than 11 percent.

Federal Home Loan Mortgage Corporation

The Federal Home Loan Mortgage Corporation was established in 1970 under provisions of the 1970 Emergency Home Finance Act to foster the flow of capital to housing markets through the creation of a buoyant secondary mortgage market. The FHLMC is governed by the Federal Home Loan Bank Board and is required to provide services to specified mortgage lenders such as depository institutions and certain mortgage banking institutions. The FHLMC augments the supply of funds flowing into the housing markets through the purchase of existing mortgages from traditional lenders. Conventional loans, participations in conventional loans, FHA, and VA loans are all handled by the corporation along the same lines as the Federal National Mortgage Association. Through its issue of mortgage backed securities, collateralized by pools of conventional residential mortgages, the FHLMC has successfully assisted in the integration of the mortgage and bond markets. The FHLMC has received wide market acceptance of its issues of participation certificates (PCs) which are pass-through mortgage backed securities and guaranteed mortgage certificates (GMCs) which are mortgage-backed bonds. The FHLMC may also raise funds to finance purchases by borrowing from the Federal Home Loan Bank or by issuing GNMA-guaranteed mortgage backed bonds, though the use of these two methods of acquiring funds has declined over the years. In 1979, the FHLMC purchased $5.7 billion in mortgage loans while sales totalled $4.5 billion. As shown in the following Table XII-14, greater emphasis,

Table XII-14   Federal Home Loan Mortgage Corporation Activity
(millions of dollars)

Year	Mortgage Transactions		Loan Portfolio (Year-end)		
	Purchases	Sales	Total	FHA-VA	Conventional
1970	$ 325	. . .	$ 325	$ 325	. . .
1971	778	$ 113	968	821	$ 147
1972	1,297	407	1,788	1,502	286
1973	1,334	409	2,604	1,800	804
1974	2,190	53	4,586	1,961	2,625
1975	1,713	1,521	4,987	1,881	3,106
1976	1,127	1,797	4,269	1,675	2,594
1977	4,160	4,647	3,267	1,450	1,817
1978	6,526	6,425	3,091	1,299	1,792
1979	5,621	4,544	4,052	1,159	2,893
1980	3,723	2,526	5,056	1,090	3,966
1981	3,800	3,532	5,237	1,047	4,190
1982	23,673	24,169	4,733	1,009	3,724

Source: U.S. League of Savings Institutions.

too, has been placed in purchasing conventional mortgages in comparison to the more standardized FHA-VA loans. This is in keeping with the fact that conventional loans now comprise the bulk of mortgage loans closed by institutional lenders. Attempts too have been made to develop more standardized packages and procedures for conventional loans.

The secondary market has also witnessed the development of the issuance of mortgage backed securities by private mortgage lenders particularly securities collateralized by conventional mortgages. These issues do not have federal guarantees and their success in the market place is dependent on market acceptance of these private issues, ratings by traditional bond agencies, and the general market evaluation of the financial condition of the particular issuing institution. In 1977, over $1.2 billion of these instruments were placed on the market by private lending institutions, in particular banks and savings and loan associations. Regulations governing the issuance of mortgage-backed bonds and pass-throughs were discussed fully in Chapter VIII. In essence, the decision to issue a mortgage backed bond as against a mortgage-backed pass-through is a balance sheet choice between borrowing through the bond vehicle or selling an asset through the pass-through mechanism.

While developments in the private mortgage-backed markets were encouraging during 1977 and 1978, current market conditions and the plight of thrift institutions during 1980-82 have brought activity in this area virtually to a standstill. A fully developed, privately originated, mortgage-backed securities sector in conjunction with an active government guaranteed sedondary sector can produce substantial benefits to the housing markets nationally in the future.

With the development of new alternative mortgages rate instruments with fluctuating interest rate provisions, more efficient methods of reducing the uncertainty to investors in the secondary market will have to be developed. Currently, activity is largely confined to arrangements on a deal-by-deal basis. The issue of due-on-sale clauses will also have to be settled nationally, since both the FNMA and FHLMC require due-on-sale clauses in conventional mortgages which they purchase from lenders. Federal pre-emption of state due-on-sale restrictions may be necessary to expand the future breadth and depth of the secondary market.

With regard to the treatment of alternative mortgage instruments, Freddie Mac has established restrictive rules governing what the agency will purchase. It will use the FHLBB index based on the mortgage contract rate for previously occupied homes, prohibit negative amortization, allow only one interest rate adjustment annually, and limit the term of loan to no more than 30 years. Fannie Mae uses more than one index, allow negative amortization and greater flexibility in terms and conditions. It will take some time before standardization of these experimental alternative mortgage packages in the secondary market can be adequately effected to reduce uncertainty and instability on these issues in the market.

In February 1982, secondary market administrators announced new programs and operating changes that would be introduced in the near future. Both Fannie Mae and Freddie Mac officials stated that they would increase the issuance of mortgage-backed securities and continue a policy of streamlining operation. Programs are planned that will seek to resolve some of the problems associated with affordability of homes for buyers. Freddie Mac also plans to increase mortgage banker participation in its activities and to expand its SWAP program to attract current loans and not only low yielding instruments. The proposed recapitalization plan now before Congress would enable the agency to undertake desired expansion and to eliminate non-member fees.

In an attempt to bolster the pool of funds available for housing finance, Freddie Mac, that is the Federal Home Loan Mortgage Corporation, in a coalition with Merrill Lynch White Weld Capital Markets Group and Salomon Brothers introduced a program in June 1982 to generate up to $500 million in funds for mortgage financing.

The new program offered growing equity mortgages more commonly known as GEM loans, which would significantly reduce the lifespan of a traditional mortgage. Monthly payments by borrowers would increase by 4 percent a year, the increases being applied to principal and not interest. In this way, the mortgage would be paid down in a shorter period of time.

Participation certificates will be issued by Freddie Mac in exchange for GEM loans bought by the institution. Merrill Lynch and Salomon Brothers will then sell the participation certificates to institutional investors creating additional housing funds through the secondary market. Plans call for expansion of the program if the initial offering is successful.

The Ginnie Mae Tandem Programs are being phased out by Congressional decree, but the agency would continue to provide financing for FHA-VA mortgage loans. It remains to be seen what the nature of the effects of the recently proposed reductions in commitment ceilings for the GNMA and the FHA will be on the secondary market in the year ahead.

During 1983, secondary market mortgage activity mushroomed, as over $253 billion in mortgage backed securities were outstanding at year end or 14 percent of total mortgages. In 1983, 43 percent of all new mortgages were channeled through these securities in comparison to 14 percent in 1980. Through various pools of mortgages, these securities are being sold to pension funds, insurance companies, state and local retirement plans, and government credit agencies. The growth in the secondary market mortgage mechanism has, in effect, fostered accelerated development of a national mortgage market and allowed fixed mortgages to be originated and later sold. Sears Mortgage Securities Corp., Residential Funding Corp., and General Electric Mortgage Securities Corp. are three major private companies that buy mortgages for resale in the secondary market. In fact, Residential Funding issued over $1.5 billion in securities in 1983.

Moreover, a national electronic mortgage market introduced by First Boston Corp. in 1983 through its Shelternet computer network, may significantly reduce the necessity for home buyers to seek mortgage finance in the traditional way. A real estate broker using the Shelternet system can, in effect, originate a loan electronically within hours, withouth the usual customer/banker meeting. Electronic mortgage technology can reduce the application processing period. The growth of the electronic mortgage marketing system will, no doubt, also facilitate the development of a timely national mortgage market system.

FEDERAL LEGISLATION GOVERNING
MORTGAGE LENDING

Since the late 1960s, a plethora of federal regulations governing the lending activities of savings and loan associations have been enacted. Most of these regulations were designed to afford protection to consumers and have increased the costs and paperwork involved in loan documentation procedures undertaken by thrift institutions and commercial banks.

Some of the more salient regulations include the Equal Credit Opportunity Act which prohibits discrimination based on race, sec, or marital status, the Truth-in-Lending Act, the Fair Credit Billing Act, the Mortgage Disclosure Act, and the Real Estate Settlement Procedures Act. The latter legislation stipulates that the lender furnish advance disclosures of all charges related to the loan to the potential borrower. Another important regulation affecting mortgage lending by thrift institutions and commercial banks is the Community Reinvestment Act enacted in 1977.

The Community Reinvestment Act requires each financial institution to prepare a designated statement outlining its community's geographic area and the institution's provision of credit to consumers in that area. This federal legislation was a response to the widespread alleged "redlining" practice of banks and other financial institutions. "Redlining" denotes the situation where financial institutions, as a matter of policy, decline to extend credit to a specifically demarcated area within a city or community. Such a practice was viewed as having deleterious and destabilizing social, political, and economic ramifications and perhaps foster urban plight. The Community Reinvestment Act sought to encourae greater community social responsibility on the part of financial institutions serving a particular neighborhood. In this way, the credit provisions of low and middle-income communities could be satisfied. Financial institutions are also required to publicly display a Community Reinvestment Act notice which solicits comments and suggestions on the institutions' credit performance from customers.

Failure to adequately satisfy the provisions of the Community Reinvestment act can result in applications for branching and new services being denied the particular negligent institution by federal and state authorities.

Chapter XIII

Future Perspectives— Outlook for the Future

OVERVIEW OF THE GROWTH AND CURRENT PROBLEMS OF THE THRIFT INDUSTRY

The thrift industry, in particular savings and loan associations, has demonstrated remarkable growth in assets since 1950. By 1975, for example, savings and loan associations were the second largest type of financial institution, after commercial banks, surpassing life insurance companies, with the numerically and geographically limited mutual banking industry ranked fourth. For savings and loan associations, total assets were 40 times larger in 1982 than assets in 1950, a growth rate over this time period surpassed only by credit unions.

Such growth, however, has not been smooth or steady on a year-to-year basis, but rather the long-term straight line trend has been punctuated by a series of peaks and troughs. During the mid-1960s and 1970s, thrift institutions experienced severe outflows of deposits as a result of competition from commercial banks and market financial instruments such as government and corporate securities. With rising interest rates and inflationary pressures, individuals shifted funds into more direct capital market instruments with higher returns than interest paid on deposits at thrift institutions. This financial disintermediation resulted in earnings pressures at thrift institutions and a reduction in funds available for housing finance. The inability of thrift institutions to undertake adjustments during cyclical fluctuations within the economy was a direct product of the legal and regulatory structure in which they operated vis-a-vis the well-known problem of borrowing short and lending long. With assets limited to fixed rate, long-term mortgages, during periods of rising and volatile interest rates, thrifts' portfolios were virtually locked in with these low yielding assets.

Various analysts, commissions, and studies presented recommendations for dealing with the problems facing thrift institutions during these periods of financial upheaval. The Commission on Money and Credit in the 1960s, the Hunt Report in 1971, The Financial Institutions Act of 1973 and 1975, the Financial Institutions and the Nation's Economy (FINE) study, and the Financial Reform Act of 1976, all addressed the subject of financial reform, but no major legislative action was taken during this period. Rather, a series of piecemeal regulatory amendments and innovations were introduced largely in response to an increasing array of financial products being offered by private unregulated institutions. The short-lived "wild card" four-year certificate in 1973 was one such attempt. In June 1978, the introduction of the Money Market Certificate (MMC) provided depository institutions with a short-term instrument which was sensitive to changes in the financial market place. A variable ceiling account, the small saver certificate with a longer-term maturity of $2\frac{1}{2}$ years, was also introduced in 1979. These two certificate accounts were largely designed to halt the disintermediation that was taking place as funds from depository institutions flowed to non-banking institutions offering higher yielding instruments.

Given an increasingly market sensitive deposit structure, the percentage of savings held in passbook accounts has declined dramatically as Table XIII-1 illustrates. While passbook accounts accounted for 91 percent of total savings in 1966, by 1980, the percentage had declined to 21 percent; to 19 percent in 1981, and 14.6 percent in 1982. Over 80 percent of the liabilities of savings and loan associations were held in the form of money market certificates, small saver certificates, large denomination time deposits, and borrowings, FHLB advances and outside borrowings in the financial market. Mutual savings banks also demonstrated a similar shift in deposit structure. While time deposits accounted for 17 percent of total savings and time deposits at the end of 1970, these accounts mushroomed to 64 percent of total savings and time accounts by the end of 1980. Money market certificates accounted for about 30 percent of deposits and for approximately one-half of total time deposits.

The "internal disintermediation" which occurred as funds were moved from lower yielding passbook accounts into higher yielding

Table XIII-1 Interest Rate Margins, Return on Assets of FSLIC-Insured Savings Associations, 1955-1981

	Percent of Passbook to Total Savings Deposits	Percent of Mortgages to Total Assets	Interest Return on Mortgages[1]	Average Cost of Funds[2]	Margin	Return on Average Assets (%)		
						Before Taxes	After Taxes	Margin
1955	95	84	5.16	2.94[3]	2.22	1.12	1.10	2
1956	95	83	5.37	3.03	2.34	1.04	1.02	2
1957	95	83	5.85	3.64	2.21	0.96	0.95	1
1958	95	83	5.70	3.38	2.32	0.98	0.97	1
1959	95	84	5.97	3.53	2.44	0.98	0.97	1
1960	95	84	5.73	3.86	2.13	0.87	0.87	—
1961	95	84	5.97	3.90	2.07	0.99	0.98	1
1962	95	85	5.92	4.08	1.84	0.98	0.98	—
1963	95	85	6.04	4.17	1.87	0.80	0.70	10
1964	95	85	5.96	4.18	1.78	0.84	0.72	10
1965	95	86	5.93	4.25	1.68	0.81	0.68	13
1966	91	86	5.94	4.53	1.41	0.49	0.43	6
1967	81	85	6.01	4.72	1.29	0.62	0.53	11
1968	77	86	6.13	4.74	1.39	0.82	0.69	13
1969	67	87	6.32	4.89	1.43	0.87	0.73	14
1970	59	86	6.56	5.30	1.26	0.74	0.59	15
1971	55	85	6.81	5.38	1.43	1.03	0.72	31
1972	51	85	6.98	5.41	1.57	1.10	0.79	31
1973	47	85	7.16	5.60	1.56	0.97	0.77	20
1974	44	83	7.43	6.14	1.29	0.68	0.55	13
1975	43	83	7.66	6.32	1.34	0.72	0.48	24
1976	40	83	8.00	6.38	1.62	0.98	0.64	34
1977	38	83	8.26	6.44	1.82	1.15	0.79	36
1978	32	83	8.50	6.67	1.83	1.22	0.84	38
1979	25	82	8.86	7.47	1.39	0.98	0.68	30
1980	21	80	9.34	8.94	0.40	0.19	0.13	6
1981	19	78	9.91	10.92	−1.01	N/A	−0.74	N/A
1982	14.6	68.3	10.68	11.38	−0.07	N/A	−0.62	N/A
1983	12	64	11.04	9.81	1.23	N/A	0.30	N/A

Source: Federal Home Loan Bank Board, United States Leage of Savings Associations.

[1]Interest earned on mortgages as a percentage average mortgage balances net of loans in process.

[2]Interest and dividends paid on savings, FHLB advances and other borrowed money as a percent of average savings and borrowings.

[3]Average savings deposit rate for 1955-1965.

Figure XIII-1   S&L Rate of Return on Average Assets,
                    1981 to 1983 (Projected)

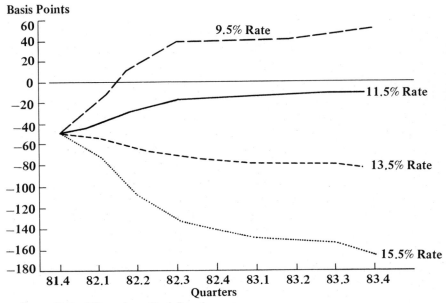

Source: Federal Home Loan Bank Board.

passbook accounts into higher yielding money market certificates, naturally increased the cost of funds to savings and loan associations. Moreover, in order to attract new deposits, high-cost market instruments had to be offered which increased both the average and marginal cost of funds to these institutions. As Table XIII-1 shows, given the fact that over 80 percent of savings and loan association assets were held in long-term mortgage instruments, a large percentage of which were negotiated at lower than current interest rates, the average yield on these assets has lagged behind the marginal yield on new mortgages. Such "portfolio drag" has had a debilitating effect on the earnings position of savings and loan associations.

As column 7 in the table shows, return on assets after taxes has declined from 0.79 percent in 1972 to 0.13 percent in 1980, and —0.74 percent in 1981 and —0.62 in 1982. The incidence of taxation, too, has also resulted in a wider spread between return on assets before taxes and return on assets after taxes. In 1980, for example, the comparable figures were 0.19 percent and 0.13 percent, respectively.

As Raoul D. Edwards, Senior Editor of the United States Banker, noted, "One simple statistic highlights the problems of the thrift industry. It costs $11.74 to attract $100 of savings, and thrifts can get only $9.91 back on each $100 loaned . . ."[1] At the end of April 1981, about 395 institutions had a net worth of 1.68 percent or a leverage ratio of 98.3 percent. According to the then Chairman of the Federal Home Loan Bank Board, Richard Pratt, these institutions were losing about 350 basis points on assets per year, with a return on net worth of —220 percent per year. At such a rate of depletion of net worth to assets, these institutions would reach a zero net worth position in a mean time of 5.38 months. During the first six months of 1981, insured savings and loan associations lost $1.5 billion, with nearly 70 percent of all insured associations recording losses over the period. As Table XIII-1 illustrates, the margin between interest return on mortgages and the average cost of funds has declined markedly, from 1.83 in 1978 to 0.40 in 1980 and —1.01 in 1981. During 1983, however, there was a marked improvement in the earnings performance of savings and loan associations, largely as a result of a decline in cost of funds associated with the downturn in short-term market interest rates. Approximately 30 percent of all thrifts continued to operate in the red during 1983.

In an economic environment characterized by accelerating and highly volatile interest rates, inflationary pressures, general economic decline and intensified competition from unregulated quasi-banking financial institutions, the thrift industry has suffered severe destabilizing shocks which threaten the viability of the nation's primary source of housing finance. The social and economic environment in which thrift institutions operate has undergone dramatic and pervasive changes which rendered anachronistic and ineffective much of the statutory and regulatory framework governing the operations of the thrift industry. It can hardly be denied that the system created in the 1930s and preserved by various legislative enactments over the years generated substantial benefits to the nation, particularly in the housing arena, during periods of stable interest rates. But given the highly diversified and increasingly competitive financial services industry of today, with many institutions operating in a largely unfettered environment, the thrift institutions were caught in an inflexible nexus of regulatory restrictions and a traditional modus operandi which militated against rapid change and innovation consonant with the contemporary competitive milieu.

---

[1]Edwards, Raoul D. "Special Report: Financing Housing," *United States Banker*, February 1982, p. 16.

CHANGING MARKET ENVIRONMENT

In 1979, for example, while financial assets of households increased by $254.9 billion, major depository institutions accounted for only 33.8 percent of this growth. Given the rapidly rising and volatile interest rate scenario in 1979, a significant percentage of the growth in household financial assets was placed in instruments offered by money market mutual funds. Money market funds invest in a mix of short-term securities such as certificates of deposit, commercial paper, banker's acceptances, and government securities. Individuals may purchase shares in the fund in relatively small denominations and, hence, obtain higher interest rates offered by these short-term instruments.

Total assets of money market funds grew by 318.5 percent in 1979 to a year-end level of $45.2 billion. In 1977, the assets of money market funds totalled $3.8 billion. By the end of 1981, total assets of money market funds increased to over $181.5 billion rising from a year-end total of $74.6 billion in 1980.

During this period, savings and loan associations and mutual savings banks recorded heavy deposit outflows, as shown in Tables XIII-2 and XIII-3. Net new savings inflows at savings and loan associations were negative for three months in 1980, and for nine months in 1981. Outflows for 1981 totalled approximately $25 billion up to December 1981, though there was some positive gain in October as a result of the tax-exampt All Savers Certificates. For savings banks, the deposit outflow was also substantial. In 1979, the mutual savings bank industry lost approximately $7 billion in deposit outflows. From August 1979

Table XIII-2   Net New Deposits at Savings and Loan Associations, 1979-1981

1979		1980		1981	
July	1,455	January	1,167	January	599
August	717	February	1,079	February	879
September	—198	March	—696	March	—2,137
October	1,314	April	—817	April	—4,638
November	732	May	1,785	May	—70
December	—700	June	—169	June	—5,759
		July	961	July	—5,538
		August	1,285	August	—3,290
		September	6	September	—3,799
		October	2,500	October	—1,601
		November	1,461	November	—1,568
		December	2,055	December	- - -

Source: United States League of Savings Associations.

until November 1981, mutual banks experienced only three months of positive new deposit growth. While there was a $4 billion gain in deposit inflows at savings banks due to the introduction of the new All Savers Certificate, in October 1981, the net result was a $65 million net deposit outflow. This outflow was a marked improvement over the $1.7 billion outflow in September, moreover when it is noted that for the first nine months of 1981, net deposit losses totalled $11.4 billion.

As Table XIII-3 illustrates for the year 1981, savings banks experienced a net savings and time deposit outflow of $13.8 billion, representing a 9.1 percent decline of total outstanding balances. Tables XIII-3 and XIII-4 also reveal that the net change in deposits excluding interest, of $1.3 billion in December 1981, was the largest deposit outflow for that month experienced by savings banks since 1971. The deposit outflow in December 1981 was equivalent to a decline of 86 basis points in total deposits outstanding.

While it cannot be denied that money market funds have attracted a substantial percentage of the deposit outflows from the thrift industry, their holdings represent a small percentage of the total time and savings deposits of depository institutions. Statistics for 1980 indicate that while savings and time deposits held by banks and thrifts amounted to over $1.4 trillion, assets of money market funds represented only 5.3 percent of this total. Money market funds were not the cause of deposit outflows from traditional depository institutions, but rather a development of the fundamental change, innovation, and diversity taking place in the nation's financial marketplace as a result of technology, volatile market conditions, and increasing knowledge and sophistication on the part of the American consumer.

It should be pointed out parenthetically that during the 1968-1969 period of rising interest rates and inflation, the growth in time and savings deposits held by households declined from $42 billion to $12 billion. The bulk of the decline in savings deposits was channelled into Treasury bills which yielded higher returns at the time. Money market funds are a product of change and a reflection of the fact that the traditional barriers between banking and commerce are slowly being eroded in an era of intense competition. Indeed, innovation and change will of necessity restructure the nation's financial services industry, including the options and activities permissible to banks and thrifts vis-a-vis the rapidly mushrooming "nonbanking" financial services' sector. Commercial banks and thrift institutions—before the passage of the 1982 Garn Act—were at a competitive disadvantage in

Table XIII-3 Net Deposit Change at Savings Banks, Past Twelve Months
(amounts in millions of dollars)

| Period | Net Change in Deposits | | | | Interest Credited | |
| | Excluding Interest | | Including Interest | | | |
	Amount	Percent of Outstanding Deposits	Amount	Percent of Outstanding Deposits	Amount	Percent of Outstanding Deposits
December 1981p	$−1,300	−.86	$800	.53	$2,100	1.38
November 1981	−1,060	−.70	−188	−.12	872	.57
October 1981	−65	−.04	789	.52	854	.57
September 1981	−1,679	−1.11	319	.21	1,999	1.33
August 1981	−1,542	−1.02	−672	−.44	870	.57
July 1981	−1,935	−1.27	−1,133	−.74	802	.53
June 1981	−1,387	−.91	542	.36	1,929	1.27
May 1981	−676	−.45	148	.10	824	.54
April 1981	−2,025	−1.33	−1,234	−.81	791	.52
March 1981	−757	−.50	1,224	.81	1,980	1.31
February 1981	−385	−.26	296	.20	681	.45
January 1981	−979	−.65	−365	−.24	614	.41
Full year 1981p	−13,790	−9.11	525	.35	14,315	9.45
Full year 1980	−4,863	−3.38	6,851	4.76	11,714	8.13

p: Preliminary.
Note: Data in Tables 3 and 4 exclude checking and certain other deposits.
Source: National Association of Mutual Savings Banks. Research analysis of monthly savings bank trends. Vol. IX, No. 1. January 1982.

Table XIII-4 Net Deposit Change at Savings Banks in December, 1971-81
(amounts in millions of dollars)

Month of December	Excluding Interest		Including Interest		Interest Credited	
	Amount	Percent of Outstanding Deposits	Amount	Percent of Outstanding Deposits	Amount	Percent of Outstanding Deposits
1981	$—1,300	—.86	$ 800	.53	$2,100	1.38
1980	—639	—.43	1,255	.84	1,894	1.26
1979	—987	—.69	830	.58	1,817	1.27
1978	—405	—.29	1,213	.87	1,618	1.16
1977	—115	—.09	1,426	1.09	1,540	1.17
1976	367	.31	1,757	1.46	1,390	1.16
1975	114	.11	1,394	1.29	1,280	1.19
1974	—37	—.04	1,053	1.08	1,090	1.12
1973	—37	—.04	1,210	1.28	1,247	1.31
1972	323	.36	1,333	1.48	1,010	1.12
1971	325	.40	1,209	1.49	884	1.09

p: Preliminary.
Note: Data in Tables 3 and 4 exclude checking and certain other deposits.
Source: National Association of Mutual Savings Banks. Research analysis of monthly savings bank trends. Vol. IX, No. 1. January 1982.

relation to the unregulated money market funds and other non-banking financial competitors, and the current evolution of new services and linkages has highlighted the polemical issue of competitive equality. The era of specialized financial institutions differentiated by product lines and markets is fast disappearing as distinctions between banks and thrift institutions and "non-banking" institutions become nebulous in the contemporary financial marketplace.

Some of the more salient developments include:

1. Sears, Roebuck and Co., the world's largest retailing conglomerate, with 854 retail department stores nationwide, 2,778 U.S. catalogue outlets and limited merchandise stores, 127 foreign stores in 12 countries, and 25 million active credit accounts now provide insurance services through its Allstate Insurance Co. subsidiary and is the largest savings and loan holding company in the United States operating the $5 billion asset Sears Savings Bank, formerly the All-State Savings and Loan Association in California. More recently, the retailing chain acquired the nation's largest real estate broker, Coldwell, Banker and Co., and the fourth largest brokerage firm, Dean Witter Reynolds. In September 1981, Sears announced that it would establish its own money market mutual fund, Sears U.S. Government Money Market Trust investing in Treasury bills and other U.S. Government instruments with a maturity of less than one year, pending approval by the Securities and Exchange Commission, which was granted in March 1982. Edward Telling, Chairman of Sears Roebuck and Co., noted that, "We can together achieve our goal of becoming the premier provider of financial services in the country."[2]

2. Merrill Lynch, with 442 offices nationwide, provides mortgages, check writing money market funds, trust and estate planning, and money management services. Its two money market funds have combined assets of over $36 billion. The brokerage giant announced in February 1982 a new financial service called "Equity Access Account" that allows customers through a special VISA credit card and checking account to borrow up to 70 percent of their home equity. Account holders would have flexibility in principal and interest payments in contrast to the fixed repayment schedule of traditional second

[2]Where America Will Bank, *Newsweek*, October 19, 1982, p. 80.

mortgages. The program was test marketed in California beginning in April 1982 and then undertaken nationwide later in the year.

3. American Express which provides travel and entertainment services nationally through 1100 offices and operates a major international bank and an insurance company, recently merged with one of the nation's largest brokerage houses, Shearson Loeb Rhoades, Inc. with 246 offices nationwide.

4. General Electric, with 300 offices nationally, provides real estate loans, second mortgages, commercial real estate financing, mortgage insurance, and leasing services.

5. Prudential Insurance Co., the nation's largest life insurance carrier, acquired the Bache Group, Inc. brokerage house.

6. In a tri-state supervised merger of savings and loan associations, Citizens Federal Savings and Loan Association of California was merged with West Side Federal Savings of New York and Washington Savings and Loan Association of Miami Beach, Florida. National Steel Corporation is the parent company of Citizens Savings and Loan Association. Citizens subsequently changed its name to First Nationwide Savings, promoting the new institutions as "first across the nation."

7. Western Bancorp in California, a 21-bank holding company with subsidiaries in 11 states, renamed its organization "First Interstate Bank." The move was largely a positioning before the fact; that is, before the ultimate advent of inter-state banking. First Interstate Banks have combined assets of over $35 billion.

8. Baldwin-United, a leading manufacturer of pianos, recently acquired a savings and loan association and a few banks.

9. Dreyfus Corp., a major money market mutual fund manager announced in August 1981 a nationwide program linking negotiable order of withdrawal accounts (NOW accounts) to one of two Drefus money market funds selected by the bank's retail customers. The service was initiated at the $1.3 billion asset Freedom Savings and Loan Association, Tampa, Florida.

10. Two savings and loan associations, the Coast Federal Savings and Loan Association of Sarasota, Florida and the Perpetual

American Federal Savings and Loan Association of Washington, D.C., filed an application in August 1981 with the Federal Home Loan Bank to establish a nationwide brokerage firm through a service corporation. The Federal Home Loan Bank Board approved the application in May 1982, and in early November 1982, Perpetual and three other associations began offering brokerage services through a new investment service known as "Invest" which will provide subscribing institutions with technical equipment, portfolio analysis, and other investment advisory services.

11. Eleven state banking associations combined to establish Mid-America Bankers Service Company to manage a money market fund.

12. Master Card and Fidelity Management Corp. are developing money market funds tied to bank deposit accounts. VISA also announced similar plans.

13. First National Bank of Springfield, Illinois, and First Interstate Bank Corp. join with Dreyfus to provide depositors with access to one of Dreyfus's money market funds.

14. Farmers and Mechanics Bank of Minneapolis merged with Marquette National Bank, the first merger between a savings bank and a commercial bank. The supervised merger was perhaps a harbinger of similar events to take place in the quest by supervisory agencies to find suitable merger partners for financially troubled thrift institutions.

15. Several commercial banks, too, have acquired stock in out-of-state banking institutions, plausibly as a preparatory measure for the advent of interstate banking. Citicorp, for example, agreed to acquire 27 percent of the stock of Central National Bank of Chicago. Chemical New York Corp. recently announced plans to acquire 32.5 percent ownership of Florida National Banks of Florida. Chase Manhattan Corp. also acquired $50 million in non-voting preferred stock of Equimark Corporation, Pittsburgh, with 15-year warrants to purchase up to 100 percent of Equimark common stock.

16. In April 1982, the Federal Reserve Board approved the merger of the troubled Scioto Savings Association with the Interstate

Financial Corporation owner of the Third National Bank and Trust Co. in Dayton, Ohio. The merger marked the first consolidation between a thrift and a bank-holding company approved by the Federal Reserve Board.

17. First Interstate Corp., a Los Angeles-based holding company inaugurated in May 1982 a new bank franchise program under which participants will be members of First Interstate's "TIPS" system, an on-line teller information and automated teller machine network that links 21 affiliates in 11 western states. First National Bank in Golden, Colorado became the first franchised bank in the United States in May 1982.

18. In September 1982, the Federal Reserve Board authorized the acquisition by Citicorp of the distressed $2.9 billion Fidelity Savings and Loan Association of San Francisco, California. The action resulted in the first interstate cross-industry merger and was approved subject to several conditions designed to preserve Fidelity operating as a thrift institution.

The Federal Home Loan Bank Board also granted approval in December 1983 for Citicorp to acquire two distressed associations, New Biscayne Federal Savings and Loan Association, Miami and First Federal Savings and Loan Association of Chicago. New Biscayne held assets of $1.8 billion and operates 34 offices in Florida while assets of First Federal were estimated at $3.95 billion with 61 offices in Illinois. Citicorp obtained approval from the Federal Reserve Board in January, subject to several stipulations. These included the operation of both institutions as savings and loans with the primary purpose of providing residential housing credit. Both institutions must also be operated as separate entities and not in tandem with any subsidiary of Citicorp, with the word "bank" not included in any name change.

Citicorp, in its expansion nationwide, now has 1032 offices in 40 states, providing services ranging from credit card operations to loan production and consumer banking offices.

1979-1982 YEARS OF CRISES AND CONSOLIDATION

The financial industry, from the above brief description of significant trends, is in the process of a revolutionary restructuring with innovative products and increasing competitive pressures. Thrift institutions have—in order to attract deposits in the face of direct competition from money market mutual funds—been forced to adjust deposit liabilities to reflect market rate sensitivities. The growth in the money market certificates and other time deposits as a percentage of deposits has already been discussed.

Some indication of the concomitant pressure which this shift in deposit instruments has created on cost of funds and earnings to these institutions is evident from the fact that in January 1981, over 30 billion of money market funds yielding 8.5 percent matured at savings and loan associations. The July money market certificate rate at the time for rollover was 14.48 percent, a 600 basis point increase in six months. Such volatile upward fluctuations in the cost of funds to these institutions has exacerbated an already converging operating income spread, given the inherent portfolio drag associated with low yielding mortgage portfolios of these institutions. For mutual savings banks in 1979, 60 percent of savings bank income was derived from mortgages, while interest paid to depositors accounted for 75 percent of total expenditures of bank income. With regard to savings and loan associations, interest on mortgage loans was the source of 79.1 percent of association income, while interest paid to savers represented 66.4 percent of the distribution of income.

As can be seen from Figure XIII-2, mortgages comprise the bulk of total assets for savings and loan associations (83 percent) and mutual savings banks (67 percent), in comparison to life insurance companies (28 percent) and commercial banks (19 percent). Such an asset concentration by savings banks and savings and loan associations in a high interest rate environment significantly impinges on earnings potential given the high proportion of markedly lower than current yield mortgages held by these institutions. The data presented in Tables XIII-5 and XIII-6 clearly depict that in 1979, over 69.2 percent of mortgages held by mutual savings banks were at an interest rate of less than 9 percent. For savings and loan associations, the comparable figure was 37 percent at 9 percent for all institutions and 66.7 percent for mortgages at interest rates of less than 10 percent.

There are, however, noteworthy variations in the general industry figures according to geographic location. Associations in Atlanta, San Francisco, Seattle, and Little Rock, Federal Home Loan Bank Districts tended to have a lower percentage of low-rate residential mortgages and comparably better earnings figures. New York associations with 64.2 percent of mortgages below 9 percent and Boston associations

Figure XIII-2   Ratio of Mortgage Loans, Including GNMAs, to Total Assets, Main Types of Financial Institutions, 1960-1980

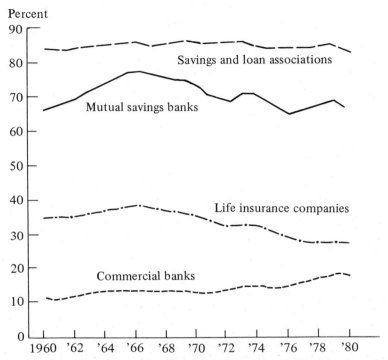

Note: Data are as of year-end. Data for life insurance companies exclude GNMAs while mutual savings bank data include all types of mortgage-backed securities.

Source: National Association of Mutual Savings Banks. 1981 National Fact Book, p. 33.

with 47.4 percent of low-rate mortgages experienced more severe earnings pressures.

Mutual banks in New York, Boston, and Pennsylvania also demonstrated higher percentages of low-rate mortgages as a percentage of total residential mortgages than the industry average. Banks in these areas, too, are also experiencing more pronounced earnings problems and erosion of net worth or general reserves. One savings bank in New York reportedly lost $114 million in 1981, and the majority of supervised mergers that have recently been effected have involved New York mutual savings banks. California associations, on the other hand, have demonstrated more favorable earnings data largely as a result of a more innovative asset policy and the widespread use of variable rate mortgage instruments.

Table XIII-5   Low-Rate Residential Mortgages as Percent of
All Residential Mortgages Held by Mutual Savings Banks,
by State, 1979

State	Less than 7 Percent (%)	Less than 8 Percent (%)	Less than 9 Percent (%)
New York	23.2	44.7	79.7
City	26.1	49.0	78.9
Upstate	15.3	33.0	81.9
Massachusetts	12.1	27.5	62.2
Boston	22.3	39.4	72.0
Other	9.9	24.9	60.0
Connecticut	7.7	21.2	58.3
Pennsylvania	21.0	38.8	67.3
New Jersey	8.1	22.2	62.8
Washington	7.6	20.9	35.5
New Hampshire	8.1	18.4	44.2
Maine	6.8	18.2	47.5
Rhode Island	10.4	24.3	60.3
Maryland	14.2	31.7	59.5
Vermont	6.1	22.4	52.0
All Savings Banks	17.4	35.5	69.2

Source: National Association of Mutual Savings Banks.

Table XIII-6   Low-Rate Mortgages as Percent of All
Residential Mortgages Held by Savings and Loan Associations,
by Federal Home Loan Bank District, 1980

Federal Home Loan Bank District	Less than 6% (%)	Less than 7% (%)	Less than 8% (%)	Less than 9% (%)	Less than 10% (%)
Boston	4.7	9.0	19.5	47.4	71.8
New York	4.2	10.0	27.5	64.2	86.2
Pittsburgh	1.5	5.1	16.5	45.9	75.5
Atlanta	1.0	3.8	13.9	43.9	71.4
Cincinnati	1.0	4.7	13.9	41.2	68.2
Indianapolis	1.6	4.7	14.0	39.4	67.0
Chicago	1.3	4.8	13.7	34.8	61.5
Des Moines	1.8	5.4	15.8	41.4	74.9
Topeka	1.2	4.0	11.8	30.9	62.3
Little Rock	1.2	3.7	11.9	33.1	79.3
San Francisco	0.3	3.8	11.7	23.1	52.7
Seattle	0.6	3.1	10.0	24.4	56.2
All Savings and Loan Associations	1.3	4.6	14.1	37.0	66.7

Source: U.S. League of Savings Associations.

Figure XIII-3   Return on Average Assets
Commercial Banks, Mutual Savings Banks, and
Savings and Loan Associations, 1955-1980

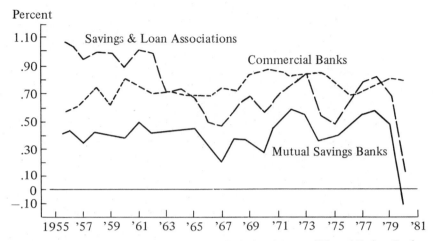

Sources: FDIC Federal Home Loan Bank Board: National Assn. of Mutual Savings Banks.

While savings banks and savings and loan associations have experienced the worst crisis in their history, commercial banks have managed to maintain and increase their profitability as Figure XIII-3 and Table XIII-7 illustrate. Return on assets for savings and loan associations was approximately 1.10 percent in 1955 but plummeted to about 0.10 percent in 1980. For mutual savings banks, the decline over the comparable period was from 0.40 percent of average assets to 0.12 in 1980. Commercial banks, on the other hand, have managed to maintain a return on assets figure of roughly 0.80. The decline in retained earnings as a percentage of total average assets for savings and loan associations and mutual savings banks is also evident from Table XIII-7.

The fact that commercial banks have generated historically steady earnings figures as a proportion of total assets since 1955, reflects the greater flexibility in asset structure of these institutions. Portfolio adjustment during periods of high and volatile interest rates can be easily effected and related to the current dictates of the marketplace. Earnings in 1981, for example, were up 9 percent at Citicorp, 6 percent at Bankers Trust and 11 percent at Manufacturers Hanover. Such comparable asset flexibility was not available to thrift institutions; and even if thrifts were granted extended asset powers, time would be required to acquire skill and expertise in these areas.

Table XIII-7 Retained Earnings as Percent of Total Assets Held by
Selected Types of Financial Institutions, 1962-1982

Year	Savings Banks	Commercial Banks	Savings and Loan Associations
1962	.41	.73	.97
1963	.44	.72	.69
1964	.44	.70	.72
1965	.46	.70	.67
1966	.33	.69	.50
1967	.20	.74	.46
1968	.37	.72	.60
1969	.35	.84	.68
1970	.27	.89	.57
1971	.48	.87	.71
1972	.60	.83	.77
1973	.54	.85	.76
1974	.35	.81	.54
1975	.38	.78	.47
1976	.45	.70	.64
1977	.55	.71	.79
1978	.58	.77	.84
1979	.46	.81	.68
1980	—.12	.80	.14
1981	—.82	.77	—.74
1982	—.73	.72	—.62

Note: Data represent retained earnings after all expenses, taxes and dividends
paid depositors as percent of average assets. Data for commercial banks are for
FDIC-insured institutions and since 1976 are based on consolidated reports. Data
for savings and loan associations are for all associations since 1976 and FSLIC-insured institutions for prior years.

Source: NAMSB.

Over the years, the fundamentals of thrift banking involved the
acceptance of deposits and lending out these funds in the form of
mortgages or investing in long-term bonds. Management skills, hence,
were limited and thin.

As Edward J. McColgan, Executive Vice President and Chief Financial Officer of the New York Bank for Savings, noted, "When I first
joined the savings and loan industry in 1960, we paid $3\frac{3}{4}$ percent on
passbook accounts and loaned it out at $5\frac{1}{2}$ or 6 percent. At that time,
even a blind man could make money."[3]

[3]Bennett, Robert A. "The Savings Banks: Deep in the Red," *New York Times*, March 8, 1981.

The chairman and president of the New York Bank for Savings, Edward Callan, also remarked that "You don't have any intermediate management or any MBAs, so if you want to start a new project, you can't reach out and get a few bright guys from the staff."[4] The New York Bank for Savings lost $16.6 million in 1980, and another $52 million by August 1981, and was merged on March 26, 1982 with Buffalo Savings Bank after exactly 163 years of operation. Such a scenario was not unique, as over 25 savings banks in New York State, among the largest 50 nationwide, reported substantial losses for 1980 and 1981.

For savings and loan associations, too, extended asset powers mandated by the Depository Deregulation and Monetary Control Act of 1980 required huge investments in personnel, equipment, and systems. At California Federal, one of the nation's largest savings and loan associations, for example, most of the association's officers had little experience in writing loans on cars, boats, and other merchandise and would require additional training. California Federal planned to hire 200 new employees to perform duties in new business operations such as consumer loans, lines of credit, credit card, and trust services. Jay Janis, former head of the Federal Home Loan Bank Board and now President of California Federal Savings, suggested that the "prime job of banks has always been to serve business. My theory is that banks will continue to serve business and that savings and loans will now have the freedom to provide a full range of services in housing and family finance."[5] The new operations would help to supplement the earnings of savings associations and generate additional deposit flows.

With the passage of the Garn-St Germain Act in November 1982, and the decline in interest rates, the pressure on earnings of these savings institutions has abated, though at the end of 1983, 38 percent of all savings and loans were still operating in the red. The Federal Home Loan Bank Board has estimated that thrift insolvencies in 1984 could cost the FSLIC $2.2 billion. Savings and loans remain vulnerable to sudden upward shifts in interest rates which could significantly increase the number of insolvencies in 1984.

HOUSING TRENDS

Thrift institutions, in particular savings and loan associations, have provided a substantial portion of the nation's housing finance for

[4]Ibid.
[5]Lueck, Thomas. "The Competitive Era in Savings," *New York Times*, January 8, 1981.

private residential purposes. As Table XIII-8 reveals, thrift institutions currently provide approximately 48 percent of total residential mortgages outstanding. Notwithstanding the fact that thrift institutions have accounted for almost half of total home mortgages outstanding over the past two decades, during periods of high volatile interest rates and heavy disintermediation, these institutions have also experienced greater fluctuations in the flow of funds for housing finance. Thrift institutions' net investment in home mortgages during these periods demonstrated substantial decline. For example, during the credit squeeze of 1973-74, net investment in the home mortgage market by savings and loan associations decreased to approximately 30 percent. Figures for the year ending 1981, also indicate this trend. Total mortgage loans closed by savings and loan associations fell from $9.2 billion in July 1979 to less than $3 billion in December 1981. Mutual savings banks also exhibited a similar decline in net flow of mortgage funds from these institutions. Available data indicate that during 1981, mortgage lending by mutual savings banks was virtually at a standstill, with no noteworthy change in aggregate portfolios of mortgage loans and mortgage backed securities. Given the unprecedented levels of deposit outflows, thrift institutions had resorted to maintaining strong liquidity positions, more so in the light of high yields on short-term, non-mortgage investments. With the passage of the Garn Act in 1982, and the decline in interest rates, savings and loan associations experienced a net deposit gain during 1983 of over $110 billion, an increase of over 176.0 percent from the previous year. Mortgage loans closed during 1983 totaled over $135.2 billion, an increase of 149.2 percent over the comparable figure for 1982.

The growth of the secondary market, mortgage pools, and federal and related agencies has augmented the traditional sources of housing funds (Table XIII-8). Mortgage pools accounted for over 12 percent of total residential mortgages outstanding in 1981. With the thrift institutions as the principal conduit to the secondary market, the current condition of the latter is partially a reflection of the demise of the thrift industry. The secondary market was virtually in a state of abeyance during 1981-82 but rebounded vigorously as a complement to the seasoned sources of housing finance in 1983.

Home ownership in the United States increased from 43 percent in 1940 to over 65 percent in the decade of the 70s. The demand for housing units will reach new heights with the emergence of the baby-boom generation as adults. The "baby boom" now accounts for one-third of the U.S. population, approximately 66 million people in the

Table XIII-8 Percent of Total Residental Mortgage Debt Outstanding by Type of Institution

| End of Period | Savings and Loan Associations | Thrift Institutions | | Life Insurance Companies | Federal and Related Agencies | All Other Mortgage Holders |
		Mutual Savings Banks	Commercial Banks			
1950	24.14	12.76	18.87	20.06	2.73	21.45
1955	29.85	15.18	15.49	20.68	3.31	15.48
1960	35.47	14.98	12.55	17.71	5.03	14.26
1965	39.72	15.56	12.57	14.90	2.90	14.35
1970	38.75	13.94	12.74	11.92	7.03	15.62
1975	42.19	10.79	14.03	6.29	8.49	18.21
1976	43.76	10.18	4.27	5.34	7.24	19.23
1977	44.71	9.50	14.89	4.37	6.27	20.26
1978	44.24	8.89	15.73	3.77	6.40	20.96
1979	42.86	8.13	15.94	3.52	6.61	12.95
1980	41.71	7.54	15.77	3.41	6.96	24.61
1981	32.75	6.31	17.97	8.70	17.43	
1982	29.19	5.72	18.26	8.33	20.79	17.43

Source: National Association of Mutual Savings Banks.

18-34 years' age range, in comparison to 40 million in that age group in 1950. With the change in demographic structure and societal values, the demand for condominiums and town house developments is expected to surge with the increase in the number of single family units. It is estimated that during the 1980s, housing for 22.5 million new households will be required. Housing construction has, however, not kept pace with the demand for housing. Production of rental units, for example, in 1971-72, totalled 1.4 million in comparison to less than 800 thousand in 1978-79. The National Association of Home Builders viewed 1981 as the worst production year since 1951, with housing starts in the region of 1.07 million. The Department of Housing and Urban Development forecasts a shortage of 150,000 to 200,000 multi-family rental units per year during the 1980-90 decade. Clearly, a restructured thrift and housing financing system will be absolutely essential if adequate sources of financing for future housing demand are to be tapped. Statistics indicate that nationally over 50 percent of deposits in thrift institutions are currently held by individuals 60 years of age or older. In the 1980s and 1990s, the future potential customers of thrift institutions, younger and more credit-oriented spenders, will have to be offered services which will foster a surge in savings habits and deposit flows. The housing slump of 1981-82 had no parallel in the past. While housing declines have often been viewed as "cyclical," many analysts doubt that the industry will return to the same pre-cycle level as in previous boom periods following housing recessions. The national commitment and capital formation required for a strong housing market were nonexistent at that time.

In the words of Jay Janis, former Chairman of the Federal Home Loan Bank Board, "Housing is more than an amalgam of land and financing and building. It is a dynamic part of the social, economic, and physical fabric of our nation. It is the bond that holds neighborhoods together; it is the all-important capital investment that makes communities viable; and it is the foundation on which our democracy rests."[6] Housing should not be viewed as competing with but rather as complementary to other national goals. If thrift institutions are to play a vital role in the future provision of adequate housing, the inevitable restructuring necessary to achieve competitive viability must be timely, effectively, and judiciously undertaken.

The President's Commission on Housing in January 1982, released

[6]Janis, Jay. "Housing for a New Generation: A Promise to Keep." Address to the Commonwealth Club of California, San Francisco, California. August 1, 1980, p. 14.

a preliminary report on housing finance entitled "Financing the Housing Needs of the 1980s." The main recommendations of the Commission are summarized next. The report recommended that the asset, liability, and service powers of depository institutions be expanded to enhance the competitiveness of these institutions in the markets for funds.

Secondly, it was recommended that tax incentives currently applicable to thrift institutions be extended to all financial institutions in order to encourage mortgage investment. The elimination of laws and regulations that limit the flow of funds to housing from any source or unnecessarily increases the cost of funds to borrowers was further suggested. The report, in addition, called for the development of mortgage contracts that satisfy the varied needs of borrowers and investors, and for the strengthening of secondary markets for mortgages and mortgage-backed securities. Finally, the Commission endorsed a re-evaluation of the roles of federal agencies in underwriting credit risks or mortgage instruments and in directing funds to mortgage markets from other participants in the capital markets.

EXTENDED POWERS FOR
THRIFT INSTITUTIONS

It can hardly be denied that the environment for home financing has changed markedly since 1930 when the basis for the current regulations and policies governing the operations of home financing institutions was originally established. There is also widespread cognizance of the need to provide thrift institutions with expanded and more flexible powers in order to secure the future viability and efficiency of the thrift industry. The ability to accept demand deposits from any source, to make commercial loans, to undertake leasing arrangements, to expand real estate activity were some areas that would provide thrift institutions with asset flexibility to effectively develop a more efficient mix of assets and liabilities, particularly during periods of high and volatile interest rates. Continued legal and regulatory protectionism would only postpone the ultimate restructuring that would be required. While legislative and regulatory relief to the current plight of the thrift industry had been adopted on an ad hoc basis, the need for pervasive and balanced re-adjustment to reflect the realities of the marketplace remained a pressing issue. The 1980 Depository Institutions Deregulation and Monetary Control Act provided thrifts with the ability to extend consumer loans, to purchase commercial paper up to 20 percent of assets, and to invest in commercial real estate loans up to 20 percent of totals. While such developments were a step in the right direction, greater flexibility equivalent to commercial bank operations must be afforded thrifts if they are to effectively meet the challenges of a deregulated environment. Several bills were, thus, introduced in Congress since June 1981 which sought to alleviate the short-term problems of thrift institutions through some type of capital assistance program, as well as address the issue of required long-term restructuring through expanded asset and liability provisions.

Various commercial banking lobbying groups had voiced negative support for expanded thrift powers without some equivalent quid pro quo. The American Bankers Association, for example, was unwilling to support any action for broader thrift "bank-like" powers without an agreeable phase-out schedule for Regulation Q and the differential. The United States League of Savings Association had, however, already endorsed such a trade-off. In any event, given the current market conditions and competitive pressures, benefits to the thrifts from the differential were virtually nugatory.

With the varied interest groups involved in influencing financial legislative reform, it could be anticipated that a good deal of intransigence would exist on the part of various lobbyists which would militate against Congress acting with much-needed celerity on these issues. It was perhaps a recognition of this fact that led to the proposal issued by the Federal Home Loan Bank Board on February 25, 1982 for expanding thrift powers through the use of service corporations.

Specifically, the proposal which had a 60-day comment period would allow service corporations to:

- Offer money-market funds and to engage in other securities brokerage activities.
- Underwrite casualty, property, life insurance, and private mortgage insurance.
- Expand the real estate brokerage authority to include the provision of these services to third parties.
- Engage in commercial lending, letters of credit, and leasing activities.
- Act as a futures commission agent and trade GNMA options.
- Manufacture mobile homes.
- Lease consumer and business goods.
- Provide debt collection services, prepare tax returns for businesses, and operate coin and currency services.

While the expanded asset powers for thrifts may be adopted by the bank board by regulatory fiat and not by law, the FHLBB proposal may have provided some stimulus for timely Congressional action on the thrift industry issues before the legislature. On October 1, 1982, the Depository Institutions Act of 1982 was passed by the House and signed into law by President Reagan on October 15, 1982. Parenthetically, too, the House/Senate Conference Report also admonished the FHLBB not to proceed with the proposed expansion of service corporation activities.

The Garn-St Germain Depository Institutions Act of 1982 authorized federally chartered savings and loan associations to make commercial, corporate, business, or agricultural loans up to 5 percent of assets until January 1, 1984 and 10 percent thereafter, to issue demand accounts and overdraft facilities in this connection. In addition, NOW accounts were authorized for commercial, corporate, business, and agricultural entities and the statutory 30-day notice of withdrawal period for savings accounts was also eliminated. The new Act also instructed the DIDC to develop a new account equivalent and competitive to money market accounts no later than December 15, 1982. The Act also contained capital assistance provisions for distressed depository institutions. These and other provisions of the 1982 Depository Institutions Act will be discussed more fully later in this chapter and in other chapters.

DEPOSIT INSTRUMENT EXPANSION

In an attempt to provide thrifts and commercial banks with more competitive liability instruments, vis-a-vis money market mutual funds and other nonbanking financial institutions, new deposit instruments, and provisions concerning deposit accounts have recently been introduced.

The "All Savers Certificate" was introduced in October 1981 as a means of halting the deposit outflows from thrifts and banks to other financial institutions. These deposit accounts were tax-exempt savings accounts that could be offered during a 15-month period through December 31, 1982. Interest up to $1,000 for an individual and $2,000 for a married couple filing a joint return would be exempt from taxation. "All Savers Certificates" carried an interest rate equal to 70 percent of the one-year Treasury bill rate. Depository institutions were also required to invest 75 percent of all net new All Savers deposits in housing related or farming loans.

All Savers Certificates would, it was hoped, provide some relief from high cost of funds to depository institutions if funds moved from higher interest rate, six-month certificates into these new accounts. Early projections forecasted as much as $250 billion flowing into All Savers Certificates. Other estimates using different tax and interest rates scenarios estimate the magnitude of funds flowing into these certificates at between $85 to $105. Preliminary data indicate that after heightened interest in the certificates during October, the All Savers Certificates did not, produce the anticipated and desired impact on deposit flows and cost of funds. All Savers Certificates were not a panacea for the current plight of the thrift industry, rather, ostensibly a short-term palliative. The certificate was not extended beyond its expiration date.

On November 1, 1981, the Depository Institutions Deregulation Committee amended the regulations governing the computation of the interest rate to be offered by depository institutions on six-month money market certificates. Financial institutions were given the option of using the current 26-week Treasury bill rate or the average of the rates for the previous four bill auctions, whichever is higher. The averaging of bill rates would allow depository institutions to be more competitive with money market mutual funds during periods of declining interest rates when rates offered on money market fund portfolios tend to lag in reflecting such declines. Analysis indicated that the maturity of money market fund portfolios averaged about four weeks.

Banks and thrift institutions were also authorized, effective December 1, 1981, to offer deregulated IRA/Keogh retirement accounts with either fixed or floating interest rates. Eligibility regulations for IRA accounts were also expanded to include individuals previously enrolled in a pension plan. Individuals may contribute up to $2,000 annually which is tax deductible and $4,000 for working married couples. Banks and thrifts may offer an 18-month interest rate ceiling free rollover IRA account, with either variable interest rates or a fixed interest rate structure. Terms governing IRA contracts should, however, be fully disclosed to participating individuals.

Under the provisions of the Economic Recovery Tax Act of 1981, these tax sheltered retirement accounts were just about made available to all American wage earners. Keogh or self-employed retirement account ceilings were also raised from $7,500 to $15,000 though maximum annual contributions to the account remained at 15 percent of income. Moreover, individuals currently enrolled in a Keogh plan were now also permitted to open IRA accounts. Contributions to IRA and Keogh accounts are deductible from taxable income up to the maximum amounts permitted, and interest earned on these accounts is also tax-exempt until funds are withdrawn at retirement when, presumably, lower tax rates would apply. The revised IRA/Keogh accounts would supplement social security benefits and provide depository institutions with a source of stable long-term funds and possibly increase deposit inflows to these institutions vis-a-vis other marketers of existing retirement funds.

In order to further expand the competitive positions of thrifts and banks in relation to nondepository institutions, particularly money market mutual funds, the DIDC sought comment on the adoption of new short-term instruments for thrift and banking institutions. While it was felt that any new market related investment account would currently exacerbate the already high cost of funds to thrift institutions and possibly increase internal disintermediation from lower yielding accounts, there would be positive long-run benefits to the viability of depository institutions emanating from these deposit instruments. Action on the DIDC proposals was, however, postponed in December until the next meeting of the Committee on March 22, 1982.

The October proposals sought comment on the following deposit instruments:

(a) A $5,000 minimum denomination transaction's account with no interest rate ceiling.

(b) A $10,000 minimum denomination, 91-day account with a 14-day required notice for withdrawal thereafter and a floating interest rate tied to the 13-week Treasury bill discount rate.

(c) A $25,000 minimum denomination account with no interest rate ceiling and a 1-day notice requirement. As the DIDC proposal states, ". . . in structuring a regulation authorizing a new short-term instrument, the relevant variables for the Committee to consider are yield, minimum denomination, maturity, and transactions' characteristics . . . In creating any short-term deposit category, major factors that must be taken into account include potential operational problems, the effect on earnings of depository institutions and the competitive viability of the instrument."[7]

At the March 22 meeting, the DIDC approved a new $7,500 minimum, 91-day certificate with a 25 basis points thrift differential. The

[7]Depository Institutions Deregulation Committee Federal Register, October 15, 1981.

account will be effective May 1, and at that time, thrift institutions may offer the 91-day Treasury bill rate at the latest auction, while commercial banks are restricted to 25 basis points less than the 91-day Treasury bill rate on these accounts.

Other proposals for new deposit instruments have included a tax-exempt housing certificate, which would allow individuals to save towards a down-payment on a home and a variation of the investment account with a transaction and an investment component, as enunciated by bankers of Chase Manhattan Corp.[8]

As previously mentioned, the 1982 Depository Institutions Act mandated the DIDC to develop a "money market account" for depository institutions. On November 15, 1982, the DIDC authorized the creation of a new account which may be offered by banks and thrift institutions beginning December 14. The account will have a $2,500 minimum denomination, no interest ceiling, no minimum maturity requirement, and would permit up to six transfers per month with no more than three through the use of checking instruments. Withdrawals from the account directly in person or by mail would be unlimited. If the balance in the new account falls below the $2,500 minimum, the NOW account ceiling of 5.25 percent would be applicable.

While the introduction of new deposit instruments will enhance the future competitive position of banks and thrift institutions, these developments do not in themselves provide an adequate short-term solution to the current problems of the thrift industry, many members of which would be hard-pressed if not unable to offer competitive market rates on these accounts given the current earnings situation.

REMEDIAL ACTION FOR DEALING WITH DISTRESSED ASSOCIATIONS

Warehousing and "Bail-Out" Plans

Various trade groups and housing analysts had supported plans for the wholesale warehousing of low-yielding mortgage portfolios of savings and loan associations and mutual savings banks. The National Association of Mutual Savings Banks had vigorously lobbied for some

---

[8]See, for example, Hammer Frederich S. "The Need Now for a New Deposit Instrument," *Journal of Retail Banking*, Vol. III, No. 4. December 1981, pp. 1-6.

form of warehousing by the temporary government purchase of the low-yielding mortgage portfolios. Based on a warehousing estimate at 500 basis points above the actual return on these portfolios, $20 billion of these mortgages could be "assumed" for a year by the government at a cost of $1 billion.

Given the desire to reduce the budget deficit of the federal government and the fact that government bail-out of failing industries appears to be anathema to the ideology of the present administration, no significant policy had been forthcoming in this direction.

Both the FDIC and FSLIC had previously endorsed capital infusion programs but lack the resources to undertake a massive assistance scheme utilizing their own sources of funding. The FDIC had previously proposed the purchasing of subordinated notes from distressed institutions, but would require a relaxation of current capital assistance criteria of impending failure and essentiality to the community, in order to provide assistance to troubled institutions.

The Federal Savings and Loan Insurance Corporation in September 1981 was authorized by the Bank Board to create income capital certificates and FSLIC promissory notes to assist ailing savings and loan associations. The income certificates would be issued by mutual associations in denominations of $100,000 minimum in exchange for five-year promissory notes of the FSLIC. The FSLIC promissory note may be treated as a cash equivalent on the balance sheet of the association and also used to satisfy net worth and liquidity requirements. The promissory notes may also be sold.

Income capital certificates have been used in one merger of two savings and loan associations in September 1981. The certificates issued in that assistance program would be redeemed by the making of annual payments to the FSLIC based on a percentage of the associations' net annual income.

The savings and loan industry has also obtained quasi-warehousing assistance from the Federal Home Loan Mortgage Corporation. The corporation has held auctions of $2 billion of its Participation Certificates (PCs) which it swapped for mortgage loans of similar coupon equivalency from lenders who require liquidity. A minimum bid of $10 million up to $100 million was required, while the FHLMC envisions the program as developing into a $30 billion to $40 billion scheme annually. Current regulations limit the corporation to 20 percent of all purchases of loans more than one year old. This restriction would seriously retard the ability of the SWAP program to effectively handle older low-rate loans. Participation certificates (PCs) may be held by the acquiring institution or sold in order to obtain additional funds for investment.

The Federal National Mortgage Association also proposed to provide liquidity to thrift institutions by the purchase of old low-yielding mortgages at market value. Sales of low-rate mortgages at substantial discounts from face value generate losses which would further weaken current net worth and earnings position of savings associations. The adoption of the Federal Home Loan Bank Board's Regulatory Accounting Procedure, however, reduces this deterrent by allowing associations to amortize loan losses or gains over the remaining life of the mortgage loan or security. Generally accepted accounting principles require such losses to be reported in the year in which the sale is made and the loss recognized. It is estimated that the mortgage industry holds over $500 billion in old mortgages. With the proposed cutbacks in federal credit ceilings of the secondary mortgage agencies, it is doubtful whether more than $5 billion a year of old mortgages could be absorbed by the market.

Other plans, too, had been proposed which would establish limited partnerships with private investors to facilitate the sale of low-yielding mortgages by depository institutions under more favorable conditions. Losses from the sale of these loans would be tax deductible by investors in these partnerships who would supply additional funds which would then be invested with proceeds from the sale of the low-yielding assets in higher current rate new mortgages. Both lending institutions and private investors would benefit from the higher earnings. The attractiveness of this type of tax shelter option for private investors would be dependent on potential tax savings to investors and the trade-offs between alternative tax shelter instruments and income generation considerations. Such a partnership plan could plausibly, however, produce positive results for thrift institutions.

At the local level, too, on a lighter note, savings and loan associations and mutual savings banks have been trying to come to grips with their current problems through the use of some rather innovative techniques. One savings and loan association, for example, the Freedom Savings and Loan Association of Tampa, Florida in May 1981 announced that it would give a 15 percent discount on the outstanding principal of mortgage loan customers with interest rates up to 8 percent if they repay the loans. The savings and loan association reported that

7,600 with loan balances totalling $121 million were eligible for the plan.

Anothe r thrift institution tried to invoke a callable clause option and require mortgage holders to repay the loan or negotiate extensions of the loans at currently adjusted rates. Buffalo Savings Bank of Buffalo, New York, tried to upgrade the yield on mortgage portfolios in September 1981 by demanding payment on 900 mortgage loans with interest rates of $8\frac{1}{2}$, which were originated in 1975 and 1976 and had a contract call provision. Holders of these notes were offered alternative new loans at 14 percent. Public outcry and castigation of the bank's action, however, resulted in cancellation of the program.

The attempt to improve yields, nonetheless, demonstrated the sensitivity of individuals to changes in terms potentially adversely affecting home ownership and the difficulties involved in effecting what would under the circumstances appear to have been a prudent managerial business decision. Many holders of the callable loans would have experienced severe hardship in meeting commitments under the higher rate loans and would face the potential loss of their homes. While the loans were 25-30 year conventional fixed rate loans, with a callable option at the end of five years, the bank had never called in these loans before and mortgage holders never expected such unprecedented action to be taken. The Buffalo Savings Bank experience, too, illustrates that widespread use of market sensitive mortgage instruments which shift the burden of interest rate risks from the lender to the buyer may very well place home ownership beyond the resources of future aspiring purchasers.

In another attempt to devise the least costly method of providing assistance to a distressed savings and loan association, the Federal Home Loan Bank Board approved the acquisition of First Federal Savings and Loan Association, Springhill, Louisiana, by eight private investors. In order to effect the purchase, a supervisory conversion from mutual to stock ownership of the association was first undertaken. While converted mutual to stock thrifts have previously been acquired by our existing thrift, the Louisiana agreement marked the first time that a thrift institution was acquired by private investors.

In February 1982, Rep. Ferdinand J. St Germain introduced in Congress a bill entitled the "Home Mortgage Capital Stability Act" which would provide capital and earnings assistance to qualified savings and loans, mutual savings banks, and commercial banks.

A Capital Assistance Program authorized by the Depository Institutions Act of 1982 contains many of the provisions of this original proposal. As stipulated by the 1982 Act, FSLIC and FDIC insured institutions may issue net worth certificates for purchase by the respective insurance agency in order to enhance net worth.

In order to receive assistance, insured institutions must satisfy the following qualifications:

1. A net worth of less than 3 percent.
2. Incurred losses for at least the two previous quarters.
3. Have not incurred losses solely to qualify for the program nor engaged in speculative activities.
4. Record a net worth of not less than $\frac{1}{2}$ of 1 percent after the FSLIC/FDIC purchase of net worth certificates.
5. 20 percent of loans must be in residential mortgages or mortgage backed securities.
6. Comply with terms and conditions prescribed by the insuring agencies.

The assistance formula stipulated by the Act will be:

Net Worth	Level of Assistance
3% or less	50% of period loss
2% or less	60% of period loss
1% or less	70% of period loss

The FSLIC/FDIC may not require management changes if applicant for assistance can demonstrate positive net worth for nine months, nor can these agencies require an agreement to merge if positive net worth for six months can be projected by the applying institution. Assistance is open to nonfederally insured thrift institutions on the condition that the deposit insurance funds of these institutions indemnify the FSLIC/FDIC for losses and charge comparable premiums.

The Federal Deposit Insurance Corporation, as of December 31, 1982, provided approximately $175 million in capital assistance under the Garn-St Germain Act of 1982 to 15 savings banks predominantly located in New York. The FDIC action was effected before year-end in order to permit these savings banks to obtain exemptions from the New York State franchise tax. The Depository Institutions Act specifically exempts thrifts from paying state franchise taxes while these institutions are receiving capital assistance under the net worth aid program. The FSLIC, on the other hand, anticipated the first exchange of promissory notes to take place in February 1983. Thus, savings and loans were be able to derive any tax exemption benefits under the program for the 1982 tax year.

Merger Policy

As was discussed in Chapter V, mergers and acquisitions represent the least cost method for the FSLIC and the FDIC to effect remedial action to beleagured institutions. In the words of the Director of the FSLIC, Brent Beesley, "We have found that the merger process most efficiently allocates our scarce resources. Approximately 90 percent of the problems are currently being solved without any assistance through supervisory mergers. With supervisory mergers of those that are solved with assistance . . ., the cost of a supervisory merger is running about 40 percent of the cost of liquidation. That figure will have to come down if we are to preserve the Insurance Corporation, given our view of what the world looks like."[9] It should be mentioned here that one forecast based on the assumption that short-term rates average $15\frac{1}{2}$ percent in 1982 estimated that 900 associations with $200 billion in assets would reach zero net worth by year-end. Another estimate by the Brookings Institution's Andrew Carron predicted over 1000 savings and loan associations and about 30 savings banks would require some form of assistance for survival.[10]

It is obvious that the FSLIC and the FDIC will have to continue to find innovative ways of effecting mergers and acquisitions of failing institutions without over-burdening the funds of these corporations—a difficult and perhaps impossible task without supplemental funding abilities. A recent study by Wharton Econometric Forecasting Associates on the financial implications of different governmental policies for the thrift industry concluded that a capital infusion or mortgage warehousing plan would be less costly than assisted mergers undertaken by the FSLIC and FDIC.[11]

More mergers across state lines will contine, as well as inter-industry consolidations between banks and thrifts in order to effect the least

[9]"Saving the Fund from Heavy 'Hits'; Beesley Spells Out Philosophy," *Savings and Loan Reporter*, Vol. 6, #30, November 13, 1981.

[10]Carron, Andrew S. "The Plight of the Thrift Institutions," The Brookings Institution, Washington, D.C., 1982.

[11]The Financial Implications of Different Governmental Policies for the Thrift Industry," Wharton Econometric Forecasting Associates. March 23, 1982.

costly supervisory action and required financial savings. The use of purchase accounting and other bookkeeping innovations will allow ailing associations to merge with each other and obtain temporary reprieves until more definitive and lasting action can be implemented. It is the philosophy of the FSLIC that mergers are business decisions and the corporation prefers the boards of directors to solve their own problems using whatever flexibility and creativity that may be necessary.

Changing Accounting/Operational Framework

As was mentioned previously, the Federal Home Loan Bank Board issued regulatory accounting procedures which permitted deferral of loan losses for savings and loan associations. In addition, associations are permitted to amortize premiums, charges, discounts, and deferred acquisition credits on loans with remaining life of ten years or less on the shorter of ten years or the stated life of the loan. In addition, profits on sales of real estate to a "permanent investor" and profit from a sale to a "nonpermanent investor" may be recognized immediately. These changes are designed to reflect positive gains in balance sheet items and enhance the "paper image" of distressed associations. The Federal Deposit Insurance Corporation also announced plans to change accounting rules of mutual savings banks in order to boost reported earnings and net worth figures. This change would involve a shift from cost basis to mark-to-market accounting. Assets would be reported at current value in the marketplace instead of value at the time of origination or purchase, more in line with LIFO or FIFO inventory valuation techniques. Considerations of valuation of goodwill could also conceivably bolster balance sheet items favorably for savings banks. One proposal also suggested giving an asset valuation to the savings banks or saving and loan associations' charter, since a charter was a valuable document for undertaking business operations. These accounting revisions can provide immediate assistance to troubled thrift institutions, as well as additional time to effect the transition to recovery.

The Federal Home Loan Bank Board also recently authorized savings and loan associations to use financial futures on a broader scale in order to reduce interest rate risk. While trading in financial futures will provide an effective managerial tool for hedging against interest rate risks, in the long run, they do not offer much to the immediate solution of the earnings problems of thrift institutions.

Increasing Borrowing Capabilities and Sources

In Chapter VIII, recent amendments to the borrowing capabilities of insured savings and loan associations were fully discussed. Borrowing limitations were eliminated and regulations governing the issuing of subordinated debt, commercial paper, and mortgage-backed bonds were also relaxed. In compliance with the 1980 Depository Institutions Deregulation and Monetary Control Act, thrift institutions were also permitted access to the resources of the Federal Reserve Board through borrowing by the use of the discount window of the Reserve Board. While increased leveraging can provide liquidity benefits when such action is desirable, the effects of such borrowing on earnings is less obvious, more so when borrowed funds are acquired at market rates and interest margins between borrowed funds and investment are considerably narrowed.

Advances from the Federal Home Loan Bank Board have increased substantially since 1979, as shown in Table XIII-9. Expanded borrowing activity by savings and loan associations and mutual savings banks, both from federal agencies and the marketplace, provide short-term operational and liquidity benefits to these institutions, particularly during periods of severe deposit outflows when there is a need to augment the traditional inflows of funds or to meet increasing demand for loanable funds.

Taxation Policy

Prior to 1962, the incidence of taxation on the earnings of savings and loan associations was virtually negligible. The Tax Reform Act of 1969 stipulated a new method for effecting deductions. Deductible additions to reserves were based on a percentage of mortgage loans outstanding. From 1970 to 1975, the allowable percentage was 1.8 percent. This percentage has been reduced by 0.6 percent each six-year period since 1975, until 1987 when the deduction for additions to reserves would be eliminated. The allowable percentage of taxable income transferable to loss reserves was also gradually reduced from 60 percent in 1969 to 40 percent in 1979. In order to qualify for tax status as a savings and loan associations, associations were required to hold 60 percent of assets in specified qualifying assets and residential mortgages. To obtain the maximum loss reserve deduction of 45 percent in any one year, savings and loan associations were also required to have

Table XIII-9 FHLB Lending Activity
(dollar amounts in millions)

Year	Advances			Advances to Associations	
	Made	Repaid	Outstanding at Year-end	Outstanding at Year-end	As a Percent of Member Assets
1960	$ 1,943	$ 2,097	$ 1,981	$ 1,979	2.8
1965	5,007	4,335	5,997	5,985	4.7
1970	3,255	1,930	10,615	10,488	6.1
1971	2,714	5,392	7,936	7,907	3.9
1972	4,792	4,750	7,979	7,960	3.3
1973	10,013	2,845	15,147	14,951	5.6
1974	12,763	6,106	21,804	21,508	7.4
1975	5,468	9,425	17,845	17,524	5.3
1976	8,114	10,097	15,862	15,708	4.1
1977	13,756	9,445	20,173	19,945	4.4
1978	25,297	12,800	32,670	31,990	6.2
1979	29,166	19,998	41,838	40,441	7.1
1980	36,585	29,460	48,963	47,045	7.6
1981	53,941	37,709	65,194	62,794	9.6
1982*	53,744	52,928	66,004	63,861	9.2

Note: Components may not add to totals due to rounding.
*Preliminary.
Source: Federal Home Loan Bank Board.

82 percent of its assets in residential loans and other qualifying assets. For mutual savings, the corresponding percentage was 72 percent of total assets. For each percentage decline in the qualifying assets' ratio below 82 percent, the 40 percent rate is reduced by $\frac{3}{4}$ of 1 percentage point and cannot be used if qualifying assets fall below the 60 percent level. For mutual savings banks, the 40 percent loss reserve percentage declines by 115 basis points for each 100 basis points below the 72 percent level and cannot be claimed if the asset percentage requirement falls below 50 percent.

The effective tax rate for savings and loan associations is higher than the comparable rate for commercial banks and other institutions. As discussed previously, net income before taxes provides the basic source of funds for addition to net worth and reserves and, hence, excessive tax rates reduce the ability of thrift institutions to bolster net worth items. Moreover, if thrift institutions are granted extensive asset diversification powers, the implementation of such abilities will be constrained by requirements of the special bad debt reserve deduction.

Both the President's Commission on Housing and several thrift trade groups have recommended a revision of tax laws affecting thrift institutions and the housing industry in general. Under the provisions of the economic Recovery Tax Act of 1981, leasing activity could provide further tax deduction benefits for thrift institutions.

FUTURE STRUCTURE AND DIRECTION OF THE THRIFT INDUSTRY

There is no doubt that consolidation and attrition in the number of operating savings and loan associations and mutual savings banks will continue as mergers and acquisitions are utilized to strengthen the structure of the industry.

In terms of function and operation, many associations and savings banks will continue to specialize in the provision of housing finance, while others may adopt a mortgage banker posture originating loans for the secondary market. In a future scenario of operating alternatives, it is conceivable that many thrift institutions will become more bank-like in function operating as one stop consumer-oriented family financial services centers offering a panoply of banking and investment services. In this regard, greater homogenization of the depository institutions' industry will be a fact of life, more so with the passage of the 1982 Depository Institutions Act.

Other institutions will develop operations similar to a full service commercial bank, engaging in commercial business lending and the provision of other business-oriented services. Start-up costs of such an orientation would be an important factor, but a thorough evaluation of the costs and benefits of shifting operations in this direction and an evaluation of specific credit needs of particular localized market, for example, will dictate whether such a course of action is desirable and feasible.

While the "plans of action" for the future are generalizations, it should be borne in mind that for each thrift institution, each situation is "sui generis" and will require a strategy tailored to the particular strengths, capabilities, competitiveness and operating ambience of the individual institutions.

Many savings and loan institutions are increasingly packaging mortgage holdings into short, intermediate, and long-term instruments and channelling these debt obligations to buyers in the secondary market. Some associations are also shifting away from traditional investment areas to develop vertically integrated real estate operations as opposed to being only suppliers of finance to the construction industry.

While the pressures on thrift earnings over the years 1980-82 have abated during 1983, the Federal Home Loan Bank Board has estimated that continued thrift insolvencies could cost the insurance fund over $2 billion in 1984. Many thrift failures have been associated with "brokered deposits," that is, deposits placed by institutional brokers usually in $100,000 denominations. In fact, in March 1984, the FSLIC resorted to the largest deposit payout in its 50-year history, after closing Empire Savings and Loan of Mesquite, Texas. Almost 85 percent of its $308 million in deposits were brokered funds. Concerns about brokers marketing the federal insurance deposit seal without regard to the financial condition of the particular depository institution led to the FDIC and FSLIC adopting on March 26, 1984, restrictions on broker deposit activities. Deposit insurance would be limited to $100,000 per broker per insured institution effective October 1, 1984. Funds deposited before the adoption of the regulation would be allowed to be rolled over within a two-year period ending October 1, 1986. The Federal Home Loan Bank Board also limited to 5 percent the amount of deposits that insured institutions with net worth less than 3 percent of liabilities could obtain through a deposit broker.

Some views on the future outlook and structure of the thrift industry by leading regulators and analysts also provide some indication of the current thinking in this direction. Frederick H. Schultz,[12] current Vice Chairman of the Federal Reserve Board, endorses expanded asset powers for thrifts and banks and sees bank holding companies being permitted to acquire thrift institutions in the near future in keeping with the increasing homogenization of the financial industry. With the rapid changes in technology and the increasing provision of financial services across state lines, there will be a concomitant decline in regulation of banking. The regulator also sees de jure interstate banking as inevitable and a reflection of de facto developments in the marketplace. The role of the Federal Reserve is viewed by Mr. Schultz as one of "trying to be flexible and orchestrate change."

Muriel Siebert, former State Banking Commissioner in the State of New York, also endorsed expanded asset powers for depository institutions. She notes that, "The thrift industry, once its current problems have become past history, should have the ability to diversify its earning powers so as to increase its stability and obviate ever again being in the position where the nature of its assets is so one-dimensional."[13] The New York State Banking Commissioner also supported broadened ability of federal insurers to assist troubled institutions and the mandated involvement of state regulatory authorities throughout the merger and acquisiion assistance in order to "assure adequate representation and input by state representatives at all stages of the procedure." Siebert also called for the merger of federal insurance agencies in order to reduce duplicative government activities given the trend toward homogenization of the financial industry.

Linda Yang, former California Savings and Loan Commissioner, is of the opinion that "Thrifts would continue to apply expertise as mortgage originators. Bank-like lending powers will not detract thrifts from their main line of business, as it requires a good deal of expertise and up front expenses to go into commercial operations. On the other hand, expanded lending powers could be useful as an auxiliary service to the existing client base. Thrift institutions would have to decide what part of market they would like to serve and then specialize in areas where they have expertise."[14]

With regard to interstate mergers as a method of assisting ailing associations, the former savings and loan commissioner of the nation's

---

[12]Rosenstein, Jay. "An Interview with . . .,*American Banker*. January 12, 1982, pp. 19-24.

[13]Siebert, Muriel S. Testimony before Senate Committee on Banking, Housing and Urban Affairs. November 1981.

[14]Telehone Interview, February 1, 1982.

leading savings and loan state, viewed these mergers as having the ". . . . effect of weakening the dual-chartering system, in particular the state system." "The stronger associations are solicited to do the merger, and for state-chartered associations such action is not possible, as the host state does not allow state associations to undertake out of state acquisitions."[15] Hence, associations interested in such mergers have to convert to federal charter. "Bureaucratically speaking, this results in a federalization of savings and loan associations in California and weakens and undercuts the state system." Ms. Yang further noted that cross-industry mergers were in a "state of fermentation."[16] If banks acquire savings and loan associations and the latter institutions disappear, then the effect is more likely to be negative in terms of sources of funds for home financing. With regard to deregulation, the Commissioner noted that the process of deregulation and its timing could be better orchestrated, especially during a volatile and high interest rate environment which weaken resources of thrift institutions.

William B. O'Connell, President of the United States League of Savings Associations, assumes "that the Housing Commission will restate the administration's commitment to housing. It would seem incomprehensible that a president coming from the largest housing state would do anything but endorse that idea."[17] The United States League of Savings Associations' President has also endorsed broadened assets' powers for thrift institutions and vigorously supported plans for the wholesale warehousing of low-yielding mortgages held by thrift institutions.

Saul Klaman, President of the National Association of Mutual Savings Banks noted that, "There is no turning back from the far-reaching-tradition shattering developments of recent years. There is no turning off the deregulation road we are now traveling . . . Adaptive change is the key to survival in this new fiercely competitive financial arena."[18] While the mutual savings banking spokesman has sanctioned a temporary governmental warehousing plan for the low-yielding mortgages held by thrifts, he also envisions builders and realtors assisting in devising "a program which relieves the thrift institutions of the dead weight of all these loans which freeze several hundred billion dollars of

[15]Ibid.

[16]Ibid.

[17]O'Connell, William H. "Housing and the Thrift Industry," United States Banker Round Table. *United States Banker*, February 1982, p. 30.

[18]Klaman, Saul B.

assets and earmark the funds so secured for housing."[19] There is also a need to keep the "momentum going on tax incentives for savings. Without a broader base of savings, you are not going to have funds to invest in housing." Finally, he asserts that, "When all is said and done, there is no better long-term solution than to get the economy in shape where we are not dealing with $100 billion deficits."[20]

There is no doubt that the problems of thrift institutions would rapidly disappear if interest rates were to decline substantially in the near future. Indeed, as Muriel Siebert, former New York State Banking Commissioner, reiterates, "The fundamental answer to the problems of the thrift industry is obvious: a reduction in interest rates. In the absence of that, there must be some legislative or regulatory relief for a condition that legislation and regulation in large part created."[21]

There are strong merits to the argument that thrift institutions were mandated by public policy to specialize in the provision of housing finance and protected and fostered over the years by Congressional and regulatory largesse. During the halcyon years of development, savings and loans and mutual savings banks did a remarkable job of meeting the housing needs of the American nation.

In the words of Representative Fernand J. St Germain, Chairman of the Committee on Banking, Finance and Urban Affairs, "There is no doubt that we created the savings and loans. We said to them, your purpose, your mission in life, is to provide home mortgage financing. And they did that for many years successfully. We assisted them with Reg. Q and we assisted them with the differential. And, yes, we said to them, "You can't engage in commercial lending. All you can do is lend long."[22]

If Congress is partially responsible for the genesis of the current plight of the thrift institutions, it seemed rational that the legislature should adopt some type of short-term action which is expiatory. The thrifts required short-term relief and prolonged vacillation would only serve to render the process of transition and change even more burdensome for these institutions. The Capital Assistance Program, as embodied in the Depository Institutions Act of 1982, was perhaps a testament to that Congressional responsibility.

[19]Klaman, Saul B. "Housing and the Thrift Industry," United States Banker Round Table. *United States Banker*, February 1982, p. 32.

[20]Ibid.

[21]"State's Savings Banks Swim in $1.25B Red Ink," United Press International. February 1982.

[22]Hershey, Jr., Robert D. "A Plan to Save the Savings Banks," *New York Times*, February 28, 1982.

Savings and loan associations have been the nation's premier sup-
plier of housing finance. In fact, 1981 marked the 150th anniversary of
the savings and loan movement in the nation, when in 1831 the first
mortgage loan for $375 was made in Philadelphia. That house today
still stands and is a monument of the role of savings and loan associations in fostering home ownership and that national goal of a "decent
home and a suitable living environment for every American family."
1981 also marked the worst operating year in the history of the savings
and loan and mutual banking industry. With expanded liability and
asset powers, as stipulated by the 1982 Depository Institutions Act and
market sensitive mortgage instruments, thrift institutions can continue
to play a vital role in the fostering of thrift and in the provision of
housing finance albeit in a restructured environment. In the words of
President Reagan, "This legislation can be the Emancipation Procla-
mation for America's Savings Institutions. With declining interest
rates, "the sun is shining on thrifts again."[23] *Tempora Mutantur Nos Et
Mutamur in illis*—Times are changing and we are changing with them.

[23]Speech before Annual Meeting of U.S. League of Savings Associations. November 1982.

Afterword

From the first day that this manuscript was written until its completion, extraordinary changes have taken place in the thrift industry. Major institutions suffering from great economic stress have been acquired or merged out of existence. Others caught in the earnings squeeze have tried creative ways to improve profits and eliminate—or at least minimize—losses. However, in an environment of continuing high interest rates during 1980–82, most found the task to be beyond their capability.

During that period of time, the situation facing the thrift industry had reached crises proportions. Great concern had been expressed about the ability of the insurance corporations to fund these losses in the event of the ultimate collapse of a large portion of the financial industry. This concern had caused both the President and Congress to affirm the commitment that the full faith and credit of the United States would back the ultimate losses which might exceed the net worth of either of the insurance corporations themselves.

The costs to both corporations had accelerated dramatically through 1981 and 1982. Both the FDIC and FSLIC had spent approximately 1 billion dollars each in purchasing assets, paying off debt or guaranteeing losses in order to attract merger partners for their ailing institutions.[1] Fully aware of the problem, at first the officers of the Federal

---

[1] *American Banker,* January 15, 1982

Savings and Loan Insusrance Corporation and later on those of the Federal Deposit Insurance Corporation had reached for ways to limit their exposure by developing new ways to sustain the thrifts at the least cost to the corporations.

Typical of this new approach has been the utilization of purchase accounting in the merger of mutual, as well as stock associations. While primarily an acounting technique, for tax purposes it provides additions for net worth of the merged entity without any change in cash flows.[2] Purchase accounting is the method by which upon acquisition of a business, all assets are revalued to fair market. The difference between the real value and the book value is attributed to good will. Since good will can be amortized for a period up to forty kyears, the reality is that the losses on portfolio, as revalued, are spread over that period of time. Since the discounted mortgages will pay off in a shorter period of time, that discount is taken in on the average life of the mortgages and on a quicker basis. While an immediate advantage is derived once the discount was fully amortized, institutions would be faced with continued write-off of the good will.

Given the use of the above technique, unprofitable mergers would seem to be worthwhile without any cost to the corporations. This lesson learned has not been lost to the government officials,k and it is entirely possible that future changes will approve this technique without the necessity of mergers. In any event, the foregoing had not been viewed as a clear solution to the problems of the thrifts.

Faced with more than nine assisted mergers up to April in 1982, the FSLIC had resorted to the use of further non-monetary solutions. Primarily the use of ICC's has seemed to postpone the inevitable. ICC's, or Income Capital Certificates, were first used by the Federal Home Loan Bank in September of 1981. These certificates were issued to First Federal Savings and Loan of Rochester on its acquisition of Franklin Society Federal of New York City by the FSLIC. These certificates are debt instruments which qualify as reserves under Section 403 of the National Housing Act and as net worth under generally accepted accounting practices.[3] The ICC's maintain the association's net worth at a steady level and are repayable as the institution becomes profitable.

[2] See the Wharton Study page 4. "The Financial Implications of Different Governmental Policies for the Thrift Industry." Wharton Econometric Forecasting Association.

[3] Income Capital Certificates are issued by mutual associations in denominations of $100,000 in exchange for 5-year promissory notes of the FSLILC. The FSLIC promissory notes may be used to satisfy net worth requirements which are currently 3 percent of liabilities. Federal Home Loan Bank Board regulation entitled "Security Constituting Permanent Equity" issued in September 1981 provides that ICC's are in the nature of permanent equity and are eligible items for use as reserves and net worth. Prior to this regulation, the definition of net worth and liquidity did not iclude such notes.

The use of ICC's had been widely used where institutions could not be marketed to willing buyers without extraordinary costs to the FSLIC. These devices, coupled with purchase accounting, have made the merger of two apparently insolvent associations appear to create a new solid entity.

At first referred to as *accounting by mirrors,* these new entities are now referred to as a "Phoenix"—at first in jest, but now serious. This name, in honor of the bird of Greek mythology, signifies the ability of the new institution to rise from its own ashes as an emblem of immortality.

Many plans had also been forthcoming for portfolio assistance or warehousing of low yielding loans for capital stabilization or maintenance plans, and for new types of regulatory accounting procedures. All of these tended to address the growing concerns for the survival of the thrift industry by government and thrift industry officials.

Whether a commitment had been made to save the thrift industry or the theory of a free market economy would prevail depended on the many forces that abound in the Washington environment. It might be correct to state that as all things outlive their usefulness, they must be abandoned so that new forms can take their place. Perhaps the thrifts were a breed of dinosaur bound for extinction. They, whether in extinction or reborn as a new mythological bird, have served well and given to this country its heritagee of housing and consumer banking.

In passing, it might be worthwhile to ponder an introductory comment made in the New York State Task Force report of April 1982 on the problems of the industry and its solutions:

"It is worth pointing out that each of the (merged) institutions traces its history back well over one hundred years indicating that it was capable of surviving 'The Great Depression' (and at least seven recessions) and two world wars but not the current situation."[4]   Those institutions faced with extraordinary losses day-by-day hoped to prolong their existence for a few months knowing that "the rules were changing each day" and that survival may bring them to the time in which a complete resscue structure was implemented. Such a plan was implemented with the passage of the Garn-St Germain Act in October 1982. Under this assistance program, ailing thrift institutions qualifying for rresistance would receive promissory notes from the FSLIC/FDIC, which would be used to bolster net worth. While many thrifts continued to operatee in the red, the majority of thrifts displayed improved earnings performance largely due to the decline in interest

[4] Report of the Thrift Industry Advisory Task Force to Governor Hugh Carey of New York, April 1982.

rates during 1982-83 and increased deposit flows through money market deposit accounts.   For the future, the financial services industry - after a bout of sustained "deregulation" — appears headed for some degree of "re-regulation" as embodied in the new St Germain-Wylie Financial Services Bill HR 5916 which was cleared for floor action by the Senate in June 1983. The new bill attempts to plug the "non-bank bank loophole" by redefining "bank" for purposes of the Bank Holding Company Act. A Bank for Bank Holding Company Act purposes would be defined as any institution eligible for FDIC insurance or that accepts transaction accounts and make commercial loans. Federally chartered thrifts, FSLIC insured state-chartered savings and loan associations, FDIC insured savings banks and non-federally insured savings institutions and cooperative banks would be specificlly excluded from Bank Holding Company Act Coverage. Savings institutions would be brought within the coverage of the Savings and Loan Holding Company Act. Other noteworthy provisions of the bill include:

1. Allowing unitary savings and loan holding companies to retain their activities if their subsidiary savings institutions meet a "60 percent qualified thrift lender" test.

2. The application of the 60 percent housing-related asset test to eligibility for FHL Bank advances.

3. Removal of the eligibility barriers to receipt of checking accounts by federally chartered savings institutions.

4. Extensionof the Net Worth CertificateProgram of the 1982 Garn Act to October 1988.

5. Place savings institutions under the Glass Steagall Act prohibition against affiliations and director interlocks between Federal Reserve member banks and securities firms.

6. Permitting bankholding companies to buy savings institutions and vice versa.

7. Authorizing FSLIC and FDIC insured mutual savings institutions to form "mutual thrift holding companies" to engage in activities permitted for multiple savings and loan holding companies.

8. Permitting savings and loan holding companies to underwrite and deal in mortgage securities and underwrite revenue bond issues.

Bibliography

1. Baxter, William F., Cootner, Paul H. and Scott, Kenneth E. *Retail Banking in the Electronic Age. The Law and Economics of Electronic Funds Transfer.* Montclair, N.J. Allanheld, Somun and Co. Publishers Inc. 1977.

2. Bellman, Harold. *The Building Society Movement.* London: Methuen and Co., Ltd. 1927.

3. Bodfish, Morton, ed. *History of the Building and Loan in the United States.* Chicago: United States Building and Loan League, 1931.

4. Bodfish, Morton and Theobald, A.D. *Savings and Loan Principles.* Englewood Cliffs, N.J. Prentice-Hall, 1940.

5. Bradford, William D. *Mergers in the Savings and Loan Industry: Structural Changes, Financial Comparidons and the Performance of Merging Savings and Loan Associations.* Ann Arbor, Michigan, 1977.

6. Carron, Andrew S. *The Plight of the Thrift Institutions.* Washington, D.C.: The Brookings Institution, 1982.

7. Conway, Lawrence V. *Savings and Loan Principles.* Chicago: American Savings and Loan Institution Press, 1957.

8. Dougall, Herbert E. and Gaumitz, Jack E. *Capital Markets and Institutions.* Englewood Cliffs, N.Y. Prentice-Hall, 1965.

9. Ewalt, Josephine H. *A Business Reborn — The Savings and Loan Story 1930-1960.* Chicago 1962.

10. Friend, Irwin. *Study of the Savings and Loan Industry.* Washington, 1969.

11. Goldsmith, Raymond W. *Financial Institutions.* New York: Random House, 1968.

12. Golember, Carter H. and Hengren, Raymond E. *Federal Regulation of Banking.* American Institute of Banking. The American LBankers Association. Washington, D.C. 1975.

13. Hamilton, James Henry. *Savings and Savings Institutions.* New York, The Macmillan Company, 1902.

14. Havrilesky, Thomas M. and Boorman, John T., ed. *Current Perspectives in Banking: Operations, Management and Regulation.* Arlington Heights, Illinois. AHM Publishing Corporation, 1976.

15. Horne, Oliver H. *A History of Savings Banks.* London: Oxford University Press, 1947.

16. Horvitz, Paul M., *et al. Private Financial Institutions.* Englewood Cliffs, N.J. Prentice-Hall, 1963.

17. Jones, Sidney L. *The Development of Economic Policy: Financial Institution Reform.* Michigan Business Studies, New Series, Vol 2, No. 1. University of Michigan, Ann Arbor, Michigan, 1979.

18. Kendall, Leon T. *The Savings and Loan Business.* Englewood Cliffs, New Jersey. Prentice-Hall, 1962.

19. Keyes, Emerson W. *A History of Savings Banking in the United States 1816-1871.* Vols. 1, 11. New York: Bradford Rhodes, 1978.

20. Keyes, Emerson W. *A History of Savings Banks in the State of New York.* Albany, N.Y.: Argus Company Printers, 1870.

21. Knowles, Charles E. *History of the Bank for Savings in the City of New York 1819-1929.* New York: The Bank for Savings in the City of New York, 1929.

22. Lewins, William. *A History of Banks for Savings.* London: Sampson, Low, Son and Marston, 1886.

23. Nadler, Paul S. *The Future of Savings Banking in New York State.* New York: New York University Graduate School of Business, 1961.

24. National Association of Mutual Savings Banks. New York: *National Fact Book of Mutual Savings Banks, 1970-1983.*

25. *New York Law Journal.* Law Journal Seminars-Press Inc. First Annual Regulatory Developments in the Savings and Loan Industry. New York, 1980.

26. New York State Banking Department. *A Bank Director's Responsibility.* New York, 1980.

27. Practising Law Institute: A Survey of Current Developments in the Thrift Industry. New York, 1980.

28. Price, Seymour J. *Building Societies: Their Origin and History.* London: Franey and Company, 1958.

29. Rosenthal, Henry S. *Cyclopedia of Building and Loan Associations.* Cincinnatti: American Building Association News, 1939.

30. Sandberg, Richard T. *Introduction to the Savings Association Business,* second edition. Chicago: American Savings and Loan Institute Press. 1973.

31. Shaw, Edward S. *Savings and Loan Structure and Market Performance.* Los Angeles: Savings and Loan Commissioner, State of California, 1962.

32. Sherman, Franklin J. *Modern Story of Mutual Savings Banks.* New York: Little and Ives, 1934.

33. Teck, Allan. *Mutual Savings Banks and Savings and Loan Associations: Aspects of Growth.* Columbia University Press, 1968.

34. United States League of Savings Associations. Chicago: *Savings and Loan Fact Book 1970-1984.*

35. Welfling, Weldon. *Mutual Savings Banks—The Evolution of a Financial Intermediary.* Cleveland: Press of Case Western Reserve University, 1968.

36. Welfling, Weldon. *Savings Banking in New York State.* Durham, N.C.: Duke University Press, 1939.

SELECTED ARTICLES

Buckley, Robert M. "There is no Mortgage Problem." *The New York Times,* November 30, 1980.

Edwards, Raoul D. "Special Report: Secondary Market." *United States Banker,* July 1981, Vol. X11, No. 7, pp 22-28.

Edwards, Raoul D. "The Cost of Financial Intermediary Supervision 1978-1981." *United States Banker,* July 1981, Vol X11, No. 7, p. 20.

Fahey, Noel "Wanted: A low-cost account to spur savings and help housing." *Savings and Loan News,* May 1981, pp. 74-79.

Faucette, Douglass P. and Kniepper, Richard K. "Income Capital Certificates: FSLIC Creates a Unique Savings and Loan Security." *Federal Home Loan Bank Board Journal,* Vol. 14 (October 1981) pp.10-13.

Hammer, Frederich S. "The Need now for a New Deposit Instrument." *Journal of Retail Banking,* Vol. III. No. 4, December 1981, pp. 1-6.

Heylar, John. "Regional Banks Search for a Niche in Face of New Rules, Competition." *Wall Street Journal,* February 4, 1982.

House Committee on Banking. Finance and Urban Affairs. "Financial Institution in a Revolutionary Era." December 1981.

Kenzie, Ross B. "Searching for our Roots, Thoughts on the Ownership of Mutual Savings Banks." *United States Banker,* July 1981 pp. 59-61.

Levensen, Irving, *et al.* "The Future of the Financial Services Industry." Hudson Institute. February 1982.

McKenzie, Joseph A. "Commercial Paper: Plugging into a new and stable Source of Financing." *FHLB Journal,* March 1971, pp. 2-5.

Melton, Carroll. "The British VRM Showes AMIs can work for Lender and Borrower." *Savings and Loan News,* June 1981, pp. 34-5.

Orr, B. "State Thrift Regulators Ponder Industry's Future." American Bankers Association, *Banking Journal,* July 1981, pp. 33-38.

President's Commission on Housing. "Financing the Housing Needs of the 1980s." January 1982.

Wallich, Henry C. "The Mutual Form has Reason to Exist and is Viable." *Savings Bank Journal,* Vol. 62, No. 9. November 1981, pp. 15-19.

Wantuck, Mary-Margaret. "Unlocking the Mysteries of the DIDC and the FIEC." *National Savings and Loan League Journal.* Vol. 35, No. 9, September 1980, pp. 10-19.

Wharton Econometric Forecasting Associates. "The Financial Implications of Different Governmental Policies for the Thrift Industry." March 23, 1981.

Willax, Paul A. "Interest Rate Flexibility, Mainstay of a Successful Future Thrift Industry." *National Savings and Loan League Journal.* Vol. 35, No. 9, September 1980. pp. 21-23.

Appendix

appendix

Agencies Regulating Banks

The federal bank regulatory structure, which was fashioned between 1863 and 1933, was distinctive in several ways. First, it divided the principal regulatory duties among three major agencies, whereas for most regulated industries there is a single federal agency which has the primary supervisory responsibility. Second, only one of the three federal banking agencies—the Office of the Comptroller of the Currency—is solely a regulatory body. The other two banking agencies—the Federal Reserve and the Federal Deposit Insurance Corporation—exercise other important responsibilities in addition to banking regulation. While it would not be correct to characterize bank regulation as merely incidental to the monetary policy responsibilities of the Federal Reserve or to the insurance responsibilities of the FDIC, in each case the effectiveness of these agencies is determined not so much by their regulatory work as by their operations in the monetary or insurance fields respectively.

Finally, mention should be made of the fact that although the federal government provided for comprehensive regulation of banks, it did not isolate banks from some regulation by other governmental agencies. Thus business concerns, banks (and bank holding companies)

*Reprinted by permission from Golembe, Carter H. and Hengren, Raymond E., *Federal Regulation of Banking,* published by the American Institute of Banking, The American Bankers Association, 1975.

frequently find themselves subject to the regulatory reach of other federal government agencies not primarily involved in banking.

The Banking Agencies

After the federal government's initial entry into the bank regulatory business through the establishment of the Office of the Comptroller of the Currency by the passage of national bank legislation, on each successive occasion when a new banking agency was created by the Congress, the banks already subject to federal regulation were linked to the new agency as part of its constituency. Thus national banks, regulated by the Comptroller of the Currency, were required to become members of the Federal Reserve System when that System was established in 1913. Similarly, all bank members of the Federal Reserve System, both national and state, were required to become insured by the FDIC when that corporation was established in 1933. The results of this evolutionary process are presented in Chart 1 which sets forth the distribution of all commercial and mutual savings banks arranged by regulatory status.

Chart 1: Distribution of Bank Regulatory Authority, December 31, 1973.

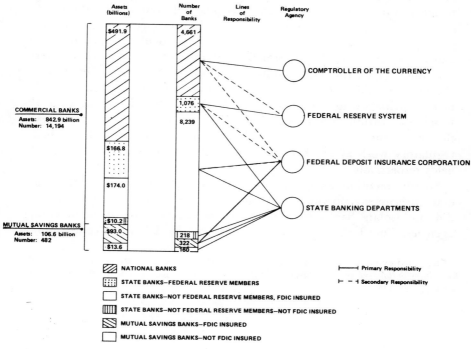

Source: FDIC Annual Report, 1973.

Insofar as the regulation of banks is concerned (as distinct from bank holding companies) Chart 1 calls attention to the considerable overlapping of regulatory authority that has stemmed from the historical development of the structure. Yet the bank regulatory chores have been more or less apportioned among the three federal banking agencies in such a way as to minimize problems arising from possible overlapping authority. Not shown on the chart but deserving of mention, nevertheless, is the coordination committee on bank regulation initially established at the direction of the President by the Secretary of the Treasury in 1964 for the exchange of views and the accommodation of differences on regulatory matters. At the outset the committee was made up of representatives of the three banking agencies. Later a representative of the Federal Home Loan Bank Board (the agency chiefly concerned with the supervision and insurance of savings and loan associations) was added to the committee, and its procedure was formalized to some extent.

Virtually all banks in the nation have their deposits insured by the FDIC, as Chart 1 shows, but that corporation regularly supervises only those state-chartered banks that are not members of the Federal Reserve System. This category includes the majority of the total number of banks in the country—more banks than are regularly supervised by the other two federal agencies combined. However, because they are typically smaller institutions, their percentage of all commercial bank assets was only 20.6 percent of the total at the end of 1973. In addition, the FDIC regularly supervises the majority of the nation's mutual savings banks, holding 87 percent of all savings bank assets. When the assets of these regulated institutions are taken into consideration, 28.1 percent of all bank assets are subject to the corporation's supervision.

While theoretically subject to supervision by the Federal Reserve and the FDIC, national banks in fact are directly supervised only by the Office of the Comptroller of the Currency, except in unusual circumstances. Although national banks comprise only about one-third of the nation's commercial banks, it will be noted from Chart 1 that at the end of 1973 the assets of these banks constituted just under 60 percent of all commercial bank assets, and over one-half of all bank assets.

For direct bank supervision, the Federal Reserve has the narrowest area of jurisdiction, measured in terms of number of banks. That is, the Federal Reserve regularly supervises only those state-chartered banks that are members of the Federal Reserve System. At the end of 1973 there were 1,076 such banks, comprising only 7.6 percent of all commercial banks. However, because of their typically larger size when compared with other banks, at the end of 1973 banks regularly supervised by the Federal Reserve held about one-fifth of all commercial bank assets.

As was mentioned earlier, the Federal Reserve is not only responsible for the regular supervision of state-chartered banks which are members of the System but also has sole regulatory authority over companies which own or control one or more banks. At the end of 1972 there were 1,607 such companies having 2,720 bank subsidiaries with assets of $467.5 billion, or 62.7 percent of all commercial bank assets.

The position of the Federal Reserve as the sole supervisor of bank holding companies gives rise to another set of possible overlapping authorities, since the banks that are members of the holding companies remain subject to their regular federal regulatory agencies. Obviously, questions might arise as to ultimate supervisory authority where, for example, the Federal Reserve supervises a holding company whose subsidiaries include national banks or state-chartered banks not members of the Federal Reserve System.

Another kind of overlap—indeed the most vexing—is found with respect to federal and state authority. As shown in Chart 1, at the end of 1973 there was a total of 9,637 banks subject to direct regulatory authority by both a federal agency and a state agency. As a matter of practice, in the overwhelming majority of cases, the federal and state agencies have devised procedures which delineate areas of responsibility and minimize overlap problems that are inherent in the structure. Note should also be made of the fact that at the end of 1973 there were a small number of commercial banks—holding only 1.2 percent of commercial bank assets—which were subject only to state authority; in addition, there were 160 mutual savings banks with approximately 12.8 percent of savings bank assets not subject to regulation by any federal agency.

One important aspect of the division of banks among regulatory agencies is the fact that the banks themselves have some option as to the federal regulatory jurisdiction in which they may be placed. Banks are able to shift among the various agencies in certain ways, although not without difficulty. For example, a state-chartered bank member of the Federal Reserve System may withdraw from that System but retain its insurance, in which case its supervisory agency becomes the FDIC. A national bank may convert to a state charter, or a state bank to national charter, in either case changing in the process the federal agency to which it had previously been subject. (See Chart 2 on p. 13.)

While bank conversions (either charter conversion or change of Federal Reserve membership status by state banks) are rarely large in number in any single year, there are occasions when both the number of conversions and the assets involved are of significance. Conversions may occur for a wide variety of reasons. Perhaps most common in recent years has been the desire of banks that are members of the Federal Reserve System to reduce the cost of carrying reserves as required by the Federal Reserve; this accounts for a number of conversions from national to state charter, and from state member to state nonmember status. Early in the 1960s, a prominent reason for charter conversion was a belief on the part of many state banks—particularly some of the larger commercial banks—that greater operational freedom was to be found within the national banking system than in the state system. Chart 2 shows, for the years 1961 through 1973, changes among banks affecting their regulatory status.

Comptroller of the Currency

The Office of the Comptroller of the Currency can be described as the only "true" bank regulatory agency at the federal level. That is, it is the only one of the three agencies which charters banks and regulates their activities in accordance with a federal statute setting forth the powers and limitations applicable to national banks. The two other federal banking agencies are not chartering agencies and exercise their regulatory powers as a result of, and in conjunction with, other responsibilities assigned to them.

The Office of the Comptroller is part of the Treasury Department but occupies a semiautonomous position within that department. The Comptroller is appointed by the President, with the advice and consent of the Senate, for a term of five years.

As is the case with the other federal banking agencies, the Office of the Comptroller is headquartered in Washington, with regional offices stationed about the country. At the end of 1971 there were 14 such offices, each of which was headed by a Regional Administrator of National Banks.

Most employees of the Comptroller's Office are engaged in bank examination or related activities. At December 1972 there were 1,639 persons so engaged, comprising 77 percent of the total employees—2,141. The Comptroller's Office maintains a legal department, banking and economic research department, bank organization division, and an insolvent national bank division.

The Office is financed by means of assessments paid by national banks. Banks are assessed at a rate of $200, plus $4\frac{1}{2}$ cents for each $1,000 of total assets and $50 for each branch, semiannually. Total expenditures for all activities in 1972 were $40.5 million. Revenues were $44.9 million, leaving an excess over expenditures of $4.4 million. The reserve maintained by the Office is known as "Comptroller's Equity" and was $27.0 million at the end of 1972.

Chart 2: Charter Conversions of
Commercial Banks, 1961–1973

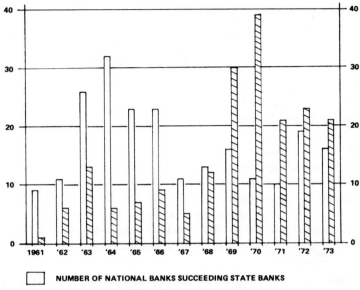

NUMBER OF NATIONAL BANKS SUCCEEDING STATE BANKS

NUMBER OF STATE BANKS SUCCEEDING NATIONAL BANKS

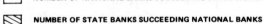

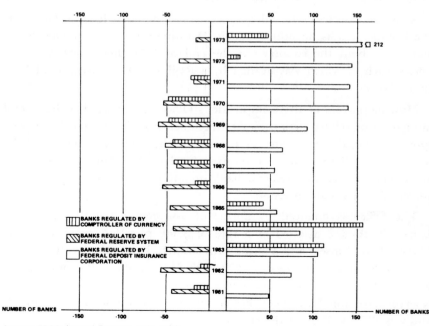

Source: FDIC Annual Reports, 1961–1973.

The Board of Governors of the Federal Reserve System has important bank and bank holding company regulatory responsibilities, in addition to its basic responsibility for the conduct of monetary policy. The Federal Reserve itself functions as an independent agency within government, headed by a seven-member Board of Governors each of whom is appointed by the President, with the advice and consent of the Senate, for a 14-year term.

A major portion of the supervisory work of the Board of Governors is carried out by the twelve Federal Reserve Banks. However, ultimate policy-making and decision-making authority resides with the Board of Governors in Washington, since many of the supervisory actions with respect to bank holding companies—and to some extent, with respect to banks—are quasi-judicial or quasi-legislative in nature. For most purposes, however, a bank holding company, or a state bank that is a member of the Federal Reserve System, regards the Federal Reserve Bank of the district in which it is located as its primary federal regulatory authority. The regional Federal Reserve Banks possess a substantial amount of authority under decentralization procedures adopted by the Board of Governors and, in addition, handle much of the regular supervisory work. For example, bank examinations are handled directly by the Federal Reserve Banks, each of which has a bank examination department. Thus, in its regional decentralization the regulatory structure of the Federal Reserve resembles that of the Office of the Comptroller of the Currency.

In addition to the Reserve Bank examinations departments (which sometimes have different names at different Reserve Banks), the Board maintains in Washington a Division of Supervision and Regulation to coordinate its various regulatory responsibilities. In all, approximately 100 employees at the Board in Washington, and 870 employees at the Federal Reserve Banks, are involved in supervisory activities related to banks and bank holding companies. Supervisory expenses at these offices in 1972 were approximately $16 million, comprising about 3.9 percent of all expenses of the Federal Reserve System. In addition, substantial cost is incurred to provide the Board with legal and research support both in Washington and at each Federal Reserve Bank.

The primary source of income of the Federal Reserve is interest earned on government obligations. The Federal Reserve does not receive appropriations from the Congress nor impose examination fees upon banks.

Federal Reserve income substantially exceeds expenses. Most of the overage is returned to the U.S. Treasury. For example, in 1972, earnings were $3,792 million and expenses only $415 million. After paying dividends of $46 million to member banks and transferring $51 million to surplus, the balance of $3,231 million was returned to the U.S. Treasury.

INDEX